MISSING

PERSONS AND POLITICS

JENNY EDKINS

CORNELL UNIVERSITY PRESS
Ithaca and London

First published 2011 by Cornell University Press

First printing, Cornell Paperbacks, 2016

Library of Congress Cataloging-in-Publication Data

Edkins, Jenny.
    Missing : persons and politics / Jenny Edkins.
        p. cm.
    Includes bibliographical references and index.
    ISBN 978-0-8014-5029-7 (cloth: alk. paper)
    ISBN 978-1-5017-0564-9 (pbk.: alk. paper)
    1. Missing persons—Identification—Political
aspects.   2. Mass casualties—Identification—
Political aspects.   3. Dead—Identification—Political
aspects.   4. Missing in action—Identification—Political
aspects.   5. Disappeared persons—Identification—
Political aspects.   I. Title.
    HV6762.A3E35 2011
    362.87—dc23   2011022286

Cornell University Press strives to use environmentally responsible suppliers and materials to the fullest extent possible in the publishing of its books. Such materials include vegetable-based, low-VOC inks and acid-free papers that are recycled, totally chlorine-free, or partly composed of nonwood fibers. For further information, visit our website at www.cornellpress.cornell.edu.

CONTENTS

PREFACE

Just before the end of my work in the archives of the postwar period, I came across an extraordinary file. Among reports of the efforts of the tracing services in the face of the overwhelming millions lost, often without trace, in concentration camps and on death marches, there is a record of a train accident.[1] On May 30, 1945, a transport of displaced persons from Hildesheim near Hannover was halted outside Rheda station in Westphalia. At about ten minutes past midnight, it was hit by another train. Four people were killed and several more injured, one badly. The badly injured person, who was taken to the American Hospital, was identified as Serge Rafalovich, born on August 24, 1909, at St. Petersburg, Russia, and a resident of Paris. One of the four killed was identified. Three were not: a man of about thirty years old, a woman of about forty, and a boy of seven or eight years old. The four bodies were taken to the Catholic Hospital and were to be buried on June 6, 1945. The personal belongings of those killed were turned over to the police and kept by the burgomaster. Further inquiries as to the identity of the three had been made without any success. For each person a form had been completed, giving a personal description and details.

In the file in the United Nations archives in New York are photographs of the faces of the three unidentified persons, with cards on which their fingerprints have been impressed and, pinned carefully to other specially designed cards, small pieces of fabric, each about an inch square, snipped from every item of clothing that they wore.

Coming across this file was extraordinarily moving. These little pieces of material, preserved in case they might one day prove useful for future identification, were here, now, in the present, hidden deep in the archive. Out there in the world was someone, maybe, for whom those traces would have significance. This was not what I found most striking, though. What struck me deeply was that in the midst of the overwhelming chaos of displaced persons, concentration camps, forced marches—people objectified, racialized, murdered in their masses—someone, somewhere, had taken the trouble to produce these records: records that could potentially serve to identify three particular persons, persons who mattered only to those who knew them, three persons among forty million. Wisława Szymborska writes:

> History rounds off skeletons to zero.
> A thousand and one is still only a thousand.
> That *one* seems never to have existed.[2]

But here, in this archive, that one *counts,* as a person, not an object, on the assumption that someone, somewhere, may be looking for them.

This book was prompted by an anger at the way prevalent forms of political or biopolitical governance both objectify and instrumentalize the person. Contemporary systems of political management are based on the administration of populations; they treat people as objects to be governed, with the aim of safeguarding populations as a whole.[3] They are heartless and *im*personal at best; at worst, they can be genocidal. The person is produced as an object of governance: as something without political standing, as something that has no voice, as disconnected and individualized. Contemporary politics does not see the person-as-such, only the person as object.

The way this objectification works becomes starkly obvious when people go missing: our systems of administration and governance cannot see the problem. When people go missing, their relatives demand action. A particular, unique, irreplaceable person has disappeared, and they want that person back. No one else will do. However, for the authorities who are supposed to act, there is really no such thing as an irreplaceable person: one person is for most purposes equivalent to another of the same sort. If a family has lost its breadwinner then some form of compensation might be in order, but the demand for the return of a *particular* breadwinner is incomprehensible.

The demand that the missing be traced inevitably challenges the production of the person as object, and it can be seen as something more: it can be seen as a demand for a different form of politics, one in which the person-as-such is acknowledged. But what is this person-as-such? When someone goes missing those left behind examine the traces that remain to try to fathom what may have happened, to try to work out what the missing person was thinking and feeling and what may have led that person to disappear. It turns out that in some profound sense the person was in any case unknowable and unknown. And that who people are is very much bound up with who they are in relation to others. It is impossible to specify what it is that makes a person irreplaceable—it is not this or that characteristic that is missed, this or that function that is no longer performed, but something singular, something unfathomable: maybe even the person's unfathomability in relation to our own. The person cannot be pinned down: *the person is missing.* It is in a sense that very "missingness" that makes the person irreplaceable.

In any case attempts to govern the person always break down. The person-as-such always escapes attempts at categorization or governance. We can see this in the ways in which the disappeared return to haunt the authoritarian systems that disappeared them in the first place. The seemingly diabolically effective tactic of disappearances rebounds in devastatingly unexpected ways. We can see it too on a more everyday level, in the ways in which the reach of systems of governance and objectification comes up against its limits in the quotidian actions of persons who insist on continuing to treat each other as such. In the New York archive, for example, that *one* counts.

* * *

Chapter 1 of this book looks at the search for those missing in the aftermath of the collapse of the World Trade Center towers in Manhattan in 2001, focusing on relatives' attempts to find out what had happened to family members, and the production of posters appealing for information about the missing. The chapter introduces many of the themes that are developed in later chapters—the contrast between the efforts of relatives and the response of the official authorities, how as persons we are in some sense already "missing" in contemporary politics, and the way in which the search for the missing became a demand for a different form of politics. The posters remained on display in New York for many weeks after the collapse, a reminder that the lives lost were *irreplaceable* lives—lives disregarded by those who organized the events of 9/11, but also in a sense lives rendered invisible by the objectifying imperatives of corporatism and public policy, lives in a sense already disappeared. Some were doubly disappeared: those who were not even supposed to be in the towers, the undocumented. But maybe even the documented existed only as objects of administration or as employees hidden behind an architecture designed to impress rather than to protect. The persistence of the missing posters constituted a demand that these lives—the lives of the missing—be recognized as such, not appropriated as heroes to justify revenge, not reduced to nothing but their ordinariness nor subsumed in numbers, but recognized as *persons-as-such,* singular lives, political in their uniqueness and irreplaceability.

Though the number of people missing in New York after 9/11 is daunting, it becomes small when set against the numbers missing after the Second World War; the end of hostilities in 1945 left tens of millions of people, many of whom had lost touch with family members, destitute and wandering from place to place. Chapter 2 recounts how following the Second World War people were herded from camp to camp as the military and civilian authorities, caught unprepared by the scale of the problem, attempted to feed and house them and organize their repatriation. It describes how the camp bureaucracy operated, excluding those considered undeserving, separating nationalities, ignoring the political will of those it was dealing with—producing a system where the displaced person *as person* went missing under a system of labeling and control. Those in the camps subverted these attempts at control by taking matters in their own hands—organizing for themselves everything from political campaigns to attempts to locate missing relatives. People trekked from camp to camp following rumored sightings of relatives. Some, armed with small photographs, approached everyone they met, asking for information. Others took the opportunity to disappear from their former lives and complicity in what had happened, and there was very little attempt to stop them.

Volunteers in the displaced persons camps, often women, did make some attempt to relate to their charges as people, and to help them make contact with family members, but the displaced were left mainly to their own resources in this regard, at least at first. Chapter 3 discusses the official and unofficial tracing services that were eventually set up, and examines the tensions and disagreements that the demand to trace the missing produced in the various military, civilian, and voluntary agencies. For many authorities the identification of the displaced as *populations* led to the invisibility of missing *persons;* the task, as these authorities saw it, was to restore order and control. While the staff of voluntary agencies insisted from the start on the search for individual missing persons, they were continually sidelined. Their willingness to help anyone, whether "enemy national" or not, was at variance with official policy, which confined what help there was to certain categories of the population. It was only once it became clear that people were not going to accept repatriation or resettlement until they had news of family members that tracing services were no longer seen by other agencies as an impediment that would slow down reconstruction, but as an essential element in the process, and that services were extended to everyone.

The conflict between the demands of relatives or survivors—and indeed the general public—and the priorities of the various authorities surfaced yet again in the 1990s in a controversy over the voluminous records from the Second World War held by the International Tracing Service. The concerns of those searching for information about what had happened to friends and relatives were not audible to those in charge of the records. Or perhaps the authorities blocked their ears, fearing that opening the records could lead to demands for restitution and justice. In the present, as in the past, it seems to take strong individuals and sustained campaigns to remove impediments to tracing missing persons and revealing the details of past abuses, and to insist on the importance of personal and family relationships. In the end it is the insistence of people themselves, searching for their missing, that disrupts the attempt to impose an order that treats people as populations.

The same tension between professionals dealing with the aftermath of disaster and those looking for people they know is described in chapter 4, which returns to the present and examines the search for the missing in the London bombings in 2005. The contrast between the deep anguish of those searching and the impenetrable bureaucratic detachment of the authorities is marked in this instance. The objectification and instrumentalization of the relatives was complete. They were made to wait hours for a telephone helpline, refused information at hospitals, and forced to fill in long and complex forms, detailing everything the missing person had been wearing or carrying and listing the person's particularities and physical characteristics. And relatives of the missing were met with not only silence but denial by the police authorities: many were sent home to wait for information even when the police already knew the fate of the missing person concerned. Alongside these reports of the apparent indifference of the authorities, whose hands were shackled by systems and protocols, we find accounts of people on the bombed trains staying for hours to sit with the injured and dying, even when there was nothing they could do for them except be there. The inquests into the deaths caused by the bombings provide a stark contrast to the actions taken by authorities in the immediate aftermath of the attacks. Not only do the inquests reveal how much people helped each other; they also demonstrate a concern for each person involved, whether victim, survivor, or relative—a concern to find out exactly what happened to each of those who died, and what it might have been like for them.

As chapter 5 makes clear, forensic investigators in New York following 9/11 showed the same respect for families of those killed as was demonstrated by the coroner's court in London following the 2005 bombings. In the immediate aftermath of the September 11 attacks families faced a system in chaos: agencies were struggling to pay out the money that had been pouring in for victims, and procedures for collecting DNA for identifications were so poor that the whole process had to be repeated in many cases. Despite the reinscription of the missing as the dead on the one hand and as heroes on the other, the focus for those working on the forensic identification of remains was on the persons involved. Staff dealt carefully and sensitively with family members. In the process, enormous amounts of money and time were spent, and new procedures for forensic identification in the challenging circumstances faced after the collapse were developed. While the money spent can be seen as reflecting the inscription of the dead as "heroes," there is little doubt that from the point of view of the forensic staff and the families the object was to reassert the significance of the personhood that had been so disregarded, and to reclaim, if not the lives, at least the deaths of those who perished. These aims were in conflict with the imperatives behind the move to restore order and control to Ground Zero, where heavy machinery was brought in to speed the process, and the remains of buildings and their inhabitants were scooped up indiscriminately and taken to a landfill site for sorting and disposal. The attempt to transform the memory of traumatic destruction into one of heroic sacrifice conflicted both with the families' insistence on the irreplaceable, grievable lives of their lost relatives and with the forensic teams' understanding of the families' anguish.

The huge sums spent on the identification process after 9/11 recall the efforts devoted to the identification of the missing in another context: the aftermath of the Vietnam War. Searches for the remains of MIAs in Vietnam continue to this day, with enormous resources, both money and personnel, devoted to these efforts. The missing in action are a unique category of missing persons: as military personnel, they belong to the state in a way that civilians do not. In service they obey orders; they have no individual voice as such; they kill and they die. However, although the military assumes responsibility for accounting for their deaths and for those missing, its accounts do not go uncontested. At times it takes people outside official channels to prompt exhumation and identification, as in the example of missing from the First World War at Fromelles in northern France. This case is discussed in chapter 6, which explores how not only the identification of remains but also the manner of burial and commemoration of casualties of war have been contested. It is a struggle over the bodies of the dead. Do they belong to the authorities or to relatives? It is a struggle too over the facts about the missing. Who is in charge of information about what happened, of gathering the details and of assessing them? And how and by whom is this information to be conveyed to the families? These struggles arise in part because of the ambiguity of citizen armies. Relatives insist on the demobilization of bodies after a conflict—the return of those lost in war to civilian status and full personhood, and the return of their bodies for burial at home. Government representatives see military cemeteries as memorials to heroic national achievements, and demand that relatives surrender the dead to this purpose as they gave the living in sacrifice in the first place.

The importance of women in the search for the missing is striking. Women volunteers are involved not only in the search process itself but also in setting up tracing systems and demanding that relatives' voices be heard. While many of the chapters in this book reveal the extent of women's involvement, in chapter 7, on the disappeared in Argentina, women's activities and activism take center stage. The political activism of women in Argentina was hugely influential not only in making the disappeared visible but in changing the political landscape more broadly. The Madres of the Plaza de Mayo took the platitudes of the regime at face value and demanded that their children be recognized as political subjects, their arrests admitted, and their supposed offenses proved. They refused to be silenced by fear or labeled as insane. They insisted that the missing be visible, that those who were disappeared be reappeared, and reappeared as persons—irreplaceable, political beings.

The case of the disappeared in Argentina reveals the stark contrast between a politics of relationality and generationality, or *a politics of the person-as-such,* and that of objectification, or *a politics that misses the person.* It also offers a concrete illustration of how instrumentalization and authoritarianism can be and is contested. In Argentina, women did not do what they were supposed to do—remain quiet and suffer in silence. They took to the streets, encircling the trauma, rendering it visible through their rejection of the possibility of disappearances, on the one hand, and of the transformation of the disappeared into the dead without an accounting of who was responsible, on the other. When exhumations began, and the disappeared were being identified, the Madres refused to accept what in a sense they most wanted—an answer to their agonizing uncertainty. In the absence of a politics that recognized their children as irreplaceable political beings, they insisted that their children remain missing.

The disappeared remained missing in another sense. In Eric Carlson's book about one of Argentina's disappeared, *I Remember Julia,* friends and family attempt to piece together a picture of who Julia was from their shared scraps of memory, only to find that this is not possible. No coherent image emerges: Julia remains missing. The loss of the missing is, to borrow Pauline Boss's term, an ambiguous loss, in the sense that no one knows whether the person lost is alive or dead. But it is ambiguous as well in the sense that some people willingly choose to leave family and friends to begin a new life elsewhere, severing all connection with the past. Chapter 8 investigates not only cases of people who walk out on their families and the impact on those left behind, but also the continuing search for answers by those whose relations disappeared for some reason after the Second World War, and by children who were separated from one or both of their birth parents. Such situations bring home how people are and remain unknown even to those who think they know them best. Extensive searching in records and places often reveals only that there is no answer, no resolution. The person-as-such is a missing person, someone who cannot be pinned down, categorized, controlled, or known, someone who always escapes capture. The final chapter of the book explores what it means to think of the person as missing, and what *a politics of the person as missing* might look like.

ACKNOWLEDGMENTS

It is with some embarrassment that I find myself completing a book about missing persons while being unable to adequately acknowledge all those who have helped. David Edkins once told me of a quotation displayed in a London coffee bar: "Happiness is good health and a bad memory." I am certainly blessed with the latter, if blessing it be, and that and the length of time this book has been in the writing are my only excuses.

The staff of the UK National Archives at Kew, Emily Oldfield at the Red Cross Museum and Archives in London, and Ndahambelela Hertha Lukileni and her staff at the archives of the United Nations in New York were most helpful during the research on the missing and displaced of the Second World War, as were participants and speakers at the conference "Beyond Camps and Forced Labour" at the Imperial War Museum in January 2009, particularly Paul A. Shapiro, Lynne Taylor, and Nancy Hamlin Soukup. My historian colleagues at Aberystwyth were a source of support and encouragement, especially R. Gerald Hughes, who gave generous help and extensive comments on areas in which I am far from an expert. Maja Zehfuss helped with German documents and much more. I had fascinating conversations with Hester Hardwick, Susan Lillienthal, Debbie Lisle, and Andreja Zevnik on this material. A grant from the Aberystwyth University Research Fund made the archive work possible.

Much of the work for the chapters on New York City, and Manhattan in particular, took place during a series of visits from March 2002 to June 2007, again funded by Aberystwyth University. As well as visiting myself, I seized on any friends or colleagues who were traveling to New York and charged them with photographing particular places and bringing back literature. Michael Feldshuh, Malcolm Hamer, Colleen Kelly, Laura Kurgan, Jan Ramirez, and Michael Schulan spoke to me on a number of questions. Some of the material I draw on for chapters 1 and 5 was first published as "Missing Persons: Manhattan 2001," in *Living, Dying, Surviving: The Logics of Biopower and the War on Terror*, ed. Elizabeth Dauphinee and Cristina Masters

(New York: Palgrave, 2006); the chapters also draw on work published in "Ground Zero: Reflections on Trauma and In/distinction," *Journal for Cultural Research* 8, no. 3 (July 2004): 247–70, and in "The Rush to Memory and the Rhetoric of War," *Journal of Political and Military Sociology* 31, no. 2 (Winter 2003): 231–51.

My initial work on the London bombings was presented at London in a Time of Terror: The Politics of Response, an international conference held at Birkbeck College in London in 2005. I had interesting discussions in London that day and elsewhere with the convenors, Angharad Closs Stephens and Nick Vaughan-Williams, and other participants. I would like to thank Marie Fatayi-Williams especially, and not just for the conversations we had but for her work more generally. Lucy Easthope shared her experiences of postdisaster planning with me. Some of the material on which chapter 4 draws was first published in "Biopolitics, Communication, and Global Governance," *Review of International Studies* 34, no. S1 (January 2008): 211-32. Mick Dillon read a draft of that piece, and a wonderful conversation, fortified by a metaphorical whiskey or two, followed.

Lucy Taylor in Aberystwyth and Katherine Hite at Vassar College shared their expertise on Latin America and commented thoughtfully on my writing on Argentina; Naeem Inayatullah's inimitable comments made me realize that this was the book I was working on; Himadeep Muppidi and his students reminded me of the particularity of my perspective; Tim Edkins prompted my engagement with Rancière; Simona Rentea shared her insights on those who go missing; Véronique Pin-Fat and Tom Lundborg read near-final drafts and provided vital feedback. My masters and doctoral students and others in the graduate community in Aberystwyth are a continual source of inspiration and good reading suggestions. Members of the Critical and Cultural Politics Group, the interdepartmental Performance and Politics Group, and the informal writing group in the International Politics Department read and commented on work in progress. Papers drawing on the developing ideas were presented at conferences of the International Studies Association; at Brown University, in Rhode Island; York University, Toronto; Vassar College, in New York State; and at the universities of Durham, Hull, St. Andrews, and Warwick in the United Kingdom, among others, and participants provided helpful and always encouraging comments.

Over the years, many others have read and commented on versions of the work, and many more have influenced my thinking. I hope they will forgive me for not mentioning them by name; my thanks are due to them all. The intellectual input was invaluable, but what was perhaps most striking was how many people turned out to have personal experience of one sort or another of missing persons, and how supportive they were of the project. Finally, that this book takes the form it does is largely thanks to the thoughtful engagement of Roger Haydon and two anonymous reviewers from Cornell University Press, and to the careful assistance of Ange Romeo-Hall and Marian Rogers.

Introduction

> Politics makes visible that which had no reason to be seen, it lodges one world into another.
>
> —Jacques Rancière, "Ten Theses on Politics"

When someone goes missing, what's happened doesn't seem possible: people don't just disappear. Sometimes all that is left to insist that the person was indeed once there is a photograph. These images are shown by those searching for the missing to everyone they meet. "This is my brother," they say. "Have you seen him?" They are enlarged and carried aloft by those protesting disappearances in authoritarian regimes. "You took them away alive. We want them back alive," they proclaim. Simple snapshots, torn from the family album, insist that this is a person, a person who exists, even though they may have been here one minute and gone the next. They challenge the traumatic disruption of time and place. They make the missing visible. But photographs themselves are ambiguous, at once present as objects yet inevitably records of an absence. Like missing persons, they cut into continuous, homogeneous time and the territorialization of space. Time stands still for those left behind, and place is unsettled: the missing are nowhere to be found.

Posters proclaiming the missing were produced in the aftermath of the collapse of the World Trade Center towers in New York City in September 2001. The search of relatives and friends of those who disappeared in the dust and debris of the towers was heartbreaking enough, but the appeal in the posters was something more than that, or so it seemed to me. The snapshots of the missing whose faces appeared on the posters were juxtaposed with quotidian details of bodies and lives torn apart by the events of that day. Time was cut short in both snapshot and missing person, time frozen in a moment that was neither present nor past, the person neither dead nor alive.

These hastily compiled posters, produced in an anguish of hope and torment, reflected the confusion and chaos of the first moments of that day, moments when no one knew what was happening. In short order, however, that confusion abated: we were told that America was under attack, that those who had died in the towers were heroes, and what is more, heroes whose deaths would be used to justify wars fought in their name. But the posters remained, not only for weeks or months afterward but for years, protesting the reimposed order, contesting the neatness of the story that was being told, insisting on the presence of the absent as ordinary people, not heroes.

In the aftermath of another event—the London bombings in July 2005—similar posters were produced, though by then the lesson had been learned, and the authorities removed them once the missing had been found. On this occasion it was not so much the posters that protested, but the friends and relatives looking for the missing. Under the protocols of disaster-preparedness, those searching the streets, phoning the hospitals, and reporting the missing had been kept waiting for over a week before they were given any information about their relatives. In this case it was not that the bodies were difficult or impossible to identify—indeed many of the missing had lived long enough to give their names to rescue workers before they died. It was rather that for the authorities charged with managing the aftermath of the bombings what mattered was not the anguish of the relatives but the careful identification of not *who* but *what* those killed were: were they innocent victims or terrorists?

There is a intriguing connection between *the politics of missing persons,* or what happens when people go missing—after violence such as wars or genocides as well as under more everyday circumstances—and the ways in which personhood is regularly produced under current forms of political order in the West, *a politics that misses the person,* a politics that objectifies and instrumentalizes. After the London bombings there was a reaction against the perceived objectification of distraught relatives searching for the missing: a call for a focus on people not process—a call for a change in a politics that forgets the person in its focus on order and security. The search for the missing, and protests surrounding disappearances more broadly, can be rewritten as a demand for, or indeed an expression of, a different form of politics, one where the person *as such* counts: this could be called *a politics of the person as missing.* What form of politics that might be, and how practices of search and protest in the aftermath of disappearances demand and produce that politics, is what this book explores.

The Western Individual

In the period following the Second World War, Europe was in chaos. Tens of millions of people had been killed or were uprooted and on the move; cities and livelihoods had been destroyed, the social fabric of a continent laid waste. Millions were missing—separated from their families. Events had happened that challenged the ways of thinking and being that had formed the backdrop of what could have been called a civilization. Yet the immediate postwar period was largely forgotten. Histories of the war were written, memorials to wartime dead erected, and new structures of national and international organization put in place. But on the whole the devastation that followed the end of the war was erased from memory. Histories of the impact of the extermination or near extermination of whole groups of people, the forced movement and resettlement of huge populations, and the multiple failures of policies of justice or restitution remained largely unwritten under the imperatives of reconstruction and the demands of the period of cold war that rapidly ensued. Revisiting the implications of that period for the lives of the people concerned—and in many senses those of us in Europe and North America at least are the inheritors of that period—has had to wait. It is only now, for example, some sixty years later, that those who were children at the time have begun to look back, and personal and regular histories have begun to be written.

And yet, despite the silence, the impact of the violence, dislocation, and disruption has arguably underpinned—and undermined—life in Europe ever since. Is it possible to trace a link between the aftermath of 1945 and the accepted ideas of personhood that became increasingly prevalent in Europe for the remainder of the twentieth century? Did the violence and upheaval give rise to a response that relied on a form of personhood that forgot vulnerability, and violence, relying instead on an atomized and limited form of being, one that could perceive fulfillment not in terms of relations or community—both of which had been thrown into doubt by the disruption of wartime—but rather through individuality and self-sufficiency? On the whole, life in Europe today does not acknowledge the impact of the events that culminated in the chaos of 1945 and reverberated far beyond. Do those reverberations strengthen the hold of a police logic that guarantees order and security, and make exclusion from or absence of its opposite, a political logic, more acceptable?

When events happen that are of unimaginable horror—events that are called traumatic—we can say, for the sake of argument, that there are two possible responses.[1] The first is a forgetting of the horror and a refusal of memory—or rather a limiting of memory to standard tropes that in fact amount to forgetting. An attempt is made to reinstate previous forms of organization, those very forms of organization that were implicated in the horror in the first place. The second is a more difficult and much rarer response: an *encircling* of the trauma, a refusal to forget the lessons, an insistence on the acknowledgement that, however impossible to understand, what happened happened. Traumatic events are those that both betray and reveal the vulnerability of existence and the impossibility of the forms of reassurance that we regularly resort to in the face of the fragility of bodies and beings. The first response covers over the trauma, pretends it didn't happen, disregards it, or medicalizes it. Perhaps this is what has happened in Europe since the Second World War, by and large. And this has had certain results. But stories from the aftermath of 1945—and especially stories of missing persons—are to be found everywhere we turn. It seemed that everyone I spoke to about my work while I was writing this book had something to tell.

For those more closely involved in the events of the late 1940s than many of us, in the end, when the dust of conflict has settled, and the antagonisms and questions—of guilt, of innocence, of revenge, of reparations—can be set aside, even if only for a time, the question of what exactly took place persists. People want to know what happened to their relations—what they did, how it turned out for them. They want to know this even when there is no possibility, because of the passage of time, of a reunion. In some cases, they want to know—though they may not want it publicly known—even if shame may accompany the discovery. We want to know how things turned out for people in the end, to complete their story and to help us in building our own. Initially there may be a reluctance—people have made new lives, concealing their past or not wanting to talk about it because of the pain involved. Or sometimes there is just no one to talk to who will listen. But the questions remain and resurface later: people cannot be allowed to just disappear.

This persistence seems, like the encircling of trauma, to contest the police logic or sovereign power based on categorization and exclusion that has itself produced the violence that leads to displacement and disappearance. It is independent from questions of reparations or retribution. It is perhaps not a question of crime and punishment (though these are important) but maybe of justice—a justice that requires persons, with all their attributes, be given respect and dignity in their uniqueness, their singularity. To achieve this may require that persons be reduced first of all to entries in card indexes alongside millions of other missing persons: a collection of those who have nothing in common other than the fact that someone else, somewhere, is searching for them. An inoperative community, perhaps.[2]

For those of us fortunate enough to have been born in Europe *after* the Second World War, and in areas and to families comparatively untouched by that conflict, its reverberations remain faint, even largely inaudible. Unlike W. G. Sebald, born in Germany in 1944 of parents who supported National Socialism, we do not see visions of a London in flames, utterly destroyed as it would have been had it ever been the subject of a firestorm such as that in Dresden, as Hitler is said to have intended.[3] Our loyalties remain undisturbed by a gray sense of guilt or the shame of survival from that era, and the violences of empire, and questions of complicity there, are too distant to echo forcibly down the generations for many among us. The "missing" have long since been all but forgotten—disappeared from our memories—and the displaced have merged into their new surroundings, absorbed without trace, at least to the casual eye, by their adopted habitat. We forget, too easily perhaps, that behind every face, even our own faces, is a vast untapped landscape—in many cases a landscape of horror concealed—that continues to contain the seeds of the past. Those of us nurtured in peacetime forget at our peril the precariousness of life and of personhood. We may turn to examine violences elsewhere, in another place or another time, in an attempt to come to terms with something we know nothing of; we often find ourselves doing so without ever wondering why. Our own transgressions are forgotten—as are the major violences in which we, as prosperous Europeans or North Americans, safe now in our warm houses, continue to be complicit.[4]

Unmissed Persons

I have talked about the missing; what about the unmissed? Not all those who are missing are reported. Some are invisible anyway. In the United Kingdom people die alone, their bodies not found until days, weeks, or even years later. No one notices that they are not there. They seem to have no ties, no relations, no one to worry about them. Estimates show that over sixteen thousand people in the United Kingdom were buried by their local authorities between 2000 and 2004 in the absence of any known relatives to pay for the funeral, and the problem seems to be increasing.[5]

However, there is a larger sense in which we could think about the unmissed: those who are not present to a Western imagination in the first place, those who are invisible to many scholars of international relations, with its focus on the world seen from a particular perspective, as if that were the only one.[6] These persons could be said to be "missing" in a different and arguably more important way than those I have been discussing so far. Their absence from our discussions is a more fundamental one, so fundamental that we don't even realize they are missing from our parochial picture of the world.[7] They are the missing missing, the doubly missing. We will encounter some of them later, the missing from the Twin Towers whose absence could not be reported, since their very presence in the United States was illegal. They are to be found in the United Kingdom as well: they are the asylum seekers who disappear from sight to avoid deportation. In the non-Western world, there are many people who go uncounted, who do not count as far as the West is concerned. If they appear at all it is as objects—of our concern, of humanitarian aid or intervention—not as persons with political views of their own.[8] Judith Butler writes of them as ungrievable lives, "lives that cannot be apprehended as injured or lost if they are not first apprehended as living."[9] Nancy Scheper-Hughes, in her book *Death without Weeping,* testifies movingly to how starvation of children in Brazil is so commonplace that the dead are not even mourned.[10]

So, amid a focus on tracing, locating, and identifying missing persons, the disappeared and the displaced, some people remain invisible to our gaze. We have spoken of the missing millions, displaced after the Second World War in Europe—and no doubt our attention could be extended to those missing in other parts of the world after this conflict or other conflicts. We will speak of the disappeared in Argentina, but nothing will be said of the disappearances in much more contemporary Pakistan. But it is not just these missing, or the doubly missing after 9/11, who are missing from our account. We have not counted those who are invisible to our (post)colonial gaze, or those whose appearance renders them invisible to our sight even when they are in plain view.[11] And yet it is to such a racialized gaze that the objectification of persons can be linked: Frantz Fanon remarks how he came to see how he was "an object in the midst of other objects"—visible only as a carrier of "tom-toms" and "cannibalism" when he encountered a metropolitan French gaze.[12] Himadeep Muppidi writes unflinchingly of his own dislocation and rage amid the specimens in the museum of King Leopold II of Belgium. Visiting the Royal Museum of Central Africa in Tervuren, Belgium, the only part of a larger project, a "World School of Colonialism," that was realized before Leopold's death, Muppidi asks: "In the European order of things, was I, could I be, only another animal-object?"[13] Treatment of the colonized as objects was common in such museums. Colonizers treated the body of an unknown African, stolen from its grave and displayed in French and Spanish museums for many years, as nothing but an object. After 170 years, the remains were finally returned to Botswana for reburial. The Botswana government was accused of undue haste—they did not wait for the man's identity to be determined, but reburied him in a public park, "making him an object of public display" once again.[14]

If politics is that which renders visible that which has no right to be seen, as Jacques Rancière claims, then a book on the politics of the missing could be deemed incomplete without some consideration of the invisible person, the person who doesn't even begin to count. There is no doubt that we need, as white Europeans or Americans, to examine the heritage we share, a heritage arguably grounded in the reduction of the majority of *persons-as-such* to the status of nothing but objects, a heritage of colonialism as much as a heritage of war. Before the U.S. residents among my readers disclaim their complicity in European colonialism, may I remind them that many of them are descendants of colonizers or reap the benefits of past repression, and moreover, that they, now, inherit the mantle of colonialism.

However, even when someone *counts* in a way westerners count, the argument of this book is that frequently they count not for *who* they are (their being in all its imponderable mystery) but for *what* they are, at least as far as the systems of accounting or governance that we have currently are concerned. I am not sure that making certain that everyone counts or is counted in ways that we currently count people in Western politics is a step forward. I would want to locate a certain homology between systems of registration, identification, and control and a process of objectification—the production of people as nothing but *objects* of administration. The messy, contradictory, intractable *person* gets in the way: a politics of the missing demands a different form of counting. Missing persons, as I examine them in this book, are not missing in some general sense. They are missing as far as those searching for them are concerned. Their lives may not be regarded as grievable in any general sense either, to use Butler's term again, but whoever they are, for their relations and friends they *are* grievable.[15] A focus on missing persons demands a focus on the specific, the particular.

Sometimes it is when people feel they count not for *who* they are but for *what* they are—or what function they fulfill, as husbands, wage earners, mothers, for example—that they may decide that their situation is intolerable and choose to go missing or to disappear. The narrator of Ralph Ellison's *Invisible Man* chose to vanish into hibernation because he realized that he was in any case invisible: "I am invisible, understand, simply because people refuse to see me.... When they approach me they see only my surroundings, themselves, or figments of their imagination—indeed, everything and anything except me." He comments: "It is sometimes advantageous to be unseen, although it is most often wearing on the nerves. . . . You often doubt if you really exist."[16] The impact of colonization on subjectivity, which is reflected in Fanon's work *Black Skin, White Masks,* is also evident in Adil Jussawalla's poem "Missing Person."[17] Like the invisible man, Jussawalla's subject is entangled in relations that are based not on *who* he is but on *what;* according to one commentator he is "a 'missing person' missing precisely because his subjectivity and agency have been substantially evacuated by colonial past and postcolonial present."[18] Persons have been replaced by masks, masks that they sometimes do not even know they wear.

In this context, the *person* is neither the *individual* of liberal political thought nor the *subject* of critical approaches to governmentality.[19] Mary Douglas and Stephen Nay point out that the person—which they claim for anthropologists has to involve relations with other people, a social context—is missing in social science, with its reliance on a concept of the solitary individual abstracted from any cultural milieu.[20] Likewise, biography and autobiography often fail to convince because they are forced to work with the fiction that the person is present, not missing: "They cannot represent what they claim to represent, namely the 'whole' life of a person," but, importantly, "this 'whole' person is in any case a fiction, a belief created by the very form of auto/ biography itself."[21] But though the dust of the archive contains only traces of the missing—material traces, in many senses—historians can and do pay attention to the gaps as much as to what is there, which anyway was not put there for their purposes.[22] It is in this dust, in the attempt at piecing together, at producing a narrative, that the impossibility of doing so appears. In the interstices of the material laid down by the bureaucracy of administration and in "what is missing from them" are to be found the traces of a different politics.[23]

Persons as Irreplaceable

The loss of someone close may appear to be a very private experience, and in that sense something outside politics, which is commonly regarded as related to the public sphere. But, on the contrary, "it furnishes a sense of political community of a complex order."[24] It does this by drawing our attention to the relations and ties that are central to questions of politics, ethics, and responsibility. Our fates are intertwined—and our existence is fundamentally composed of and through relations. Our responses when someone goes missing—or when people go missing, but when we say it like this we must be careful, because people go missing *one by one*—our responses when this happens can tell us something about what a politics that insists on or assumes these relational ties, rather than one based on treating people as inter-changeable individuals, might be like. Each missing person is missed as this or that unique and irreplaceable person, and is missed by those close and by those further away as well. They are not missed as abstract individuals.

For some purposes, and for most of what we ordinarily call politics, the person as a unique being is not what is important—notionally what is needed is any individual with certain abilities or characteristics. In recruitment for a particular job, for example, considerations of fairness and equal opportunity require those doing the hiring to be blind to the particularities of the per-son and look only at someone's ability to satisfy the "person specification," which is expected to be drawn up in terms of readily definable and measur-able qualifications, experience, and skills. The economic individual too is exchangeable one for another, and ranked by wealth, purchasing power, or entitlements.[25] The market principle allows us to ignore the needs of some-one who has no money and who thus cannot express those needs in terms that the economic system can recognize. In democratic politics, individual votes are counted, but once the election has taken place, there is no onus on the winning group to take account of the wishes or feelings of the minority. The democratic system of contested elections based on "one man, one vote" allows for a polarization, rather than an accommodation, of views. What matters is ensuring that one's party has sufficient votes to win, not listening to the views of those who might disagree with the majority, in order to take their thoughts on board. A simple majority voting system means this is not necessary. The law is also blind to personhood, in that it applies to all equally. Of course, in the search for justice, it will not suffice if just *any* person is punished; it has to be the one who is found guilty of the crime. In this sense, despite its seeming abstraction, justice when expressed in a court of law requires that attention be paid to details of evidence and nuances of judg-ment, to determine that the crime was committed by this one and not that one. Nevertheless, broadly speaking, ordinary politics and market economics rely on substitutability: we have *a politics that misses the person,* a politics of the *what,* not the *who.*

When someone goes missing the threads that connect our stories and our lives are strained, even broken. The loss of someone we love shows us some-thing about who we are, and how closely we are bound to each other. Indeed, it shows us that who we are comes in large part from our ties to others. Judith Butler observes: "It's not as if an 'I' exists independently over here and then simply loses a 'you' over there, especially if the attachment to 'you' is part of what composes who 'I' am. . . . On one level, I think I have lost 'you' only to discover that 'I' have gone missing as well."[26] Butler is writing here, it seems, of those to whom we feel closest—our nearest and dearest, those whose loss will strike us hardest. But is it possible, if we are thinking in terms of the ties that compose us or the encounters that make us who we are, to limit ourselves in this way, to draw a line around those whose loss affects our sense of who we are and those whose disappearance has no impact on us? Isn't our response to the loss of our immediate friends and relatives symptomatic of something wider? Do not the ties through which we find ourselves extend indefinitely around us without any obvious end point? Do they not contest the notion of an order that relies on roles, categories, and exclusions, an order of objectification and instrumentalization? What we lose, then, when anyone goes missing, is a part of the warp and weft of the relations that constitute us—a part of what tells us who we are, as irreplaceable beings, irreplaceable in a sense only because of the relations within which we have our being and the encounters that have taken place and that compose them.

This is not to say that fairness and equality are not important, or that struggles for such values should not have been undertaken. It is to point out that to focus on being evenhanded and fair can lead to the person being treated as nothing more than an object or a commodity. Sometimes the lack of final information about a missing person leads to financial difficulty—a pension may not be forthcoming, or an insurance policy may not pay out. But for most people searching for someone who is missing it seems that the money is not what is at stake or what leads them to pursue their questions about what has happened. Many insist that nothing can replace the person who has been lost. When a determination of the fate of the missing is made and compensation paid, some are even "insulted" by the paltry sums offered, and one suspects that this is not to do solely with the way in which the money will not replace the earnings of the husband or father, wife or mother. It is more a reaction to the singularity and uniqueness of the person lost. It is not any child who has been lost—who could be replaced by another child conceived later—but a particular child, who is irreplaceable. In response to the "flat-rate pay-out of £11,000" offered by the Criminal Injuries Compensation Authority for "a young unmarried man" after the London bombings, Marie Fatayi-Williams "was in no frame of mind to go through the ordeal of filling in countless claim forms [or] ready to subject Anthony to further injustice and injury." Writing three years later, she expressed surprise that "no one in authority has shown any concern about the absence of my application for this compensation."[27] But if she hadn't applied through the formal bureaucracy, then it could not even recognize her existence.

Protests on behalf of the displaced, the missing, and the disappeared produce a political subjectivity—the person—and an interruption of the social order, the form of order that philosopher Jacques Rancière calls a police order, an order that cannot see the person-as-such.[28] What I am calling the person-as-such—and metaphorically, the missing person epitomizes the person-as-such—is always the subject of a lack, never complete, always relational, never fully known, never "at home." This notion of the person draws on Lacanian thinking.[29] What we call social order or social reality is also, in this view, structured around a traumatic excess or lack that is rendered invisible. Rancière's police order relies in a similar way on the production of a series of roles or categories that form a society or social reality apparently without supplement or excess, complete in itself. Politics, for Rancière, is the disruption of that order in the name of that which is not seen by that order, that which has no part in it, that which is not a part of the particular "partition of the sensible," the particular way of seeing the world, upon which it is founded.[30] The person is a political subjectivity whose production—merely through the assumption that it exists as an equal speaking being—disrupts the police order.

According to Rancière, "Political subjectification is an ability to produce...polemical scenes...that bring out the contradiction between [police logic and political logic], by positing existences that are at the same time nonexistences—or nonexistences that are at the same time existences."[31] In Argentina, in the aftermath of the production of the "disappeared"—perhaps paradigmatic "nonexistences that are at the same time existences"—the Madres of the Plaza de Mayo produced such scenes initially by visiting police stations and demanding to know where their children were held, taking at face value the provisions of the law, demanding that their children count. Later, by taking their protest to the public square, yet wearing the head scarves of women, they demanded not only that their children count, but also that they themselves count. By acting as though mothers and grandmothers are capable beings, by *assuming* equality in other words, they altered the relationship "between the ways of *doing,* of *being,* and of *saying* that define the perceptible organisation of the community, the relationships between the places where one does one thing and those where one does something else, the capacities associated with this particular *doing* and those required for another."[32]

For Giorgio Agamben the political order of the West—which he calls sovereign power—was based on an exclusion that produced a particular form of life: "bare life" or *homo sacer,* a form of life with no part in politics, a form of life that belongs to the home, not the public sphere.[33] However, this form of life has the potential to turn into "an existence over which power no longer seems to have any hold." It seems as if "the bare life of *homo sacer*...in assuming itself as a task" becomes "explicitly and immediately political."[34] In a similar way to that in which bare life or *homo sacer* is the product of the social order that the order cannot tolerate, so missing persons are the product of a social order without supplement whose existence (or, in this case, non-existence) disrupts that very order. Whether we phrase it in Agambenian terms as the assumption of bare life or in Rancière's as the assumption of equality as speaking beings, relatives speaking in the name of that which is not there (the displaced, the missing, or the disappeared) are producing a political subjectivity (the missing person, the subject of a lack). Action or speech on behalf of the displaced or the disappeared creates the demand for a place for the person-as-such in politics. But, as Rancière warns us, "The resistance of any police order... is a matter of principle."[35] There is always the risk—indeed the likelihood—that the partition of the sensible will recompose itself and another police order will be put in place. We can see that taking place in the way in which "the missing" are first largely ignored and then themselves become a category within what remains a police logic.

Categorizing the Missing

Whereas the response of those in authority is to provide information that can lead to closure and to moving on, and compensation that can restore the financial stability of those left, and, sometimes, criminal prosecutions that can provide a form of justice, the relatives of the missing are responding to something quite different: to the unique person who is missing or lost. What is missing is the *who*—the *person-as-such* not the *subject* of the law or a compensation claim. In their procedures in relation to the missing, even voluntary agencies risk making the missing into objects once more—objects of policy, measurable and accountable. In 2002, the International Committee of the Red Cross (ICRC) began a review of its activities, and those of other agencies, in regard to missing persons, and set up an agenda with clear objectives to highlight the issue. Of course, in order to do this, a definition was necessary. This is what they came up with: "A 'missing person' is anyone unaccounted for as a result of an armed conflict or a situation of internal violence."[36] The ICRC remit under international law relates to those affected by conflict— prisoners of war, the wounded, and civilians—hence the way in which missing persons are defined here in relation to conflict or internal violence. But the use of the phrase "anyone unaccounted for" situates the person missing in relation to some formalized "accounting" procedure, whatever that might be (lists of the missing in action, perhaps; lists of those presumed dead but where evidence of death is not available). The definition pays no regard to the way in which someone (not "anyone") is only ever missing *in relation. People are not missing in the abstract. People are only missing* in relation to those who know them and are concerned for their well-being and want to know their whereabouts. The ICRC report locates responsibility for preventing disappearances and tracing the missing on the shoulders of government authorities and armed groups. It becomes a question of the administration of populations—those in authority are required to keep adequate records of their populations. But in the process persons become objects of administration. Defining and pinning down missing people as "The Missing"—as in the title of the ICRC report—becomes another categorization, another supposedly universal category, like "citizen," "refugee," "asylum seeker," and the *who* can disappear into the *what.* People go missing one by one, as someone, not as "anyone." The move to account for the missing may be a response to the insistence by relatives on the importance of the *who*—the unique person who is missing—but defining missing persons and establishing a bureaucratic mechanism for dealing with them, while laudable in many ways, risk missing both the point and the person. Such actions reinstate the very form of police order that protesting the missing person, with its insistence on the person-as-such, challenged.

However, missing persons disturb; their ambiguity deranges not only those who search for them, but also those who seek to impose administrative or political classifications or categorizations. On September 10, 1945, Colonel Bowring, at that time head of the Search Bureau in the British sector of occupied Germany, sent out "General Instructions for All Officers Engaged in Tracing and Search." The tasks of the bureau were listed. The first task listed was "to trace and search for Military and civilian missing persons of the United Nations." Fair enough. Interestingly though, the second task was "to establish the fate of those persons who cannot be found."[37] Surely, this was by definition impossible. More intriguingly still, the instructions were clearly set out under distinct headings: search for living persons, search for children, search for deceased persons, and search for missing persons. The list is reminiscent of the extract from a "Chinese encyclopaedia" with which Michel Foucault begins his study *The Order of Things.*[38] What we have perhaps is a heterotopia, where there is no common ground upon which the various terms make sense. As Foucault suggests, "Heterotopias are disturbing, probably because they secretly undermine language, because they make it impossible to name this *and* that, because they shatter or tangle common names."[39]

The attempt to delineate "missing persons" as a category among other categories disrupts the logic—it throws into disarray the police order built around a categorization with no remainder. The missing *are* the remainder. For the police order, there can be nothing missing. But the missing are the part of no part, those "existences that are at the same time nonexistences—or nonexistences that are at the same time existences," existences that the police logic neglects, those that are invisible within that logic and yet that "bring out the contradiction between two logics," police logic and political logic.[40] While Rancière sees "the people" as the political subjectivity that deranges par excellence, "the person" perhaps disturbs in a different and potentially more profound manner. The person as missing cannot be pinned down by a police logic, and we are all potentially missing persons in that sense.

The missing disrupt in another way. They are between two deaths: the symbolic space they occupy cannot be closed, although their biological existence is assumed, at least potentially, to have ended.[41] They are virtually *homines sacri* in that they are occupants of a zone of indistinction between life and death.[42] In the state of emergency become rule, "we are all virtually *homines sacri*."[43] For sovereign power, then, there is no difference between the missing and the rest of us. Except that *the missing reveal the status of the rest of us.* The responses vary: on the one hand, the authorities may ignore the missing and hope they may be forgotten or seen as irrelevant politically; on the other hand, they may pursue them with huge resources, in an attempt to bring them back within control.

The missing are whatever beings, loved ones, and "the principal enemy of the state"—hence, perhaps, the huge resources devoted to finding them and turning them from the missing to the dead or the living.[44] So, in an uncanny way, the drive of relatives searching for their loved ones and the drive of the authorities to secure the missing and account for them run along parallel tracks, but for very different reasons. One is a challenge to administrative or police organization and logic; the other its reinstatement. Administrative organization wins when it can categorize the missing, give them an identity and a belonging, as "the missing." Relatives insist on the importance of the missing person-as-such. But the move that so often accompanies any response by those in power to demands for tracing and identification—the move from "missing persons" to "the missing" as a category—signals a new police order. Missing persons as such are from a different world, a different distribution of the sensible, invisible to governmental categorizations, and they demand, this book argues, a politics that takes into account the person-as-such—a politics of the person as missing.

CHAPTER 1

Missing Persons, Manhattan

We all lost you all, and mourn together. We are not
"sightseers."

—Mariette, WTC Viewing Platform, January 26, 2002

Coming face-to-face with the photographs of
those who disappeared in the rubble and dust of the World Trade Center
towers in September 2001 is a disturbing experience, even for people not
intimately involved with the events, and I write from that perspective. Word
of what had happened spread quickly in London, where I was that day, meeting old friends and going to see exhibitions. Those who had heard the news
were compelled to tell others about it. We were visiting the British Museum
that afternoon and approached an attendant for directions to a particular
Roman mosaic. He told us where we could find the mosaic but then added
in an urgent undertone: "They've hijacked four planes and crashed two into
a skyscraper in Manhattan and two into the Pentagon. There's a fifth plane
flying around with six hundred people on board…" My first reaction was that
this was impossible; it must be a misunderstanding or a bad joke: the museum
attendant must be crazy. Or could it be true? We had to find out more. It
was impossible to continue with our mundane activities. My own immediate
instinct was to head home. Outside, London appeared normal, but snatches of
conversations overheard along the streets confirmed that the impossible had
indeed taken place: "…at least four planes…" "They've evacuated the Stock
Exchange…" "London is a target too…" And on the train home, the same
gesture repeated: people sitting in silence, hands over their mouths, reading the
account in the evening paper, thinking.

The first time I visited New York after that was around the time of the six-month anniversary; this proved to be the start of a series of visits over the following months and years from which much of the material in this chapter is drawn. Looking again at the photographs I took during those visits reminds me of my own first encounter with what was at the time, for me at least, stunningly unexpected, unbelievable even: the use of passenger planes, full of people, as weapons to be flown deliberately into skyscrapers. Schooled in the politics of hostage taking, threats, negotiations, and demands, all based on some notion of the value of life, I found it difficult to comprehend how anyone could find it possible to do such a thing—to disregard life so utterly. I'm not sure I would call it courage, as Susan Sontag famously implied, but certainly it entailed a way of thinking that for me was beyond the imagination.[1] Recalling the bewilderment and horror that followed, amplified of course by the totally unexpected collapse of the towers, brings back how at the time the hospitals were put on alert to receive thousands of casualties, people flocked to donate blood, and rescue squads rushed to recover the survivors assumed to be buried under the rubble. It was a while before it became clear that of the majority of the thousands killed only the smallest traces would remain, if anything remained at all. The missing would disappear. The cloud of dust that hung over Manhattan for some days would be all that lingered of many of the dead.[2]

The line between presence and absence cannot be drawn clearly, certainly not for some time for those whose relatives or friends cannot be found after a disaster, and maybe not at all for any of us. Photographs are interesting in this context. A photograph appears to record a moment that has inevitably passed, but in itself, as a photograph, it is equally clearly present. The eyes in the photograph still gaze determinedly directly at us, undaunted by the impossibility of this look.[3] The photograph "is" the person. As Roland Barthes points out,

> Show your photographs to someone—he will immediately show you his: "Look, this is my brother; this is me as a child," etc.; the Photograph is never anything but an antiphon of "Look," "See," "Here it is"; it points the finger at a certain *vis-à-vis,* and cannot escape this pure deitic language.[4]

We find this same language used with the New York photographs: "Have you seen this man?" "If you see this person…" "If you see or have seen this person, please contact the following people…" The inscription "Attached is a picture of…" is much more unusual. The photographs of the missing are a precious remnant, a trace, a proof that the person exists. This is a person, a missing person, they proclaim. Here is my sister, my husband, my son, my friend. Here they are: *I did not just imagine them.* They have not come home, but they must be somewhere. "Please help!" say the inscriptions. "Please call if you have any information."

Searching for the Missing

It was in the chaos and confusion of the first few hours after the Trade Center towers collapsed that the missing posters came to be produced. People who were worried sick about relatives and friends they had not heard from and who had failed to return home gave up watching television, with its repetition and lame attempts at making sense of what had happened in terms of "attacks" and "terrorists," and took to the streets. One of those searching, Tommy Mackell, was quoted as saying: "We're not interested in watching any more TV. We have no time limit. We'll just keep walking."[5] There was a general move for people to gather in public spaces, notably Union Square. This park was the closest people could get to the site where the World Trade Center had been—the whole tip of Manhattan Island below that point, in other words below Fourteenth Street, had been closed off.

Union Square became a focal point where groups congregated to talk and to begin to absorb what had happened. Immediately after the events, impromptu memorials of candles and flowers were set up in the square. The gatherings offered the residents of Manhattan an opportunity to attempt to think, communally, about what had happened. These impromptu meetings provided an arena for an openness of political discussion and debate not allowed in the media, and the discussions that took place, though heated, were notable for their sensitivity and tolerance.[6] It seemed almost as if the aim was to counter the closed, violent, insensitive actions that had happened earlier. And they also represented a general feeling that there was a need for unmediated discussion, away from the repetition of the events of the impact and the collapse that by then were being replayed incessantly on television channels. Union Square became "the quintessential public square—a meeting place for New Yorkers to exchange their thoughts and ideas, political and spiritual insights and personal tributes."[7] Some people laid out rolls of paper on which anyone and everyone could write their thoughts and messages; others chalked on the sidewalks or attached notes to fencing or lampposts. The atmosphere was one of tension, almost excitement, in the face of the new, alongside a quiet, intense mourning of a loss that was not yet fully grasped, let alone accepted.[8] Political life was being reclaimed, and community reconstituted.

For those searching for the missing, there was no official coordination at first, no central place to go to. It was not until late on Wednesday, more than twenty-four hours after the collapse of the towers, that the New York Armory was opened to allow those seeking information on friends and relatives to complete forms with details of the missing.[9] In the meantime, people took to the streets in search of anyone who might have information, who might have been in the towers and escaped, or who might have seen the people they were looking for. They took photographs of their relatives with them, to show to those they came across. An obvious next step, given the availability of photocopiers and computers, was to make flyers to hand out and to post on the walls by the hospitals, where people came to check lists of those admitted. Under the circumstances, everyone wanted to do what they could to help, and copy shops were providing as many free copies as relatives wanted.

David Friend asks: "What impulse drove so many to craft such similar signs in such abundance?"[10] With no operational cell phone networks, overloaded emergency response numbers, and television and radio being very much "one-way media,"

> the missing posters in those first days were makeshift attempts at cutting through the havoc so as to plead one's case directly, concisely, individually. [People] had to do *something* concrete to broadcast the vital statistics of the missing—*their* missing. So, watching others do the same...they concocted their own grassroots medium, collectively.[11]

Patty Lampert's cousin Bobby Baierwalter was one of those missing. She saw television coverage of people putting up posters, got a photograph, and made a poster. She and other relations were convinced that the flyers would find him: he was in a hospital somewhere. When they went downtown on Friday, clutching the "magical" bundles of posters, they were full of hope. But when they arrived

> there was dead silence. This was Manhattan but there wasn't a sound from anywhere. No one spoke to each other. It was eerie....Everything was covered in dust. You passed people, people holding flyers just like you, everyone in a daze. But you were almost afraid to look at them because looking would make it too real, and this was like a dream you were in. As I walked I saw one flyer taped on scaffolding. Then another, and another. You read one and then had to walk on. It was too painful to take in more than one at a time. Then we walked and saw papers everywhere...One long unending tunnel of papers. With pictures...up and down every street, like Post-It notes. It slowly hit me. There were too many pictures like ours, like Bobby. We weren't going to find him. And we just broke down crying on the street corner—I

don't know where. We were in a dream but the pictures were what was real. The faces in the pictures were the *only* thing real. I knew then. Bobby's gone and we're never going to see him again.[12]

As well as handing out posters, relatives talked to the press and to others searching. It is the conversations with the press that I remember. I wasn't in New York until quite some time later, as I've said, so I didn't see the posters appear on the streets, on bus shelters, on cars, on pizza restaurants. But I did see the broadcast interviews with the relatives. The press had nothing much else to show. There were no injured being ferried to hospitals, no people being dramatically recovered from the rubble, no dead bodies being pulled out from which we could avert our eyes, though we did have our eyes averted for us from the body parts that lay in the streets and on the roofs of surrounding buildings—and, in the replays, from the images of those falling from the towers. There was only this chaos of people needing to walk the streets with their flyers, searching—hopelessly, endlessly searching. I remember one interview with someone who actually found the person she was looking for. I cannot remember the details for certain, but I think that a reunion was in fact filmed. One minute we were talking to a woman with her son looking for the missing father, and the next he had miraculously appeared. I don't know if this was staged or what. I remember thinking at the time it seemed highly improbable. Maybe I dreamed it. Mostly what we saw were people anxiously but determinedly giving details of the person they were looking for, holding the picture close to their chest to make sure it was in view of the camera, refusing to surrender what hope remained, refusing to cry out.

On the whole the flyers people produced were basic and all very similar: each carried a photograph, accompanied by text. A full name was always given, with alternative names or nicknames too; sometimes the correct pronunciation was even spelled out. Then there were details of where the missing person worked; personal information such as age, height, weight, and distinguishing marks; and finally a contact telephone number or numbers. Some flyers were handwritten, most produced on word processors. The photographs were for the most part in color, only occasionally black and white. The posters were overwhelmingly the same size, printed on standard white letter-size paper.

The language on the posters is direct and unambiguous: "AON Insurance. 101 floor. Missing. Please call...Last seen 78th floor waiting for elevator. Anyone from AON who knows Edward please call"; "5ft 10in, 175lbs, brown hair, brown eyes; WTC 104th floor—Junk Bonds. Contact..." Personal details are given without flinching: "6+ ft tall; Heavy set; Blond; Pale skinned; Wedding band"; "Extremely overweight approximately 6 feet tall, wearing a navy blue polo shirt, black pants, and black Rockport lace shoes"; "Tattoos: panther—left forearm (looks more like a dog's head), 'Jim'—upper right arm (both poorly done); Gold wedding band; Watch with gold band; Dressed business casual"; "Female, Indian (Brown complexion)...prominent mole on upper right cheek below eye, a mole on right thigh"; "Small gap between upper two front teeth."

A confusion of tenses betrays the uncertainty the relatives are trying to hold on to. While what the missing were wearing or where they worked is described most usually in the past tense ("Hugo was an employee on the 84th Floor of the Second Tower. He was last seen wearing a Black Shirt and Blue Jeans"), their distinguishing marks are detailed in the present ("He has a tattoo on his right shoulder..."). The type of information given on the posters changed as speculation about likely outcomes altered. At first they were hopeful, giving just name, picture, and workplace; later, less optimistic, people listed information about scars, dental implants, tattoos.[13] Of course, with hindsight it is obvious that certain locations were an almost automatic death sentence. People didn't know that at the time.

Occasionally, as well as the information to help identification, we are given other details: "Expecting first child this week"; "Wife is pregnant with twins and due next week. He also has a two year old son at home who has just said his first sentence: 'I want my daddy'"; "Her family is in Bermuda and unable to come to the USA due to restrictions. PLEASE HELP." We are often told where people were last seen: "Possibly seen outside the WTC after the crash"; "Last heard evacuating the 86th floor of tower 2." And sometimes we are given the whole story as far as it is known: "The last call we had from her was that she was trapped in the elevator on the 12th floor #2 WTC and she couldn't get out since about 8:50am. Then we lost contact with her. If anyone was with her at that time and was able to escape from the elevator, please contact us and tell us what happened." There is a desire to know not just whether a friend or relative is alive, but what happened to them. How did they die? How come they didn't get out? *What was it like for them?* We can never know, of course, and we know that, but we want to get as close to being able to imagine as we can.

It is difficult to read these details, but it can be easier to read the inscriptions than to look at the photographs themselves.

Most of those who died were people who either worked in a particular office block or were visiting it for one reason or another that day, or those who had come to rescue them. The photographs on the missing flyers do not show these people. They show a woman with her child, in a garden; another woman in a strappy dress with a bouquet of flowers; a man in a tuxedo and bow tie. A man sitting back on a leather sofa, relaxed, arms spread wide, a broad smile on his face. A couple in dark glasses, arms around one another, smiling. Another couple in a garden, older, but also happy and smiling. A graduation photo. Another in a bow tie. A couple and their baby. Another couple with two children gathered round the table to blow out the candles on a birthday cake—a third birthday, it looks like, though the child seems too small. A family on a beach, the daughter riding high on her father's shoulders. A wedding day. Another celebration: champagne. An evening out in a restaurant. A couple at home at Christmas, she sitting on his lap. A father holding his newborn child. More parties. A backpacking trip. A boat trip. And one that really haunts me: someone who has a look just like someone I know.

Occasionally there is a posed, official photograph, but for the most part these are intimate, personal photographs, snapshots intended for the privacy of the album, not the walls of New York City. Taken by family or friends, they recall holidays, celebrations, births, marriages. The people are smiling, happy, relaxed, if occasionally a little awkward at being photographed, but sublimely unaware of what the future is to bring. These are the people that worked in the World Trade Center, the people New Yorkers saw around them every day, on the subway, the buses, the sidewalks, in the parks. But these are their private faces. They are not the public, city-walking, streetwise New York faces that people show to the world. Yet here they are, torn from the private world and pasted on walls, bus shelters, lampposts. They are faces that do not suit the context in which they now appear, exposed to public gaze alongside the sometimes embarrassing details of their distinguishing marks.[14]

In the aftermath of the Second World War missing posters prepared by the German Red Cross appeared in post offices and railway stations, as we shall see in chapter 2. In the Asian tsunami of December 2003 and the Kosovo crisis in the late 1990s, similar forms of missing posters were found.[15] The United States Holocaust Memorial Museum in Washington contains what is called the Tower of Faces.[16] The tower displays hundreds of photographs from the Yaffa Eliach Shtetl Collection, depicting Jewish life in a small town in Lithuania.[17] The three-story tower is "covered with a pastiche of photographs depicting ordinary people in ordinary situations: weddings, new babies, school and religious rites of passage, working, or playing—simply people living."[18] Visitors are told that all but twenty-nine of the Jewish residents of the town were killed in 1941, and that no Jews live there today. Like the New York missing posters, these photographs show people before the disaster, unaware of what was about to happen, and disconnected from the context in which their images would be shown. This is felt to be one of the most powerful exhibits in the museum.[19] The photographs are from a period where the snapshot photograph was much rarer. They are posed photographs taken by a professional photographer. They depict family groups and individuals from the Jewish community, and as in the missing posters in New York, the sitters smile out at us or sit composed and reflective, ignorant of what the future is to bring. These photographs contrast starkly with those elsewhere in the museum, taken when prisoners were admitted to the camps, or when victims were shot, like those seen in the Tuol Sleng Genocide Museum in Cambodia.

Already Invisible

The workers in the World Trade Center were normally concealed behind the corporate facade of the buildings. Much of the shock on September 11 could be traced to our most basic fantasies about buildings.[20] As Mark Wigley puts it, "Buildings are seen as a form of protection, an insulation from danger. They have to be solid because their occupants are fragile. Keeping the elements and enemies out, they allow bodies to have a life."[21] In the same way as clothing, they are fashioned with care to provide protection for the human body; as Elaine Scarry points out, "A made object is a projection of the human body."[22] Scarry contrasts practices that "make" the world—practices like making a coat to keep out the cold for example, in which the sentience or feeling of the human body and its frailty are taken into account—with the violence of torture and war, or other forms of violence, which "unmake" the world. A woman making a coat, for example,

> has no interest in making a coat per se but in making someone warm: her skilled attention to threads, materials, seams, linings are all objectifications of the fact that she is at work to remake human tissue to be free of the problem of being cold. She could do this by putting her arms around the shivering person... but she instead more successfully accomplishes her goal by indirection—by making the freestanding object which then remakes the human site which is her actual object.... The coat-maker... is working... not to make the artefact... but to remake human sentience.... She enters into and in some way alters the alive percipience of other persons.[23]

To construct a building would be to sense the vulnerability of the human frame to cold, wind, and rain and to provide protection from the elements with walls and ceilings. This "making" is a response to sentience. Violence and brutality in torture and war are the precise opposite of this. They are an "unmaking" of the world and reflect a lack of sentience: those responsible must cultivate a nonawareness of the feelings of those they brutalize. In this sense, perhaps, Wigley proposes, "the terrorist is the exact counter-figure to the architect."[24]

However, buildings, more than clothing, can allow or even encourage us to forget our vulnerability. And buildings, like clothes, are made for reasons other than those Scarry describes: commercial reasons that can lead the architect and the fashion designer to ignore or even exploit the vulnerability and sentient awareness of their clients. In a corporate building, for example, "the occupants . . . are irrelevant"; the design acts as a screen to conceal those working within: "The corporation veils the actual bodies of those whom it networks together and controls from afar and even those who carry out that control."[25] As an exemplar of such construction, the World Trade Center towers were not there to protect their occupants from the weather. The point is not just that the architects of corporatism construct buildings that have everything the client finds attractive—a high profile; a smooth, modernist appearance; open-plan spaces at a low cost—at the expense of a structure that is quick to evacuate or able to withstand fire. It is that their work also conceals the people that inhabit the buildings, rendering them an anonymous mass of faceless workers behind a screen or facade. It is in this sense that terrorists and architects can be equated: both "distance themselves from the flesh and blood experience of mundane existence" and for both "reality distils itself to the instrumental use of physical forces in the service of an abstract goal." Both "bombers and master-builders . . . view living processes in general, and social life in particular, with a high degree of abstraction."[26]

When the towers collapsed two things happened. First, buildings that should protect killed—structures that should have held and outlived their occupants fell, crushing those who relied on them for survival. What became clear was what was already there but unacknowledged: "The devastating spectacle of September 11 was a simultaneous destruction of body and building and the distinction between them."[27] It was not just that everything was revealed as vulnerable.[28] What was revealed was the impossibility of a sustained distinction between body and building, flesh and object, protected and protector, vulnerable and invulnerable, animate and inanimate:

> The everyday idea that architecture keeps the danger out was exposed as a fantasy. Violence is never a distant thing. Security is never more than a fragile illusion. Buildings are much stranger than we are willing to admit. They are tied to an economy of violence rather than simply a protection from it.[29]

Second, the collapse suddenly revealed the faces of workers, which had been previously concealed.[30] The way that corporate culture instrumentalizes those it exploits became plain. These normally concealed faces suddenly appeared on the streets. As Wigley puts it very graphically,

> When the façades came down the faces of the invisible occupants who were lost came up, filling the vertical surfaces of the city in pasted photocopies and covering the surfaces of televisions, computers, and newspapers all around the world. They formed a new kind of façade, a dispersed image of diversity in place of the singular monolithic screen—each face, each personality, each story, suddenly in focus.... It was precisely those who were missing, those who the building did not protect, who had their horrifying disappearance marked by a sudden visibility.[31]

In other words, those who had been presented as faceless and invisible by the system within which they worked were suddenly given particularity. Those of us wandering the streets could see clearly the mix and variety of people who had been in the buildings that day. We could see them as private people, with their families, their children, their dogs, their special occasions. All things that the corporation lives on and makes its profits from yet chooses to ignore. We may not have felt that they were people we had much in common with, or would have been particularly likely to have as friends, but that was unimportant. We now knew who they were, and that they had been disappeared, rubbed out, vanished. It was shocking the way this disappearance revealed to us their inevitable invisibility—they were in any case the disappeared, the bare life of the city-state.[32]

Some of the people who died in the towers were not represented in the missing posters: "Families of undocumented workers... did not dare display their photos."[33] Diana Taylor calls this a double disappearance: missing from the towers and missing from the missing posters. She tells us how sometimes Mexicans would put up a picture of the Virgin of Guadeloupe to stand in the place of the missing person. A lone bicycle, abandoned on the street, appeared as a memorial to the undocumented, who were often delivery workers. Two images of this bicycle appeared in Angelika Bammer's exhibition "Memory Sites: Destruction, Loss, and Transformation," at the Schatten Gallery, Emory University, in 2003. One of the images shows "attached to the abandoned bicycle... the American flag, the Mexican flag, an epitaph, and a plastic-wrapped image of the Virgin of Guadalupe."[34] The plight of immigrant workers was recognized in the press very early on, with reports that alongside the stockbrokers and investment bankers would be "a small army of poorly paid Hispanic immigrants" who were now among the victims.[35] These people worked in the World Trade Center restaurants and shops or as office cleaners, or made deliveries to the buildings from businesses outside. When disaster struck, their relatives could not get support from traditional sources, and employers often would not name undocumented workers for fear of a backlash. Relatives of these workers went to their own organizations, which provided help and support and campaigned to get the undocumented onto the official lists. The main organization involved, Asociación Tepeyac, a Mexican community group, provided "the city's alternative emergency system for the immigrant workers, families and bi-national communities whose lives and livelihoods" had been taken away.[36] Tepeyac had been founded in 1997 as a collaboration of existing groups to provide a resource for the Mexican community in New York, and serves Latino immigrants, particularly the undocumented.[37]

After the collapse of the Trade Center, survivors who worked with Tepeyac converged on the headquarters and set up an emergency response, appealing to the undocumented to come forward for help. The Immigration and Naturalization Service announced that it would "not seek, and local authorities will not divulge, any information provided in the rescue and recovery efforts."[38] An appeal was put out to employers to declare their undocumented workers, and a list of sixty-five *desaparecidos,* the doubly disappeared, was eventually compiled. The majority of those names appeared on the medical examiner's list of the missing by 2002.[39] As news of its work spread, Tepeyac received funding from other organizations, which it dispensed as emergency help to those with no other source of funds; and the American Red Cross also became involved. Tepeyac sent volunteers to South American countries to obtain DNA samples from relatives to assist in identification. It supported those who had survived but had lost their jobs, and helped when the aftermath of 9/11 led to a revival of anti-immigrant feeling and a suspension of moves towards an amnesty for the undocumented. However, there were most probably others whose relatives and friends never came forward. Of the sixty-five cases that Tepeyac identified, some twenty-odd cases were never proved and never received federal aid. These were mainly Mexicans, but three Colombians, two Peruvians, three Ecuadorians, four Dominicans, and two Hondurans were among at least twenty-five who remained unlisted and uncounted.[40]

These people's stories are very different from those of most of the New York missing who appeared in the "Portraits of Grief" published by the *New York Times.* In a precarious situation before September 11, many of the immigrant families living in New York had severe difficulties coping with their grief, which was compounded by enormous financial problems and isolation from their extended families. In other cases, the loss of a son or a husband who was supporting family in his country of origin meant the sudden end of that support, and the future plans and dreams attached to it. Tepeyac has been able to provide support in these cases, often with small sums to invest in businesses that can provide income to replace that lost.[41]

These people were not only rendered invisible by the architecture of corporatism, then, as all those working for companies located in the Trade Center were; they were invisible anyway, in hiding from the authorities, living their lives in the shadows. However, to focus our concern too much on the doubly missing would perhaps enable us to conceal from ourselves the much more troubling way in which even the documented were invisible, disappeared. They appeared only as employees, voters, and consumers, not as persons. That was one of the things that was so shocking about the posters: they revealed that it was not anonymous workers or heroes that died, but our neighbors.

From the point of view of the hijackers it mattered not one iota exactly who was in the buildings at the time; it is not even certain that it mattered greatly how many lives were involved. What mattered to the hijackers was the spectacle, and the impact of their own suicides as a "counterstrike weapon," which would render any response powerless or counterproductive.[42] Loss of other lives was random and to a great degree incidental. Those on board the aircraft and those in the target buildings had not just been killed; they were "disappeared," wiped out, erased. Their lives had been totally disregarded. They were treated as worthless—as bare life, life already in some sense invisible. There were no bodies to be retrieved.[43] Most had not had time to speak to their relatives. The horror was that in being treated instrumentally, as bare life, the victims had been deprived not only of their lives but also of their deaths. They were not the dead. They were the missing.

On September 20, Americans were instructed by their president to live their lives and hug their children and, by implication, to leave political concerns to others.[44] The resentment this pronouncement led to wasn't clear until some years later, when the response to Barack Obama's 2008 campaign for president revealed an intense and widespread desire for renewed political involvement. Indeed, in the immediate aftermath of 9/11 New Yorkers found things to do that expressed their desire to be involved. If they could not volunteer as rescuers or support staff, if their blood was not needed, then they lined the streets to cheer the rescue workers; they encircled Ground Zero; they formed organizations to contest the politics of revenge. They took part in a myriad of extraordinary—and political—activities of witnessing, mourning, and protest.

Witnessing, Mourning, Protest

It was only through reading accounts written later that I learned how those in New York reacted to the missing posters. Marshall Sella recounts how he was drawn time and time again to one image—that of an older man with a beard, Mark Rasweiler.[45] Sella was not alone in this: "Everyone seemed to lock on to one face in particular." When he mentioned to a friend "the happy older man" the friend knew immediately whom he was talking about. It wasn't that the man resembled someone Sella knew, but, as he tells us, just that he was "Mark, a guy I knew by sight. Neighborhood fellow." In the midst of all the "icons of flame and rubble" that made no sense, Mark's face did. Sella reports that "ever since I laid eyes on Mark Rasweiler's 'Missing' poster, I wanted to steal one. I felt it was partly mine. I wanted to have it, not as a mawkish souvenir but, for some irrational motive, as the best and only picture I would ever have of him." Of course, stealing the poster—taking it down off the wall where it had been painstakingly posted—was out of the question. But finally, Marshall comes across one lying on the pavement next to a bus stop. He picks it up and takes it home. Suddenly, he tells us, "it felt as if I had lost him."

Writer Vivian Gorlick, who lived near the corner of Twelfth Street and Seventh Avenue, reports how, three weeks after the events, she stood staring at the missing posters, day after day: "By now, they are my intimates. When I don't know what to do with myself, they are the company I seek out."[46] She noticed that she wasn't the only one; other people were congregating to look at the posters—the same people, regularly. It is the details on the posters that first compel attention, but what holds it, she says, are the revisions that appear—additions and amendments to the descriptions on the posters, entered by hand, in brackets:

> The poster that drives all this home is for Colleen Supinski, 27, last seen on the 104th floor of Tower 2. She has, we are told by her relative, Noreen Supinski (whom we are to call), "large blue eyes, long thick eyelashes, long blond hair, tiny wrists and fingers, small frame, petite features; small gap between upper two front teeth." And oh, yes, a "small flower tattoo on right lower abd." Then, beside the sentence about the tattoo, penciled in, is "all black."

Gorlick continues:

> I have this image—it's with me often as I go about the day—of Noreen reviewing her composition (extraordinary enough with its "long thick eyelashes" and "tiny wrists"), nodding, walking away, and then, like any writer driven to self-correction, coming back. "No, that's not right," she

thinks. "It needs a few more words. Only a few more, and it will have delivered itself of its task."

Gorlick reflects that the reason that these revisions hold her, and compel her to revisit the posters time and time again, is that when the planes flew into the Trade Center towers it was "as though the narrating intelligence of the race had ceased to exist." It is the return of Noreen to her poster, and others likewise to theirs, to pencil in details, to make sure that everything is there, "the narrative drive" behind the posters, it is this that contests the disappearances: "That impulse to get it right, make words register the vital distinction, insist that clarity of thought matters. The relief I feel in its presence! The relief we all feel, that the city feels." It is as if the posters, with their ordinary faces, their specific personal details of appearance and hidden characteristics, can reinstate the value of personhood and the specificity of the person that the events of September 11 had threatened to obliterate.

The posters also made an urgent plea for information. As we have seen, people not only wanted to find out whether their relatives or friends had survived, but *how* they had died, what had happened to them. The horror was not just that bodies had been reduced to particles of dust and scattered to the four winds, but that *all* those who were there had disappeared. There was no one left to tell the tale. Everyone had seen what happened—at least from the outside—but almost no one who had been there—on the inside— had got out to tell what had happened. The voices on answering machines and in voice mail, the e-mail messages in in-boxes, the paper descending slowly down to the street after the collapse of the towers, the remnants of artifacts and of bodies—these were all that remained. Poor material for the necessary work of mourning, for composing stories of the ends of lives. The posters were perhaps both an appeal for something to fill that gap and a beginning of the narrative of death, and, perhaps most important, a response to those who would deny personhood as such. As Amy Waldman wrote, "The first wave of paper rained upon the city from the World Trade Center like death's disembodied proxy. As if in answer, a second wave rose up from the photo albums and word processors of thousands of desperate families."[47]

Of course, it was not just those in New York who were taken with the images or who responded to the appeals on the posters. A news photograph of two friends of Amy O'Doherty holding her picture with her distinguishing marks and her mother's contact numbers clearly visible prompted condolence calls from distant parts of the globe for many months.[48]

From the beginning, newspapers published accounts of individual victims. While this appears a laudable attempt to restore individual significance to lives lost, I think it is more ambiguous. The *New York Times* began the process of publishing mini-obituaries of the dead, called "Portraits of Grief," on a day-by-day basis. This was an unusual step. In general only celebrities or those who have in some way made a particular contribution are honored by an obituary in the *New York Times,* not those who would be described as ordinary people. Obituaries detail accomplishments: everything that made the person whose life is being celebrated unusual and worthy of distinction. The profiles given in the "Portraits of Grief" were different. They focused not on the exceptional, but on the banal: "She dressed impeccably and had her nails done once a week. She entertained regularly, making all the food herself. She took great pride in her small apartment."[49] In other words, they brought out the commonplace, the ordinary and the unoriginal. This style borders easily on the trite, but what it also does is remove any political significance. In emphasizing people's ordinary, everyday lives, it glosses over the political commitments or affiliations they may have had and fails to mention anything that might be controversial. It presents them as bare life, life without a political voice. In bringing out the ordinary, the obituaries stress the similarity of the victims. The "Portraits of Grief" offered up "a cultural ideal" and revealed the values and attributes considered important in the particular context: "devotion to family; passion, talent, or interests outside work; a work ethic; generosity, humour, and humanity; and good health or energy."[50] They did this at the expense of more specific, more challenging entries that would have brought out differences and particularity. In a sense, as David Simpson notes, "They seem regimented, even militarised, made to march to the beat of a single drum."[51] Simpson proposes a somewhat different argument from mine, but again drawing on the notion of bare life. He argues, persuasively, that in making the dead into heroes and emphasizing the plenitude of their lives, "Portraits of Grief" and other forms of memorializing after 9/11 may betray an anxiety that we do indeed routinely produce life as bare:

> The hyperbole with which it has been proposed that the victims of 9/11 were not bare lives, were lives of plenitude and national significance (significance for the nation), becomes then not simply the expected tendency to speak only good things of the dead but also a hint of an anxiety, a hint that we ourselves may be more prone to disposing of bare lives than we should be—the bare lives of those in other parts of the world and perhaps in the midst of our own national plenum, perhaps

even the lives of some of the 9/11 victims—the firemen who were not given functioning radio equipment, for example.[52]

Judith Greenberg suggests that "the intimacy produced by the 'Portraits of Grief' section in the *New York Times* and the 'family album' quality of the missing person fliers publicly attempted to bring the grief of the broken private home to the broken public home."[53] The "Portraits of Grief" focused, as did the photographs, on family life. In the majority of cases, the men and women were remembered for their connections to family members, and rather than just mentioning those who survived the deceased, as happens at the end of a traditional obituary, family relationships were vividly portrayed. But the function of the "Portraits of Grief" was in a sense the opposite of that of traditional obituaries. While the latter "typically highlight what the deceased did to distinguish themselves, to set themselves apart, the portraits celebrated *ordinary* qualities."[54]

Other newspapers produced extended profiles of individuals, but again they were drawn to the typical not the extraordinary. One reporter described his search for a suitable subject for an article: "I need to find someone who has a missing relation who is a quintessential New Yorker."[55] The eventual profile (of Barbra Walsh) was entitled "An Ordinary Life." What these reports sought to glorify was how unexceptional and how ordinary these people had been. This approach makes it easier to portray them as nothing but innocent victims. It is similar to the way images of tragedy focus on children. What is at issue here is not in any sense a suggestion that the victims were themselves responsible for their fate, far from it. The question is whether, by reducing the dead to nothing but bare life, these forms of remembering are not repeating the very disregard of the person-as-such that characterized the events that killed them in the first place. For those piloting the planes that struck the World Trade Center, the nationalities, political commitments, and religious affiliations of those they killed were immaterial; only their pure existence as lives that could be taken mattered. Forms of memorializing that stress the ordinariness of the lives of those killed risk repeating or even reinforcing this gesture.

In parallel with the spontaneous meetings in Union Square and elsewhere, two notable projects based around photography sprang up after 9/11, operating with similar aims but disagreeing as to how best to accomplish them. Both wanted to democratize the display of photographs, and take the control of images out of the hands of the commercial media. They aimed to provide a platform for people to display their own photographs and to view those put up by other people. The September 11 Photo Project was initially based in

New York and later opened at Arlington National Cemetery in Arlington, Virginia (in March 2002), and then at other sites around the United States. This project invited submissions of photographs from anyone and everyone.[56] People submitted three photographs, with written text if desired, and all submissions were displayed. A selection was later published.[57] Another project, Here Is New York, had similar aims, though it was curated differently.[58] It opened in an empty storefront in downtown Manhattan and invited submissions from professional and amateur photographers alike. The organizers were conscious of the project's role in the rebuilding of community; they noted that in the end "it became a rallying point for the neighbourhood and for the community at large."[59] However, there were limits to its democracy. Not all submissions were displayed; the project's volunteer staff selected material from each submission. The photographs were digitized, reprinted in a common format, and displayed without any text or title. Observing visitors to these exhibitions myself, I sensed a feeling of intense engagement and reflection—an attempt to think through what had happened, and to do this not in isolation but in company, not through the narrations of those in the media but through unmediated images.

Both projects wanted to provide ways for images to circulate uncensored and independently of media interest. It was coverage on television and in the *New York Times,* however, that created enormous interest in the Here Is New York project. Ironically, then, although the aim had been to create a new setting for pictures, outside of the media, the images went immediately right back into the media.[60] Nevertheless, the images themselves remain hugely powerful and evoke the traumatic as only images can.[61]

The gatherings in Union Square were the occasion for heated and heartfelt political debates about what had happened and what the response should be. They were also a space where more organized, though still in many senses spontaneous, political actions took place. An example of this was a group of artists around a hundred strong who staged a protest against the way their shock and sorrow (and those of others) was being co-opted by the federal government and translated into a call for revenge. Dressed in black with white dust-masks over their mouths, they stood in silence in a semicircle. Around their necks hung placards reading: "Our grief is not a cry for war." This performance or demonstration took place in Union Square on September 22 and again in Times Square on September 25 and October 5.[62] The Times Square performance on October 5 was at 6:00 p.m., just the time when the vast screens there were filled with news broadcasts about the war on terror. The symbolism was interesting. The figures were voiceless: they stood with their mouths gagged, speechless in the face of trauma perhaps, but also rendered dumb by the rhetoric of war and its attempt to silence dissent through a summons to patriotism and revenge. Speechlessness and bare life go together; language and voice are a feature of politically qualified life, the life of the citizen, the life of those who claim equality as speaking beings. The activists, in the silence of their grief, stand up for their right to a political voice, in opposition to others claiming to speak for them. They both emphasize their bare life—and its roots in feeling and emotion—and use it politically. They are rendered silent by their grief, but it is *their* grief, and they lay claim to the right to speak of it, or, rather, in this case, of what it is not.

Many of the official ceremonies included a reading of the names of those lost. Like the listing of names on war memorials, this practice is an attempt to recognize each person as an individual. However, as with other attempts to reclaim individuality, such as the *New York Times* "Portraits," it is ambiguous. The use of names both distinguishes individuals as equal and of value and, at the same time, in a sense reduces each person to bare life. Differences of political view, religious affiliation, or role are glossed over. The inclusion of the names of rescue workers on a general memorial listing of all those lost was contested for precisely this reason: it failed to mark out those who were voluntarily risking their lives from those they fought to save. It implies "that there was nothing but victims that day."[63] This points up the way in which lists of "victims" in general produce people as helpless and innocent, with no political voice.

The inclusion of a person's name can imply a silent support of actions that person might well have disagreed with. Amber Amundson wrote an open letter to President Bush that was published in the *Chicago Tribune* on September 25, 2001.[64] In it she explicitly requested that her husband's name not be used in such a way. She wrote: "My anguish is compounded exponentially by fear that his death will be used to justify new violence against other innocent victims." Addressing those leaders who advocated revenge, she said: "If you choose to respond to this incomprehensible brutality by perpetuating violence against other innocent human beings, you may not do so in the name of justice for my husband."[65] Her husband's political views and his pacifism while working at the Pentagon motivated her stand. Craig Scott Amundson saw his work as an enlisted specialist with the U.S. Army as contributing to peace rather than war. Mrs. Amundson was much vilified for taking this stand.[66]

A wider campaign grew up based around the slogan Not in My Name, which gave voice to those, not necessarily victims or relatives of victims, who felt silenced by the way in which the Bush administration claimed to speak for the whole nation. Participants were invited to take a pledge that begins: "We believe that as people living in the United States it is our responsibility to resist the injustices done by our government in our names." It goes on with a series of refrains: "Not in our name will you... wage endless war... invade countries" and so forth.[67] This was, at least initially, a powerful repoliticization.

Afterlife

By the time I first photographed the missing flyers posted outside St. Vincent's Hospital on West Eleventh Street it was more than one year after the tragedy. The original flyers had been joined by others saying things like "Loved and missed by all... 12.22.69—9.11.01" rather than "Missing." People had added newspaper cuttings ("Reality-TV champ missing in rubble") or memorial cards ("In loving memory of..."). Others posted what they hoped were helpful poems ("Gone but Not Forgotten"), messages from children, or religious or patriotic symbols and mottoes (Proud to be an American). For the most part though, the initial posters were still there, and still the same. Still asking for information, still telling us dates of birth, eye color, distinguishing marks. New York was indeed "a city that lived alongside its missing and dead."[68] When I traveled through New York in March 2005, the posters I had photographed two and a half years before were, to my surprise, still there. They were much faded then, with some colors bleaching more rapidly than others to give a blue tinge. Marshall Sella notes: "Decay was necessary. Symbols of grief are not designed as instruments of cheer. Candles, for instance, are not prized merely for the flickering vitality of their light. They must also melt and vanish—the flame must consume the flesh. Flowers are offered up because they bloom and rot."[69] However, when the skies opened on the Friday after the collapse of the towers, and it rained heavily, people rushed to protect the posters. They remained, for years afterward, a haunting presence on the streets. Nobody felt it appropriate to take them down.

Why did New Yorkers do this? Why were the missing posters left up for so long, and even annotated or replaced? The explanation generally given is that by the time people realized that for "missing" they should read "presumed dead," the posters had become shrines where people could remember those killed. There was a range of different types and forms of impromptu memorial that appeared around the city, as the New-York Historical Society and City Lore chronicled in their exhibition "Missing."[70] But I think they were more than memorials.

In New York there had been a swift move to resolve the missing into the dead. Death certificates were offered rapidly in the aftermath. This is not generally the case; it was not the case in the Asian tsunami of 2003, for example. Why was there this contrast? And why then did the missing posters remain on the streets of New York for well over a year after the event? Remember that the posters included not only pictures of private events and personal moments, but also details of old surgical procedures, intimate tattoos, pregnancies, personal peculiarities. This is not the sort of information that is usually placed in a memorial context.

Perhaps the persistence of the posters was like a collective scream, an open wound, a refusal to close over the trauma of loss, a refusal of the incorporation of the bodies of the missing as heroes of the state. Those people who had turned off the television to take to the streets had a view of what had happened that was starkly different from the account that was by then being broadcast by government and media:

> When the only president we have talked to us about "terrible sadness" New Yorkers weren't impressed. When he gave us clichés about the day's events many of us were furious. "We know what happened, we weren't in a bunker," one shouted at the set. As for the government functioning and the economy continuing... "Who's he kidding? Wall Street is under dust."...In lower Manhattan at least, it's clear that this president has no idea what happened today. "That's the scariest part of all," some people said. There was no leadership coming from politicians tonight. Nor pundits, try as they might.[71]

On the morning of September 12, Secretary of State Colin Powell said on ABC's *Good Morning America*: "The American people have a clear understanding that this is a war. That's the way they see it." Laura Flanders wrote: "I beg to differ. In Manhattan, we aren't in a state of war, we're in a state of mourning. And for the whole country to join us right now would be a really good idea."[72] In the aftermath of what was being called "the attacks" the federal authorities had moved swiftly to reestablish narratives of nation, sacrifice, and heroism. In fact, these attempts began even as the events were still unfolding.[73] Contemporary political order can only survive with its legitimacy intact if the trauma of violence is concealed. The persistence of the missing posters on the streets was testimony to the trauma, to the ineffectiveness of the authorities in safeguarding those they claimed to protect, and to the lies of heroism and sacrifice. These were ordinary people who went to work and were overtaken by disaster, not heroes who sacrificed their lives for America. *Just take a look at the pictures.*

Bare life was exposed in the missing flyers, in the portrait photograph, and in the details—scars, eye color, race. Through the display of flyers, the life of the home has insistently become life that demands its place in the public sphere.[74] The collective scream, with its insistent display of the life of the home in public, reminds us that it is this very bare life that in the end is what is important to us. All our politics, all our systems of government or economics, all these pale in value when set alongside our personal lives. These posters do not ask us to look out for the person who was in charge of the office, the one who had the biggest paycheck, the one from the most prestigious family or with the most qualifications. Each and every life represented in the flyers has its own value—as a life that is interwoven with other lives, none of which will any longer be the same.

The flyers are a symbolic reminder too that these people are indeed *missing*. There are no remains, they are not "dead"—the dead have corpses. It is expected that up to one thousand people will remain missing; that not even the smallest remains of these people will be identified, despite the best efforts of forensic scientists. Many bodies were fragmented on impact and burned or crushed and mixed with other debris on the huge site. Increasingly, fragments located and identified by DNA are linked to people who have already been identified, with as many as two hundred body parts matched to one person.[75] The missing are not dead; they are not alive either. They are neither dead nor alive. *There are no bodies to insist that these people once lived, only the pictures.* These pictures assert, alongside the Madres of the Plaza de Mayo: "They took them away alive—we want them back alive!"[76]

As we have seen, there was a move to issue official death certificates very early on in the process, ostensibly to help relatives. It took a while for a final count of the dead to be decided. Two weeks after the attack, 6,886 people were reported missing. This number diminished rapidly at first and then remained at 2,792 from December 2002 until October 2003, when 40 unsolved cases were removed from the list. The number settled on in January 2004, when 3 more names were removed, was 2,749, the same as the number of death certificates that had been issued.[77] This is no doubt a tidy solution, but it does not reflect the uncertainties that are bound to remain. A number of people have been prosecuted for falsely claiming relatives missing in order to benefit from compensation payments, and there are, as we have seen, people killed on September 11 who have not been listed as missing by anyone.

The missing posters protested this tidiness and insisted on the raw, traumatic brutality of loss. The photograph exaggerates the non-sense that death makes. How can someone be there one minute and have vanished the next? The photograph demands action, refuses easy ways out—the missing must be found. But in some sense all the dead are missing. There is no place for them in our politics; the dead and the unborn are excluded. Our attitude is that since they can no longer feel pain or know what's going on, what happens doesn't matter to them, and their views don't count. Though the dead, like the unborn, have certain rights in law, the respect they are accorded is limited: they do not fully count. The bereaved do not behave like this. Often they carry on as if responding to someone who is no longer there. Of course, once anonymous, the dead can be co-opted into political projects. They can be the heroes who sacrificed their lives in a noble cause or the victims whom we invoke as triggers of retributive action.

Not only did the posters remain on the streets long after everyone had realized that none of the people depicted were going to return, but people took photographs of these photographs: "I took pictures of pictures, of people looking at pictures, of people taking pictures."[78] This practice seemed incomprehensible, but it was widespread. It was perhaps in part a record of the politicization of bare life, and in part the need to record what the journalists were not recording. What was missing was not images of the disaster but images of those bearing witness to the disaster—bearing witness to the missing, protesting their exclusion from politics. It was not a question of remembering the dead, but of bearing witness to their deaths, and the manner of their deaths. It could not be done the usual way; these were not usual deaths.

Photographs also appear on government websites.[79] An exhibition of missing posters was put together, and two versions of it toured the country, attracting some controversy.[80] Photographs of the missing posters appear in books and exhibitions. Credit is given to the person who photographed the photograph, but not to the person who took the photograph itself. Nor is permission sought from the relatives of those whose photograph is shown, just as I have not sought their permission to talk about their photographs here.

Not only had the Twin Towers disappeared; their occupants had "disappeared" too: "In the cacophony of 9.11, the bodies that allow us to mourn have vanished, or merged with polluted air, or simply turned into construction debris."[81] Only the posters remained.

Born out of necessity and public silence, the posters became a call to a different form of politics, one that starts in the street, in the home, a politics that was reactivated in a number of ways in the streets and squares of Manhattan. The posters contest the neat boundaries that the authorities wanted to impose in the form of death certificates. The posters remind us of our responsibility to the missing, a responsibility that can be fulfilled only to each as a person, a responsibility to resist the invocation of the missing en masse in support of causes or nationalism. The folk memories embodied in the missing posters are not to be dismissed as sentiment. They remain dangerous. They invoke the betrayal of the World Trade Center workers by their buildings, and their incorporation by state remembrance, as well as their victimization by those piloting the planes. These people were obliterated in the name of what? The answer is twofold: they were obliterated by those who killed them and by those who write their deaths as sacrifice. They did not sacrifice their lives. What would that mean anyway? They went about their ordinary business. They were always already missing—excluded from our politics.

Practices of memorialization, debate, and protest in the aftermath of 9/11 in New York can be seen as an insistence on a different form of politics, one that begins from the *person-as-such*. We detect this insistence in the search for the missing and in how the missing posters, used initially by relatives in their search, became, in the end, a protest against the instrumentalization of the missing, their exclusion from politics. We saw how persons-as-such were missing in the practices of those who attacked the Twin Towers; those who co-opted the missing into narratives of sacrifice, revenge, and war; and those who had anyway already concealed them behind the facade of corporate America.

In the aftermath of the Second World War in Europe we find another instance where persons-as-such were missing from politics. The millions displaced by war and Nazi persecution were herded into camps where they were registered, objectified, and denied any form of political status. They were deloused, disinfected, fed, and housed, and then categorized by nationality for repatriation. But the displaced themselves had different priorities. In some cases they were desperate to find family members who were lost in the postwar confusion; in others they wanted to disappear into the chaos to escape retribution for wartime allegiances or crimes. The next two chapters examine, first, the displaced persons camps and individual efforts to trace missing persons and, second, the eventual establishment of tracing services. Though these services attempted to respond to the demand from relatives for assistance, they can be seen in the main as part of the reestablishment of a biopolitics of control of population and territory after the disruption of war.

We revisit New York later, in chapter 5, when we examine how families of the missing, voluntary organizations, and official bodies confronted the lengthy process of attempting to gather and identify the remains of the missing.

CHAPTER 2

Displaced Persons, Postwar Europe

He was certain he could find his father as he had
found the other members of his family scattered like
leaves over the map of Germany. He had bicycled
after them one by one, going forward by hunch and
by hearsay from camp to camp.

—Kathryn Hulme, *The Wild Place*

In the aftermath of the Second World War, nearly
forty million people, most of them civilians, were on the move across a dev-
astated Europe in search of home or refuge. Many were walking from camp
to camp, seeking news of relatives they had lost touch with in the turmoil;
others were the uprooted and unwilling subjects of forced deportations
from the East; yet others were escaping repatriation to the Russian zone.
Invariably they were hungry, ill, exhausted. Prisoners of war awaited release,
and victorious armies potential redeployment to Asia. Families had been
separated, relatives killed, children lost or forsaken. Most estimates suggested
by the summer of 1945 there were almost 7 million displaced civilians in
western Europe, another 7 million in the Soviet areas of control in central
and eastern Europe, 95,000 in Italy, and 141,000 in Norway; in addition,
7.8 million Wehrmacht prisoners of war were held by the Western Allies
and 2 million by the Soviet Union. To these figures should be added, by
late summer, some 12 million expellees—ethnic Germans forced to return
to Germany from areas of eastern Europe and areas that were part of Germany itself in 1937.[1] It was a state of chaos that exceeded the predictions
of those planning postwar relief, and the mechanisms in place to help those
displaced from their homes and separated from their families were nowhere
near adequate. Difficulties were compounded by the competing priorities and different ways of working of military, governmental, and voluntary

organizations, and sometimes it seemed as if the voices of those in need of help were the last to be heard.

At most, displaced persons were offered food and shelter; at worst, they were forcibly repatriated to face death or persecution in former homelands. For those in the Nazi concentration camps, liberation did not bring an end to their suffering or ensure their survival. For many it meant long periods in other camps, where their basic needs may have been met but where they continued to be treated as objects of bureaucracy and administration, not subjects with a political say in their own future. The bare life of the concentration camp became the bare life of the displaced persons camp. Thrown back on their own resources—when not prohibited from acting by regulation and restraint—people began their own efforts to address what were priorities for many: reestablishing contact with family members and plotting their own route through the politics of the altered world that they faced.

In this chapter I examine how the camp bureaucracy and organization worked to objectify and constrain, looking through the eyes of one of those trying to make their way home after the "liberations," Primo Levi, and reading accounts of volunteers drafted to the camps who wrote later of their work. I explore stories of those in the camps who refused to sit on their hands and wait but began searching for relatives themselves, using a plethora of informal approaches, and others who seized on the confusion to escape identification.

Liberation

Despite what had been known or rumored about Nazi atrocities for some time, coming across abandoned concentration camps shocked the Allied armies and the Red Cross workers summoned to help.[2] The conditions in Belsen, entered by the British on April 15, 1945, were horrific: the unburied bodies, or those hastily buried in open pits, and the living, who were "so weak and listless that they just lay on the ground and took no notice of what was going on, and in fact were difficult to distinguish from the corpses which lay everywhere."[3] Ten thousand corpses lay unburied in Belsen Camp 1, with a further seventeen thousand dumped in shallow pits; the daily death rate was five hundred, and twenty-five to thirty thousand of the forty thousand remaining inmates urgently needed medical attention.[4] Evelyn Bark, a relief worker with a British Red Cross team, records her reactions:

> The ghastly sight was beyond anything I could imagine. . . . Pitiful wrecks of humanity were still dragging themselves around; their frames, weighing next to nothing, were mere clothes-hangers for the filthy

striped pyjamas which appeared to be the uniform of the internees. . . .
Everywhere there were mounds of litter, stinking puddles, heaps of dis-
carded footwear, and corpses hidden under tattered rags, for many lay
where they had dropped, unnoticed by the living ghosts around. . . . The
living had not had the strength to bury the dead, nor the means of
burning the corpses.[5]

From inside the wire, the surviving inmates of the camps noted the
uncertainty of the first outsiders to arrive. Four Russian soldiers on horse-
back entered Buna-Monowitz, one of the three main camps of Auschwitz-
Birkenau, on January 27, 1945. Primo Levi, one of those who remained,
barely clinging to life, tells us how

> when they reached the barbed wire, they stopped to look, exchanging
> a few timid words, and throwing strangely embarrassed glances at the
> sprawling bodies, at the battered huts and at us few still alive. . . . They
> did not greet us, nor did they smile; they seemed oppressed not only by
> compassion but by a confused restraint. . . . It was the shame we knew
> so well, the shame that drowned us after the selections, and every time
> we had to watch, or submit to, some outrage: . . . the feeling of guilt that
> such a crime should exist, that it should have been introduced irrevo-
> cably into the world of things that exist.[6]

Levi explains how "face to face with liberty" the survivors felt themselves
"lost, emptied, atrophied," unfit for their part: "an unexpected attack of mor-
tal fatigue . . . accompanied the joy of liberation."[7]

What followed for Levi was a succession of tortuous train journeys, packed
into goods wagons in a rerun of the Nazi deportations, taken by mistake east
into Russia and then north, to a series of temporary or not-so-temporary
camps. His journey from Auschwitz to his home in Turin, less than eight
hundred miles as the crow flies, lasted almost nine months. In the chaos,
improvisation had been the order of the day in the attempts of the military
authorities to deal with the flow of displaced persons; things had definitely
not proceeded according to plan. Camps for the populations on the move
had been set up "in any suitable, or sometimes unsuitable, accommodation
that survived. . . . Barracks, labour camps, concentration camps, schools, gym-
nasia, factories, airport buildings, barns, granaries, groups of villages from
which the Germans had been evicted, all were used." Most of this accommodation had suffered serious damage, and "in the rubble and ruins there
was rarely any water, electricity, or sanitation. Still less frequently was there
any furniture or equipment."[8] At the camp at Warendorf displaced persons

were lodged in what had been a stud farm, "and in several of the stalls were whole families, women, children and males. . . . Outside cooking by means of dixies and camp kettles was being carried on."[9] The teams in charge of the camps were improvised too, with food and equipment requisitioned from German civilians, and camp inmates recruited to run things themselves. "The actuality of conditions . . . fell sadly short of the hopes and excitement" of liberation, and refugees were "frequently worse off than they had been under the Nazis."[10]

Levi describes how each time they reached a new camp they had to succumb to "the unconscious desire of the new authorities, who," he tells us, "absorbed us in turn within their own sphere, to strip us of the vestiges of our former life, to make of us new men consistent with their own models, to impose their brand upon us."[11] The process of disinfection—"a form of purification and exorcism"—is a source of wry amusement to Levi as he recounts the admission of his group of Italians to their final staging post, a camp run by the Americans at St. Valentin in Austria, where "the only efficient equipment was in the baths and the disinfection room":

> A few gigantic, taciturn GIs, unarmed, but embellished with a myriad of gadgets whose significance and use escaped us, were responsible for this ritual task. . . . They took us to a vast brick room, divided in two by a cable on which ten curious implements were hanging, vaguely similar to pneumatic drills; we could hear an air compressor pulsating outside. . . . Ten officials appeared on the scene, with a science-fiction attire, wrapped up in white overalls, with helmets and gas masks. They seized the first of the flock, and without wasting time stuck the tubes of the hanging instruments into all the openings of their clothes in turn: under collars and belts, into pockets, up trouser legs, under skirts. They were a sort of pneumatic blower, which blew out insecticide: the insecticide was DDT, an absolute novelty to us, like jeeps, penicillin and the atomic bomb, which we learnt about soon afterwards.[12]

On May 8, 1945, when the end of the war arrived, Levi was in a transit camp at Katowice; he notes that "from that day . . . our homes were no longer forbidden us, no war front now separated us from them, no concrete obstacle, only red tape; we felt that our repatriation was now our due, and every hour spent in exile weighed on us like lead."[13] At that point confined to bed by a debilitating illness, Levi was persuaded to entrust a letter home to another inmate of the camp who had decided to make his own way back to Turin rather than wait for repatriation. The letter reached his family, but the messenger then asked for two hundred thousand lire to go and help Levi and bring him home. Fortunately, his mother and sister "were not wholly taken in by the messenger."[14] They told him to come back in a few days when they would have the money; he disappeared, stealing the sister's bicycle on the way.

It was another month before the Italian contingent at Katowice, Levi among them, was finally put on a train for repatriation. He arrived home in Turin on October 19 after twenty months' absence. His house was still standing, his family alive. But "no one was expecting me. I was swollen, bearded and in rags, and had difficulty making myself recognized." The ordeal was not over, though; indeed, it seemed to be just beginning. Levi describes the period of "wandering on the margins of civilization" between his so-called liberation and his arrival in Turin as a period of truce, an interlude before facing the uncertainties and demands of return.[15]

Organizing the Camps

One of those who staffed the camps through which refugees like Levi passed was Francesca Wilson. A Cambridge graduate, teacher, and relief worker with experience in Holland, France, Corsica, and Tunisia after the First World War and later in Serbia, Austria, Russia, and Spain, she joined the United Nations Relief and Rehabilitation Administration (UNRRA) in January 1945 as a welfare officer. UNRRA had been established in November 1943 to deal with the relief needs of United Nations civilians, victims of war.[16] As we shall see in chapter 3, planning for postwar requirements had begun even earlier: a British government committee of surpluses established in 1940 became the Inter-Allied Committee on Post-war Requirements in 1941, based in London, and an equivalent organization existed in Washington.[17] The term "United Nations" in the context of UNRRA referred to the forty-four Allied governments (later forty-seven) that had signed the agreement: the Axis powers were not included, and UNRRA predated the United Nations Organization, founded two years later.[18] Funding came from member governments, the United States and the United Kingdom being the largest contributors, and UNRRA operations were at the request of national governments or the Allied military authorities.[19] UNRRA was "an intergovernmental service agency" mandated to "act with and through the member governments."[20] This meant, for example, that the demands of governments for the repatriation of their citizens were difficult to refuse, despite the obvious reluctance of some of the displaced to return to their homes, especially when those homes were under Soviet control.[21] Full-scale UNRRA relief operations were carried out in Greece, Yugoslavia, Albania, Czechoslovakia,

Poland, and Italy, and other operations elsewhere.[22] In occupied zones of Germany, the mandate extended only to displaced persons who were United Nations nationals (in the limited sense used here), not to "enemy" civilians, unless they had been persecuted by the National Socialist regime for their religious or political affiliations.

From the beginning UNRRA faced many criticisms. The limited nature of its mandate, its relatively well-paid staff, a perceived incompetence in its operations, the diversion of some of its supplies to the black market, and a general reluctance to support relief elsewhere, particularly in former enemy territory, when there was hardship at home were some of the grievances expressed.[23] It was recognized that UNRRA would work in conjunction with the military authorities, though at the start precisely what that relationship would be had not been made clear. As the British chancellor of the exchequer put it, in his request for a vote of funds for UNRRA in the House of Commons on January 25, 1944, "the first period of liberation... must, to some extent, be one of improvised arrangements and nothing must be allowed to interfere with the main object, which is the advance of our arms."[24] In the first instance, the military commanders in the field would administer relief through their civil affairs staff. In the debate that followed the chancellor's speech, a number of the drawbacks that the organization would indeed later face were raised—that relief was organized by a body answerable to governments and hence was subject to political influence, that the mandate was limited to certain nationals, and that funds, supplies, and staff might not be adequate to the task. There was a general recognition of the importance of handling things better than had been the case in November 1918, after the First World War.

Always intended as a temporary body, UNRRA surrendered its responsibilities for displaced persons in 1947, its obligations passing first to the International Refugee Organization (IRO) and then, after a further four years, to the Office of the United Nations High Commissioner for Refugees (UNHCR), which remains the organization charged with refugee matters some fifty-five years later.[25] The military authorities, in the shape initially of the Supreme Headquarters, Allied Expeditionary Force (SHAEF) and later of the discrete military governments in the various zones of Germany, had also been working with the displaced. As had been foreseen, military commanders initially worked separately and only later enlisted the help of UNRRA. Both the International Committee of the Red Cross (ICRC) in Geneva and the National Red Cross Societies in Britain and elsewhere were involved, too. The British Red Cross had set up an umbrella organization in the autumn of 1942 at the request of the British government: the Council of British Societies for Relief Abroad (COBSRA), designed to coordinate voluntary activity, which of course was funded from independent charitable donations.[26] The way these arrangements were supposed to work was at many times confused, and the result was chaotic, with the various organizations, institutions, and authorities, military and civilian, governmental and voluntary, all with their different priorities and terms of reference, vying sometimes acrimoniously with each other (and their own internal colleagues competing among themselves) to recommend procedures and claim expertise and authority—and to apportion blame when things went wrong.

After some weeks of stasis at the UNRRA Training and Mobilization Center in Granville, Normandy, Francesca Wilson describes how she formed part of a team of eight designated to go to the recently liberated concentration camp at Dachau.[27] Although impatient to start the job for which she had signed up, she "felt exhilarated" not only by the "escape from England" but the prospect of "something exciting to do ahead."[28] She spent her time at Granville getting to know her fellow recruits, most of whom seemed to be retired army officers. She remarked with surprise on the lack of women in the groups. In her experience women were often better suited than men "for all the improvisations and make-do-and-mends that relief work entails." Whereas "a man wants a real, clear-cut job, relief work is temporary, messy and clamorous."[29] Wilson's group eventually set out from Normandy on May 7, 1945, in two reconditioned army trucks, which were, in her description, "packed tight not only with us but with all our paraphernalia, our camp-beds, blankets, water-bottles, personal kit, and, because on the morning of our start the war was still on, even helmets and gas-masks."[30] As they traveled through France "Peace broke out.... Flags came out of windows, people waved and shouted."[31] Crossing into Germany, she seemed surprised that jubilation was replaced by "a strange silence, as though people were stunned.... No one smiled or waved."[32] At Heidelberg the team was redirected to Starnberg, and a camp at Feldafing housing deportees from Dachau. The Americans in authority, whom team members had been directed to seek out, had no idea they were coming, "had never heard of UNRRA," and did not know what to do with them.[33] However, living accommodation was hastily requisitioned in the houses of local Germans, and the new arrivals were shown around the camp, a former Hitler Youth School.[34] Wilson's account reflects the ambiguity Levi noticed in the Russians at Auschwitz. She writes:

> As for the inmates of the camp—at first it was hard to look on them without repulsion. I have seen victims of famine before... but this was worse, for these people were victims of more than famine, they were

victims of cruelty. They were wearing the convicts' striped blue and white pyjamas, and had the shaven heads and the number tattooed on the left arm which were the marks of Auschwitz. Some were walking skeletons, most had hollow cheeks and large, black expressionless eyes, which stared and stared and saw nothing. They had the furtive look and gestures of hunted animals. By years of brutal treatment, by the murder of relatives, by the constant fear of death, all that was human had been taken away from them.[35]

A period working in Feldafing camp and later in the towns and villages of Upper Bavaria with scattered DPs—the term quickly adopted among the "liberators" for these displaced persons[36]—was followed by Wilson's transfer with part of her team to the camp of Föhrenwald, originally a garden village built in 1939 for German munitions workers. In her account of her experiences at Feldafing and Föhrenwald, Wilson describes the tension between the attempts of the authorities in the camps to bring order to the chaos, and the needs of the displaced persons themselves. While many of the refugees seemed to prefer to fend for themselves through what they called "organising"—for Wilson this was "the slave word for looting"—the relief agencies "wanted them medically examined, deloused, registered," and brought into the camps.[37] The efforts at welfare work were frequently disrupted by military orders—which UNRRA personnel could not quarrel with of course—to evacuate certain groups from the camp to make way for others who were arriving.[38]

Kathryn Hulme tells us in The Wild Place, her account of her work with Polish DPs at Wildflecken camp, how, from her first day in 1945 to when she finally left in December 1950, though she wept for "all the refugees on the planet," each of them impressed her in their "single plight."[39] Her first assignment on arrival at Wildflecken was to screen requests from people who needed a pass to leave the camp temporarily. "Never again," she says, "would I be able to look on a refugee mass, even in pictures, and see it collectively, see it as a homogeneous stream of humanity that could be handled with the impersonal science of the engineer.... Each new individual encounter would repeat the misery in a slightly different form.... The 'DP problem'... had as many faces as there were people composing it."[40]

Personal relationships and attempts to get to know the refugees as people were seen as less of a priority by those in charge of the camps, though relief workers like Hulme and Wilson did what they could: Francesca Wilson made an effort to walk around the camps and talk to the refugees. How successful they were in establishing relationships one might doubt, given, for example, the way in which, in Wilson's account at least, comments detailing the distinctive characteristics of Jews, both positive and negative, sit alongside her remarks on the residual anti-Semitism of Poles and Austrians, which she describes as "the effects of years of... propaganda."[41] Reading the writings of that immediate postwar period, I found it striking how readily national characteristics are described in very definitive terms, and how strong an anti-Semitism remains, even among those sympathetic to the plight of survivors of the concentration camps.

There were anyhow tensions in the camp bureaucracy between the desire that displaced persons be organized in groups according to their national origin, and the sense that, because of the way that "Jews" had been persecuted by the Nazis as Jews, and not as Germans, Greeks, Poles, or French, a separate category might be necessary. Officials or administrators could not decide how those imprisoned as Jews should be housed in the camps: should they be treated separately, repeating the Nazi categorization, or grouped together with fellow nationals who had arguably suffered much less under the German regime and who in any case might harbor anti-Semitic sentiments? National categorizations would make repatriation, the chief aim of UNRRA, much easier. The "Jews" themselves were not all of one mind, of course. Notes on a visit to Hohne displaced persons camp (housed on the site of the former Bergen-Belsen concentration camp) compiled by Lt. Col. R. B. Longe contain a section entitled "The Jewish Problem." It is unbelievable, from my perspective now at least, that he should use such terminology. But there clearly were difficulties. The Hohne DP center actually consisted of four separate "camps" (apart from the Belsen "dirty" camp, Camp 1, which had been burned to the ground within a few weeks of liberation, as soon as survivors had been evacuated): Camp 2 contained Poles; Camp 3, Poles and Jews of mixed nationalities; and Camps 4 and 5, "segregated Jews of Polish origin... administered by the Central Jewish Committee." Longe notes that "the Hungarian and Rumanian Jews regard themselves as nationals first and Jews second.... The vast majority of the Polish and German Jews however regard themselves as Jews first and last and are unanimous in demanding to be sent to Palestine." A "non-Zionist" organization had been set up in Camp 3 "for watching over the interests of those Jews who wish to emigrate elsewhere than to Palestine." And, from the opposite faction, "a demonstration was staged by Jews from Camps 4 and 5 to protest against the Jews from Camp 3 who have not opted for Palestine."[42] The non-Jewish Poles were not all of one mind either—some were willing to return to Poland, in accordance with the wishes of UNRRA and the agreements that had been endorsed by its member governments, but others were adamant they would not return to a Poland under Soviet rule. There seemed to be no way out of these "problems," but, despite this, the need for some form of categorization, whether racial, national, or religious, remained unquestioned.[43]

A flowchart detailing the sequence of procedures in "assembly centres," as the camps were officially known, shows the importance attached to determining the category of displaced person being dealt with.[44] After disinfection and a medical, everyone had to go through a full registration process, including the verification of their nationality, before their claim could be accepted or refused, and full registration, including the filling in of a DP.2 card, completed. The camp authorities were on the lookout for those who were enemy nationals, Soviet citizens, or suspects. Enemy nationals were to be transferred to detention camps, Soviet citizens to "treaty centres" for deportation to the USSR,[45] and suspects handed over to the relevant national authorities. United Nations prisoners of war and civilian internees were transferred to the prisoner of war executive. Once this selection process had been completed, once people had been categorized, checked, and processed through the various stages shown in the flowchart, the displaced were ready for the final stage: "disposal"—as if they were some form of unwanted object, which indeed I suppose they were in the eyes of the authorities. Many of these people had already been through horrendous experiences of dehumanizing categorization and "selection" during their persecution in other, Nazi- or Ustaše-run, camps.

That the camp authorities were taken by surprise by the way in which the displaced persons organized themselves politically, and were unable to react appropriately to their demands, reflects an assumption that often forms the basis of relief organizations: that their business is to provide the material necessities of life, no more. Those in camps are on the whole not seen as persons, with their own views about what should happen, but as passive recipients of aid—objects of charity or objects to be disinfected.[46] UNRRA saw its chief task as providing medical care, food, and shelter for the displaced and then returning them, more or less automatically, to what had been their homes. UNRRA's job was to bring order, organization, and form—welfare, not politics—to the chaos it encountered. The displaced saw things differently. Many of them had come to the decision not to return "home" and had their own decided views as to where they wanted to live and what future they saw for themselves and their communities. UNRRA's approach led the camp authorities in Hohne to some incomprehensible actions. Incredibly, German Jews, as soon as they were free from illness and fed, were regarded as enemy nationals, not nationals of the United Nations. Once recovered, they were no longer the responsibility of UNRRA and could be released to the surrounding German communities, which were supposed to absorb them.[47]

Later, independently of the question of national categorizations, UNRRA, perhaps to formalize and justify its work or perhaps as a signal of its own authority alongside that of the military, which ran the camps, began to issue questionnaires demanding statistical information and additional forms of categorization of the displaced. According to Francesca Wilson, "Their [Bavarian Area] headquarters in Pasing, near Munich, began to pour out questionnaires to us. What about our Personal Counselling Service? To how many people did we give personal counselling every day? How many handicapped had we discovered?" Wilson clearly found this a strange intrusion; she remarks: "Social science has neat labels and appropriate pigeon-holes for everyone: handicapped, under-privileged, maladjusted, deprived, introvert and extravert. Does it sometimes forget the person in his label?" Had the displaced persons themselves gone missing, as persons? It is ironic, though, that despite this insight Wilson continues her account with the instinctive use of a national categorization: "The Americans, who predominated at Pasing, laid great stress on labels."[48]

Historian Caroline Moorehead, writing many years later, echoes these reflections on the methods of gathering information. For her, the paperwork gave the whole enterprise "an Alice in Wonderland quality":

> As if forms and documents, properly filled in, could somehow contain the chaos, though the methods adopted then are still considered the most efficient. "Who has been displaced?" read one form. "When? Where? Why? Who, while displaced, has died? . . . married? or had a child born? Who, having been displaced, remains displaced? Where? Why?"[49]

Francesca Wilson does grant these methods a certain utility, despite her criticisms, in raising standards within UNRRA, for example, and notes the way in which documentation and statistics helped to locate unaccompanied children and signaled that "UNRRA was starting its search for the kidnapped and the lost. . . . In hundreds of cases relatives were found and the child restored to them."[50]

Locating the Lost

Locating missing relatives was only a small part of the task for most relief organizations working with the displaced after the Second World War, but it was a very important part as far as the displaced themselves were concerned. When an official visitor to the DP camp at Warendorf, where families were housed in animal stalls, spoke to the inmates in April 1945, what they requested was not more space or better rations but notepaper and envelopes: "There seemed to be a universal desire to communicate with friends."[51] As Mark Wyman points out, for DPs "questions of food, clothing, and even health were secondary to locating their loved ones."[52]

It was not just children who were missing or lost. Caught up in what Primo Levi describes as "the confused vortex of thousands of refugees and displaced persons,"[53] other people had become separated from their relatives or didn't know for example whether or not their husbands or wives, brothers or sisters, grown sons and daughters, or elderly parents had survived the transportations, forced labor camps or fighting. Indeed, many who were still alive at the end of the war did not make it home—or to a new place of settlement—in the aftermath: nearly three million of the forty million refugees "died in the turmoil that followed" the end of the war.[54]

For those in the field, reuniting people who had been separated often seemed a hopeless enterprise. In the summer of 1945 Evelyn Bark was one of those summoned to help at Belsen. With the more immediate needs of the inmates being dealt with, the daily death toll swiftly reduced from eight hundred or so to nil, and the "dirty camp" burned to the ground, Bark's task was to begin the work of tracing and reuniting families.

The retreating Nazis had destroyed all the concentration camp records at Belsen. In the early days of liberation eighteen thousand corpses had been buried without recording the camp numbers tattooed on their arms, and there was no record of the names corresponding to those numbers in any case, so the work of compiling lists of the names had to start from scratch "from the daily returns of deaths and hospital admissions, and by making inquiries among the surviving internees":

> It was a colossal task to discover the surname, Christian name, date and place of birth, last known address and next of kin of every single living person in the camp—it was absolutely impossible to get accurate information about the dead....I almost despaired at the seemingly endless difficulties; information written on dreadful old scraps of paper in a dozen languages was brought in from the various blocks; nothing was in alphabetical order; and while we were struggling to make sense of what we had found out, new inquiries rained in on us from both outside and inside the camp. Thousands of people wanted to know whether we had found any trace of this or that missing relative or friend.[55]

Francesca Wilson remarks: "We had been given excellent training in the methods of setting up Information Bureaux—but what was the use of that when there was never any information to give?" They wrote down details of the missing—"Sara Rotstein, aged 50, last heard of at Teresienstadt in 1943, looked for by her son Josef, late of Auschwitz and Dachau, now in Feldafing"—but there was at that time no central tracing agency, and everything relied on the exchange of details between local displaced persons camps and by word of mouth within the camps themselves.[56] Newcomers to any camp were questioned by those already there, and names and details were published in camp newspapers or posted on notice boards; people listened to radio broadcasts giving the names of displaced people trying to contact relatives, and these names were added to the camp notice board.[57] During the daily half hour given over to loudspeaker announcements, everyone would fall silent:

> All activity stops. People stand still listening and hoping. Every now and then a voice screams 'Me! That's me!' And somebody who has ceased to be a lost soul rushes wildly toward the administration building. At other times a couple of men will look at each other, then one will go to the office to report how so-and-so, mentioned over the loudspeaker, was killed at Dachau.[58]

Of course, it is often bad news, and only more rarely good. Very occasionally there is a story of success in all the searching—Francesca Wilson drove a young Polish refugee by the name of Joseph to a camp not far from Feldafing, where he had heard through the refugee grapevine that his sister and cousin were working. The two had moved on from the camp just before Wilson and the young man arrived, but they were eventually traced through word of mouth to another camp. The girls had not been registered there, and the search seemed to have come to a fruitless end. Joseph would not give up, though, and "suddenly . . . a door [opened] and there they were, and in a trice brother and sister were in each other's arms." "There was something in the scene," Wilson tells us, "which made it belong to the ancient world, or at least to an era before letters, telegrams, trains, all the communications of our modern world existed." For her, this "ordinary scene—a brother meeting a sister—was so miraculous" that it seemed to emphasize the extent to which the chaos of the aftermath of the war was a return to the "Dark Ages" in Europe.[59]

Many parents seeking their missing children traveled from camp to camp, endlessly searching. At Hohne camp "some hundreds turn[ed] up daily looking for relatives."[60] In the summer of 1945, "refugee centres were full of men and women holding snapshots, battered, faded little photographs, left over from family holidays or kindergarten gatherings, wandering round and round, asking all new arrivals whether they had ever seen their child."[61] Others made their own missing person posters—of the kind that remain familiar to us today—in their attempt to trace their relatives. Parents put up posters seeking missing children:

> Sigrid Bork, born 1940. Brown-grey eyes; dark blond curly hair.... The last time we saw her she was wearing a small black coat, red slippers, a blue cap, dark grey muff, red scarf, grey-brown gloves.... On 2 March 1945 we had to leave her in a hospital... from there she was taken away by nurses.... Who can help us? Getrud Bork. Mother.[62]

Small passport-sized photographs appeared alongside the "anguished pleas from distraught parents" that "were to be seen in 1945 in every post office, bus terminus and railway station."[63]

It must have seemed at times that finding out where to send an inquiry about a missing person was as fraught as setting out to find the missing person oneself. A plethora of organizations existed, in a more or less coordinated, that is, uncoordinated way. If inquirers were unlucky enough to send their inquiry to the wrong organization, it would be laboriously returned to them, for them to send on to the right one themselves. Inevitably what people did, quite sensibly, was send their inquiries to everyone they could think of. Fey von Hassell tells how in 1944 she managed to get a message to her mother that she was in the process of being deported. She had been arrested by the SS and forcibly separated from her two children. Her father, Ulrich von Hassell, a former diplomat and German ambassador to Italy, was one of those involved in the July 1944 plot to assassinate Hitler and had been executed. Fey scribbled her mother's address and a brief message on a scrap of paper and dropped it from the train onto the tracks at a small station: "Incredibly enough... the note with no stamp on it arrived at my mother's house about a month later."[64] Tracing her children after the war was not as easy. Her path was blocked at every turn by travel restrictions and the lack of a postal service. She and her Italian husband, Detalmo, were frustrated at their inability, despite their diplomatic connections, to get a pass to travel to Germany:

> To help overcome our frustration, [we prepared] pamphlets and papers giving details of Corradino and Robertino, along with their photographs. These we sent everywhere we could think of: to all the bishops and archbishops of Germany and Austria; to the Italian, German and International Red Cross; to the secret services of America, Britain and France; to the Italian ambassadors in Washington and Warsaw; to Vatican Radio; and to a hundred other addresses. Each leaflet was written

in German, English, French, Russian and Italian. But there was nothing, no response at all. It was like throwing pebbles into the sea.[65]

Von Hassell's two sons had been taken from her when she was arrested, and it was not until September 1945, a year later, that she was finally reunited with them. Hers was a personal search, unaided by relief agencies or tracing bureaus, carried out, when she was unable to travel herself, by her mother, still in Germany, who visited orphanages and cross-questioned staff, armed with pictures of the two children.

Again, it was of course not just children who were sought. American reporter I. F. Stone, in his book *Underground to Palestine,* describes how names and questions were written on the walls of staircases in an UNRRA building in Czechoslovakia: "One saw this kind of scrawl in every reception centre in Europe.... Refugees wrote their names and home towns on every wall they came to with the hope that some friend or relative might see them."[66] Photos of the missing were shown at cinemas and sometimes attached to messages: "This is my husband. I have had no word from him for four years. Does anyone know where he is now or whether he is still among the living?"[67] In most cases, the search was in the desperate hope of a reunion, but in one case at least, a wife was seeking news of the fate of her husband because she wished to marry a British Red Cross worker and return with him to the United Kingdom. The marriage could not take place until proof of her first husband's death had been produced. She was forced to undertake the difficult and dangerous journey back to Eastern Europe herself before her life could continue.[68]

And it was not only the parents who did the searching. Kathryn Hulme tells of her encounter with a little Polish boy who had succeeded in securing the transfer of his mother from one camp, his sister and brother from another in a different zone, and was now seeking permission to venture out once more in search of his father, who had been reported to be wandering the ruins of Munich. This boy traveled from camp to camp "sustaining himself on pilfered fruit from German orchards and his passionate faith that the people who belonged to him were not dead."[69]

In her book on the history of the International Red Cross, Caroline Moorehead describes one set of missing children posters:

> There was Bruno Schwartz, who stares out anxious and waif-like from his photograph, his ears protruding from close-cropped hair. "Born 4.3.42. Eyes blue, hair very fair. The child was wounded in Heiligenbeil, East Prussia, and taken to the district hospital." There is Stella Falck, a "quiet and calm" child with a particularly deep voice and a doll

which had real fair hair, could say Mummy and Daddy, and to which she was very attached; Siegfried Rzegotta, a solid, plump baby, "born 1.7.43, eyes pale blue, hair... last seen February 1945... wearing a dark blue romper suit with his full name printed on it"; and Norbert Wolf, a laughing fair child in a Peter Pan collar, "born 8.6.42, eyes blue, hair blond. Went missing on 7 May 1945 on the Czech border." The descriptions give little away: one can only guess at the anguish of their parents.[70]

Clearly, even after all these years, these images and their descriptions are heart-wrenching to those who come across them, including the historian in the archive. From her descriptions we can see that Moorehead was moved; and she reprints the poster itself in her book, perhaps in memory of the lost, perhaps to recover something of the rawness of the time. More is to come though—her account of what happened next, presumably gleaned from the archives of the International Committee of the Red Cross. Here is the story in Moorehead's words:

> Bruno Schwartz, the waif-like little boy with protruding ears who had been left in a doctor's care in the hospital in East Prussia while his mother Therese took his sisters to safety, died of his wounds. After the war, his mother waited for him in the West, begging the various tracing services to find him and endlessly trying to discover the names of nurses who... might have come across him. Only in April 1958, when the boy would have been sixteen, did she learn the truth. The director of a cemetery in Celle wrote to say that they had found a grave with the name of Bruno Schwartz. Therese Schwartz, fleeing with her daughters from East Prussia, had lost another son, aged six, in the bombing. Her husband, missing in Romania, has never been found.[71]

Choosing to Disappear

Of course, not all of the missing—whether German nationals or others—wanted to be traced. There were those who were content to disappear—from their families, from their former lives and their complicity in what had happened, or what they feared might be regarded as complicity, and from their homelands, which were no longer the same as far as they were concerned.[72] Even those who found themselves, eventually, at home—and a home not destroyed but still standing—like Primo Levi, still had to rebuild a new life and find a way of accommodating their experiences.

There is a temptation to tell the story from the perspective of the victors—
especially for someone from the postwar generation in the United Kingdom
like me—and to forget the complexities hidden by the words "liberation"
and "occupation."[73] Even for the "defeated," as one German commentator
notes,

> experiences regarding 8 May [1945] do not correspond one with
> another. Everyone experienced it in their own way. One person
> returned home, the other lost his *Heimat*. This one was liberated, for
> that one captivity started. Some were embittered by shattered illusions,
> others grateful for the gift of a new beginning.[74]

In the DP camps, as in the concentration camps before them, the law did
not apply. Those thought to have been camp guards or minor collaborators
were often subjected to summary justice from fellow inmates. The authorities sometimes did not intervene; sometimes so-called trials of suspected
war criminals were held but were far from fair, and the death penalty was
demanded for minor offenses.[75] And in some instances the treatment of
German prisoners of war by the French and the Americans was far from
the standard laid down by the Geneva Conventions. Figures for the number of German POWs who died as a result of their brutal forced labor
and starvation rations vary between three hundred thousand and over a
million.[76]

In contrast, the justice that was supposed to have been meted out in the
form of war crimes trials of senior officers in charge of the concentration
camps, and the extermination program overall, never fully materialized. The
fate of Gustav Wagner, deputy commandant of the Sobibor extermination
camp, who lived comfortably in Brazil after the war, was typical of the majority who escaped prosecution.[77] Tom Bower contrasts the meticulously well
organized "Project Paperclip," which succeeded in tracking down and evacuating nine thousand of Germany's top scientists and putting their expertise
to immediate use, despite the chaos in Europe in 1945, with "the operation
to hunt down the murderers of twelve million people [which] did not even
boast a codename. It had no trained staff, no headquarters and no priority."[78]
The disputes and stalemates that Bower draws attention to in British government departments were similar to those encountered in the attempts to set
up tracing services, which we examine in chapter 3. There were questions of
what could count as a war crime, where and by whom such crimes should
be prosecuted, whether crimes against stateless persons—which by then
included most of the Jews of Europe—could be considered, who should be
responsible for detaining suspects, and so on. A United Nations War Crimes
Commission (UNWCC) had been established but proved ineffectual. As a

result, no arrangements had been made for arrests or for the collection of evidence to support prosecutions, and in the meantime the SS and camp guards just melted away into the populations on the move. Going missing—choosing to disappear—was not too difficult.

Although millions were effectively under arrest—held in internment camps where they were supposed to undergo questioning as to their identity—there was no organized briefing for the interrogators, and many of the culpable escaped the net. Gustav Wagner was in a camp in Bavaria, but "no one questioned him and he was released at the end of May," despite the fact that his name appeared on the UN list of wanted men.[79] And no one thought to convert the summary beatings of suspected camp guards and others into opportunities to obtain eyewitness statements from former camp inmates, which could have led to formal prosecutions. Questioning of those who were found in the field was rough and ready—there were few safeguards, and testimony would have sometimes been obtained under duress.[80]

The situation at Belsen reflected the British reluctance to get involved in the prosecution of war crimes, and its incompetence in handling them.[81] The need for British involvement was ducked first on the grounds that no British subjects were among the victims. Potential witnesses among the former inmates were asked to stay in the vicinity in case their evidence was needed in the trials, but quite naturally "after years of suffering [they] didn't want to wait around any longer," and "vital witnesses were formally allowed to disappear."[82] The trial of the commandant and forty-four staff finally began in September 1945. It was a shambles. Charges did not include murder, but only "ill-treatment" of the internees by those "responsible for [their] well-being."[83] Procedural disputes, disputes about definitions, and challenges to the credibility of witnesses were interminable:

> Witnesses testifying that they had seen someone beaten to the ground were unable to prove that the victim had actually died of the wounds. They were unable to give dates and times for the assaults. Their explanation, that there was no sense of time in a concentration camp, did not seem to be understood.[84]

The summing up focused on the need for specificity, the absences of witnesses in person, and on what was "reasonable conduct in the circumstances." The reaction was an uproar: "As a means of uncovering the monstrousness of a system dedicated to murder [the trials] looked absurd."[85] They reflected the same disastrous and inappropriate concern for certainty and the same desire to avoid doing anything that plagued British bureaucratic procedures in other matters, as we shall see in chapter 3. Retrials were demanded but proved impossible: those acquitted had been released immediately and swiftly vanished.

Formal trials were held by the American, British, French, and Russian military authorities, and in total over ten thousand perpetrators were estimated to have been legally convicted.[86] A Central Registry of War Criminals and Security Suspects (CROWCASS) had been established in January 1945 and was supposedly to contain three lists: the wanted, those detained for specific crimes, and all prisoners of war. The lists were to be compiled using an IBM Hollerith card index machine.[87] In 1947 lists containing over fifty thousand names were published and circulated; the volume was reprinted and generally released in 2005, despite the original embargo for seventy-five years.[88] At present, there seems to be both a desire to believe that Germans implicated in horrific crimes have been brought to justice—and in a fair and accountable way—and a feeling that there must still be thousands at large in the community, whom we must somehow track down. Not infrequently, newspaper articles highlight instances that have come to light, and questions are asked in the British parliament, for example.[89] While it was convenient at one time for all concerned that people disappear, it seems necessary to deny that this could have happened or to pretend that we can still track down those who escaped.[90]

In the chaos of the aftermath of the violent upheaval of war, people lose touch with friends and relations, and many have a compelling and urgent need to reestablish contact. But this is often not a main concern for the authorities. Feeding, housing, and attending to the medical needs of the displaced, and returning them to their countries of origin, take priority. But should this lack of interest in tracing the missing after wars surprise us? Is it not a reflection of how, even in times of peace, governments are concerned with populations, not particular people? In their eyes, and even sometimes in our own, are we nothing more than objects to be kept alive, organized, and controlled, rather than people who have their being within an intricate web of relationships?

In the displaced persons camps, inmates struggled to reestablish family connections and make a life for themselves in changed circumstances, in spite of, rather than aided by, the efforts of those organizing the camps. On the whole there was no organized protest against the dehumanizing practices to which they were subject, unlike the protests against the instrumentalization of the missing in New York. Instead people evaded bureaucratic procedures and constraints and found their own ways of sidestepping categorization and depersonalization—or of escaping the camps altogether. Such protests as there were surprised those who thought they were helping, and it was only much later, and for their own purposes, that the authorities in occupied

Europe came to understand the importance of tracing services. We examine how this came about in the next chapter.

Though the women employed in relief work often seemed to be the ones who saw those they helped as persons, not objects, the distance between them and their charges remained considerable. For these women relief work often provided an escape from mundane lives or family problems. Francesca Wilson's relief work with UNRRA led to exciting adventure and travel.[91] Susan Pettiss, an UNRRA worker from Alabama, observes: "The idea of getting away from it all and into the arena of post-war Europe as a participant in efforts to pick up the pieces was intriguing—a great and socially acceptable escape."[92] Her escape was from an alcoholic husband and an abusive marriage, however, not just an escape from boredom to adventure. Evelyn Bark's memoirs of her service as head of Red Cross Foreign Relations Department work in northwestern Europe were called *No Time to Kill*—under ordinary circumstances, women like Bark often had nothing but spare time to kill. When she was congratulated on receiving the OBE after the war, she remarked: "I should perhaps feel rather diffident about accepting a decoration for work which I so whole-heartedly enjoy."[93] Evelyn Bark became the first woman to be awarded a CMG: women had only recently become eligible for the Order of St. Michael and St. George.[94] The foreword to her memoirs was written by the Duke of Gloucester.

As we shall see in the next chapter, the concerns of the junior women working on the ground in displaced persons camps were reflected in the attempts of senior women in the British Red Cross and UNRRA to bring a particular sort of order to the chaos that was Europe. But these women's ideas about how this should be undertaken were not the same as those of the military planners or the men who were largely in charge of the organizations and governments involved. To the chaos on the ground was added conflict as to priorities and of personalities, conflict between the abstractions of military precision, the pragmatism of government bureaucracies, and the needs of those whose lives had been disrupted or destroyed. Organization—or the fate of particular organizations, their influence, and standing—seemed to some as important as effective action, and debates over who should do what and when all too often meant that nothing was done, and those searching for relatives were left to their own devices. The authorities prioritized the control of populations on the move—both so that they would not disrupt military operations and so that they could be repatriated as quickly as possible—rather than the business of tracing the missing, and the politics of who should be helped conflicted with the concern of voluntary agencies to help everyone, even former enemies.

CHAPTER 3

Tracing Services

> A plan could have been made that would have pre-
> vented at least two-thirds of the distress of mind
> which is going on at the moment.
>
> —S. J. Warner, Director, Foreign Relations Depart-
> ment, British Red Cross

For many in Europe who had lost touch with
family members after the Second World War, reestablishing contact was a
first priority, taking precedence over other concerns. While the military
authorities in charge of postconflict reconstruction were first oblivious to
this need, focusing instead on military priorities and on repatriation, voluntary agencies took an active role in tracing missing relatives. Jacques Rancière
reminds us that "in order to enter into political exchange, it becomes necessary to invent the scene upon which spoken words may be audible, in which
objects may be visible, and individuals themselves may be recognized."[1] It
was the voluntary agencies, together with some in the military, who insisted
on the visibility of missing persons and the audibility of the voices of those
searching for them. The occupying authorities finally acknowledged the
importance of tracing services, albeit on their own terms.

In 1945 a confused and confusing network of tracing organizations all
over Europe, including the United Kingdom, was hard at work responding to the challenge presented by the huge volume of inquiries about
the whereabouts of friends and relations that were received as the armies
moved forward. Official decisions about who was in charge, or what form
services should take, had little impact at first in a chaotic situation where
there were tensions between the various authorities involved and communication was difficult, while at the same time anxious relatives were

urgently pressing for information—and searching independently as often as not.

The archives contain a number of reports of the disputes about the organization of tracing services, each produced by a different group and reflecting a concern to exercise some control over the contentious history of tracing. The "primeval Chaos" into which the European continent had dissolved,[2] with the movement of millions of people and the lack of any overall administration or authority, was reflected in the disorder of tracing services. It seems that everyone did what they could—while disagreeing fundamentally about what could or should be done or why, and who was to be helped and how. It was only later, when the immediate urgency had died down, that any coherent administrative organization or framework could be agreed on—or, as it turns out, imposed.

A number of organizations had been set up rather hastily and often had little or no previous experience in the field, which led to confusion. Duplication and chaos grew: "Tracers were now everywhere. . . . It rapidly became clear that some kind of overall authority was needed."[3] But when it came to setting up a central tracing bureau, not only were there disagreements as to priorities and methods, but there were clashes in terms of the overall aims of the exercise and the values that drove it. The resourcefulness of voluntary organizations, praised often for being able to turn their hands to anything and find ways around whatever obstacles they came across, conflicted with the attempted precision of the military planners, who were trying to foresee any and every eventuality and to put in place systems so robust that they could cope, through a series of intricate directives and regulations, with everything. On top of this was the politics of repatriation: governments had an interest in tracing their own nationals to ensure their return home, willingly or otherwise.

Governments were not interested in tracing particular persons, who might or might not want to return to where they had come from, but in tracing their nationals and repatriating them: displaced *populations* were the concern, not displaced *persons*. Persons-as-such were invisible, as we saw in chapter 2, and *missing* persons doubly so. Voluntary organizations sought to reunite families and to respond to the mental distress, as they saw it, of those searching. Military planners wanted to control refugee movements and focused on military objectives—for them, civilians were largely in the way. Governments were keen to rebuild nations whose populations had been decimated in the conflict. The people working for voluntary organizations, the military, and governments each had an eye on their particular priorities. And those seeking missing relatives made their own decisions as to what to do, enlisting help where they could, often impeded in their efforts by artificial barriers and insensitivities, but driven by their own imperatives. For some people, the chaos provided a welcome opportunity to evade those looking for them and quietly disappear.

Outline Planning

Tracing military personnel missing in action had been an ongoing concern throughout the war, with organizations such as the British Red Cross closely involved both in hospital searching and in listing prisoners of war, as we shall see in chapter 6. However, although it was evident that vast population movements would mean that families would become separated and many people would be unable to maintain contact with their relatives, other objectives than connecting displaced persons with their families seemed more important to those planning for postwar requirements. In 1944, a paper from the European regional office of UNRRA, based in London, on communication between displaced persons and their families formed the basis of initial discussions about tracing services. The paper arose from a meeting involving representatives of the British Red Cross, UNRRA, and the International Red Cross (IRC), organized in London on June 1, 1944, by Sir Herbert Emerson of the Inter-Governmental Committee on Refugees. In the revised document, dated August 1944, overarching priorities were clearly stated:

> It is necessary to bear in mind the two principles governing all arrangements for displaced persons:
>
>   1. That nothing should be done which will slow down the process of repatriation; and
>   2. That every inducement should be offered to displaced persons to obey the "stand still" orders of the military authorities, so that they can be brought within the organised scheme, instead of "trekking" in an unorganised fashion.[4]

The people on the move were seen as a potential obstacle, and a threat to organization and control. It was recognized at the start that as soon as territories were liberated, inquiries for the missing would begin, but "to attempt to answer these enquiries, or to trace the exact whereabouts of the displaced persons newly liberated, would clog the repatriation machinery and slow down the process of sending displaced persons home; this...cannot be allowed."[5] The Red Cross postcards, through which people could register inquiries, were seen as "inducements to persuade unorganised displaced persons to come to Assembly Areas."[6] Innocuous enough, maybe, until one remembers that entering the assembly centres, as the camps were called, could be the first step in a surrender to Allied military control, which could lead, and indeed in some cases did lead, to forcible repatriation or resettlement, and death. In Slovenia, for example, those forcibly returned by the British were subsequently massacred.[7]

The separate outline plan for refugee and displaced persons put forward by Supreme Headquarters, Allied Expeditionary Force (SHAEF) in June 1944 had also emphasized the priority of military operations. The object of the plan "for the control, care and disposition of refugees and displaced persons" was the following:

a. To eliminate or reduce interference with military operations.
b. To permit a smooth transfer of responsibility from military authorities to civilian agencies at the earliest practicable date.[8]

Those persons on the move were either "refugees" if within the boundaries of their own country, or "displaced persons" if outside. The types of refu-gees and displaced persons were listed as "evacuees; war or political fugitives; political prisoners; forced or voluntary workers; Todt workers and members of other para-military organizations not treated as members of forces under German command;[9] deportees; intruded persons; extruded persons; civilian internees (other than BR or US); ex P/Ws; stateless persons."[10] Estimates at the time were as follows:

> There are 11,332,700 displaced and refugees in Belgium, Denmark, France, Germany (excluding German refugees), Luxembourg, the Netherlands and Norway. Of these 2,397,300 are refugees within their own countries. 8,935,400 are displaced persons in foreign countries. They speak at least 20 different languages, come from 20 countries and are the concern of as many governments.[11]

As part of the military priorities, "stand still" or "stand fast" orders were to be issued, requiring "refugees and displaced persons...to stand fast until their movement can be organised by military or Allied national authorities." Those interned or imprisoned by the Germans were to be "freed from confine-ment...and transferred to Assembly Centres where they will be held as may be appropriate."[12] From one camp to another, one might say.

When the SHAEF outline plan was circulated for comment, a number of concerns were expressed. One was that the security issues had not been addressed, and in particular that collaborators could slip through the net and escape. Further, a commander with experience of displaced persons in Italy, Lt. Col. L. R. Hulls, noted his concern that voluntary organizations such as the Red Cross had not been involved in the current plans as yet, though their help would be essential.[13] Hulls brought a touch of practicality to the situation with his comments that stand fast orders could not be expected to have any effect in one of the cases envisaged, opposing armies in combat. He noted: "Refugees in a battle zone cannot normally be instructed to remain where they are until their movement can be organised"; rather, movement must be organized immediately, and the way to do this was to use transport returning from delivering troops to the front. The outline plan's suggestion of directing refugees to minor roads and lanes was neither necessary nor practicable. Hulls summed up the difficulties to be faced, from his experience: "great numbers; little or no notice of what may happen next; evacuation by road, rail and sea; transportation and transit camps; security, medical, feeding; co-ordination between armies, commands in rear, and Allied national authorities."[14]

By the time the SHAEF outline plan had been revised, in November 1944, the general aims had been expanded to include, alongside the prevention of disruption of military operations, relieving disease, want, and ill-treatment and facilitating repatriation.[15] The categories of persons had been refined too and were now listed as comprising refugees, displaced persons, United Nations displaced persons, and stateless persons. The term "United Nations displaced persons," as we saw in chapter 2, applied only to citizens of the forty-odd Allied nations—enemy or ex-enemy displaced persons were not UN nationals at this point. SHAEF responsibilities to DPs and refugees in general were confined to preventing disease; relieving want and organizing repatriation was to apply only to UN displaced persons. The German authorities were to be required to deal with enemy or ex-enemy DPs, though UNRRA's charter did allow it to deal with enemy nationals who were persecuted because of race, religion, or activities in favor of the United Nations.[16] There was still no engagement by SHAEF at this point with the need for tracing facilities; concern was centered on the processing of displaced populations. There is no place in the numerous categorizations for persons who are missing to their relatives—they are displaced persons like other displaced persons, nothing more.

Tracing Machinery

Although SHAEF had not yet tackled the question of tracing, the UNRRA European regional office paper, produced alongside the SHAEF outline plan, had proposed the setting up of "machinery for the tracing of displaced persons in Europe," and it envisaged a central tracing bureau, based on expanding the existing International Committee of the Red Cross (ICRC) register at Geneva, a role to which the Committee had agreed, which would operate alongside national tracing bureaus in member countries based on the British Red Cross model.[17] The UNRRA invitation to the International Committee to undertake this role was contained in a telegram of September 26, 1944, which suggested an expansion of its Section on Dispersed Families. The use of the International Red Cross registration card P.10.027 was also envisaged.[18]

The ICRC,[19] established originally to assist soldiers wounded or taken prisoner, had four million names in its card index files by September 1940 and was receiving fifty thousand letters a day concerning the identity and treatment of prisoners of war.[20] The card index did not at first include civilians. The Committee had been pushing for some time for an extension of treaties to cover civilians. However, only verbal agreements were made at the Tokyo Conference,[21] and a commitment to treat "enemy civilians"— nationals of enemy countries who happened to be in the territory when war broke out—with the same rights as prisoners of war. This lack restricted what the International Committee could do, and particularly limited its attempts to obtain access to the concentration camps, which after all contained "detained civilians," not "enemy nationals."[22] The ICRC operated on the principles of neutrality and discretion—principles that gave it access to prisoner of war camps and the right to talk to prisoners, but that arguably prevented it from speaking out against the plans to exterminate the Jews. Caroline Moorehead describes how the Committee knew a great deal about what was going on in this regard at every stage of the war, despite not having been admitted to the concentration camps; she points out that by early 1942 "knowledge of the camps [was] circulating freely throughout Europe" with "details of the train transports and extermination camps... regularly reaching London."[23] She sets out carefully a number of reasons why the Committee decided, at its meeting of October 14, 1942, not to issue a public pronouncement or protest but to remain silent, but its decision that day continues to reverberate.[24] Despite its considerable efforts to obtain access to the camps and to obtain the release of the inmates as the end of the war approached, the International Committee is widely regarded as having failed.[25]

While it was recognized that enemy prisoners of war were entitled to humane treatment and in particular to the exchange of messages with their families, the same was not accepted for enemy civilians in postwar camps. Even German armed forces who had surrendered were not considered prisoners of war by the Allies, but rather "belonged to a category specially created for them:'surrendered enemy personnel.'"[26] In 1943, in anticipation of the need for families of all nationalities—and mixed nationalities—for a means of tracing relatives from whom they had become separated, the ICRC set up a separate section for dispersed families, and arranged for the printing and distribution of a special card designed for the purpose, the P.10.027 card.[27] The ICRC informed UNRRA of its actions, and was invited to operate as a central tracing bureau and distribute its cards in displaced persons camps. It agreed to this, while expressing its regret that a whole category of DPs—former enemies—were to be excluded.[28] By the spring of 1945 everything was in place for the ICRC to act as a central bureau.[29] In line with this expectation, ICRC asked SHAEF to enable its delegates to be installed in occupied Germany and printed a supply of a million cards.

A memorandum setting out the procedure to be followed for inquiries from displaced persons was circulated to SHAEF from UNRRA and the ICRC on June 2, 1945, noting that, "by agreement between SHAEF, UNRRA and the International Red Cross Committee, the last named acts as a central link in the system of tracing missing persons."[30] On July 23, 1945, International Red Cross tracing expert, Maurice Thudichum, who was eventually to become the director of the International Tracing Service in Bad Arolsen from 1947 to 1951, arrived in Germany "with two lorries loaded with half a million IRC Tracing Cards (P.10.027) and large quantities of instructions in fourteen languages" for distribution in UNRRA Assembly Centres. However, by this point the military authorities had become interested in the question of tracing, and since the visit by Thudichum "had not been properly approved by SHAEF...he had to be sent back to Switzerland with his lorries. From that time onwards, the IRC was virtually excluded from the field of civilian tracing." A history written in 1947 speculates that the reasons might have been that "as a neutral organisation it was unpopular in belligerent circles and...it seemed too hasty to set to work without following closely the military procedures."[31] UNRRA accounts of 1946 indicate that there was disagreement among the occupying powers, and that the ICRC was unacceptable to the Soviet Union for political reasons: the Soviets saw it as a national, Swiss organization, not an international one.[32]

It seems that one of the chief reasons that the British Red Cross and the International Committee were excluded from the operation of the Central Tracing Bureau was the question of the nationality of the displaced and the link with repatriation. The overriding aim of the Allied tracing services was political—or biopolitical—not humanitarian: the control of populations, and their repatriation or resettlement in line with the wishes of the member governments of UNRRA.[33] Tracing missing persons and reuniting families were not the prime motivation of the official services.[34] A series of uncoordinated actions by officials of UNRRA and the military organizations had perhaps been partially responsible for a general misunderstanding that led to approval of ICRC involvement in the first place. Yet priorities, particularly those relating to repatriation, made it almost inevitable that the military and UNRRA, as an intergovernmental body, would take control of tracing services, sidelining both the International Red Cross and, to a lesser extent, the British Red Cross too.

The UNRRA European regional office paper of August 1944 had suggested unofficially that the British Red Cross Foreign Relations Department—which was already involved in tracing—would be an appropriate organization to undertake this work in the United Kingdom.[35] In October 1944 the British Home Office concurred with the Foreign Office that the British Red Cross should indeed take on that role and be the lead organization in the United Kingdom for dealing with inquiries about the whereabouts of refugees and for transmitting messages to family members.[36] The machinery that existed at that time included the Foreign Relations Department of the British Red Cross Society, the Citizens' Advice Bureaux, and the United Kingdom Search Bureau,[37] all of which were in touch with other organizations abroad, including the Central Register at Geneva. It was argued that setting up a new organization to serve as the British National Tracing Bureau would make it necessary "to duplicate the extensive records already in the possession of the Red Cross and other bodies," and there seemed to be no reason for this.[38] A similar motivation seemed to have been at work in the original suggestion that the International Red Cross should provide the central resource. However, in the end the conflict between national state and military priorities and those of independently funded voluntary organizations proved too great.

When the Joint War Organisation of the British Red Cross and St. John had set up its Foreign Relations Department in May 1940, there were already the beginnings of a tracing service within the organization, and this had expanded as more and more civilians were displaced by or entangled in the war.[39] By 1944 it was an extensive and full-fledged service, staffed with expert linguists and experienced searchers and dealing with numerous inquiries under the careful eye of its director, Miss S. J. Warner, whose personal involvement and assertiveness were to prove important as things developed. There were separate sections for handling inquiries about civilians of different nationalities, and eventually British Red Cross activities covered the whole of the liberated territories of Europe. The United Kingdom Search Bureau for

German, Austrian and Stateless Persons from Central Europe, set up in June 1944, became a section of the British Red Cross Foreign Relations Department and brought together fifty-seven affiliated organizations throughout the United Kingdom. These included several specifically Jewish organizations or those dealing with particular nationals, such as the Jewish Refugee Committee, the Austrian Centre, the Czech Trust Fund, the Polish Jewish Refugee Fund & Federation of Jewish Relief Organisations, and the Association of Jewish Refugees.[40]

The British Red Cross tracing service involved more than just office work. Its workers took to the streets. In the autumn of 1944, Evelyn Bark, then a junior volunteer, was posted to the Foreign Relations Department in the field headquarters of the Red Cross Commission for North West Europe in Brussels. She took with her "eleven and a half pounds of Red Cross enquiry forms on thin paper with details of missing people last heard of in Belgium."[41] On arrival, she untied her parcel of forms, sorted the inquiries by area of the city, and began to make her calls to the last-known addresses of the relatives sought, helped by friends who transcribed the names onto file cards for indexing. She also made use of information in the documents left behind when the Gestapo evacuated in haste in the building the Red Cross had taken over.

When the Allied armies advanced into Italy, British Red Cross work of tracing was made easier through the cooperation of the Civil Affairs branch of the military authorities: "Bureaux staffed by specialist tracers had followed close behind the Allied forces as they made their way up Italy. . . . Everywhere the army went, trained tracers went with them."[42] A bureau for recording displaced persons, together with a tracing service run by the British Red Cross under the Military Control Commission, had been set up at Bari in southern Italy and had worked very successfully.[43] However, the situation was not to be as straightforward when forces advanced into Germany. There was no specified role for the British Red Cross or other voluntary organizations that might be working with UNRRA; indeed, the British Red Cross Society was said to "resent having to submit to UNRRA control," and it seemed that "an impasse" had been reached.[44]

The debates and disagreements around the setting up of zonal tracing services and a central tracing agency for all the Allied zones in Germany came to a head in the summer of 1945. The military command was surprised at the volume of demand from displaced persons in Germany to be put in contact with their relatives, as were the departments at the British War Office and the Foreign Office that had of course been set up to deal with prisoners of war, not civilians. The scheme proposed and largely agreed on by all parties in 1944 for a central tracing bureau run by the International Red Cross and national bureaus on the British Red Cross model did not envisage any kind of tracing bureau within Germany; it was assumed that the DP.2 registration cards, filled out for each displaced person in assembly centres and "deposited centrally with SHAEF," would provide the information that could be married with inquiries.[45] It soon became clear that this would not work and that "this limited conception of tracing had to be actively supplemented by actual search among German records and in Assembly Centres and other places in Germany, while at the same time, the DP.2 Cards proved entirely unworkable for any tracing or Central Record purposes."[46]

During the summer of 1945 various groups at SHAEF and its successor in charge of displaced persons, the Combined Displaced Persons Executive (CDPX), as well as officials in the British and U.S. sections of the Control Commission for Germany, continued to discuss the question of displaced civilians. Meanwhile the situation in the field was becoming desperate, as an official from the British Red Cross noted:

> The greatest need among DPs now is for facilities to enable them to trace their relatives. The doctors agree that anxiety about their families is an even greater factor in preventing recovery than the very rough conditions under which they still live, or the strain of previous experiences. Lists, facilities for transport, and for *exchange of letters* are all essential to tracing relations inside Germany. The making of lists is extraordinarily difficult when camps are perpetually subjected to changes of policy and unexpected influxes of population.... The attitude of the Russians in denying the normal facilities for tracing people in their camps and for arranging to re-unite families remains the same. It causes great distress and suffering and discredits them inevitably.[47]

At this point inquiries from the United Kingdom and the United States were being received by a central office at SHAEF, which forwarded them to the relevant army group. Some of these inquiries were then dealt with, but a large number were just filed.[48] SHAEF had neither the staff nor the machinery to cope with the numbers of inquiries it received, and had discussed the problem with the G-5 Displaced Persons Branch.[49] The creation of a central records office in Germany was being considered. This idea was pursued at a conference on July 11, 1945, and it was envisaged that UNRRA would eventually take over responsibility for its organization.[50] In the meantime a copy of a directive entitled *Inquiries concerning the Whereabouts and Welfare of Individuals,* issued on July 5, 1945, reached Miss Warner at the British Red Cross Foreign Relations Department.[51] The directive stated that "no records of individuals are held at this headquarters" and requested no further inquiries be addressed to the department but instead referred to national agencies, with the results being reported to the ICRC Records Bureau in Geneva.

The directive prompted an explosive response from Miss Warner deploring the fact that "it seems impossible for the officers in charge of Civil Affairs in the Army to consult the actual people who have for years been working on this enquiry and tracing system" and remarking that their suggestion that Civil Affairs officers send a copy of every inquiry they receive to the ICRC in Geneva was "deplorable."[52] In Miss Warner's view there was "no doubt that enquiries should go between the National Tracing Bureau direct, without a copy of every enquiry going to Geneva." However, she thought there was little prospect of convincing the ICRC of this: "They will find out by bitter experience, as a large part of their records are bound to be dead before they have even got them on to their cards. We know here how difficult it is to work even with the lists we have received from the camps, because by the time the lists have reached London almost invariably people have moved from camps."[53]

Miss Warner wrote to Lt. Col. E. M. Hammer, at the War Office, Civil Affairs, on July 20, 1945, noting in no uncertain terms the concern of her department "at the lack of any system in the territories in Germany occupied by the United Nations for enquiries from relatives and friends of the many thousands not only of displaced persons but of German nationals with whom it is desired to get in touch." She pointed out that, despite the ignorance of other parties on this, the British Red Cross was the National Tracing Bureau for the United Kingdom, and that it had been permitted to set up central tracing bureaus in other areas—Italy and Austria—with some success, but that as yet there was no central system in Germany: "The lack of any enquiry/message system or registration system is causing misery and unhappiness to individuals, which I think will shortly reach such a volume that both the Government of this country and the reputation of the United Nations as a whole will suffer considerably."[54]

She was scathing about the deficiencies of the "field postcard" inquiry form in comparison to the Red Cross form used in Italy and Austria. She proposed the setting up of a system based on the Red Cross forms immediately, "without waiting for any more elaborate system that it may be found necessary and possible for UNRRA to set up for the future."[55] Her suggestion found support at the Foreign Office.[56]

What angered her most was the way in which, "if there had been some willingness on the part of the Civil Affairs Administration of the Armies to make use of the experience and personnel of voluntary Societies," then existing organizations, including her own, could have helped. She issued a warning that she didn't think that "the British Red Cross, which has had a reputation of success in this work up to the present, should continue to take responsibility for a failure which it has no control to prevent." She proposed that she should advise her executive to make a public statement to this effect on the BBC, though "it would be extremely difficult to word it without indicating that the lack of organisation about communications is really to a large extent unnecessary."[57]

She ended by noting that the British Red Cross was "faced with a situation in which we now have some thousands of enquiries waiting to be dispatched, and a good many hundreds already dispatched as directed by SHAEF to what was SHAEF Headquarters from which up to the present we have had no reply." "We also," she added, "have hundreds of patient enquirers who come in daily or who write to us and to whom we have to reply that there is no way of assisting them."[58] The frustration she felt on behalf of those who relied on the Red Cross for help was palpable.

The Central Tracing Bureau

Whether as a result of Miss Warner's intervention or not, organization of a central tracing bureau began to move ahead rapidly, though the confusion had by no means abated. On July 24, 1945, a circular was sent out reporting the establishment of a Central Tracing Bureau and a Central Records Office by the CDPX at Hoechst near Frankfurt, to be run by UNRRA and responsible for "promoting the development of a National Tracing Bureau in each country."[59] The CDPX seemed unaware that the British Red Cross had been acting as National Tracing Bureau in the United Kingdom for some time. By August 6, 1945, a Zonal Search Bureau under the Control Commission for Germany, British Element, based at Bunde, was operating with Col. J. R. Bowring as its director. The British Red Cross had been instrumental in helping set up this bureau in the British zone, supplying trained staff and advice. A circular had been issued directing future inquiries to the new bureau and noting that the British Red Cross Foreign Relations Department was associated with it, and that Red Cross forms could still be used.[60]

In a memorandum of August 13, 1945, Bowring circulated his own plan, called "The Tracing of Missing Persons of Allied Nationality throughout Germany." He set out the problem again: "The great number of prisoners of war, the mass deportations of workers and political suspects, the actual fighting coupled with the barbarous conduct of the Germans has created a situation whereby a vast number of persons are classified as 'missing'. Their fate is known neither to their governments nor to their nearest relatives."[61] His memorandum gives the following reasons for tracing these missing persons:

a. To reunite families. There are many families so broken up that, unless an official organisation is created for bringing them together, their reunion may never be achieved.

b. Where applicable, to establish beyond doubt the fact of death so that pensions may be paid to dependents, widows may re-marry, estates may be appropriately administered.

c. To establish for all time the enormity of the German crimes and to make available to those concerned with this problem such evidence as is collected during the course of routine search.[62]

The same memorandum notes that the Central Records and Tracing Bureau set up using UNRRA personnel under the direction of CDPX in the U.S. zone was "developing slowly and does not appear to be in a position to co-ordinate the activities." In contrast to Miss Warner's intervention, which unashamedly espoused the needs of the relatives of the displaced, Bowring attempted to establish the shared concern of both governments and relatives to locate the missing, and noted additional administrative and judicial reasons for this action that would appeal to governments: to enable bureaucratic processes of death to proceed and to gather evidence for criminal prosecutions.

A memo to the British Red Cross from Col. A. H. Moffitt of CDPX on August 26, 1945, set out the procedure to be followed with regard to the Central Tracing Bureau in Hoechst.[63] The three zonal bureaus in Germany were to be coordinated with this central bureau, and British Red Cross inquiries were to be transmitted through the British Zonal Bureau to the central agency. By this time the British Red Cross had accumulated some twenty thousand inquiries, which had been passed to the British Zonal Bureau at Bunde and were being processed. Working out the details of the Central Bureau took somewhat longer, through a tripartite working group, with UNRRA invited to participate. Where the organization should be located took a while to work out too: representatives of the different Allies spoke out for their own preferred locations.[64] Meanwhile, relatives waited in frustration and distress, their searches stalled, their multiple inquiries to different organizations receiving no answer.

Miss Warner responded to Colonel Moffitt on September 12, 1945, saying that although the UNRRA idea was a good one, it would take time to set up, and there would be a need for trained and experienced personnel.

She noted her general agreement with the principles and made one or two suggestions as to the details of the system proposed, in particular with regard to whom original inquiries should be directed.[65] An agreed paper was finally prepared by the Allied Control Authority to present to the Coordinating Committee on September 17, 1945.[66] At some point tracing had become big business, and the new category "missing persons" had come to be used not just in relation to soldiers missing in action but in relation to civilians.

The extent to which there was an attempt to sideline bodies like the Red Cross, and the very competent women who ran them, focused as they were on getting the job done on behalf of relatives, is laid bare in a letter from Lt. Col. F. C. Davies, Prisoners of War and Displaced Persons Division, Control Commission for Germany, to Lt. Col. E. M. Hammer, enclosing his "distribution list," he says, "merely in order to give you an idea of some of the bodies that I have unearthed and who are interested in missing personnel in Germany. You will note that British Red Cross is not included on the Distribution List as, for obvious reasons, I want to keep my distribution list confined to official bodies." He continues, somewhat disingenuously: "There are doubtless other unofficial bodies interested in this question that I have not yet unearthed."[67] Clearly, certain organizations were to be excluded: their advocacy on behalf of relatives of the missing had to be silenced.

However, by the end of November 1945 Colonel Bowring had become head of the Central Tracing Bureau (CTB) at Hoechst.[68] Somehow, the concerns of relatives slipped under the wire: Bowring was not unsympathetic to their cause. The activities at Hoechst are recorded in a series of UNRRA public information photographs currently lodged in the archives of the United Nations in New York.[69] The captions of the photographs describe what went on, or at least, what was supposed to be going on—that is, what the official methods of work were—and the images themselves bring these activities to life for us. We see Bowring, "Chief of the UNRRA Central Tracing Bureau and former British staff officer," posing with a clipboard in front of a chart that shows the connections between the CTB and various national tracing bureaus, including the British Red Cross in London. The chart has the International Red Cross in Geneva ominously disconnected from the network. The caption explains that "the network locates United Nations Nationals displaced during the war and reunites families and friends."[70]

Subsequent photographs trace the processes of dealing with inquiries received by the Bureau, from those, a minority presumably, where inquirers visited the bureau in person and were received at the reception desk, to inquiries received by mail. The incoming mail is first sorted by language and country. From the mail room, the inquiries go to the records room, where "data is sorted and filed, case histories made up, and folders prepared on each case."[71] The captions tell us that the master index is checked for information about each missing person. If a person still has not been located, the inquiry is passed to the staff in the correspondence room, who send out letters to town mayors and others who might have records or some knowledge of the person's whereabouts. "If this method fails," we are told, "field searching parties are sent out from the Central or National Tracing Bureaus, in a final attempt to locate the person. These parties investigate places where the missing person is known or suspected to have been, and check with local citizens to locate the individuals."[72] We see from surviving records held elsewhere that this was of course a somewhat idealized view of what happened: the reality was not as organized, thorough, or straightforward according to some observers—Miss Warner at the British Red Cross, for example. Indeed, the numbers of missing at that time, and the even greater numbers of those searching for them, would clearly overwhelm the resources of the tracing service shown in these images. The staff of the Bureau did what they could, perhaps.

By January 1946 the CTB had moved from Hoechst near Frankfurt to Arolsen near Kassel. The buildings at Arolsen had been an SS training facility—the local aristocracy was happy to see a continuation of a major center in the town. It was February 15, 1946, before the British Foreign Office received confirmation that the UNRRA Tracing Bureau had been officially established, and February 26 before a letter went to the British Red Cross offices informing its staff that they were to be the National Tracing Bureau for the United Kingdom. Miss Warner's misgivings about the efficiency of the Central Tracing Bureau proved justified—by August 1946 concentration camps records held there had not yet been entered onto cards and alphabetized.[73] Miss Warner had been on a temporary assignment to Arolsen for three months and had proposed a method by which such cards could be produced and sorted, using the services of the ICRC, but her advice had not been acted on. Worse, the CTB was forwarding inquiries to other bureaus without first checking the inquiries against its own records.[74]

Enemy Nationals

In her letter to Colonel Hammer in July 1945, Miss Warner had pointed out that the UNRRA plan failed to deal with German displaced persons.[75] This was a crucial point. Not only were British Red Cross staff acting as advocates for families, their work was not confined to nationals of the Allied powers.[76] They were willing to respond to all inquiries, irrespective of the category of missing person sought. This was in complete contrast with the actions of other organizations, such as UNRRA. There were gray areas: women British by birth but who had married German nationals, for example, or those Germans—enemy nationals—who had been persecuted by the Nazi regime, or who were relatives of United Nations nationals eligible for help.[77] UNRRA did eventually help in some of these cases. But enemy nationals were not to be helped by UNRRA or by the British government. A telegram of August 27, 1945, from the Foreign Office to Washington noted that the War Office did not accept inquiries about German civilians not related to UN subjects but passed them on to the British Red Cross, whose staff, though they lacked any official means of dealing with them, nevertheless were known to contrive "by unofficial means to get some messages passed into and out of Germany."[78] As we saw in chapter 2, UNRRA had been set up by the Allied powers to help their own nationals—misleadingly named United Nations nationals—while the Red Cross, and particularly the International Red Cross, were obliged, given their stance of strict neutrality, to help everyone equally, regardless of nationality and, given their independence from government or military control, were free to do so, as long as this independence lasted.

Both the ICRC and the British Red Cross regarded it as fundamental that searching should extend to all, including Germans. It is not clear to what extent Colonel Bowring at the CTB agreed with this view. The British Zonal Bureau, which he ran for a time, was clearly influenced by the British Red Cross, and Miss Warner in particular. Although Bowring and Warner disagreed on operational matters, they may have been quite close in terms of the question of the inclusiveness of searching. It is clear that Bowring was regarded as somewhat of a loose cannon by the officials in CDPX: his view was "not always in accord with" that of Her Majesty's government.[79] By the time he had been appointed head of the Central Tracing Bureau at Hoechst, Bowring was said to have been "carried away by his enthusiasm,"[80] and a new policy statement was issued that "emphasised that UNRRA could only trace persons falling under the definitions of the Council Resolutions as eligible for UNRRA care. UNRRA could not accept responsibility for tracing any Germans except victims of Nazi persecution."[81] A proposal, in 1946, to establish a tracing bureau under CDPX dealing only with missing Germans was never approved.

A 1946 report on tracing in Germany noted that governments had been slow to realize the importance of tracing.[82] Initially tracing was regarded as a humanitarian problem—a simple case of putting people in touch with each other and thus, presumably, not the job of governments. It was only much later that it became clear that the ramifications of *not* tracing in terms of "long range political, legal and social" questions were "of such magnitude as to necessitate a careful scrutiny and adjustment."[83] The "verification of claims for insurance and pensions," for example, ideally should not be based solely on a presumption of death. One of the chief conclusions of the report was that "the problem of tracing missing German nationals is of primary importance for the Occupying Powers as a pre-requisite for the settling of the population necessary for any basic social or industrial re-organisation."[84] The document elaborates: "Thousands, many not aware of the names of their next of kin, are wandering from place to place and creating added difficulties in the economic life of the country. No real progress of social or industrial re-organisation can be carried through until the population is definitely settled. An effective tracing service for the German population is essential for obtaining this objective."[85] Reconstruction could not take place, according to the report, until "basic human relationships had been restored," because it was only this that would produce a settled population, amenable to the reinstitution of state forms of control and administration by the Allied powers.[86] The report also details the "multiplicity of unauthorized bureaus" that were operating in Germany at that time and "which hopelessly confuse the situation": "Some of them are unscrupulous in their intent and methods; others are well-intentioned but ineffective because of the decentralisation of information and the duplication of effort." Some operate "under the auspices of religious organisations," which are "widely distributed, but for the most part the 'Bureaux' are local in nature and extremely limited in their operation."[87]

A permanent exhibition at Foundation Haus der Geschichte der Bundesrepublik Deutschland in Bonn gives an account of the missing persons tracing service in Germany in the postwar period.[88] The origins of the tracing service are credited to individual initiative. The exhibition quotes an account from a report by Hellmuth Unger, an ex-soldier who was eventually put in charge of the Munich tracing service. He and two comrades, Heinz-Herbert Müller, an old friend from Dresden, and Lance Corporal Dr. Schulze-Menz, had come up with the idea during the idle period before the end of the war. Not knowing where their families were, and wondering who was going to tell them that they were alive, they resolved to set up a central point where people could register for information and which would help them establish contact with their relatives. His two friends moved on, but Unger, based in a small rented room in Schwaberwegen with an old Wehrmacht typewriter, set to work putting a plan on paper and "on 20 June 1945... got a ride on a milk-truck to Munich, asked and found the way to the Red Cross, and presented [his] proposal for setting up a tracing service."[89]

Other agencies established though private initiative were run by unscrupulous profiteers and were "springing up like mushrooms after a warm rain."[90] Eventually authorized search bureaus were established in three centers: two bureaus in Hamburg, one in Munich, and one in Berlin.[91] Hamburg and Munich were the main centers, with the Berlin bureau serving mainly as a local service for the Berlin area. The British were the first to realize the need for an authorized bureau and set up a service in September 1945 to put German prisoners of war in contact with their families. Civilians communicated with the bureau, and the service operated on a "meeting of cards" principle: when inquiries received matched the records held the search was successful; there was no active searching by bureau staff. This service was extended to the whole of Germany in October 1945, under the supervision of the British Army of the Rhine, and was known as the Central Postal Enquiry Bureau, apparently based in Hamburg. A second bureau, the German Zonal Search Bureau, was operated by the German Red Cross under the supervision of the British military government. This also worked on the "meeting of cards" principle but was supplemented by some searching through radio broadcasts and a limited field search. Also based in Hamburg, the German Zonal Search Bureau covered northeastern Germany and the northern part of the French zone but worked in cooperation with the Bavarian Red Cross, which was by then operating in southern Germany.

The Bavarian Red Cross ran the German Search Service in Munich under the supervision of the Public Welfare Branch of the Office of Military Government for Bavaria, and together with the Hamburg search bureau covered the whole of Germany. Again, it operated on the basis of the "meeting of cards" principle, but it ran, in addition, "field searches for special cases through investigation of police and burgomeisters' records, churches, the Red Cross, and other welfare agencies."[92] The Berlin bureau was set up on March 1, 1946, but was of limited effectiveness. Although the need for a centralized service for tracing Germans had been recognized in 1945, and discussions between various bodies, including the Allied Control Authority Directorate of Internal Affairs and Communications, the Civil Administration Committee, and its Missing Persons Bureau Sub-Committee, continued into 1946, there were no positive outcomes.[93]

The private and charitable organizations that sprang up in 1945 were brought together under the German Red Cross as the Munich Tracing Service in January 1950. The Munich service established records of and actively investigated both the missing in action and prisoners of war still in captivity. It interviewed those who returned and a total of 2.6 million former soldiers.[94] It still deals with inquiries today. The German Red Cross itself had not been officially reestablished until 1951. During the war, the organization had become part of the Nazi regime and was implicated in horrific medical experiments, though its current website mentions none of this.[95] The German Red Cross now constitutes the main source of information for those wishing to trace relations who served in the Wehrmacht.

Five years after the end of the war, following an appeal by the Federal Republic of Germany in February 1950 to citizens to register missing persons, 2.5 million soldiers, civilians, and children whose whereabouts were unknown were listed, and the German Red Cross Tracing Service set about trying to establish their fate. Volumes were published listing the missing. The fifty-one-volume *German Prisoners of War and Missing Members of the Wehrmacht* was completed in 1955, and the *Illustrated Lists of Missing Persons* consisting of 199 single volumes with personal information of 1.4 million persons and 900,000 photos went to press in 1957.[96] In some cases where specific information about an individual was not available, "expert opinions" were given as to the presumed fate of missing persons, based on exhaustive inquiries through the available records and testimony as to the fate of the groups or units to which the individuals belonged.[97] By 2005 around 1.2 million cases had been clarified; 1.3 million remained unresolved. Registration of the missing had not included families in the German Democratic Republic or countries in Eastern Europe.[98] Information on them became available only when records emerged from 1992 onward with the reunification of Germany and the opening of the Soviet archives. Collaboration between the Russian State Military Archives and the German Red Cross began in 2004 and involved the scanning of records of some two million prisoners of war and civilian internees on both sides. Since the new information became accessible in the 1990s, around two hundred thousand further cases of missing persons have been resolved. Efforts to trace and incorporate further records continue, as do inquiries from those seeking missing relatives.[99]

The Opening of International Tracing Service Records

Many of the surviving concentration camp records from all over Germany and beyond eventually found their way to the offices of the International Tracing Service (ITS) at Bad Arolsen, where they remained entombed for over sixty years. After a long and at times bitter campaign, these archives were eventually opened to researchers. The records had been exclusively used to respond in confidence to inquiries from those seeking relatives or proof of their own imprisonment, a process that could often take years, with inquirers having to wait patiently for a response from the staff working their way slowly through a huge backlog. In 2008–2009, records were computerized and copies lodged in each of the treaty countries, and the archives themselves were opened for the first time to the public for historical research in January 2008.[100]

The ITS was set up under the International Refugee Organization (IRO) in 1947 and transferred to an International Commission in 1955, under the Bonn Agreement.[101] It took over the records of the concentration camps and forced labor organizations, the records of the DP camps and resettlement, and other miscellaneous material. Administered by the ICRC, funded by the West German government and answerable to the eleven-member International Commission, for some years it responded reasonably well to inquiries from relatives and survivors.[102] Up until the mid-1960s, under the leadership of Nicolas Burckhardt, successor to Maurice Thudichum as director, there was a period of openness—researchers were allowed access to the records on an informal basis, and the records relating to Belgian nationals were even copied onto microfilm and located in Belgium.[103]

At some point this relative responsiveness ceased. The change seems to have followed an application from Yugoslavia to join the commission, and thus obtain access to the records. Fearing that the records might be put to use in unacceptable ways, the ICRC and the ITS management made the decision that no one should be allowed in.[104] By the late 1990s the records were closed to researchers, and the response to inquiries from survivors and relatives of those persecuted was very slow or nonexistent. A backlog of 450,000 requests developed, with inquirers having to wait up to a dozen years for a response. Survivors were growing old, and the delays became increasingly unacceptable. The problems were the outcome not so much of funding problems or lack of staff or searching tools, but of a deliberate policy of the then director to set a quota limiting the number of inquiries members of staff could process.[105]

In 1998 the International Commission responded to the increasing concerns by agreeing that the records would be opened. By this point the United States Holocaust Memorial Museum (USHMM), in the person of the director of its Center for Advanced Holocaust Studies, Paul Shapiro, had become involved in the discussions as a strong advocate of opening the records. At a commission meeting in May 2001, draft access guidelines were produced, but in Shapiro's view these were so restrictive as to entirely inhibit access.[106] The central question that was raised concerned how to accommodate the various privacy regulations of member countries, and the proposed guidelines seemed to Shapiro to represent the most restrictive common denominator. It became clear to him that the commission was not the place where progress could be made. The delegates were diplomats from the member countries, serving for short periods, sometimes as little as one year, and the commission itself met only annually. Those serving on the commission knew very little about what the ITS records contained, or how significant they were— not only to Jewish survivors, but to victims of Nazi persecutions of many nationalities and, of course, to the increasing number of historians of the period. In December 2003 the Holocaust Task Force (in full, the Task Force for International Cooperation on Holocaust Education, Remembrance, and Research) met in Washington. Shapiro decided to use the Task Force to attempt to break the logjam by suggesting that copies of the ITS records be made and lodged in each of the member countries—with access granted under the privacy laws of that country. This suggestion, if adopted, would have the advantage of ensuring that the ITS would not be able to backtrack on access at some future date. At the commission meeting in Rome in 2004 Shapiro presented a description of the records and the evasions that had been experienced.

The pace and pressure for change began to accelerate. A Task Force resolution to open the archive was passed, a visit to ITS took place, and yet more Task Force resolutions were passed.[107] A friend of Shapiro published an article in the *Minneapolis Star Tribune* on May 9, 2005, just before the opening of Germany's Holocaust memorial; it was widely circulated on the Internet.[108] This was followed on May 19, 2005, by an article in *Die Zeit* by Frank-Uwe Betz entitled "Das andere Mahnmal." Betz explicitly contrasted the closure of the ITS with the opening of the memorial to the murdered Jews of Europe in Berlin: "The huge Holocaust memorial next to the Brandenburg Gate in Berlin may be impressive. But what use is it if the other monument, the true memorial at Arolsen, remains closed?"[109] The June 2005 meeting of the ITS commission opened amid controversy. Germany, Belgium, Italy, the ICRC, and the director of the ITS remained opposed. After acrimonious meetings—with frequent breaks for tempers to cool—a vote was taken, and a working group, to be chaired by France, set up. According to Shapiro's account, the first meeting of the Working Group was the setting for a heavy-handed attempt to derail the whole process. Two points were raised. First was the question of confidentiality: the records would reveal who had been persecuted as a homosexual, and who had collaborated. Did we want this known? Second, there was the question of the ownership of the records: their provenance was German, and therefore they belonged to Germany, but Germany was opposed to open access. If this claim were put forward, Shapiro pointed out, it would be the first time that the German state had made a claim based on direct descent from the Third Reich.

Germany's opposition continued into 2006, as did that of the ITS management. A short documentary contrasted the resistance of the ITS director
with the needs of Holocaust survivors. Knowingly concealing information
was aligned with Holocaust denial. Articles appeared in the *New York Times*
and other major newspapers.[110] Gradually countries added their agreement
to access. Change in Germany's position came with the change in the German chancellor. Under the new chancellor, Angela Merkel, the German
justice minister, Brigitte Zypries, listened to the case and then initiated
moves that overcame the legal objections that Germany itself had raised. In
2006 Germany signed the agreement, and all was set for the records to be
opened.[111]

Why had all this taken so long, and why had it been such a controversial move? Why had the needs of those searching for information about
what had happened to their families and friends, and for confirmation of
their own persecution, been overridden or ignored for so long, and by an
organization—the Red Cross—set up precisely to help such people? Shapiro identifies a number of key reasons. First, none of those involved in
the decision-making process knew the full range of material involved, and
the concerns of those asking for information were not given due weight in the
discussions. They were not heard. Second, the reflex action was to remain
with the status quo. Every one of the countries involved had a rationale of
its own for this. Shapiro, reflecting on his experience of the process at a
conference at the Imperial War Museum in London in January 2009, gave
some examples. As far as Germany was concerned, the motto of the previous administration had been one of finishing with the Holocaust—moving
on. The United States was reluctant to engage in a battle with Germany, and
reluctant to get into a fight with the International Red Cross at a point when
its own actions were under scrutiny. In Belgium there was an unwillingness
to do anything that might exacerbate interethnic tensions—and tensions over
degrees of involvement in the Nazi period. The Italians had placed DP camp
records at ITS in the 1980s—at a point when the way in which many war
criminals had evaded capture by working the DP system was under investigation; the records had been lodged at Arolsen precisely because they would
then be inaccessible. Israel, according to Shapiro, remained silent throughout
the whole process. In the early 1950s, when the Allied High Command was
still in charge, copies had been made of the records of camp incarcerations.
The Israeli archivists at Yad Vashem were happy that they had what they
needed; they were unaware of the existence at Arolsen of records concerned
with forced labor. And Israel did not want to lose the support it had from
Germany at that time.

Whether or not Shapiro's surmises as to the precise reasons each of the member governments acted as it did are accurate, it seems that what happened was a continuation of the approach we saw in the immediate postwar period. Then it is clear from the archives that the priorities of the military authorities and Allied government objectives had come first. The needs of the displaced and their relatives for an effective tracing service had come a very low second to the demand that DPs be contained, controlled, and finally disposed of according to the wishes of the Allied powers. Even when the importance of tracing was recognized, it was left in the hands of a few individuals, mainly in voluntary organizations, to push for effective organization and funding of the services. Now as then, it has taken the intervention of an individual with a strong sense of the needs of survivors and those searching for the missing, Paul Shapiro, backed by a privately funded organization, the USHMM, to bring pressure to bear for change to take place and for impediments to searching to be removed.

Of course, the records at Arolsen contain not only details of the victims but information about their persecutors, and about the corporations who worked with the Nazis or who benefited from slave labor. Writer and former international lawyer Anna Funder argues that there may have been other pressures, behind the scenes, leading to the reluctance to release the records to the public.[112] Insurance claims might be one factor—without information from the records, the heirs of those killed could not pursue claims on life insurance policies held by their relatives. Former U.S. federal prosecutor John Loftus argues that the archives remained closed for so long "so as to conceal the identities of Nazis who were helped to escape using the identity documents of dead Jews obtained with the assistance of the Red Cross." If the files were released, Loftus observes, "many of the dead Jewish victims would show up 'alive' in allied countries."[113] A fully open and Internet-searchable archive could have enormous consequences, as Funder points out. The USHMM is proposing a closed system that is only accessible through its Washington premises or through its own searchers.[114]

Nevertheless, the vast archive at Bad Arolsen is now open for public access. Of the 17.5 million people whose lives are documented around half are non-Jews. In addition to the records of concentration camps and forced labor sites, the archive contains some 3.2 million displaced persons cards, 450,000 displaced persons files, three-quarters of which have never been looked at, and details of resettlement. There are also various miscellaneous records—of cemeteries, analytical studies, and testimonies taken on liberation. Finally, there are 2.5 million postwar inquiry files: records of inquiries received by the ITS and its predecessor bodies since the end of the war. Digital copies of the archive are being made and lodged at the United States Holocaust Memorial Museum in Washington, at Yad Vashem in Jerusalem, and at the Institute of National Remembrance in Warsaw. It is unclear whether copies are to be lodged in other countries too. Although the records are open, they are not yet properly indexed or catalogued for historical research. The main finding guide is the Central Name Index, which contains some forty million cards. It is still not possible for individuals to use the records themselves, except by visiting Bad Arolsen, and it seems that in the interests of conservation the originals of documents will not be made available. The USHMM has set up its own inquiry service—or rather expanded the service it already offered to survivors to cover this new material.[115] Staff are being trained in the details of the records, and the obscure Nazi coding systems used in them, and inquiries are answered through a combination of the new material and the existing searching expertise of USHMM staff. Since January 2008, 7,500 inquiries have been received at USHMM, and the response time is said to be between eight and twelve weeks.[116]

Response times at the ITS are said to have greatly improved, and the backlog of material there is being dealt with. During the period from 1998, the backlog of unanswered requests was never less than 303,227, with a maximum figure of 443,423 reached in 2004.[117] It is noted in the 2008 annual report that "while by the end of 2006 there still was a mountain of over 149,000 unanswered enquiries, by the end of 2007 it had been reduced to less than 48,000. In 2008, all letters were answered."[118] A decision was taken by ITS, USHMM, and Yad Vashem to focus inevitably limited resources initially on addressing the needs of those seeking information about individual people—and dealing with the backlog of inquiries—as opposed to cataloguing and indexing the entire collection. The latter is a process that will take some years. The ITS remit covers "Germans and non-Germans detained in Nazi concentration or labour camps and...non-Germans displaced as a result of the Second World War;"[119] displaced Germans are the responsibility of the German Red Cross.

In an interesting development, and one that in a curious way brings the story full circle, at the ceremony marking the opening of the ITS archive on April 30, 2008, the ICRC indicated its desire to withdraw from its administrative role. The ICRC's vice president, Christine Beerli, said that "for the ICRC, this new task and the gradual decline in the number of cases of humanitarian concern processed by the International Tracing Service raises the question of the organization's future role in the Service."[120] A new international agreement replacing the Bonn Agreement of 1955 is being drawn up, and the future tasks of the ITS discussed.[121] On May 18, 2009, a meeting at Lancaster House in London, opened by what appeared from the video to have been a far-from-dynamic address by Foreign Office minister Lord Malloch-Brown, marked the end of the United Kingdom's year as president of the ITS.[122] The contrast with the interest generated by the appearance of Paul Shapiro at the conference at the Imperial War Museum earlier in 2009 was stark; clearly, governments on the International Commission remain nowhere near as enthusiastic about the value and significance of the Bad Arolsen records as scholars, historians, and the representatives or descendants of those who suffered under the Nazi regime.

By 1947 the British Red Cross was winding up the work of its Foreign Relations Department, which finally closed its doors on May 31 of that year. Miss Warner attended a meeting at Arolsen in Germany in February 1947, when UNRRA announced a reduction in the staff of its Central Tracing Bureau in Germany from three hundred to forty.[123] At that time the location of a more permanent bureau, and its funding and administration, had yet to be decided, though the Preparatory Commission for the International Refugee Organization had begun work on the establishment of an International Tracing Service to replace the Central Tracing Bureau run by UNRRA, which had closed on June 30, 1947.[124] The resolution to establish such a tracing service was adopted on October 30, 1947.[125]

The debate about the future location of the ITS went back and forth— Berlin would be more accessible, but there were no suitable buildings there. Only the voice of the British Red Cross, specifically that of Miss Warner once more, brought the discussion back to basics:

> A suggestion has been put forward from time to time that the Central Record Bureau in Germany should be situated in Berlin. This would seem inadvisable. Every attempt should be made to regard the work as the united effort of civilised nations to provide information to assist in re-establishing the family life of the millions whose present and future existence has been altered and in many cases imperilled by uncertainty regarding the fate of their family and friends. For this reason alone the present peaceful place in which the Bureau is situated would seem to be an admirable choice.[126]

Miss Warner, known as "Auntie" by her staff, was clearly a formidable woman, and her influence considerable.[127] Her focus remained the job of work to be done—the service provided to those in need of help. When Colonel Bowring resigned his post in 1947, she sent him a message noting that they had not always seen eye to eye but thanking him nevertheless for his help in those matters on which they did agree.[128] Evelyn Bark recalls being introduced to Miss Warner on her first day as one of the five hundred staff, mostly women, of the Foreign Relations Department, "the 'Foreign Office' of the British Red Cross" in Clarence House, premises that had been lent by King George VI:

> After a few words of greeting, she removed her spectacles and peered closely at my Red Cross recommendations and the references from my previous employers. Then she replaced her spectacles, and during an uncomfortably long pause gazed at me quizzically. Finally she asked: "Do you like people?" For the last few hours I had been rehearsing silently what I should tell her about my past activities, so that all I could think of in reply to this unexpected question was a flat "Yes". The interview was over.[129]

In the end what seems to have been the case is that two contradictory processes were happening side by side: on the one hand, the attempt by government authorities, in the form of military and occupying powers, to take control once more of their own national populations and extend this control to former enemy populations; and, on the other hand, the efforts by people such as those working for the British Red Cross to respond to and act as a voice for relatives searching for missing family members, wherever they came from. On the one hand, a resumption of a biopolitics of populations, a police order; on the other, a struggle for and insistence on the importance of personal and family relationships. It was only when people refused to give up on their search for relatives that it became clear no reconstruction would be possible without some recognition of the need for ongoing tracing services. The Red Cross also had to insist on the importance of a proactive tracing strategy: it was not enough to wait for a "meeting of cards." Searchers had to take to the streets, to talk to people, to follow up leads. If they didn't, people would continue to trek from place to place. It was people themselves, in the end, who had disrupted the imposed order, demanded to be heard, and acted on their own behalf.

In the next chapter we turn to the search for the missing after the London bombings in July 2005. Here again we find a tension between the objectives of the professional teams handling the disaster and relatives and friends trying to establish the fate of people they knew.

CHAPTER 4

Missing Persons, London

> Nobody in authority seemed to be thinking of us as
> people with emotions.
>
> —Marie Fatayi-Williams, *For the Love of Anthony*

On July 7, 2005, nearly four years after the col-
lapse of the World Trade Center, there were three explosions on the London
underground during the early morning rush hour. Initially a power surge was
blamed, but it was apparent to many Londoners from the start that this was
likely to be something more. What exactly had happened remained unclear
for some time. Communication with workers and passengers underground
was hampered by the absence of radios or phones that worked, and emergency
workers did not enter the tunnels at first for fear of secondary explosions or
contamination. The injured on the trains were left to help each other as best
they could, with the assistance of train drivers and London Transport staff.[1]
There was confusion as to the number of incidents too—passengers who
evacuated themselves from the trains began to appear at stations on both sides
of each blast. Just over half an hour later, when the top deck was blown off
a London bus in full daylight in Bloomsbury, outside the headquarters of the
British Medical Association in Tavistock Square, it became clear that some sort
of terrorist episode must be in progress. By then, emergency services and police
were overwhelmed, mobile phone networks shut down or severely overloaded,
and public transport completely closed down. By early afternoon, people had
begun to make their way quietly home from central London on foot.

In the days following, tributes were left at King's Cross Station, which is near
Tavistock Square and close to the site of one of the underground explosions,

and gathered together in a small memorial garden, temporarily supplanting what had been a cycle park. A book of condolences was provided just outside the garden. In the garden itself, the space surrounding a small tree was lined with flowers, flags, and messages. It was possible for visitors to enter and make a circuit of the area to read the messages, though there would not have been room for more than a few dozen people at a time in the garden. Instructions at the entrance asked that people refrain from taking photographs. The garden was separated from its surroundings by metal railings, and messages and flags were attached to the railings too. The London authorities had obviously learned the lessons of the aftermath of Princess Diana's death in 1997 and the street memorials in Manhattan in 2001: by July 2005 memorial activities were allowed but closely circumscribed, in this case by iron railings.[2]

From outside the garden it was possible to photograph those visiting the interior, and to take shots of some of the messages that were facing the outside. The garden—later returned to its familiar role of cycle park—is situated at a corner of the facade of King's Cross Station, adjacent to a very busy crossroads, with traffic signals for pedestrians and vehicles. There is and was a continual flow of people past the area; the pavement outside would regularly be dozens deep with people weaving to and fro. The small area of contemplation was somewhat incongruous in the middle of the city bustle, apparently unnoticed by most passersby. Visitors, however, were thoroughly absorbed.

Prominent in the garden were messages from other cities or different national or religious groups offering sympathy and understanding: messages from the Turkish community, the Afghan community in Walsall, from religious groups, from visitors to the city. "We are with you: All Indians in UK & all over"; "Our heart is with you just like your heart was with us"; "America stands united with London against terrorism"; "To you brave Londoners...your friends from Norway"; "Our prayers are with you. Keep the faith. From all South Africans"; "We fought together in the last war and we will always be with you till the end. Maltese Community"; "We are all Londoners: Christian, Muslim, Jew, Hindu, Sikh, Buddhist"; "London: Madrid's heart is with you: Be Brave." A message in Japanese from someone called Katahira, from Sayama City Fire Station, Saitama Prefecture near Tokyo, reads: "I pray for the souls of the dead and for the speedy recovery of the injured, for peace in the UK and the world. 7 July 2005." One message summed up the general feeling: "It wasn't necessary to have been born here to feel sadness for what happened in London." It seemed at first glance different from New York after 9/11: less insular, perhaps, with

messages from all over the world offering support. There was little condemnation and no demand for retaliation: "Only one race is harmed by this:
the human race."

A little further along the same stretch of road, on the other side of the
station entrance, was a hoarding on which details of missing persons were
posted, behind clear plastic. The posters were not as numerous as those in
New York, of course, and seemed more controlled: specific sites were provided, and the posters were systematically removed as the missing were identified. The wording was much the same, though: "Missing: James Mayes.
White, slim build, 5' 11". Hazel eyes and short curly brown hair. Last seen or
heard from before London Bombings. Was travelling on the Piccadilly line
from King's Cross at 8.30-9am on Thursday 7 July. If you see him please
call us urgently on…"; "Have you seen this man or his car? Christian Small
(Age 28). Black male. Athletic build. 5' 01". Short black hair. Brown eyes.
He left home at 7.55am on Thursday 7 July 2005. Car: Mitsubishi Colt
Hatchback (silver). Stations: From Blackhorse Road or Walthamstow Central via King's Cross and Finsbury Park to Holborn. Contacts…" Scattered
posters also appeared in nearby parks, attached to gateposts: "Missing: Neetu
Jain. Last seen at Euston/Tavistock Square on the morning of 7th July.
Please contact…"; "Karolina: Her appearance… White female, short blond
hair, distinct blue eyes, 1.6m (5ft 4ins), belly-button piercing, Polish nationality (speaks very good English). She was wearing… Black trouser suit, with
long-sleeved round neck black jersey, several silver rings on both hands, silver
fine-medium linked chain, black heeled shoes. Personal belongings… Black
handbag, keys with London Olympics 2012 key ring, pack of cigarettes, Sony
Eriksson mobile phone (silver, with falling autumn leaves screen saver). Karolina is still missing!!! Karolina is still missing and if anyway can help please
contact anyone of us on the following contact details…" The *Guardian* later
reported that "Magda Gluck, whose 29-year-old twin sister, Karolina, was
killed at Russell Square, said the aftermath was a 'big mess. It took us more
than a week to find out that she was killed. It was too long to find out that
kind of information.'"[3]

This chapter looks at the disaster identification protocols used after the
London bombings and how these served more as a tool for the authorities
in their search for suspected terrorists than as an aid to relatives. It examines the concern to establish order and control rather than to communicate
with those missing their relatives, a concern that reflects priorities we saw
earlier in post–World War II displaced persons camps. Although the enormous practical difficulties with identification experienced in New York were
not encountered in London, friends and relatives of the missing were kept

waiting for up to a week or more for information about where their sons and daughters, friends and family members, might be.

Information Withheld

In contrast to the authorities' silence in naming the dead, detailed information was demanded from those searching for friends and relations. Everyone was treated as a suspect; the priority was the search for the "perpetrators," not the needs of the "victims." Families were plunged into a world of Disaster Victim Identification forms, police liaison officers, and stonewalling by officials. People were angry, and one of the most prominent protests against the way in which people were handled came from Marie Fatayi-Williams.[4] She made an impromptu speech on Monday July 11 near Tavistock Square. Her address was a compelling indictment of all those who use violence to try to change the world, and of the needless suffering this brings about: "What inspiration can senseless slaughter provide? Death and destruction...can never be the foundations for building society."[5] It was also a moving lament at the added anguish caused when information about the missing is withheld, and a plea for that information.

Mrs. Fatayi-Williams begins her speech by holding up a photograph of her son: "This is Anthony, Anthony Fatayi-Williams, 26 years old, he's missing." The photograph stands in for the person: "This is Anthony." *Here he is. He exists. I cannot find him; no one will tell me where he is, but he exists. I did not just imagine him.* Marie is an imposing, charismatic figure, powerfully emotional and hugely strong in her grief and her conviction. She stands surrounded by relatives and supporters and a press of media in the middle of the street leading to Tavistock Square itself, as near to the site of the explosion as she can get. Behind her are large photos of Anthony. She continues:

> We fear that he was in the bus explosion...on Thursday. We don't know. We do know from the witnesses that he left the Northern line in Euston. We know he made a call to his office at Amec at 9.41 from the NW1 area to say he could not make [it] by the tube but he would find alternative means to [get to] work. Since then he has not made any contact with any single person.

And she, his mother, has been able to get no information whatsoever about where he is or what happened to him:

> My son Anthony is my first son, my only son, the head of my family. In African society, we hold on to sons.... This is now the fifth

day, five days on, and we are waiting to know what happened to him
and I, his mother, I need to know what happened to Anthony. His
young sisters need to know what happened, his uncles and aunties need
to know what happened to Anthony, his father needs to know what
happened to Anthony. Millions of my friends back home in Nigeria
need to know what happened to Anthony. His friends surrounding me
here, who have put this together, need to know what has happened to
Anthony. I need to know.

She enumerates the web of relationships in which Anthony is entwined. He
is not just a statistic, an unidentified victim of a terrorist bomb. He is a person
who is missed, someone with relatives, friends, sisters, uncles, aunts, a father, a
mother, friends, his mother's friends. They all need to know what happened.
This need is urgent, pressing. It is an entitlement, a right. It should not be
suspended or held in abeyance.

Like other relatives, Marie Fatayi-Williams is told to wait. She is told that
identification is "a highly complex and sensitive process,"[6] that it takes time,
that she must go home and wait. As if this were something quite simple and
easy to do. It is not. As Anthony's friend Amrit Walia says: "We understand
the police have a job to do, but it is agonising to sit and wait, which is all they
have advised us to do."[7]

Difficulties and delays started on the day of the bombings. To begin with,
there had been unforeseen delays in opening the Metropolitan Police Service Casualty Bureau telephone lines. This service was designed for people
to report relatives or friends as missing. According to the London Assembly
report of July 7, delays in opening Casualty Bureau phone lines were due to
an incorrect connection at the New Scotland Yard switchboard.[8] This meant
that the line was not working at all until after 4:00 p.m. on the day of the
bombings. By then people were frantic with worry about those missing, and
those with injured relatives had no means of finding out about them and
getting to the right hospital other than contacting hospitals directly. When
the phone lines did open, there were forty-two thousand attempted calls in
the first hour. The system was hopelessly overloaded and it was taking people
more than three hours to get through, even with their phones on automatic
redial. According to one man whose wife was seriously injured, this was
unforgivable:

The thing that caused me absolutely unnecessary extra anguish and
grief on the day, and I think many other people, was something that to
me is incomprehensible and inexcusable, and that is the failure of the
Central Casualty Bureau emergency number....It took me slightly

more than three hours, if my memory is correct, to register my wife as somebody who was missing and presumably involved. That needs to be addressed. It really really really does need to be addressed.[9]

The delay could have meant someone with a relative in a critical condition not getting to their bedside before they died. To add insult to injury, the Casualty Bureau number was not a free number.

However, delays, technical inadequacies, and overload were not the chief problem. The main difficulty was that there was in fact no organization intended specifically to help families locate their friends and relatives. Neither the Casualty Bureau nor the ineptly named Family Assistance Centre set up in Victoria two days later was dedicated to that job. The Casualty Bureau was the "first stage in the criminal investigation and formal identification process,"[10] not a mechanism for providing worried members of the public with information. Although counselors and other advisers from voluntary organizations like the Salvation Army, the Red Cross, and Victim Support were present at the Family Assistance Centre, its prime concern was just as clear as that of the Casualty Bureau.[11] Its focus was on "gathering information: personal and forensic details of people who were potentially injured or killed in the attacks, to assist in the identification process."[12] The phrase "gathering information" is crucial here. As the London Assembly report points out, "This met the needs of the Metropolitan Police in conducting their investigation and identification process,"[13] but it was absolutely no help to those searching for family members:

> The Centre was not prepared to give out information, only to collect it. People searching for their loved ones have one primary need: information. They may also have practical needs, but their main concern is to find out the whereabouts of their loved one. They may not need bereavement counselling in the first few days—the need for information is paramount.[14]

Among other things, "families and friends need a reception centre to provide a central contact point, when hospitals and other authorities identify survivors."[15] Unlike New York in 2001, in London all that was provided were various understaffed and difficult to access points where families could register details of missing persons. Indeed, families were more likely to get help and feedback by posting missing persons posters on park railings and standing outside stations pleading for information than from filing an official missing persons report, and they knew it.[16] Outside King's Cross Station, a reporter spoke to Craig Laskey, whose friend Lee Baisden was missing: "My hope is that Lee is OK, is traumatised and is wandering around somewhere. We have tried the hospitals but they are very resistant to telling you everything. It has been very frustrating dealing with the authorities. The information flow is all one way. They are willing to take information but not to release anything at all."[17]

At this point, according to the same report, the number of confirmed deaths in the bombings was fifty-two, and there were still fifty-six people being treated in seven hospitals: "Staff said they had all been identified, dashing the hopes of those clinging to the belief that their loved ones may be alive." This was on Wednesday, July 13.[18] Such announcements increased the confusion and the anguish.

The chaos is clear in the story of Gladys Wundowa, an administrative secretary with the charity African Development Agencies in Hackney and a student of housing management at Hackney College, who also worked as a cleaner at University College London.[19] By the day after the bombings, her husband, Emmanuel Wundowa, had visited five hospitals in his search:

> I suspect Gladys either took the train or the bus but we have no idea. If she has been picked up we just want to know where she is. We have gone from hospital to hospital to establish whether she is there but each time the lists have come out negative. I feel almost helpless. We do not know where to go, who to talk to. . . . I have been very frustrated at the lack of support from the police. The emergency number that has been given doesn't give information in return. Tell me what happened to my wife, if they have picked her up where have they taken her to, please, help me? All they have told me is that if I happen to see her they will eliminate her from the missing list. That is offensive.[20]

This was only the beginning for Mr. Wundowa. On July 12 the *Guardian* newspaper reported that one of the victims had been identified, but the remainder had not.[21] However, in a press release University College London confirmed that one of its employees, Gladys Wundowa, was among the dead, and this was followed by television coverage. Her husband was distraught and angry:

> The police have not identified my wife. What the heck is going on? The BBC and Sky News are saying that Gladys is dead but no one has told me that. It's not what the police told me, they have not identified her. I have been sitting down here and nobody is telling me anything. If they have got some information that is of benefit to me, why don't they pass it on to me? We are in pieces here. We are still waiting for

news of Gladys. People are going on air and telling the whole world that she is dead and she hasn't even been identified.[22]

University College later apologized for its announcement: they had believed the police had already notified Mr. Wundowa.

It turned out that Gladys had been a victim of the Tavistock Square bombing. However, she had not died immediately but had been treated by paramedics on the pavement before being transferred to an ambulance to be taken to hospital. She died on the way. Later, when he discovered what had happened, her husband wanted to get in touch with the paramedics who helped her, to find out more about how she died, but the police told him they couldn't help. Eventually the BBC intervened, contacting the London Ambulance Service on his behalf.[23] One year later, Mr. Wundera still hadn't received any money from the Criminal Injuries Compensation Board; he was told they were checking whether he had a criminal record in Ghana.

Anthony Fatayi-Williams's father and uncle (a former Nigerian foreign minister) were informed of Anthony's death by two police officers on Wednesday, July 13; they were invited to identify him.[24] When they saw the body, they noted remarkably few injuries and described it as "well-preserved." According to the inquest opened on Thursday, July 14, identification had been made from dental records.[25] There would seem to be no reason why the family could not have identified the body before July 13. According to Marie Fatayi-Williams's account, her first contact with the Metropolitan Police was when she was phoned in Nigeria on Friday, July 8, by an officer asking whether she would be flying to London and when, but saying nothing in response to her questions.[26] When she arrived at Heathrow on Saturday morning, she was met by another Metropolitan Police officer. Again she got no response to her questions, though she later wrote "it's obvious to me now that the tragic news could have been delivered straight away. Instead, his bureaucratic bosses had dispatched this man not to end my agony of uncertainty, but to ascertain that Mrs Fatayi-Williams had arrived as intended."[27]

Relatives of Samantha and Lee, a couple who died as a result of the bombings, did not get a formal identification of Samantha until July 16, nine days after she gave her full name to her rescuer at Russell Square. In the words of a letter from the family to the London Assembly, this is the story:

> Sammy was found alive and gave her name, Samantha _____, to her rescuer, and he then passed her on to the emergency staff in the ticket hall of Russell Square, where she died. When we were phoning every hospital in London, it came to one and we asked if there was a Mr Lee _____ or a Samantha _____ and they said there was a Miss

Samantha _____ and they would find out more details for us. When she came back she said she was mistaken. If a person is found alive there needs to be a way of transferring their name with the person, ie: plaster, pen, anything. As this mistake built up our hopes so much. It then took until 16 July to be notified of her identification. We were never asked if we could or would like to see her or be with her. We do not know where her body was kept. Was it in every way being looked after humanly and with respect?[28]

The story of another woman, this time someone who was killed at Aldgate, was similar.[29] During the "identification process" prints and DNA swabs were taken from the victim's house; CCTV pictures were obtained of her on her way to London on the morning of the bombings. Finally, after ten days, an identification was made. This person too, like Samantha, had been alive after the bombing: a fellow passenger sat with her waiting for the emergency services to arrive. When they did arrive she was still alive, and they treated her; she died a few minutes later. Clearly her injuries cannot have been so horrific that her parents could not have identified her by sight. Why was it necessary to delay the identification by ten days? After the Madrid train bombings, most of the 190 dead had been identified within twenty-four hours, and almost all were buried within three days.[30]

Disaster Victim Identification

The London Assembly report highlights some of the stories of the search for the missing after July 7.[31] The committee made a point of asking survivors and relatives for their views, in person, in public hearings or private, and by written submissions—the first time this had been done in the aftermath of a disaster, amazingly. The report stretches to 157 pages, with the second volume (279 pages) devoted to transcripts of meetings and correspondence with organizations, and the third volume (296 pages) to views and information from individuals. It is a report that raises many questions and makes a series of important recommendations. However, on the question of the identification process, it seems to be the view of the committee that given that "this was the first time a Resilience Mortuary had been set up in the UK" and that "the Mass Fatalities Plan had only been completed a few weeks before 7 July," "the establishment of the Mortuary by 10 pm on 8 July was a remarkable achievement. The correct identification of the deceased was a highly complex and sensitive task, and this was completed within 7 days."[32]

The brief report known as "Lessons Learned," published later by the Home Office and the culture secretary, which runs to only thirty-two pages,[33] can be seen as a response in many ways to some of the issues raised powerfully by the Assembly Report. Some of the suggestions it makes are laughable. For example, it suggests that a recorded message should be made available for callers trying to get through to the Casualty Bureau. When it comes to the question of identification, the report suggests that more could be done to explain the process:

> It is essential to ensure absolute certainty before a family is told about the death of a loved one and this may take time. We hope that, by explaining the nature and complexity of the Disaster Victim Identification (DVI) process to families in full, and by improving the way the police communicate with families, we will be able to make the experience less distressing for them. We are working up a series of information sheets for victims of major emergencies that we will collect together in an online library. These will include a sheet about the DVI process, to be distributed by Family Liaison Officers and at Assistance Centres. In addition, the police are reviewing the training for Family Liaison Officers so that they are better aware of the DVI process and the issues for families.[34]

The International Criminal Police Organization (INTERPOL) manual on Disaster Victim Identification (DVI) was first published in 1984 and later revised and circulated to all INTERPOL member countries "to encourage the compatibility of procedures across international boundaries, which is essential in these days of ever-increasing world travel."[35]

As a process, the system of Disaster Victim Identification (DVI) is eminently straightforward and clear. There are three forms to be completed: a yellow Ante Mortem (AM) form, a pink Post Mortem (PM) form, and a white Comparison report. When all three forms are completed, and an identification has been made, they are filed together under a set of cover pages provided, the AM and PM forms being interleaved to make comparison of data easier. The cover pages and the Victim Identification Report, on white paper, are the final parts to be completed. They are filled in by a panel of experts (police officer, pathologist, odontologist) before a death certificate can be issued or a body released for burial. The final stage links a particular "DEAD BODY," identified by nature, place, and date of disaster and number, with a particular "MISSING PERSON," identified by name and date of birth.

The Ante Mortem and Post Mortem forms each comprise fifteen pages,[36] arranged in seven sections covering personal data (AM form only),[37] recovery of body from site (PM form only), description of effects (clothing, jewelry, etc.), physical description and distinguishing marks (tattoos etc.), medical information that may assist identification, dental information, and "other." The assumption here is clearly that we are dealing with dead bodies: there is no provision for people who die during the rescue process, only for those who are already dead. The two forms are completed separately. The AM form is completed by those interviewing the relatives, and the PM form by those recovering bodies from "the disaster site." The instructions ask that the AM forms be completed and forwarded as quickly as possible and that full and detailed information is obtained, since "it is impossible to know what data will be found from the disaster site." The onus is on the relatives to put down everything they can think of. And the AM form is extremely detailed. For personal effects, details of all clothing, shoes, jewelry, watches, glasses, personal effects, and identity papers carried must be given, down to details of keys carried, purse/wallet etc. This section covers three pages. Then a full physical description is needed, beginning with height, weight, build, race, and hair.[38] The description required includes great detail. For example, the nose: Is it small, medium, or large? Pointed, Roman, or alcoholic? Is it concave, straight, or convex? Turned down, horizontal, or turned up? Are there marks of spectacles or not? Any other peculiarities? The same details are required for other facial features: forehead, eyes, eyebrows, ears, facial hair, mouth, lips, teeth, smoking habits. And it goes on: chin, neck, hands, feet, body hair, pubic hair, scars, skin marks, tattoos/piercings, malformations, amputations, circumcision. Finally, it asks for a full list of medical conditions: AIDS? Addictions? Pregnancies? IUD?

This type of information, in this amount of detail, was presumably being collected from relatives in the London bombings, perhaps even over the phone, by the Casualty Bureau.[39] It is recognized that there will be a far greater number of people reported missing in the early stages than there are casualties in the end, so that it doesn't make sense to complete AM forms in great detail at an early stage. In London, the total reported missing was 7,823.[40] Even if the information was collected later, one has to ask how necessary the detail was in all cases, when it appears that the majority of victims were in the end identified by dental records. Much of the information included in the form would not be regarded anyway as satisfactory confirmation of identity. According to a newspaper report in the *Independent* at the time, "primary" evidence, sufficient on its own for identification, includes fingerprints, dental records, DNA, or "a unique identity feature, say, a pacemaker with a serial number on it." If none of these is available, then some combination of "secondary" forms of evidence may be acceptable: "marks and scars, blood group, jewellery, X-ray, and deformity."[41]

As relatives noticed, the collection of data through the Casualty Bureau or the Family Assistance Centre as part of DVI is a very one-sided process. Relations of the missing provide more or less exhaustive details of their family member on the AM forms, which are immediately passed to the police. The primary role of the family liaison officer allocated to relatives of the missing is as part of the investigation: the liaison officer works on behalf of the police, specifically to assist in the gathering of information. The police and forensic experts working with the bodies of victims also collect information and complete forms. However, these PM forms are not made available to relatives. Indeed, relatives are not given any details, even of the most general sort, of the bodies recovered. They are kept very much in the dark until they need to be contacted for further information. A matching process takes place behind closed doors, and it is only when a positive identification has been made that family members are informed. Remains are released for burial, and death certificates issued at this point. Before then, the bodies belong to the coroner, not to the next of kin. The information belongs to the coroner too. There is no provision for identification of the body by relatives as part of the process. The rationale for this is that "visual recognition" is "unscientific" and prone to inaccuracies. The face has disappeared as a means of identification: tattoos can be used, but face recognition by someone who knows the person is not allowed.[42]

Survivors and relatives of those killed in disasters of all types have engaged in a long-standing battle to ensure that the authorities dealing with the aftermath of the disaster pay attention to their needs.[43] Members of the group Disaster Action, all survivors or people bereaved in disasters—including, as they note on their website,[44] the Zeebrugge ferry sinking, King's Cross fire, Lockerbie air crash, Hillsborough football stadium crush, Marchioness riverboat sinking, Dunblane shootings, Southall and Ladbroke Grove train crashes, the September 11 attacks in the United States, and the Bali bombing—offer guidance on issues related specifically to disaster victim identification. They stress the importance to the bereaved, both relatives and friends, of knowing the cause of death, in some detail, and the need to be with the person after death or to view the body, whatever its condition. In the case of missing persons, Disaster Action members emphasize that "friends and family members may go to great lengths to find them themselves, regardless of other efforts or advice by the authorities. This may include travelling to disaster zones, temporary mortuaries, hospitals, etc. It is important that their families feel reassured that all that could be done is being or has been done to find, recover and establish the identity of all the victims."[45]

In New York in 2001, the decision had been made early on that the Office of the Chief Medical Examiner (OCME) would not concern itself with cause of death, but purely with identification: "After the first few days we knew that the OCME effort would focus exclusively on identification. Other than the identity of the victims, there was not much mystery about the cause of death in this homicide investigation. Everyone in the world who owned a television set had witnessed the crime, and within seventy-two hours, we also knew who had done it."[46] On September 27 the FBI released photographs of those it believed to be the hijackers.[47] Eventually, positive identifications of four of the hijackers were made by matching DNA samples provided by the FBI to postmortem DNA found at the site. In doing this, the OCME was responding to the concerns of the families that the remains of the attackers be separated from those of their victims. There was some difficulty in obtaining the DNA profiles from the FBI. According to Robert Shaler, director of the DNA lab at the OCME:

> A reasonable time frame within which to expect this information should have been a couple of weeks, maybe a month. Instead, it took longer than a year.... At one point I questioned whether [the FBI] truly empathized with the families. I wanted to believe they did. The delay likely had something to do with national security; I'm sure the DNA profiles of these cowards was felt to pose a national threat. How? I had no clue.[48]

In the case of the London bombings of July 7, a convincing argument was made—the London Assembly inquiry found it convincing—that in the circumstances all that could be done to expedite identification of the victims had been done. But what were these circumstances, and how did they come to be defined as such? In the end, two things seem to have been important. First, it seems to have been the treatment of what happened on July 7 as a disaster that led to the invocation of the DVI process for the identification of the bodies of those killed. To what extent was that appropriate? It may seem obvious that what happened was a disaster, an outrage, "a terrible and tragic atrocity that has cost many innocent lives," in the words of the prime minister, Tony Blair.[49] The government's Emergency Committee met without hesitation that morning. There is no doubt that a large number of people were affected by the bombings: 56 people died, including the bombers, 700 were injured, "1,000 adults and 2,000 of their children...suffered from post-traumatic stress as a result of their experiences on 7 July [and] 3,000 others are estimated to have been directly affected."[50]

However, what counts as an emergency or a disaster is not largely a question of numbers. In the bombings at Aldgate and at Edgware Road taken separately, the numbers of fatalities were no greater than a bad traffic accident.

There is a choice as to whether an incident should be treated as a disaster and whether, for example, all the intricacies and complexities of the Disaster Victim Identification processes need to be invoked. This is, or rather should be, a matter of judgment. As such, it needs to be justified; delays in the identification of bodies cannot be argued to be the result of the circumstances when those circumstances are established through a political judgment. What had happened on July 7 was appalling. It was arguably made worse at least for the relatives of the missing by invoking the bureaucratic apparatus of disaster management.

Criminal Investigation

The second circumstance that led to delays and the strange treatment of relatives and friends of the victims was the priority given to the criminal investigation, and the fact that, in London, the police authorities were concerned with both the identification of the missing and the criminal proceedings. The police search for a suspected criminal is perhaps the exemplary case in which the authorities are concerned to identify and apprehend a particular individual—though even here of course they are concerned with *what* a person has or may have done, not with *who* that person is more broadly, though the latter may become an issue at a trial or at least in the sentencing process. Who exactly the victim is is often less important than who the perpetrator is, in the eyes of the investigators. In New York the situation was different. The FBI investigation into the disaster appears to have been largely separate from the OCME's work. Indeed, in New York this is the general policy. As Shiya Ribowsky explains,

> Cops focus primarily on the *perpetrator* and on the questions: *Who did it?* and *Why?* We at OCME focus on the *victim: Who is dead?* and *What happened?* Each death therefore must be treated by us with the same care, attention to detail, and dignity as any other. This difference of focus is a further reiteration of the status of the OCME as not being part of law *enforcement,* though one of OCME's functions is indeed to support the criminal justice system.[51]

In London on July 8, 2005, "an Identification Commission was established, chaired by the Coroner and consisting of the Senior Police Identification Manager, a Pathologist, a Orthodontist, a Home Office representative and anyone else who the Coroner wishe[d] to sit on it."[52] Formally, it was this commission that was responsible for identifications, but the process was, it seems, very much under police control.[53]

One of those in charge was Andy Hayman, then the assistant commissioner recently made responsible for counterterrorism for the Metropolitan Police at Scotland Yard. Hayman gives a detailed account of the events of July 7 in his book *The Terrorist Hunters,* a book that was banned by the British government before it went on sale.[54] Extracts from the book had already appeared in the *Times* by then. Hayman's description of what happened during the forensic investigation makes the focus on the perpetrators in the London case clear:

> It may sound insensitive and callous, but as the bodies were removed, our forensic science teams paid most attention at first to those we suspected might have been the bombers. We needed to identify them fast to track any accomplices and check links to any other potential terrorists. . . . At 10.19pm the family of one Hasib Hussain reported him missing. An hour and a half later a police exhibits officer, who was putting together documents and possessions found near the bombs, phoned the Anti-Terrorist Branch with a number of names identified on cards and personal items. Among them were gym membership cards that bore the names Sidique Khan and Mr S. Tanweer. The proximity of these cards to the rucksacks that we believed had contained the bombs meant we immediately suspected they were those of the bombers.[55]

Further information followed: Hasib Hussain's property was found in Tavistock Square, and his family reported that he had traveled to London with friends, including Khan and Tanweer, and on July 10 and 11 pathologists reports indicated that the men later identified as Hussain, Tanweer, Khan, and Lindsay "were in possession of, or in close proximity to, the bombs at the times of the explosions."[56] Warrants were obtained for searches of their home addresses and vehicles, and CCTV images at King's Cross and Luton railway stations located. Jermaine Lindsay's wife reported him missing on July 13 and told police that he knew the occupants of addresses she had seen being searched. Identification of the remains of the four at the sites of the bombings was confirmed by DNA analysis between July 13 and 16.

It seems likely that the release of all identifications was held until the identity of the suspected bombers had been confirmed. There is some confusion in the London Assembly report about exactly how long identification took, but it was certainly somewhere between seven and ten days before relatives were notified and the bodies of victims identified and released for burial. In one place the report notes: "It took ten days for all those who were killed on 7 July to be formally identified by the police"[57] In another comment on the same page, the report says: "The correct identification of the deceased was a highly complex and sensitive task, and this was completed within 7 days."[58] Since neither the full details of the forensic investigation process nor the forensic report have yet been made public, details are sketchy. Pictures of the investigators at work were published in the *Daily Mail* in July 2009.[59] According to a report in the journal *European Hospital,* "Over a 17-day period, 56 bodies and 1162 body parts were examined."[60] Radiographers undertook "primary surveys," using fluoroscopy to help them locate personal effects, document injuries, and retrieve foreign bodies—presumably by this they mean forensic evidence such as bomb parts—swiftly. Secondary surveys focused on "intra-oral dental radiography"—teeth X-rays—and this was the primary means of identification employed. The scene was examined closely by police forensic officers, evidence carefully collected and mapped, and body parts recorded and sent to the mortuary.[61]

Although according to one report Inner North London coroner Dr. Andrew Reid had said the bodies of the presumed bombers would be treated in exactly the same way as those of the victims, their bodies were in fact held for much longer.[62] All four were released in the last week of October 2005. The body of Shehzad Tanweer was buried in Pakistan; relatives of Mohammad Sidique Khan asked for the body to be kept in the mortuary pending another postmortem.[63] It seems he was buried in Pakistan some months later.[64] Hasib Hussain was buried in Leeds.[65]

There was no account of what happened to the bodies of those victims who identified themselves to rescuers before they died, or who died on their way to hospital, and no reasons were given as to why their relatives could not have been informed immediately. It was only with the preinquest hearings in 2010 that these questions were raised again. The hearings brought to light information that had clearly been known to police officers for some time but that many relatives had not suspected at all. Seventeen of the fifty-two people killed had survived for a period after the explosions. Behnaz Mozakka, for example, "was conscious after the blast and spoke to a police officer."[66] In other instances "clear identification of the loved ones was found at the scene" but relatives were not informed: "In one case there was medication found with the name of the injured person, in another case there were identification cards found on the body. Yet, for many days, they were anxious and worried and telephoning hospitals and visiting hospitals enquiring into whether or not their loved one might still be alive."[67]

Dates for inquests into the deaths of July 7 were set and postponed numerous times, despite protests from the families. In May 2009, following the collapse of the trial of three people accused of having collaborated with the suspected bombers, when the jury failed to agree, the coroner then responsible, Dr. Andrew Reid, wrote to relatives indicating that full inquests might never be held. An earlier attempt by the justice secretary, Jack Straw, to put in place legislation to allow the inquests to be held in secret was dropped after protests.[68] Demands for a public inquiry to investigate in detail what happened and to establish guilt had been rebutted.

By early 2010, however, preinquest hearings were under way, and things seemed more promising.[69] Coroner Lady Justice Hallett's initial rulings opened the way for full inquests, approaching in detail what might have been expected of a public inquiry. It became clear that inquests regarding victims and suspected bombers would not take place together as originally planned—a result of pressure from families—and that the inquests would include the examination of whether those killed in the bombings could have been saved. The actions of the security services prior to July 7 were to be scrutinized, to see whether more could have been done to prevent the bombings, and what was done after the blasts to save those who were injured but not killed outright was to be examined.

The full inquests finally began on October 11, 2010. Lady Justice Hallett had interpreted her remit broadly and inclusively, and she strongly contested suggestions from the Home Office and the Security Services that she hold some of the proceedings in secret. The evidence presented revealed much that was not previously known about what happened on July 7, and confirmed much that had been suspected. In particular, the evidence showed that many of those who died had been alive for some time after the explosions, and that fellow passengers had stayed with them in the trains, treating their injuries as best they could and comforting them as they awaited the emergency services. In stunning contrast to the DVI process, the testimony given at the inquests adds up to a harrowing but hugely detailed account of what happened to each individual person involved. Numerous witnesses are called: survivors from the trains and staff who attended before the emergency services arrived. Reconstructions are provided by the police, for example, of where each individual person in the carriage was sitting, where the injured were found, exactly what spot in the tunnel the explosion took place. People speak slowly of what they saw, heard, and felt; who else they saw; what they and others did; and of course, what they can't remember. The ethos is one of total concern for all persons-as-such—who they are, how what happened affected them, what they did afterward—in a completely nonjudgmental way. The aim is to produce a thorough account of how each person died. The horror is not ducked but faced, carefully. Details are required, but with sensitivity. Alongside this is a palpable concern for the relatives and friends of those who died, who are sitting listening to all the evidence.

Despite initial skepticism from many about the value of inquests into these deaths, the stories that have emerged, thanks to Lady Justice Hallett's "particular skill" and courage, have provided an insight into "how generously human beings can behave towards each other in extreme conditions."[70] Mary Dejevsky writes of the testimonies:

> Invariably they have described the actions of ordinary members of the public who found themselves, on that one day, in extraordinary circumstances—people who, to put it mildly, were tested and not found wanting. While many ordinary individuals displayed superhuman compassion and strength, many of those who were trained and paid to be heroes appear to have fallen grievously short. Time and again, passengers have noted—some with regret, some with anger, some simply as a matter of fact—how official help was for an excruciatingly long time simply not there....The most obvious [failures] are material....Far, far more damaging were the formalistic attitudes that seem to have governed the response: a built-in fear of breaking rules, a retreat to learnt formulae that demanded caution, and an absence of the very qualities that defined the passengers' response: resourcefulness, flexibility and sheer grit.[71]

It was not just the resourcefulness of surviving passengers and the help they provided to their fellows that was striking, but the way in which that help was offered. Despite—or perhaps because of—extreme circumstances, ordinary civilities were remembered. Passengers introduced themselves to each other—even shook hands—and spoke about family and friends. They stayed with each other even though there was nothing they could offer other than the comfort of their presence. And they refused the label "hero." The response was from stranger to stranger, person to person. They did nothing more than they had to do.

On one issue that the families were concerned to raise—the delay before postmortems were held and families informed—the judgment of the preinquest hearings was that such concerns, while appropriate for a public inquiry, were outside the scope of an inquest designed to determine cause of death. Counsel for the families pointed out that "in the hours and days that followed the explosions, there were concerns that the families had as to the whereabouts of their loved ones and telephone calls that were made...didn't get the answers that it was hoped they would get." However, although "a degree of flexibility, having regard to the humanity of the situation" was possible in an inquest, the coroner ruled that answers to these questions should be sought outside the framework of the formal proceedings.[72]

During the first session of the inquests themselves, counsel for the inquests reiterated that the question of delays in identification would not form part of the remit of the inquests. Although it was admitted that "the process by which their loved ones were identified, how they were informed of their deaths and how they were informed only after the formal disaster victim identification process was complete has given rise to a huge amount of anguish on the part of the families," the issue was to be addressed by way of a separate report prepared by the Metropolitan Police. The detailed report would, it was said, "explain how the complex disaster victim identification system works and that it's obligated to conform with a number of internationally agreed protocols and that explains why the deceased were removed from the scenes in the way that they were, why the scenes had to be forensically searched in the way that they were and why there were then necessarily delays in informing their loved ones of their deaths."[73]

In May 2009 the second report of the Intelligence and Security Committee was published.[74] That report draws attention to the difference between the "evidential process by which the police linked evidence found at the bomb sites with the identities of the bombers" and the use of the term "identification" by the security service MI5.[75] The committee was charged with examining why previous encounters with two of the presumed bombers, Khan and Tanweer, had not been followed up. MI5 said that "they had not identified Mohammed Sidique Khan prior to 7/7." When questioned in detail by the committee, this apparent contradiction was put down to how, for MI5, "formally identifying someone involves both *who* and *what* they are":

> For MI5, *what* they are comes first. If an unidentified person is assessed to be an *attack planner,* it is vitally important that MI5 then verify *exactly who they are.* To do this they look at details such as date and place of birth, nationality and addresses [and] the person is then formally "identified", in MI5 terms. . . . However, the opposite is not true. If an unidentified person is *not a threat,* it does not matter to MI5 *who* they are.[76]

If MI5 have information about someone they have assessed not to be a threat, they will not bother to pursue the question of *who* he is: they are content to have determined *what* he is. In fact, it was said that at that time MI5 had the resources to cover only 6 percent of those "known to be involved in attack planning."[77] Not only did MI5 not follow up on Khan and Tanweer, then, because they were not assessed as a threat, but MI5 might not have done so anyway, given that resources to follow up every "threat" were not available.

Forensics was of course originally developed not to assist relatives searching for the missing but precisely to assist the police in their criminal investigations. The tensions between the two were recognized in exhumations that took place in Bosnia. Eric Stover and Rachel Shigekane tell the story of British investigator Kevin Berry and his team, working on behalf of the International Criminal Tribunal for the former Yugoslavia (ICTY) in southwestern Kosovo in 1999:

> One hot summer evening [they] suddenly found themselves surrounded by a throng of angry villagers.... "It was a tense moment," Berry recalled. "We'd received orders that afternoon to move on and somehow the villagers had caught wind of it. They were concerned that we would leave with our work unfinished." Faced with a clash between the evidentiary needs of the ICTY for only certain kinds of evidence and the needs of the villagers, Berry opted to stay in Mala Krusa and finish all of the exhumations. "The villagers were right," he said later. "They were waiting for their loved ones to be recovered. It would have been disrespectful to leave."[78]

For the criminal proceedings in the international tribunal, what was needed was evidence to substantiate charges of genocide or crimes against humanity. *Such charges do not require personal identification of the victims.* For such mechanisms of justice, *as for the perpetrators of the genocide,* it is not necessary that particular individuals were killed, only that those targeted were perceived as members of a particular ethnic, racial, religious, or national grouping. The forensic evidence needed is what category the victim belonged to, and the cause and manner of death. The identification of the person is not necessary.

President George W. Bush expressed his condolences on the morning of September 11 at around 9:30 a.m.—before the buildings had fallen in Manhattan and before the plane had crashed in Pennsylvania. In a statement at 5:30 p.m. on the evening of the London bombings, Tony Blair, the British prime minister, said: "I would like once again to express my sympathy and sorrow for those families that will be grieving so unexpectedly and tragically tonight."[79] Those to whom Blair offered his condolences on July 7, 2005, could not have been grieving that night, though they would undoubtedly have been distraught. Families were still trying desperately to find out what had happened: calling friends, going from hospital to hospital, trying to get through to the Casualty Bureau, taking the first flight to London. They couldn't get any news of their missing sons, daughters, mothers, fathers, brothers, sisters, friends, or partners. They could not possibly begin to mourn. No one could or would tell them whether the people they were looking for were dead or alive.[80]

The distress friends and relatives suffered is a symptom of a more deep-seated problem. Persons are not seen as important in themselves, each for *who* that person is or might be, as what I have been calling *persons-as-such*. They are only either survivors that can go home and carry on, walk away from the disaster, or dead bodies that can be matched in due course with names and dates of birth of missing persons and filed away. If what went wrong after July 7 is to be put right, this is what needs to change. It is a major change. As the London Assembly report put it,

> There is an overarching, fundamental lesson to be learnt from the response to the 7 July attacks, which underpins most of our findings and recommendations. The response on 7 July demonstrated that there is a lack of consideration of the individuals caught up in major or catastrophic incidents. Procedures tend to focus too much on incidents, rather than on individuals, and on processes rather than people. Emergency plans tend to cater for the needs of the emergency and other responding services, rather than explicitly addressing the needs and priorities of the people involved.[81]

The conclusion is that "a change of mindset is needed to bring about the necessary shift in focus, from incidents to individuals, and from processes to people."[82] What is being suggested here is a rethinking of how we expect our policing and emergency services to behave in relation to us, and by extension, how we would like our governments to behave.

This is a change that is not only needed at a time of emergency; it is needed all the time. The same type of governance can be found in attempts to set out rules for humanitarian intervention in conflict zones, to "do no harm," to deal with famines and other events perceived as exceptional, as failures of the system, as disasters. It can be seen in the planning for the displaced persons of Europe in the aftermath of the Second World War. Indeed, the argument is that our politics has become little more that a permanent state of emergency or exception, where the respect owed to each and every life has disappeared. Life becomes nothing more than bare life, to be used instrumentally.[83] If life dares to disagree, if people challenge the government or the processes of governance, then the solution is to persuade, to educate, to patronize, not to listen and debate. If people don't like the Disaster Victim Identification process, for example, if they want to make sure the bodies of the dead are "treated humanly," then all we need apparently is a library of online information sheets that explain the DVI process to them and a fully trained family liaison officer to make sure they go along with it.

John Tulloch, an academic at Brunel University and one of the people injured in the London bombings, ends his account of the events of that day with a postscript in the form of a letter addressed directly to Mohammad Sidique Khan, the alleged Edgware Road bomber. He refuses to accept the labels of "innocent victim" given to him and "mindless psychopath" given to Khan.[84] He talks about the three images he has of Khan. The first is the person he met briefly in that "faceless, too-busy everyday world" on July 7. The second two are from the media: the image of Khan as a contemplative, patient, teaching assistant at a primary school in Leeds, and the image in the al-Jazeera video where Khan is "talking the talk of a soldier straight to camera."[85] Tulloch wants to address Khan as a person, as someone who decided, quite mistakenly in Tulloch's view, to explode a bomb on a train in London. He refuses to write him off, to objectify him, but insists on "what is so nearly lost to us: the dignity of humankind."[86] What Tulloch calls "dignity" is nonnegotiable: it has to extend to those we call victim and those we call perpetrator alike. The alternative is the acceptance of "a conformism of fear."[87]

In their study of Basque political violence, *Terror and Taboo,* anthropologists Joseba Zulaika and William A. Douglass note that 73 percent of victims of violence want to meet with their aggressors: "They long for that face-to-face interaction . . . [that] would entail a recognition of each other's humanity."[88] In contrast, both terrorist organizations and counterterrorism experts inhabit a world of objectification and depersonalization:

> It is in a world of secrecy, masks, and hidden agendas that violence prospers. . . . Counterterrorism's policy of defacing the activist and reducing his/her narratives to sheer criminality only replicates the violence's original logic of secrecy and dehumanization. Both the terrorist and the counterterrorist . . . are engaged in systematically ignoring the human condition of the other.[89]

And of course of the public, those who suffer the consequences. For Zulaika and Douglass, both the terrorist and those who attempt to govern terror are engaged in the process of turning other people into mere instruments of their own agendas. They are not in the business of granting that their opponents may have thought through the implications of their actions, or may be entitled to a hearing.

Relatives of the missing do not just accept what they are told. They do not just go home and wait. They walk the streets, they put up missing posters, they protest the injustice to anyone who will listen. They know what is at stake. Those in political authority assume that their task is that of dealing with people as objects to be governed, not as persons: as far as they are concerned *the person-as-such is missing*. We need to take note before we all become nothing more than a list of physical characteristics and distinguishing marks, dead bodies in all but name.

CHAPTER 5

Forensic Identification

> We have the technology to identify and fit a name to
> even the smallest human remnant, but we also have
> the technology to create more such remnants or to
> make bodies disappear altogether.
>
> —David Simpson, *9/11: The Culture of Commemoration*

In the first few days after September 11, it was impossible for ordinary New Yorkers to approach Ground Zero.[1] Manhattan below Fourteenth Street was cordoned off, inaccessible at first even to those who lived there. To get past the official barricades required a firefighter's badge or some subterfuge. The formerly open city had been closed, fenced, and guarded. This inaccessibility was one of the things that generated feelings of powerlessness in those affected but unable to help. Groups of people gathered in the squares and parks closest to the scene: Union Square and later Washington Square were focal points. As restrictions were further lifted, Ground Zero itself became a focus of attention. People came to volunteer their services, to bring gifts of food and medical supplies, and to try to help in whatever ways were allowed. Rescue workers were the "heroes" of the day. They had the hardest job and were exposed to extremes of horror, but they were also in some sense the most privileged: they at least were able to help, to do something. As the official emergency team got organized, and the work was contracted out to commercial organizations, volunteers were progressively excluded. Not only were they barred from the site, but they were accused of voyeurism—wanting to help was seen as a morbid fascination with death and destruction. Indeed, some people made the decision not to visit the site, perhaps because they agreed with the view that it was a voyeuristic activity.

Some of those who were unable to visit Ground Zero themselves, those outside New York or even outside the United States, sent surrogate visitors in the form of objects mailed to rescue organizations.[2] Surveillance web-cameras were set up so that the world could watch the recovery effort, and rescue workers could watch what was going on when they were on a break. Those who did visit left objects—for the dead or for each other—messages inscribed on T-shirts or flags, garlands of paper cranes, teddy bears, flowers, and photographs tied to the railings or left at impromptu shrines around the site. Viewing platforms were set up, one for the public and one with restricted access for the Port Authority.[3] By February 2002 it was necessary to have tickets to visit the public platform. People queued for an hour or so for the free tickets allocating them a time, returning later at the allotted hour to queue once more before ascending the wooden viewing platform. Each group of visitors was allocated three minutes at the site. They wrote messages on the wooden sides of the viewing platform, took photographs of each other and of the "pit," and descended again to street level. By March 2002 the boundaries of the site had shrunk to the extent that the recovery operation could be seen from a number of points around the site, and visitors circled the area, stopping to look at what was going on and to inspect the temporary memorials set up on police barricades and construction fences. A map was produced to document the moving boundaries and show visitors where they could walk and where the impromptu shrines were.[4] Street stalls sold images of the towers before their collapse.

As time went on and the perimeter of the site shrank further, certain features and practices followed the shrinking borderline. New maps were produced, charting the moving shrines that surrounded the site. The platform built to accommodate tourists finally disappeared, and by the time of the first anniversary in September 2002 visitors could walk around the edge of the pit itself. In commemoration of the anniversary, people gathered again in Union Square and Washington Square. These gatherings reflected the same impetus to debate and reflect that had motivated the original gatherings, though much muted and semiformalized. Official spaces were provided where messages could be left. Overnight vigils were again held at these places. The anniversary was marked by silences in the squares parallel to and in protest of the official ceremonies at Ground Zero itself. Memorials were still in place around Lower Manhattan, and missing posters still hung outside the hospitals. A remnant of the shrines that at one time surrounded Ground Zero was still evident on the fences around St. Paul's, but elsewhere the authorities were trying to reclaim public space from the public. Notices signed by the City of New York Department of Parks and Recreation appeared on fences, asserting: "This is not intended to be a memorial site. Do Not Place Candles, Flyers, or Posters. They will be removed." Or, in Union Square, the rather improbable sign on railings and stone ornaments: "No Candles Please. Permanent Damage will Result. Thank You."

Kevin Bubriski was fascinated by the combination of "a remarkable sense of community" and "the deepest kind of personal reflection on loss and mortality." He visited Ground Zero several times, photographing not the site itself and the recovery effort but the faces of visitors as they "came to a full stop, planting their feet firmly as if to keep themselves from wavering or falling."[5] In his images we see reflected in visitors' faces their response to what they saw. They stood silently trying to make sense of what had taken place at Ground Zero—to remake their inner world—and trying to heal the wound by their presence. As one visitor to the viewing platform put it in the message she left, "We all lost you all, and mourn together. We are *not* 'sightseers.'"[6]

People needed to see for themselves, to domesticate the imagination in a sense, but also to see the enormity that cannot be shown in television images or documented in eyewitness accounts. The reality on the ground was both incomparably worse than and not as bad as people had imagined. The experience brings home what New York filmmaker Ken Jacobs described as follows: "What I don't want is that the mass tightens into a thing. I prefer it porous, airy. To preserve the everyday and the ordinary that always accompanies the extraordinary, keeping it accessible."[7] Like other New Yorkers, Jacobs visited Ground Zero. He remarks: "My need with many others here with camera in hand was to hold on to some of the strangeness of our days."[8] The contradiction is plain: the need to preserve or hold on to the openness—what Jacobs calls "the strangeness"—alongside the need to respect the very impossibility of that openness being a "thing" that we can hold to. By encircling the site of the trauma the traumatic event is both in one sense located—it is specific, it took place *here* and nowhere else—and in another dislocated. Recognized as a hole, a gap, a lack, or an excess, it cannot be grasped, pinned down, specified in language.

This chapter examines the work of recovery and the tensions it embodied. Alongside the encircling of Ground Zero, a project of identification and accounting began. Families were required to produce objects that might contain the DNA of the missing, and teams clearing the site worked to separate fragments of human remains from the vast pile of rubble. The development of DNA technologies is one thing; their uneven use in various cases and for a variety of political purposes, in Bosnia, New York, Vietnam, Argentina, and post–World War II remains, another. The Bosnian investigations after the Srebrenica massacres resulted in powerful new technologies and had varying impacts on the families, the national community, and the international community.[9] These techniques were employed in the aftermath of 9/11, and the political implications of the extensive and costly identifications are considered, as are their impacts on relatives of the missing.

The chapter begins by exploring accounts by those who were involved in the huge Family Assistance Center. These reveal an enormous attempt to bring order to the chaos, to reclaim control, and to deal with the trauma through processes of memorialization, ritual, and grief that might bring about a reinscription of the missing as the dead.

Families of the Missing

Like ordinary New Yorkers, the families of the missing were also visitors to Ground Zero. Their experience was organized separately—they had their own viewing platform, situated at another corner of the site, and their visit was an accompanied one. They were taken in groups by barge from the Family Assistance Center, situated some way away at Pier 94, to Battery Park, where they walked to Ground Zero. Rene Marcus, an American Red Cross volunteer, gives her description of these visits. The families and friends meet in a "staging area" where they are given a bouquet of flowers and a teddy bear and briefed as to what to expect. The visitors are accompanied by Red Cross mental health specialists, chaplains of various religions, and an escort of armed and uniformed state troopers. The trip to Battery Park on a double-decker boat takes about half an hour.

> They walk, wearing their hard hats and goggles to the site. Face masks are available. Soldiers stand at attention saluting until all pass thru the boundary gates, climb up some stairs to an observation area. It is from here that those who lost loved ones have the opportunity to gaze across all the destruction, cranes, bulldozers, smoky areas and workers to say their last goodbyes. Many are weeping, others clutch themselves or each other, and almost everyone is dabbing tissues at their eyes. It's awesome and terribly sad. After 15 minutes or so, they turn to go to a makeshift memorial. No one is talking. It's quiet except for the sounds of recovery taking place at "Ground Zero". Families and friends leave a picture, a note or letter, a teddy bear, a candle, or some special memento and flowers on the huge collection of all that has been left by others before them. They are allowed a few moments there. They return to the boat. It is quiet. No one is talking or making eye contact.[10]

The implication is that this helps to bring some form of closure. I doubt it. These regimented visits—with hints of the military and heroism close to the surface—risk incorporating the missing into the narratives of attacks on America that make a military response seem inevitable.

The Family Assistance Center had originally been located opposite the Office of the Chief Medical Examiner and was set up to house other agencies as well. Staff at the OCME had realized that their headquarters was not a suitable place to deal with the families. Later the center was transferred to the Lexington Avenue National Guard Armory, a few blocks away, before finally being moved to Pier 94 on Fifty-Seventh Street. The main government Emergency Operations Center dealing with the World Trade Center disaster was next door at Pier 92.[11]

At Pier 94, the assistance center was "set up like a trade show with full carpet, poles with drapes, and some 75 agencies with all their staff and stuff: service agencies, government, immigration, FBI, child care, etc." It was "a comfortable building in order to be welcoming and calming as it can be to the families," and the dining areas had "donated fresh flowers daily, tablecloths, and an ambience of peace and calm different from the noisy, bustling activity everywhere else."[12] One of the most noticeable things about the center, apart from its huge size and the amount of activity going on there, seemed to be the degree of security, which volunteer workers described as the most stringent they had ever encountered. There were three checkpoints to pass through. Authorization badges had to be renewed every day, and lengthy queues endured. Robert Munson, a member of the International Family Linking On-call Team, which he describes as a specialty group of the American Red Cross International Disaster Response Team, recounts, in an e-mail home to his family and coworkers in the Red Cross, how workers and family entered the building every day:

> We all stand in lines with our own thoughts—waiting to get into the huge building on Pier 94. To get into the building, one crosses a highway, passes by the media area separated from us by portable iron fencing. We pass by the wall you have seen on TV with all of the photos of missing loved ones. Many such walls are all over NYC. Yellow ribbons are beginning to fill in all of the fencing. You wait in line while guards check credentials of workers and ID papers of family members. All bags are searched. Cameras are forbidden. I don't know what else they are looking for. I don't ask. You cross a small parking area which contains the WORLDCOM semi-trailer housing the banks of telephones from which family members can call worldwide for free. Also in this area the Salvation Army has a large canteen and snack tent.

One enters the building—family members in one door, workers through another. Family is greeted by uniformed guards who check papers again and pass them into a line to the Reception Desk at which they learn what services are available and where they are. They get a dated, colored badge reading "Family". Red Cross has a First Aid station there staffed by both nurses and physicians. They are stocked like a neighborhood drug store. Families then go to the service they want, and sit in large waiting areas for the next available government or agency worker. Red Cross Mental Health workers, Chaplains and Therapy Dogs wander throughout the building—are all clearly marked as to who they are; even the dogs have their own picture ID.[13]

There could be up to a five-hour wait before families were finally seen. In the first few days at least the workers were completely overloaded. Later too, when death certificates began to be issued in alphabetical order, the crowds were even busier, with "much more open weeping everywhere" than before.[14] There was an area set aside for a two-hundred-foot wall of missing posters, with candles, teddy bears, and flowers, roped off from the bustle of the center. The idea was to give family members somewhere peaceful to go, and perhaps limit the challenge that the posters, with their invocation of bare life, represented. Red Cross workers on rotations lasting a few weeks are working flat out. Each case that they deal with is differ-ent. There is a Japanese woman who has lost her only son and whose main concern is to have "something tangible of his to take back with her to Japan for the Buddhist memorial service that is scheduled on her return to Japan"; a man originally from Poland whose identical twin worked in the World Trade Center and whose widow cannot bear to look at the brother's face or hear his voice; and a young Mexican woman looking for her hus-band, a waiter in the Windows on the World restaurant. "I try to help her through the paper of death certificates, return of personal effects, and any other benefits to which she might be entitled," Munson tells us. "She is not ready. She still completely believes they will find her husband alive. It has now been 20 days."[15]

It was hard for the Red Cross workers and others interviewing family after family after family, and dealing with those who had survived. Survivors' stories could be horrific, and as Rene Marcus explains,

Their nightmare continues. One woman I interviewed lost her front teeth and fractured her tibia as well as losing her job. Another saw an airplane part plummeting to earth and causing grave injury to another, and others told me of the sight of people and paper in the air. They could only shake their heads in disbelief and downcast their eyes. Do you wonder how I managed? Me too.[16]

Marcus's main job was helping those searching for the missing, first opening an ARC 901 file, then preparing "cash gift" paperwork and seeing to immediate financial needs: "This would sometimes take 2–3 hours and could be very emotional for families."[17] Paperwork of all sorts was involved: death certificates, bills, mortgage and loan papers. The heartless, impersonal administrative bureaucracy of death.

The American Red Cross's role seems to have been to translate grief and disbelief into the paperwork of financial claims and to turn away any politics or protest, despite what its volunteers might have felt. Like UNRRA in the displaced persons camps, the Red Cross was not concerned with the families as people with political views or agendas, but only as "victims." As an organization, it did encounter considerable criticism and controversy, but not over its complicity in such a process of depoliticization—rather, over its raising and distribution of funds. Immediately after the events of September 11, people were keen to give whatever help they could. This eagerness to be involved meant hugely generous donations to organizations like the Red Cross, who were involved with the recovery effort, but it translated only a short time later into bitter criticisms of the use to which these enormous funds were being put.

The American Red Cross was founded in 1881 by Clara Barton, following her experiences in the American Civil War.[18] I return to her work with the missing in action in chapter 6. The Red Cross grew rapidly, and in 1900 it was granted a United States Congressional Charter. The 1905 revision, in addition to stating the organization's duty "to provide volunteer aid in time of war to the sick and wounded of the armed forces," mandated the Red Cross "to carry out a system of national and international relief in time of peace, and apply that system in mitigating the suffering caused by pestilence, famine, fire, floods, and other great national calamities, and to devise and carry out measures for preventing those calamities."[19] Interestingly enough, the reason for the congressional charter was in part at least the controversy in the early twentieth century surrounding Clara Barton's leadership of the organization, and specifically, her accounting practices. Barton was "highly popular in the public eye," but some "viewed her personal management style with concern" and "considered her financial record-keeping sloppy and incomplete."[20] Very similar concerns over leadership style and financial irregularities led to the revision of the charter in 2007. The history of the federal charter on the present-day Red Cross website recounts the 2007 revision, but without revealing any of the leadership controversies of the twenty-first century, which presumably remain too raw. The board was downsized, and new provisions put in place for accountability and annual reports to Congress.

In the immediate aftermath of September 11, the American Red Cross launched a fund called the Liberty Fund, which was designed to keep new donations separate from its normal Disaster Relief Fund. The Red Cross website announced at the time that this new fund would "support the immediate and emerging efforts of the American Red Cross to alleviate human suffering brought on by the attacks of September 11."[21] However, in a memo written to local Red Cross branches, or "chapters," the president of the Red Cross, Dr. Bernadine Healy, who had been personally responsible for the launch of a separate fund, noted that several million additional dollars would be needed to prepare for future terrorist attacks. This work would include developing "preparedness standards," "training and development in response to weapons of mass destruction," "assuring blood readiness," "volunteer recruitment, training, and development, continued engagement, retention, cultivation, re-training and deployment," and being prepared for "future terrorist attacks and catastrophic events which may be multifaceted and which may occur concurrently in multiple cities and regions."[22] Many donors felt that this was not what they had given money for—what they had assumed was that their donations would be used to help victims and their families. Nor did they necessarily agree with Healy's defense of the Liberty Fund as "a war fund." "We must have the ability to help our troops if we go into a ground war. We must have the ability to help the victims of tomorrow," Healy told a congressional hearing.[23]

By October 26, Bernadine Healy had announced her resignation. Her leadership style had been described as "autocratic and arrogant,"[24] and she was seen by some in the Red Cross as "too driven and steely for an organization that they considered an affair of the heart"; or, put another way, "Dr. Healy was not people-oriented, and the Red Cross is all about people."[25] She was said to have "caused morale at the national organisation to drop to an all-time low," with a number of senior and long-serving employees having left since she took over.[26] *New York Times* reporter Deborah Sontag, who interviewed Healy shortly after she announced her resignation, noticed "a saying attributed to Clara Barton [displayed] above the mantle: 'It irritates me to be told how things have always been done....I defy the tyranny of precedent.'"[27] In the interview, Healy compared herself to Barton, though admitting that while she had served only two years, Barton had served twenty years before being forced out. Supporters would have seen the board's choice of Healy in 1999 as the choice of "a driven professional who ruffled feathers but made things happen," and according to one board member, "We hired a change agent for a culture resistant to change."[28] One change Healy implemented immediately on appointment was an external investigation of embezzlement at one Red Cross chapter, an action that prompted internal criticism from those who thought the matter should have been handled more discreetly. She also introduced more professionalism into the handling of blood donations.

It seems that what led in the end to Bernadine Healy's loss of the support of the board, in addition to the groundswell of criticism in the wake of September 11, was that, although professional, her style of leadership and her seemingly heartless approach annoyed too many, within the organization, in the broader American public, and overseas. She seems to have been oblivious to the way in which her priorities were not neutral. Her proposed use of the 9/11 funds were clearly supportive of one particular approach: that of the Republican administration. This lack of neutrality was also apparent—and counterproductive—in her stance regarding the withholding of contributions to the International Red Cross in a dispute over the exclusion of Israel's Red Shield of David from the International Federation of Red Cross and Red Crescent Societies, which surfaced at roughly the same time. Healy managed to annoy the board by firing long-serving staff, creating the Liberty Fund without consulting the board, and taking an uncompromising stance on the Israel issue. According to Red Cross board chair David T. McLaughlin, "Bernadine brought discipline, authority and accountability to the American Red Cross. But every time she took a strong position, a little more of her capital with the board was spent. At a certain point, you can't recoup."[29]

In a November 14 briefing, McLaughlin, speaking alongside interim CEO Harold Decker, announced a complete U-turn on the Liberty Fund:

> It has been made increasingly clear that there is a significant gap between the focus of our efforts and the expectations of the American public. And regrettably, it took us sometime, somewhat longer than I think probably it should have, to address that credibility gap. But today we are making a course correction for the Red Cross Liberty Disaster Fund. One hundred percent of that fund and our efforts will be devoted to support those who are affected by the terrible tragedies that occurred on September 11. And with this action, we hope to restore the faith of our donors, the trust of the American public and to empower thousands of Red Cross workers and volunteers on the front line.[30]

Decker apologized that Red Cross activities had not been "as sharply focused as America wants and the victims of this tragedy deserve," and promised that from then on the victims would be "our only priority."[31] Other efforts—for future provision—would be funded separately. Assistance to families would be speeded up, and information would be shared with other organizations to help coordinate efforts. Prior to this, the Red Cross had refused to release the names of families it was assisting to other voluntary organizations out of respect for confidentiality.

In a further attempt to restore confidence in the Red Cross and its methods, Senator George Mitchell was appointed as Independent Overseer of the Liberty Fund. He met with donors and recipients and discussed their needs and expectations. In January 2002, in conjunction with the Red Cross, he produced a plan detailing how the remaining money in the Liberty Fund would be spent, and issued quarterly reports up to February 2003. A Liberty Oversight Commission carried on his work. In a short promotional video on the American Red Cross website, Mitchell underlined his support: "I was involved because of criticism of the Red Cross but I must tell you my admiration for the Red Cross grew during the process, because while, yes, there had been mistakes,... it was all out of the right attitude: people wanting to help, people trying to help, people doing the best they could to help.... Not much in life happens perfectly."[32]

The audited financial statements produced in 2004 reflect the resolution of the controversy; indeed, they seem to be an attempt to make it appear that all had been straightforward from the beginning. They show cash contributions from the public of just over $1 billion, of which $136,134,000 had been spent on immediate disaster relief, $384,287,000 on direct financial assistance to families of the dead and the seriously injured (3,500 beneficiaries), and a further $282,225,000 on assistance to displaced residents, economically affected individuals, and disaster responders (55,000 people).[33] These figures, we are told, reflect the definitions of the scope and purpose of the fund by the board and the executive committee at various points up to and including November 10, 2001, and applied retroactively. The board decided that the fund was to be used "exclusively to meet the immediate and long-term recovery needs of people directly affected by the terrorist attacks on the United States on September 11, 2001."[34] Donations received between September 11 and October 31 and not designated by the donors for other purposes were regarded—again, presumably, retroactively—as intended for response to the September 11 attacks.

Part of the controversy over the American Red Cross relief effort had been to do with delays in providing assistance to families. In the November 14 briefing, Decker had assured his audience: "Families only have to fill out a one-page, single-page form that tells us what needs they have now. The Red Cross then verifies the identities and sends out checks, working with our social workers, often within 48 hours."[35] Some applications did fall through the cracks, however—paperwork got lost or was not dealt with promptly. But, on the other hand, checks were necessary to prevent fraudulent applications:

> Cyril Kendall, a father of 12 children, claimed that a 13th child had died in the WTC attack. He told the Red Cross and Safe Horizon that his son was in the North Tower for a job interview with the American Bureau of Shipping, a legitimate company. To prove the existence of his "son," Cyril showed Red Cross workers a picture of himself as a young man. He stole over $119,000 from September 11th Recovery Program and $190,000 in total.[36]

The Red Cross reopened many files after the event to check for possible cases of fraud. Around 140 cases relating to the Liberty Fund were taken up by federal prosecutors, and ten in civil suits by the Red Cross itself. Nearly $400,000 was returned.[37]

Recovery

Like the visitors to Ground Zero, the Red Cross assistance and other "rescue, relief and memorial efforts were also symbolic repair work [in an effort] to unscramble, reconstruct and reorder the damage done in our symbol system along with the damage done on the ground,"[38] according to Eric Rothenbuhler, who analyzes visits to Ground Zero in terms of boundary practices linked to the "contagious magic and dangerous powers of the sacred."[39] Social practices having to do with the creation and crossing of boundaries around the site of destruction included "the definition of the impact zone with Ground Zero at its centre, the sending of volunteers, goods, funds, and gifts from around the country, and the celebration of the fire fighters and rescue and recovery workers who crossed the boundary and represented us at Ground Zero."[40] What is produced is a series of concentric circles:

> At the centre is the place of death, those who have been touched by it and those who touch it. At the barricades are those who came to pay tribute and bear witness—to be within proximity, as if to touch, those who crossed the barrier. In the larger community is the place of the smell and the ash, the missing posters, candles, flowers, and public shrines. This territory extends out communicatively across the country.[41]

And to the wider international community, some would say. Ground Zero, in this account, is "the anchoring centre of a meaningful organization of experience: in other words, a sacred place."[42]

Many New Yorkers were mourning the buildings themselves, as well as the people whose lives were lost in the collapse. Visitors to Ground Zero were like "loving family members of the buildings who needed to see the actual body of the buildings to accept their loss."[43] The image of the buildings appeared alongside the posters for missing people at shrines and impromptu memorials around the city. There were those who complained that the "Towers of Light" that shone upward from Ground Zero to commemorate the six-month anniversary of the collapse were inappropriate and insensitive in their focus on the loss of the towers rather than the loss of those killed. As a result the temporary memorial was renamed "Tribute in Light." However, the two events are intertwined.[44] When the buildings collapsed, flesh and structure became indistinguishable. The towers and their contents were uniformly destroyed.

The aim of the rescue teams once it was clear there were to be no survivors was to reverse the indistinction between bodies and steel through painstaking sorting of the remains at Ground Zero. They were not working to recover the materials from which the buildings had been constructed, but rather to separate the remains of the built, insentient structure from what was left of sentient human beings who had been in the buildings at the time of their collapse. Though according to Elaine Scarry the world could be remade after violence and destruction, there was of course no way in which those human remains could be used to remake living human beings; all that could be done was to identify and give a name to those who had disappeared.[45] In the end of course even that was to prove impossible for many of the people who had been lost. The unbuilding of the World Trade Center towers was taking place alongside a reassertion or remaking of the distinction between sentience and nonsentience.

Initially at least this remaking was undertaken by rescue squads who knew where certain people would have been, and had a personal stake in the recovery of their remains. Within less than two months it became apparent that the city authorities in charge of the operation had different priorities. Their concern appeared to be to clear the remains of the buildings as quickly as possible—to speed the unbuilding—so that reconstruction could begin and the city environment could be remade as ordered and under control.[46] The anxiety of firefighters to recover with as much honor as possible the remains of their own comrades and other victims of the collapse was making the whole process too slow. On November 2, 2001, Day 52 of the rescue effort, the city announced that the number of firefighters allowed on site was to be reduced to twenty-five. Concerns for safety were cited as the reason for the proposed reduction in firefighter numbers. The city planned to continue scooping and dumping at all times, with remains being separated out when the mix was examined at the Staten Island Landfill site.[47] On Day 56, November 5, Dennis Smith, a retired New York City firefighter and author, wrote: "Ground Zero not only looks like a construction site, it *is* a construction site."[48] The announcement by the city led to a demonstration by firefighters and "scuffles" with police, following which—incredibly—firefighters were arrested for trespassing on Ground Zero. On November 12, representatives of families of firefighters expressed their views in an emotional confrontation at the mayor's office. One widow remarked: "Last week my husband is memorialized as a hero, this week he's thought of as landfill?"[49] As a result a compromise was reached: the force of firefighters was increased from twenty-five to seventy-five, and the huge crane known as "Big Red"—regarded as too indiscriminate—was removed from the site. The remaking of the world takes time and is not to be hurried. The unmaking of the world by violence of one sort or another can be undone only by a slow painstaking remaking, brick by brick.

Firefighters were not at Ground Zero, Rothenbuhler argues, as "already given away life"[50] or what is called, following philosopher Giorgio Agamben, bare life.[51] Although they were treated in public discourse and particularly in the rhetoric of the Bush war as citizen-soldiers, as far as the general public and the firefighters themselves were concerned they were there on a personal basis, as indeed many had been on the day of the disaster itself. They were there looking for their sons and brothers, rhetorically and literally. Their role was that of "inside outsiders, defending to the very last day the irrational, the symbolic, the sentimental, and the memorial against the bureaucracy."[52] Their involvement demonstrated "the contrast of instrumental rationality and universalism, on the one hand, and the logic of the sacred and personalism," on the other.[53] The instrumentalization of life could be contested only by courtesy, reverence, and personalization.

In March, six months after the collapse, ironworkers remained at the site alongside the reduced contingent of firefighters, and bodies were still being recovered. The final piece of steel was removed with ceremony on May 30, 2002. The family of one of the missing firefighters, Michael Lynch,[54] had set up a website in September in the hope of finding him alive, but slowly realized that the best they could hope for was that his remains would be identified. They had a long and agonizing wait, like so many others. A memorial service was held on December 7, 2001, although by then nothing had been found. On March 21, 2002, Michael's father, Jack, had been working on the recovery effort at Ground Zero as usual and was on his way home when he got a phone call. Some of his fellow firefighters had found Michael's remains.

The family arrived and insisted on going down to the base of the pit to accompany Michael up. They still could not bury the body immediately—Michael's remains were commingled with those of a woman he had been carrying or shielding with his coat at the time of the collapse, and the family had to wait until DNA tests had taken place to identify her. Commingling of remains was a major problem with DNA identification, as we shall see later. Michael's funeral service took place on May 3, 2002.[55]

In the weeks after the commemoration of the first anniversary in September 2002, attempts to reclaim Ground Zero as ordinary space increased. Surrounding streets were cleared of shrines and memorials, and the tarmac and sidewalks repaired, even before the anniversary. Once the ceremonies had taken place, a fence was constructed around the site—the construction site, as it now certainly was. Rebuilding of transportation arteries had already been under way for a considerable period, although plans for the final structures on the site were still being debated, as was the future of Manhattan and indeed New York as a whole.[56] The fence was planned as an opaque structure, but there was resistance to this.[57] What was eventually erected was a steel fence that allowed visitors to observe the site, although the leaving of objects was discouraged by a notice that asked: "Please understand that all articles left behind must be removed." The names of those reported killed were listed, and the fence also carried panels giving the history of the Trade Center and previous attacks. It was no longer the place of spontaneous or disorganized activity it once had been. Gradually it had been reclaimed and order reimposed.

Identification Forensics

Efforts to reclaim the dead continued long after the site had been cleared. As Episcopal chaplain Charles Flood remarked, the exhaustive process of forensic identification was "all wrapped up in feelings of wanting to conquer death. It is very American. It is a way of saying we will prevail: This dust shall have a name again."[58] The very possibility of the identification of fragments of flesh and bone raised the public expectation that death should no longer be anonymous: "A nameless death seemed an affront."[59]

Forensic human identification, using a variety of methods, is required in three main situations: criminal investigations, where an unidentified corpse must be identified if the investigation is to proceed; accidents and mass disaster incidents, which involve the matching of antemortem and postmortem data under protocols developed by INTERPOL, the International Criminal Police Organization; and war crimes and genocide, where the Geneva

Conventions of 1949 specify establishing the identity of the dead as part of the obligations of parties to the conflict.[60] The credibility of identification is regarded as increasing as one moves from circumstantial evidence (personal effects such as clothes or jewelry or the visual identification by a relative, for example) to physical evidence, either external (skin color, sex, tattoos, scars, fingerprints) or, more credible still, internal (healed fractures, pathological conditions, blood groups, DNA, dental records).[61]

The use of DNA for identification began with the discovery in 1985 that although 99.5 percent of DNA—the molecule that "carries the hereditary information that an organism requires to function"—is identical between individuals, specific regions of DNA vary significantly from person to person, giving everyone a distinctive "DNA fingerprint," or "profile."[62] While other methods of identification rely on measurements or images of the body or body parts, DNA profiling "unlike all the other practices... —from anthropometry, to fingerprinting, to iris recognition—...allows investigators to capture, store and use not just the representation or documentation of the body but bodily matter.... Actual aspects of the body itself."[63] This appears a stunning change—we are used to thinking of the body as an integral whole, bounded and contained, not as an object that sheds parts of itself wherever it goes, leaving traces, and traces that can be identified. However, it is not so much this aspect that makes DNA profiling unique—after all, forensics has worked with traces of the body—hair, blood, fingerprints, semen—before, in different ways. What is distinctive is the way DNA is specific to one individual with a strong degree of certainty: if the DNA matches, the person is considered identified beyond doubt.

However, things are not quite that simple or straightforward—or speedy—in practice, and in particular in situations like the World Trade Center collapse.[64] DNA matching relies on comparing DNA from the missing person—ideally collected from personal items such as a toothbrush or hairbrush—or, failing that, DNA from close blood relatives, with DNA found on the human remains. Problems can arise either with the collection of antemortem DNA or DNA samples for kinship analysis, or with the DNA from the remains that are found. The public perception that minute fragments of tissue can be identified as having come from a particular individual is correct, but only up to a point.

The process of identification after the collapse of the World Trade Center towers in Manhattan in 2001 was extraordinarily difficult. The first and most challenging problem was the degradation of the DNA on the remains that were found. The accounts of what made for the basic technical difficulties make gruesome reading for those of us not familiar with forensics. The complicating factors included "the force and velocity of the initial impact of the aircraft; the abnormally high temperatures generated by the aviation fuel explosions; and the extraordinary devastation wreaked by the subsequent destruction and collapse of the buildings." If that was not enough, in the aftermath "the recovery process took many months, leading to prolonged exposure of the remains to differing weather conditions; subterranean fires (and the continual application of water to douse these fires); and the extremely deleterious effects caused by heavy machinery used in the excavation and recovery process." Taken together these factors led to "extraordinarily high levels of fragmentation, commingling, and varying stages of decomposition, mummification, and cremation."[65] Even DNA often could not survive such conditions intact.

The likely problems with identification had become apparent to the chief medical examiner, Charles Hirsch, on the day itself. He had been caught up in the events, arriving at his office covered in bruises and lacerations and with pockets full of dust. He told a reporter later that he had realized at that moment, emptying the debris from his pockets into an ashtray, that "if rein- forced concrete was rendered into dust, then it wasn't much of a mystery as to what would happen to people."[66]

By Wednesday, September 12, a Family Assistance Center was operating at the New York University Medical School, staffed by Red Cross and New York Police Department (NYPD) personnel. When two staff from the Office of the Chief Medical Examiner of New York (OCME) visited,

> what they found was appalling. Grieving family members were filling out a seven-page questionnaire by hand and supplying a photograph of a missing person. The form had information about the missing person, such as physical characteristics—including scars, tattoos, birthmarks, injuries, workplace address, relatives, and jewelry and clothing worn.[67]

The reason that the visiting staff from the OCME were appalled does not seem to have been mainly that relatives were being put through the totally unnecessary anguish of trying to specify what the missing person had been wearing that morning. It had to do with how the recording system would work—or rather what problems could be anticipated. These records were to be transferred to the OCME records unit, but there was no system to ensure that DNA collections, which would have to take place later, would be coor- dinated with this information. And there was no means of dealing with the collection of samples from relatives outside New York.

Clearly the management of information flows was very important—indeed, crucial in ensuring correct and speedy identifications—but, as we saw when we examined the procedures after the London bombings in chapter 4, no attention whatsoever was being paid to what the relatives were being put through. They were presumably being asked to fill out antemortem Disaster Identification Forms similar to those used later in London. This procedure, it seems to me, accounts at least in part for the form that the missing posters took—the details the posters gave reflected the details relatives provided at the so-called Family Assistance Center. However, it had already become apparent to the OCME that the vast majority of identifications would be made, or, in the very few cases identified by scars or tattoos, confirmed, by DNA analysis. The other information was largely superfluous. In London most identifications, it seems, were made without recourse to obscure details—bodies were often easily identified. In New York the reverse was the case—there were very few bodies at all. The general public had not realized this by September 12, but the chief medical examiner had.

There is ample evidence that people working at the OCME were in the end hugely aware of and sympathetic to the needs of the families, holding regular meetings and carefully explaining their work, but it was first necessary for the OCME to put in train a process for the collection of what they called antemortem DNA—swabs from family members and collections of personal items (toothbrushes, hairbrushes, etc.). This involved designing forms and preparing guidance on the DNA process for the NYPD. Although an official from the OCME was delegated to attend the Family Assistance Center to assist, the NYPD assumed complete control of the process. This, according to Robert Shaler, led to the collection of many inappropriate samples: "When politicians, police and medical examiners figure out what we learned—mass fatalities are all about families—they might get it right."[68] Again though, it seems to me that in the end Shaler is more concerned with the efficiency of the process than with the needs of the families. Except of course that their prime need seems to be for an identification. The problems of coordination between the NYPD and the other organizations involved, in particular the OCME, did in fact lead to other problems and to misidentifications. By late November or early December 2001, according to Shaler, it became clear that "it was a mess": there were clerical errors, but, more significantly, hundreds of families "did not have sufficient ante-mortem DNA from either kinship swabs or personal effects to make identifications."[69] In fact, only 35 percent of families had given sufficient samples for identification purposes: the NYPD had not understood what was needed.[70]

This was mainly due to a failure to understand the process, and the necessity, for example, to have DNA not only from a victim's father but from a mother or siblings too. There were instances of personal effects brought in by relatives being muddled up or misidentified. Confusion reigned, as every time a relative contacted the Family Assistance Center or the NYPD a new case number was assigned. All these had to be somehow linked together correctly. The whole thing became, in Shaler's words, "a numbers confetti."[71] The first misidentification through this route was spotted in April 2002: the wrong remains had been returned to a widow in November 2001, and the mistake was not discovered until five months later.[72]

Mistakes did not end with problems in the collection of DNA antemortem samples by the NYPD. Alongside these challenges were the initial unpreparedness for such a huge investigation, institutional infighting, infighting among the families, and cases of fraud (both among "victims" and among OCME officials) and misidentification.[73] The chief challenge, however, was the appalling condition of the remains that were to be identified, along with the policy decision by the mayor of New York that an attempt should be made to identify all the victims. A number of private DNA laboratories were recruited to assist with the identification process, and new software was designed and developed to enable matching of samples from families with profiles from victims. In October a Kinship and Data Analysis Panel was set up to oversee and advise on the whole process. The latter was a panel of scientific experts assembled by the National Institute of Justice to review, discuss, and advise on the available systems; the panel was responsible for the final report produced in 2006.[74] The software developed in Bosnia by the International Commission on Missing Persons had not been designed to deal with the problems being experienced in New York; something that could handle multiple comparisons was necessary.[75] A new accepted statistical standard for making an identification needed to be developed, as most of the degraded World Trade Center DNA did not yield enough information for the standard matching protocols.

While identification is possible with ease under well-established probabilities where a complete antemortem DNA sample from an individual is compared with a full profile obtained from a set of remains, such was rarely the case in New York. Degradation of DNA from remains meant that only an incomplete profile was obtainable, a profile containing only some of the relevant information. Agreement had to be reached as to what would be regarded as constituting a match in such a case. Commingling of remains was commonplace—the nature of what had happened on September 11 meant that it was often the case that part of one person's body might be imbedded in the flesh of another person. Isolated teeth were often found within the remains of other victims, but flesh and bone were commingled too: in one case, for example, "an isolated finger, together with an amputated hand wearing a metal ring on one finger, had become embedded in the chest" of another individual.[76] This difficulty meant that in the end it was largely DNA from bone that had to be analyzed, drawing on methods developed by forensic scientists working on mass graves in Bosnia, and extensive retesting of earlier results was carried out.[77] And in addition to problems of degradation and commingling, the tragedy was not "closed" but "open": the list of victims was unknown. One year after the events, the Kinship and Data Analysis Panel recommended that the population could by then be considered closed—with the number of missing persons put at 2,802. This meant that the statistical calculations of probabilities used in determining the threshold for a match or an identification could be revised.[78]

Two years after the collapse of the towers the Kinship and Data Analysis Panel recommended that "completion of ongoing work with current technologies be viewed as a stopping point in the identification process."[79] It recognized that existing technologies had reached their limit, and that some of the victims would not be identified. Work continued for a while, but an announcement of the end of the process was made on February 23, 2005, with 1,161 victims unidentified.[80] By then identifications had slowed. The new techniques so painstakingly developed had not been as successful as had been hoped, only adding a small number of new identifications to the total.[81] However, identifications continue to be made: in September 2007 a Qantas Airlines employee who was on the first plane to hit the World Trade Center was identified from bone fragments that were part of the original recovery.[82] And remains continue to be recovered from the site: in 2006 remains were discovered in two locations—on the roof of the Deutsche Bank building and in two manholes—and in 2008 more remains were recovered under a road that had been paved after the collapse.[83] In April 2010 a three-month renewed examination of remains from parts of the site made accessible by new construction work was announced; when the search ended "72 human remains" had been found, according to officials.[84]

Grieving the Body

The relatives of the missing grieved in two ways. First, and obviously enough, they mourned the loss of a member of their family—a sudden, totally unexpected loss. Shock, incomprehension, and disbelief—that the person who was there this morning is no longer here. The suddenness of such a death is always bewildering. But the relatives of the missing had a second grief, a grief that did not dawn immediately but crept up on them gradually, as the days drew out into weeks and months: they might have to grieve the loss of their relative's body. They had to face a second loss. Logically, rationally, the corpse is an inanimate object. It has no feeling, no awareness of the dignity or otherwise with which it is treated. When one views the body of a relative, what is most striking is that the *person* is no longer there—there is a clear sense of absence. The body is not alive. It is not living. It is a dead body. And yet our cultures tell us otherwise: the body may not be alive, but it is grievable.[85] If there is no body, its loss is felt. In whatever form our beliefs and customs suggest, we pay our respects to the remains.

Shiya Ribowsky of New York's OCME gives us an intensely sensitive record of his interviews with family members during the identification process.[86] Ribowsky was familiar with meeting family members of New York's everyday victims of crime, but the meetings with WTC families were different. There were two types of interview—depending on whether remains had been identified or not. If they had not been identified, the interview was *easier,* from Ribowsky's point of view—though he stresses, not *easy.* Occasionally the OCME staff had to deal with anger at the lack of progress, or unrealistic expectations as to the simplicity of DNA identification.

If remains had been found and positively identified, the encounter was different. Some people maintained the belief and the hope that the missing person would be found alive. Even in 2005, after remains were found, a relative told a reporter: "Well, I guess that's it, I guess he's not running around New Jersey somewhere with amnesia. I guess he really is dead."[87] More common was a feeling of release. As Ribowsky recounts,

> A great many family members, after receiving notification that their loved ones had been found, sagged with relief, because now at least they knew. . . . Families yearned for positive identification, if only so that they could have certainty about the death and something to bury. As one firefighter's widow expressed it to a reporter, in a sentiment I heard in a thousand variations from grieving relatives, "If he's not laid to rest, it's like he never was. I want something that marks that he was alive. It makes him real. It says he was."[88]

This very moving comment brings home the way in which the missing and the disappeared are different from the dead. When someone goes missing, it seems almost as if their whole existence had been a dream, as if the person missing them just imagined that they had a husband, a son, a sister, a brother. To vanish without trace seems inconceivable, and yet of course it is very easy, and many people do every year.[89]

Relatives of those missing scoured photographs taken on September 11 for evidence of those they knew. David Friend tells the story of a couple who

found what they are sure is an image of their son, Luke, in a photograph of
people gathered on windowsills of the Trade Center upper floors before the
buildings collapsed.[90] They came across the digital image on the Internet
several months afterward, a picture taken by Jeff Christensen for Reuters:

> It shows some three dozen World Trade Center tenants, having smashed
> through the glass, standing clustered on windowsills at the highest levels
> of the north side of the north tower. Most are standing and seem to be
> straining for air. Some have collapsed, possibly dragged to the windows.
> Others appear to be propped up by their colleagues. A thin ribbon of
> smoke, blown sideways by the wind, rings the building like a lasso.[91]

Luke's parents calculated from other photographs that these figures were
on the 103rd floor, where Luke worked, and are convinced that one of the
figures is their son. Friend asks another woman, Jean Coleman, who lost
two sons that day and is positive that she can see both of them in this same
image, why she is so set on contacting Christensen three years afterward to
get originals of the picture. Her response was as follows:

> Who knew what [we] were looking for? I guess for me it was impor-
> tant to have a sense that they didn't go into oblivion, that the essence
> of the person you knew was somehow intact. So many people died and
> disappeared. That's truly awful. From my point of view, I *wanted* them
> not to have been nameless and faceless.[92]

This was difficult for the relatives. Geraldine Davie lost her daughter Amy
O'Doherty who worked on the 104th floor of Tower 1. As she recounts,
four years after the events she was still trying to put together a picture of
her daughter's life from accounts of her friends and photographs they sent
her. She was trying to put together a picture of her life, but at the same time,
she says:

> I am also trying to put her back together again. I have a lot of remains.
> I got the first call in December 2001, another call a year later. We had
> buried the first group of remains. Then two weeks ago they identified
> her left foot. It's horribly difficult. In one sense they're trying to piece
> her together—the medical examiner—and I am too. Eventually, some
> time this year, we'll put her all together in Virginia, reinter her, so that
> she's not all scattered around this earth.[93]

When remains were positively identified, and the families were interviewed, they were full of questions: "Did my loved one suffer? Was my loved
one among the jumpers? Was my loved one burned to death?"[94] Ribowsky

at the OCME answered these questions as best he could. For the most part death would have been instantaneous—people were killed the instant the floor above came down on them. The towers fell in six to nine seconds, so that each floor crashed on the next in a microsecond. In most cases there was no evidence of vital response to trauma—the body reacting to injury—so it was possible to conclude that the injuries occurred at the time of death: "The vast majority of victims were not injured severely or even at all until the buildings fell down."[95] However, it was impossible to know whether someone was among the jumpers, or whether a particular person had burned to death, since all the remains were subjected to fires in the burning buildings after their collapse.

Something that upset many of the family members, with Ribowsky at the OCME sharing their dismay, was the setting up of a second site for the examination of remains at a recently closed rubbish tip on Staten Island, which goes by the name of Fresh Kills. Some 1.7 million tons of debris was taken to Fresh Kills to be sifted for human remains. A total of 2,411 remains were recovered, of which 1,228 have been identified as belonging to 648 individuals.[96] Ribowsky tells us:

> I was not at the meetings that led to Mayor Rudolph Giuliani's decision to have the rubble from Ground Zero loaded onto trucks, then onto barges, taken across the bay, and finally spread out and sifted through on a garbage dump. It was part of the city's great and noble effort to retrieve every possible bit of human remains, but... the location could not have been more ill-chosen. The name of the site alone should have made any responsible public official shudder.[97]

This decision remains controversial and still leads to emotionally charged exchanges between family members, furious that their relations' remains have been consigned to a rubbish dump, and city officials attempting to justify the policy. There is concern that although the debris was sifted, there will inevitably still be human remains that have not been separated from the rest of the debris, which in the end was leveled out and spread over the forty-acre site. To add insult to injury, some of the debris was used for road fill. There are plans to erect a memorial at Fresh Kills. One of the leaders of the protests, Diane Horning, a Catholic whose son died in the North Tower, is "enraged" by suggestions that the site will be a symbolic cemetery: "Only if my son is 'symbolically' dead... but if he is really dead then I really want him buried."[98]

The unidentified fragments that made their way to the OCME in Manhattan are stored there, ready for future testing, and eventual "burial" in the

Ground Zero memorial. The area, between East Twenty-Ninth and East Thirtieth Street, along Franklin D. Roosevelt Drive, became known as "Memorial Park." The mayor's office renovated the area in 2006 in an attempt to give families who didn't have anything to bury "their mausoleum, their cemetery, their sacred space."[99]

The OCME continues to work on recovery and identification. In a February 2009 press release, figures were given for the operation so far.[100] A total of 1,773 "potential human remains" had been recovered in the Phase II search of the immediate Ground Zero area, which began in January 2006. New methods were used for testing these and for retesting 6,318 bone samples from the original recovery effort. There were 23 new victim identifications as a result. DNA testing continues on 5,394 samples. Of the 2,752 people reported missing, 1,126 remain unidentified, their death certified only by judicial decree.

Several times during the account of his work as a medicolegal investigator before and during the 9/11 events, Ribowsky talks about the need to distance himself from the traumatic impact on families he was dealing with—and yet the impossibility of doing so. Reflecting on his interviews with the World Trade Center families, he says:

> Today, though, recalling the family suffering those interviews entailed, I feel the weight of emotion more heavily than perhaps I did then, perhaps because I no longer have to struggle to preserve myself for the work of seeing the next family, and the next, and the next. . . . Recalling those interviews and their extreme emotionality now, I move slowly, as though under a great weight, and each step feels enormously difficult to take.[101]

Ribowsky tells us that the total cost of the identifications at OCME was $80 million,[102] which by my calculation is about $80,000 per person identified. Of course, the process included the development of new methods of organization, DNA techniques, and computer software that will be invaluable in future work. But those engaged in the identification process were able to assure the families that their efforts would not be impeded by lack of funds. A clue to why the cost was felt to be justified lies in Ribowsky's own reflection that what engaged him in the whole process was the job of creating order out of chaos. When the aircraft flew into the Trade Center towers people were indiscriminately slaughtered and their bodies turned to fragments. The work of identification, carried out with the highest regard for the feelings and needs of the families, was a way of reconstructing order out of chaos that was far more significant to my eyes than any rebuilding at Ground Zero. Each missing person was unique, irreplaceable. Identification restored them to the family and social relations within which they had had their being.

Amidst the confetti of numbers, what happens to the person who is missing? Where is the *who* that each was? Is it lost in the objectification of biological data: DNA sequence, toothbrush, hairbrush, buccal swab? Perhaps, as Jasmina Husanović argues, the data are part of a biopolitical form of governance.[103] But as far as the families of the missing are concerned, these objects are of huge, and emotional, significance. They are not just "objects." It is not any old bone that is sought, but the bone that was once part of the flesh and blood of the being they call husband, son, brother, wife, daughter, sister. These objects, these "remains," are saturated with meaning. Objects are not just "objects" in this context, numbers not just numbers, bar codes not just part of a mechanism of control, any more than people are just members of a population to be administered.

The attempt to identify the missing after the collapse of the World Trade Center can be seen in part as an attempt to overcome death, to assert human control, to reinstate order. But it is also a recognition of the significance of the person-as-such, and the need for those searching to be able to retrieve at least some remains, however small. Ribowsky tells us how one family received the remains of their relative, James Cartier: "When at last we identified some of James' remains, two of his brothers showed up to claim him. Michael Cartier donned a pair of gloves and held and cradled his brother's remains. It was as touching a scene as I've ever witnessed."[104] It seems that the processes of recovery and restitution were profoundly ambiguous. They were both a restoration of order and certainty, a rebuilding of what had been destroyed, and, at the same time, a recognition that that order could never be reconstituted. In one sense the search for the missing after 9/11 is similar to the search we examine in chapter 6, the search for those missing in action. In Vietnam, for example, disproportionate amounts of money and effort are expended in an attempt to show that "heroes" will not be abandoned, that the lost will always be brought home and honored for their "sacrifice." On the other hand, the families and those working with and for them were responding to a need to reclaim those who had been wiped out, whose existence as persons had been disregarded by those who killed them—a need to reassert the importance of the person-as-such.

CHAPTER 6

Missing in Action

> By all means have memorials. Make them out of
> Government stone if you like. Make them uniform.
> But you have no right to employ, in making those
> memorials, the bodies of other people's relatives.
>
> —Viscount Wolmer, House of Commons Debate,
> 4 May 1920

In July 2010 a project to identify and reinter British and Australian soldiers missing in action in the First World War culminated in the ceremonial burial of the final unknown soldier at a newly constructed Commonwealth War Graves Commission cemetery at Fromelles in northern France. This chapter opens with the story of this project. In this account, we find in microcosm many of the questions that arise in relation to missing military personnel, questions that have been raised in the aftermath of many conflicts: To whom do the bodies of the missing in action belong?[1] Who should decide how they are to be buried and commemorated? To what lengths should attempts to exhume and identify the missing in action go? Who is entitled to set limits on these attempts?

These questions arise at least in part because the missing in action are not quite the same as other missing persons. A debate arises around repatriation of the remains of those killed in action because of the assumption of ownership of bodies by the military; Michael Sledge notes that the term "repatriation" implies that "the desired object is subject to another's control and must be 'freed' in order to be returned."[2] We could say that servicemen and servicewomen belong to the nation-state. They have been taken out of the everyday realm of civilian life. They serve the nation: they kill and die for it. They must follow orders; they cannot quit their posts. They have no views as individuals but exist only as part of the hierarchy, obedient ultimately to political leaderships. They remind us of Giorgio Agamben's bare life or *homo sacer:* they are life that can kill and be killed without it being seen as homicide; they are life that has no political voice.[3] However, for Agamben, *homo sacer* is also life that cannot be sacrificed. Narratives of heroism and sacrifice in the aftermath of war underscore the strange position of military personnel, especially civilian conscripts: they have no choice but to die, yet their deaths are scripted as sacrifice.

Like the relatives of other missing, most families of the missing in action want to know what has happened and want to find and mourn a body. Though ambivalent in relation to missing civilians, military authorities seem ready, at least nowadays, to assume responsibility for locating and identifying their own missing personnel. Perhaps this is because, for the military, these missing complicate the account of military action, the count of the dead, and must be accounted for if only to ensure their absence is not desertion. In this distribution of the sensible, the count must be complete: there must be nothing missing, no void.[4] For the relatives, on the other hand, the missing in action must count *as persons:* They must be treated as equal speaking beings (citizens), not as beings with no voice (soldiers). They must be returned to civilian status.

What relatives demand is the removal of combatants from production as *homo sacer,* "sacred life," life that can be killed without homicide, and their return, or the return of their remains, to the everyday life of the family and the home. A return from the realm of the sacred to that of the profane, or what Agamben calls profanation.[5] Luc Capdevila and Daniele Voldman have another term for this process: "demobilisation." For them it was the desire of veterans and relatives "to demobilise the dead, which was as crucial to them as the demobilisation of the living," that led them to demand the repatriation of bodies and their return to families for burial and commemoration.[6]

Capdevila and Voldman describe how civilian practices of burial replaced those of the military during the twentieth century, in what we could see as the playing out of profanation or the challenge to the police order of the military.[7] In France during the First World War, though not without "bitter negotiations between society at large and the civilian and military authorities," there was a move to the treatment of military casualties according to civilian traditions—individual burial in a coffin of identified remains—and a recognition of the right of families to seek repatriation of bodies.[8] At the start of the conflict the military hierarchy was working on the assumption that communal graves would be used. However, the great majority of combatants—who were after all only civilians in uniform—were not prepared to adopt military practices.... Whenever they could do so, soldiers buried their comrades in individual graves and informed their relatives by letter...as to the place and circumstances of a son's death or the disappearance of a husband.[9]

Such "civilian" practices posed organizational problems for the military, but nevertheless they were officially accepted in France by 1915, and indeed implemented throughout the conflict.[10] The repatriation of bodies was eventually accepted too. In North America it was during the American Civil War that it first became the practice to account for missing soldiers. Drew Gilpin Faust sees this as a response to pressure from relatives as well as from the soldiers themselves, who took to wearing forms of identification.[11] The United States also repatriated remains from the First World War onward if families requested it, though not until after the cessation of hostilities. The adoption of this policy had been controversial in the United States, as in France. The U.S. Army went further, instituting a policy of "concurrent return"—return during hostilities—from the Korean War in December 1950 onward.[12] The question of who should decide how remains of the missing are to be buried and commemorated—the authorities, acting in the name of the Empire (or now the Commonwealth), or the families—was also the subject of controversy in the United Kingdom, and, as we shall see, there, in contrast to France and the United States, the views of the military and the political authorities prevailed. Repatriation was prohibited, and burial in official cemeteries with standardized headstones mandatory.

It has not always been the case that missing military personnel are traced and identified at the time, never mind long after the event as at Fromelles or in Vietnam, and the extent to which identification processes are pursued still varies.[13] If someone is missing in action, strong circumstantial evidence will often make it quite clear that there is a firm basis for the presumption of death. Yet most contemporary militaries in Europe and the United States go to considerable lengths to verify that evidence—and to assure themselves that there is no possibility of desertion. Usually presumption of death is made in the absence of identifiable remains. But in some cases, extraordinary efforts are made, and other personnel put at risk either physically or emotionally through their work with the decomposed bodies of their comrades, to ensure identification and sometimes repatriation of remains. Where official agencies do not act, there are voluntary organizations dedicated to the search.[14]

For Michael Sledge the question of ownership applies "not only to physical remains but also to information about the dead and their memory."[15] Later in this chapter, I shall look at how gathering information about the missing, and evidence of death, led to a contest of strength between the Red Cross and military and governmental authorities over who had the rights to that information, and who was entitled to convey it to the next of kin. The Red Cross provided useful resources to help with interviewing witnesses but their staff members were expected to hand over information they gleaned to military authorities. A tension exists between official verification, with its standardized form of notification, and the more personalized approach adopted by the Red Cross—a tension we also observed in chapter 3 in relation to the work of tracing civilians. However, while with civilian missing the military had a take-it-or-leave-it approach, with missing service personnel there is no doubt as to the military's claim to ownership.

Mass Graves at Fromelles

On July 19, 2010, the ninety-fourth anniversary of the battle of Fromelles in northern France, over five thousand people gathered to witness the burial of an unknown soldier at Pheasant Wood, the first new military cemetery to be built by the Commonwealth War Graves Commission since the 1960s.[16] The ceremony was attended by a full slate of dignitaries from the three countries involved, and wreaths were laid by the Prince of Wales; the Duke of Kent, president of the Commonwealth War Graves Commission; Quentin Bryce, governor-general of Australia; and Hubert Falco, French minister of state for defense and veterans. In his speech, the Duke of Kent noted: "It is right and fitting that these men—comrades, Allies and even two brothers—lie side by side in this beautiful cemetery. . . . They are lost no longer, and are here at last at peace."[17] However, like many stories of the missing, the recovery, identification, and reinterment of the soldiers buried at Pheasant Wood is not the straightforward account of unprompted official action that it appears, but one of controversy and struggle, and one in which the actions of particular unaffiliated individuals played a crucial part.

The search began with the work of Australian schoolteacher and so-called amateur historian Lambis Englezos.[18] He became convinced that there were graves of those who died at Fromelles—many of them Australians—that had not been discovered by Graves Concentration Units immediately after the war. His research located aerial reconnaissance photographs taken before and after the battle that showed that pits—possibly burial pits—had been dug behind the German lines just after the fighting. He presented his work to the Australian military, but it remained unconvinced, and it was not until documentary evidence came to light that the military could be persuaded to take the investigation any further. A chance meeting between Englezos and military historian Peter Barton, who was on a lecture tour in Australia, led to the location of that further evidence: a document in the Bavarian military archive that contained detailed instructions from Col. Julius Ritter von Braun to the troops of his Bavarian Reserve Infantry Regiment 21 regarding the construction of mass graves for the burial of enemy dead at Pheasant Wood.[19] The burial parties were instructed to remove soldiers' identity tags for forwarding to the Red Cross in Geneva, and hence to the families, but on no account to remove other items from the bodies.

At this point the Australian army was finally persuaded to take things further. It commissioned the Glasgow University Archaeological Research Division (GUARD) to carry out a noninvasive survey of the site of the pits. This survey turned up evidence that the graves were there and intact, and confirmation in the form of two Australian military medals was found by Barton himself.[20] The initial investigation was followed later by a trial dig.[21] After the trial dig, a full excavation was commissioned from Oxford Archaeology, a group with experience of work on mass graves in Bosnia and elsewhere.[22] The excavation uncovered the remains of 250 soldiers. These bodies, and artifacts found alongside them, were removed for careful examination and DNA sampling in an attempt to establish identity in as many cases as possible, before reburial in the new cemetery. The recovery followed protocols of the type that are standard in forensic identification: careful prevention of contamination by placing an exclusion zone around the excavation; a strong "chain of custody" system in which remains are kept together and signed for as they travel from grave to mortuary; and detailed photography and recording.[23] The information relating to identification was examined by a Data Analysis Team and was collated with DNA samples collected from surviving relatives who had come forward, with recommendations submitted for scrutiny by identification panels. The process remains open until 2014, and further panels will be held. Relatives who have not yet provided samples are invited to come forward.

In the course of his work to compile lists of the missing in action that could help identify the soldiers of Pheasant Wood, Barton came across what he saw as a hugely significant archive in a basement at the Red Cross Museum in Geneva: the ICRC First World War index card archive. He was amazed that its existence was not widely known. The records contain details of servicemen captured, killed, or buried during the First World War—details passed on to the Red Cross by combatants during the conflict and carefully collated and recorded before being sent on to the families. Particulars include such information as the exact location of field burials and the identities of those interred—even with home addresses and next of kin. The Red Cross is digitizing these records, which apparently have lain virtually untouched for almost a hundred years.[24] In a strange reversal of what might be expected, the discovery of a grave site had led to the location of paper documentation of burials—and potentially, back again to the location of many more mass graves.

The objectives of the Fromelles project were officially described as "the dignified recovery of the remains of those soldiers who have lain in the field at Pheasant Wood for the last 93 years so as to provide them the same courtesies that were extended to their colleagues when the battlefields were cleared at the end of the War—an individual burial with military honours and their name on their headstone whenever possible."[25] The Commonwealth War Graves Commission notes that "165,000 Commonwealth soldiers killed on the Western Front during the First World War are still missing."[26] In the battle of Fromelles, described by Peter Barton as "one of the most appalling military blunders of the First World War," it is thought that some 1,660 men disappeared. According to Barton another thirty or so mass graves exist in the area.[27] The Australian-based Fromelles Discussion Group pushes for the exhumation and attempted identification of *all* the missing from Fromelles, not just those in the Pheasant Wood burial pits.[28] But, according to the Commonwealth War Graves Commission, "UK and Australian Governments do not actively search for the remains of those missing in action"; if bodies are found, attempts are made to identify them.[29] The limit set by these governments to their responsibilities is clear—bodies become their concern only once found—and it seems any further identification will rely on individuals like Lambis Englezos and Peter Barton coming up with evidence of the existence of new graves and forcing action to recover and identify those buried in them. Bodies already located and interred as "unknown" in other war cemeteries will not, it seems, be exhumed for identification.

A documentary broadcast to coincide with the ceremony at Fromelles takes us through the background to the opening of the new cemetery. It is scripted like a murder thriller:

> The bodies of over 900,000 First World War soldiers were never found or identified. In an astonishing discovery, 250 of these men were discovered in 6 un-marked mass graves in Fromelles, a tiny village in Northern France. The search is on to reveal these men's identities and give them the military burial that they never had when they fell 90 years ago.[30]

Despite this framing, the program does more than solve the mystery. Surviving relatives of three of the missing soldiers are interviewed. There is no
mistaking the depth of emotion as they give accounts of how their families
reacted to the news—or lack of news—after the battle, and express their desire
to see the missing relative identified and at least metaphorically brought home.
The interviews bring out how the impact of these deaths reverberated down
the generations, and the curiosity the families felt even now to find out not
only what had happened to the missing soldier, but what had been the fate of
others involved in the story. To see their relatives identified and buried with
honor was only one part of the puzzle presented by the disappearances. For
one woman, the death of her grandfather had led to hardship for her mother,
who was separated from her siblings when her father failed to return and
her mother could not make ends meet. This woman's uncle could remember
clearly the father's departure for the front—for her it would be "a dream come
true" if he were to be identified, finally. Another woman wanted to know what
had happened to the missing soldier's fiancée, and was pleased to find out that
she had married and had named one of her sons after her lost love.[31]

Of course nearly a hundred years after the event, families had found ways
to carry on—and one wonders whether the impact of the new investigations was entirely positive, especially when, in the end, many of the dead of
Fromelles were not identified, despite hopes being raised.[32] Comparatively
few families of the soldiers came forward, so that there were many cases
where perfectly good DNA profiles were obtained from remains, but no
contemporary samples from relatives were available for matching. For the
authorities, the whole exercise must have been a costly one, but one that they
were more or less compelled to undertake, given the implicit promise that
founded organizations such as the Commonwealth War Graves Commission: the promise that all the dead would be treated the same. The commission's principles are the following:

Each of the dead should be commemorated by name on the headstone
    or memorial
Headstones and memorials should be permanent
Headstones should be uniform
There should be no distinction made on account of military or civil
    rank, race or creed.[33]

The commission is responsible for more than 935,000 named graves and
almost 212,000 graves of unnamed individuals; moreover, "the names of
almost 760,000 people can be found on memorials to the missing."[34]

The Commonwealth War Graves Commission, formerly the Imperial War Graves Commission, was not conceived by the government, but rather founded by one individual, Fabian Ware. At the beginning of the First World War, in the United Kingdom, as in France,

> the very thought that every soldier who died serving his country should be commemorated at public expense had received no serious attention from any army or government. Indeed, the immense task of satisfying a growing sentiment among the people of the Empire by caring for the unprecedented number of graves of an army that was, for the first time, a citizen army, was quite unforeseen.[35]

In 1914, Fabian Ware was working as a volunteer with a Red Cross Mobile Unit, and as part of his work he instructed his men to record where the dead were buried. The Red Cross had a mission to collect information they could convey to next of kin about the dead and missing in action. But Ware took this further, insisting on the importance of this work and the need for his unit to be granted access to battlefields to complete the task. By 1915 his unit became the Graves Registration Commission, the recognized body responsible for finding, recording, and marking the location of graves and, eventually, acquiring land for military cemeteries in France.

The commission's work did not meet with universal approval at the time. There were those who wanted the bodies returned home to the United Kingdom for burial, and indeed, some of those who could afford it were quietly repatriating the remains of their fallen. Ware's conviction was that officers and men shared a camaraderie in the trenches, where divisions of rank and class had begun to break down, and that officers would wish to remain buried alongside their men. When the Graves Registration Commission became the Directorate of Graves Registration and Enquiries and, by 1917, the Imperial War Graves Commission, instituted under Royal Charter, the "radical departure from earlier tradition, when officers had been buried in individual graves and men in mass graves...became the cornerstone of the Commission's philosophy," and it was determined that no distinction of rank should be made in the erection of memorials.[36]

The demand for the repatriation of remains continued, however, despite the success of the commission's work in general. Added to this was an insistence that relatives should be able to choose the form of headstone, rather than merely being allowed to add a few words to a standard "government stone." The discontent was expressed in a debate in the House of Commons on May 4, 1920.[37] The commission was proposing a uniform headstone to be used for each grave, thus insisting on equality for all, without distinction of rank. In the debate, Viscount Wolmer retorted: "They claim equality for all. That is a claim which we...endorse to the full. We demand equality for all. Uniformity is not and never can be equality....There is an absolute distinction between uniformity and equality, and, indeed, an antagonism between them, which the War Graves Commission almost entirely miss."[38] Uniformity meant conformity with military order; equality meant the demand for equal treatment of persons-as-such—persons with their own views and wishes. Another key argument put forward by those in favor of the plan was that the commission's cemeteries, with their massed ranks of uniform headstones spread across Europe, and indeed the world, would form a magnificent monument to the Great War. Some had called it a memorial to freedom. Wolmer retorted: "What freedom is it if you will not even allow the dead bodies of people's relatives to be cared for and looked after in the way they like? It is a memorial, not to freedom, but to rigid militarism; not in intention, but in effect."[39]

In the end Wolmer's arguments failed; members deplored the way a sensitive topic had become a source of controversy. Winston Churchill, as secretary of state for war and air, closed the debate with a reminder that the scale of the operation required standardization if it were to be completed in a reasonable time, and if it were to ensure permanence and durability. As he saw it, the benefit would be that "even if our language, our institutions, and our Empire all have faded from the memory of man, these great stones will still preserve the memory of a common purpose pursued by a great nation in the remote past."[40] The fact that "this may bring a measure of comfort and consolation to many of those who have lost their dear ones" seemed a secondary concern, and Churchill called on those who disagreed with what was planned to regard themselves as called upon to "make only one further sacrifice amongst the many great ones they have made already."[41] To sacrifice the bodies of their sons as well as their lives, presumably.

By the time of the reburial of the Fromelles soldiers, these controversies had all but been forgotten. The commission's war cemeteries had become part of the landscape, and the construction of the new cemetery on the basis of existing tradition was not questioned. However, some relatives remained unhappy with the emphasis on identification and individual commemoration. One relative, Alastair Matheson, reflected: "The notion that it can somehow make things right by finding the remains of the dead is not true....While finding people is great, and it's important that we should do it, the greater truth is the truth of people lost. Even when we find a few, the loss is the thing that is more important to remember."[42]

The attempt at certainty, at identification, can be seen as an attempt to conceal loss, loss that nevertheless remains, even when the remains of those lost are found. As an insistence on the person-as-such, as something that belongs not to a group of comrades at the front, as the Commonwealth War Graves Commission wanted to insist, nor to the nation, whatever that might be, but to a place and people—home and family. And as a memory, not as a collection of bones.

Tracing Military Personnel

At the beginning of the Second World War, the British Red Cross Society, operating jointly with the Order of St. John throughout the war, worked in close collaboration with the British government and the military service departments in tracing missing military personnel. It had been decided that "the proposed joint body," the War Organisation of the Order of St. John and the Red Cross, "would again be entrusted with the duty of tracing the wounded and the missing," as it had been during the First World War.[43] The writers of the *Official Record of the Humanitarian Services of the War Organisation of the British Red Cross Society and Order of St. John of Jerusalem* recognized the contradictions inherent here, which were to give rise before long to some serious disagreements, misunderstandings, and disputes. The British Red Cross saw itself as trying to satisfy at one and the same time the needs of the service departments and those of the relatives of the missing service personnel: "To meet the wishes of all parties was at times not easy—indeed upon occasions it was impossible, for they were irreconcilable. To anxious relatives, news about a missing man or a dangerously ill patient was a personal matter. To Service Departments, the established procedures of notification could not be disregarded."[44] It was the relatives of the missing who, after all, provided the voluntary contributions that funded the Red Cross. But the service departments insisted that official notification to families that a person was presumed dead remain their prerogative, and they attempted to limit the information the Red Cross could provide to what the services considered appropriate.[45] And indeed they tried to prevent communication by anyone else too. The Red Cross wrote to one of its senior volunteers: "The War Office does not encourage the communication by casualties to the relatives [of the missing] in case the information is not accurate."[46] Information about the missing in action belonged to the military authorities, and they claimed the right to hand it out or not as they saw fit.

The British Red Cross remained an officially recognized partner during the huge increase in the wounded and missing following the fall of France in the summer of 1940, but just before the end of 1941 the policy of the War Office (but not the Admiralty or the Navy) changed. The British Red

Cross Society was excluded, and the War Office from then on approached the International Committee of the Red Cross (ICRC) in Geneva and the protecting power for information on prisoners of war, and service personnel for eyewitness reports, directly. To the British Red Cross this appeared as a unilateral action on the part of the War Office.[47] The War Office spokesman claimed in the House of Commons that responsibility for tracing its missing had always rested with the War Office, not the British Red Cross Society: "The War Office is and always has been responsible for this service. While it is very grateful to the British Red Cross Society for such additional help as it is able to give, the War Office has in no way farmed out its responsibility to any outside organisation."[48] According to the official British Red Cross history, controversy over who was or should be responsible continued for some months, with lengthy correspondence and questions in the House of Commons, culminating in a letter from the Army Council in June 1942 setting out that "enquiries which the Wounded and Missing Department [of the Red Cross] had been making of the International Red Cross Committee on behalf of the War Office were no longer necessary, as the notification of names [of prisoners of war] by the German and Italian Governments had become regularly organised."[49]

The position of the British Red Cross on this controversy is elaborated more forcefully in the confidential supplement to the official history, published in a limited edition of fifty copies.[50] The War Organisation of the Red Cross and St. John was an independent organization funded by public contributions. Though "recognised by Government," it was "not under Government direction," and its association with the International Red Cross gave it "a status and channels of communication" not open to government departments.[51] In 1939 it had in hand only a balance of £2000, and during the First World War expenditure had totaled £17 million. An appeal at the start of the Second World War produced an even more generous response from the public than before, and these funds enabled the organization to meet the costs of all it was required to do. Funds were sought for "relief... for the sick and wounded of the Fighting Forces, prisoners of war interned in enemy and neutral countries, and civilians injured or sick as a result of enemy action."[52] As a voluntary organization the British Red Cross Society was part of the extensive network of national Red Cross Societies, which together with the ICRC made up the International Red Cross movement. Established by Henri Dunant after the battle of Solferino in 1859 as a philanthropic organization to assist victims of war, particularly wounded soldiers, the ICRC's aim was not to contest violent conflict but to ameliorate its effects. From the start it relied on contributions and volunteers, and from the start it appealed to "aristocratic ladies" who believed "that rank entailed duty as well as privilege."[53] It appealed to women in general at a time when the areas of work open to them were severely limited, and opportunities for travel and leadership almost nonexistent. Clara Barton, born in 1821, was an influential figure in the development of the American Red Cross: "Between 1881 and 1904...the American Red Cross *was* Clara Barton."[54] Interestingly, she was the first to realize, in the course of her work during the American Civil War (1861–65), that "prisoners returning from captivity...needed news about their families, just as the families were desperate to know what had happened to their sons and husbands."[55] In 1865 Barton established a search service for missing prisoners of war, and later any missing men, which recorded inquiries, published lists, and interviewed returning veterans. The military authorities had kept no record of the dead or wounded. Some 20,000 names were included in Barton's lists.[56]

Given its status as a voluntary philanthropic organization, the British Red Cross Society acted on behalf of the public, not the government, and it did not take kindly to Maj. Gen. Alfred Knox's accusation in the House of Commons on February 10, 1942, that it was "meddling" in the work of the War Office.[57] An apology was demanded. As far as the Red Cross was concerned, it had a mandate to act on behalf of its individual donors—and in particular on behalf of the relatives and friends of the missing. If anything, it was the government that was at fault, for its lack of action and inefficiency—and its reluctance, or inability, to expedite communications with relatives. It reached the point where the Red Cross contemplated closing down its activities if it were unable to continue to give the public the information it expected.

The separation of the activities of the War Office Casualty Branch and the Red Cross Wounded and Missing Department in 1942 was in large part due to disagreement as to priorities, though each perceived the other as in some way inefficient and badly organized, which contributed to the rift. There were also personality issues, as we shall see later. According to the Casualty Branch, there were "fundamental differences between the Casualty Branch's approach to the Missing problem and that of the B.R.C.S. [which] lay in the latter's tendency to precipitate action and assumption (unchecked by responsibility for the legal, financial and other effects of any incorrect official recording of deaths that had always to be borne in mind by the Casualty Branch) and their freedom to concentrate on the proportion of 'missing' cases in which they were at any time in contact with the relatives."[58] From the Casualty Branch's point of view, the main problems were the Red Cross's tendency to send inquiries off to Geneva as soon as they were received rather than waiting "for the names of the residue of the true Missing to emerge"; to accept "much less than complete reconciliation of detail in identifying missing personnel"; and to take as useful prisoner of war lists issued by the Germans, which tended to prove inaccurate.[59]

It was widely acknowledged that the move of the Casualty Branch from London to Liverpool had not helped its operations, with the new staff being untrained and robust procedures lacking. The account of the history of the Casualty Branch shows that it was sensitive to its relations with other organizations, including the Red Cross, and with members of the public, as well as to the often conflicting views of service personnel. Some of the wounded did not want any information at all passed on to their relatives, for example, and others wanted to control what was said themselves. The notification procedures of the Casualty Branch bypassed these views, and it did pass on information.[60]

The Casualty Branch's exhaustive methods of confirming the circumstances before official presumption of death could be arrived at meant that it would be likely to flounder amidst a plethora of written reports from eyewitnesses. It seems to have been more concerned sometimes about whether the accounts of all witnesses tallied exactly, rather than with what the balance of probabilities as to the fate of the person missing was. The sinking of the *Gracie Fields* during the evacuation from Dunkirk took place on May 30, 1940, according to the Admiralty, and a number of the soldiers on board had been reported missing.[61] However, discrepancies were noted between the various reports of those called on to give eyewitness accounts. There were differences as to what date the ship sank, how many bombs had hit the ship (two or three), and whether the ship was towed into harbor after the transfer of those on board to other vessels, which took place over a period of hours, or whether it sank—and whether the dead sank with the ship. Officials assessing the case eventually accepted that the evidence was strong enough to presume the men dead, but then debate ensued as to what the proper date of death should be. "This is a matter of fact and should be established...beyond doubt....It is very undesirable that there should be two dates for a thing like this," wrote one official.[62]

In the case of one of the missing, there is a statement on file by a witness that notes: "I boarded the "Gracie Fields" on 28.5.40, and it was bombed. No. 3513516 Pte. Maile. H. was badly wounded, and C.S.M. White ordered me with Pte. Mc.Dermott to dress his wounds. Pte. Maile died about 10 minutes afterwards, in my presence."[63] Other witnesses reported seeing Private Maile "in agony" and his eyes glaze over. Not satisfied, Officer in Charge, Infantry Records, Casualty Section, Preston, writing on November 15, 1940, notes discrepancies in the account: Maile was listed as a corporal not a private, and it was not known whether Maile's body had gone down with the ship. Further inquiries produced an explanation (Private Maile had asked to return to the rank of private so that he could serve as a driver, and the ship had indeed gone down with all the dead on board), but one wonders what value the extra investigations served. Presumably the intention was to cover the War Office's back so that it couldn't be accused of mistakes.

Hospital Searching

The Red Cross's methods were no less meticulous. Red Cross volunteers and staff did, however, seem to be more engaged and better placed in some cases at least to make accurate and speedy judgments. Yet there were severe problems with the Red Cross service too, as we shall see shortly. A marvelous account of exactly what the work of Red Cross searchers involved in the somewhat drily titled *Official Record of the War Organisation of the Red Cross* reveals some of the demands of what was a far from dry task.[64] The account is taken from the personal report of one searcher—a woman whose name remains missing in the official history, perhaps ironically, but who was in fact Mrs. Hilda M. Pickard-Cambridge.[65] Searchers were allocated to particular hospitals that received the wounded—in France, initially, and, after the evacuation of the British Expeditionary Force, in the United Kingdom. Some nine hundred searchers, all voluntary, were working under the direction of the Wounded and Missing Department of the Red Cross in London by the summer of 1941, organized by counties and hospitals.[66] The searchers were subject to a careful selection process; qualities sought were "tact, sympathy, an ability to obtain from the patients...the information required, and a skill in weighing the value of such information as the patient supplied."[67] The work was confidential. Each searcher visited a particular hospital regularly, armed with indexed lists of the missing by regiment, to interview patients and obtain statements about those reported missing. The searchers were issued "a book of instructions" as to what questions to ask and what information to obtain, and special confidential forms on which that information was to be reported.[68]

The searcher's first task was to ask permission of the nursing sister to visit, and then to obtain the names of patients who had arrived since her last visit. With each man, having established his front, regiment, and battalion, she would explain what she was doing: "I told him that the Red Cross would like his help; that he had come back, and his friends had not, and that it was up to him to help in any way he could."[69] They went through the list of missing in the man's battalion together, marking with a cross all the names he knew. Then, for each name in turn, the searcher would ask the patient:

Whether he was there at the time when the man was missing and, if not, when he saw him last? The date? The place? The names of his officers, the padre, N.C.O.s and other men in his platoon? Whether we held the ground? Whether he saw the missing man wounded? Whether there were any stretcher-bearers there or medical officers? What their names were?[70]

Hilda Pickard-Cambridge noted down all the details, trying to keep up with the great speed with which her informants talked, and at the same time to form a picture for herself of what had happened. She read back the coherent narrative she had produced to her informant, who corrected her as she went along.

If a man had witnessed the death of a comrade himself, a further step was necessary, as set out in a War Office letter of May 29, 1943:

The War Office request that searchers will act on the following suggestions: We are finding these [hospital searching] reports especially helpful, and in some cases we hope to accept the statements as reliable evidence of death and to record death on that evidence alone.

(i) If the witness states he was an eyewitness of death, we should like to know the precise grounds on which he believed the man to be dead (e.g. examination of the body or length of time the subject was observed by the witness after being hit).
(ii) We should like to have the witness's signature to any definite eyewitness report of death ... (on a separate piece of paper, e.g. "I certify ... was killed etc.").[71]

Sometimes of course this process was difficult. The witness may have been badly injured, and so unable to write. Nevertheless, witnesses were often determined to make the effort. Pickard-Cambridge records supporting one man's hand to steady it as he tried to sign a statement: "His hands were both severely wounded. I wanted the sister of the ward to sign for him, but he insisted on doing it himself. I held the pencil, while, with two fingers of his left hand he gave me a quavering little signature."[72]

In her account of her work, Pickard-Cambridge stresses the importance of "infinite patience and concentration," of giving the respondents time to take their minds back and think through all the details, of encouraging them to draw diagrams to make their accounts clearer:

A searcher must always be thinking hard, and trying to get the names of the men who were most likely to have been with the missing man last, also to ask for a description of the man the informant is thinking of. As there are so many men of the same name it is absolutely necessary to make quite sure he is thinking of the right man. He is often able to give a very good description as to height, colouring, his home town, the work he did before the War, his nickname, adding "he was well educated, always carrying books"; "a very good musician, he played the trombone"; "he was good at all sports"; "a scar on his left cheek"; "a tattoo on one of his arms of the Pyramids with a sphinx"; "very jovial". They could always think of something to prove he was the man enquired for.[73]

It is interesting how these reports drew more on *who* the missing person was—as a person—than on *what* his military status or role was.

The album Hilda Pickard-Cambridge put together at the end of the war contains examples of the forms she completed. It is not clear what exactly happened to these reports—which give meticulously detailed accounts of the fate of men who lost their lives during the war, information that would be sought by next of kin—or where the reports are now. According to the system at the time, the confidential report forms were sent through the county officer to the Red Cross headquarters, which forwarded them to the War Office Casualty Branch. We are told that "these reports, *which were never made public,* often formed but one part of the whole information about a man's fate."[74] The Casualty Branch would coordinate all reports it received before arriving at its conclusion and communicating officially with the missing man's next of kin: "Many thousands of BRCS Hospital Searchers' reports relating to 'missing' officers and men were received and filed . . . for consideration with other evidence."[75] The Red Cross experience shows, however, that valuable though an official notification was, people also wanted reports, even hearsay reports, of what had happened to their relatives—*how* they had been killed or captured, or how they were faring in the hospital. But there is no evidence that the reports collected so carefully in the hospitals (and elsewhere) from fellow soldiers ever reached the families.[76] The hospital searchers pieced together the story of what had happened, alongside the physical piecing together of damaged bodies by the medical staff. One of Pickard-Cambridge's reports from the First World War, relating to Private Eric Gauntlett Steele, appears today on an Internet site that collects letters and other records of ordinary Canadian service personnel.[77] It is interesting that in this case the hospital searchers, three of whose reports are included in the online archive, only confirmed the information that was given in a letter from Private Steele's commanding officer to his relatives, written the morning after he was killed in action.

The importance that people attach to letters or other messages from family or friends is brought out in the Red Cross account of its attempts during the war and the period afterward to put people in touch. Not only were family members put in touch with each other, but the Red Cross could help by forwarding messages that mortally wounded soldiers had asked their fellow soldiers to pass on to their families.[78] In the period after the end of the war, as we saw in chapter 3, Red Cross efforts extended to civilians, as well as to the armed forces, but clearly drew on the expertise that had been established earlier, particularly from 1940 onward, in dealing with military casualties or the missing in action.

Despite these considerable successes, the supplement to the *Official Record* reports some fairly severe problems with the hospital searching service, and it seems that the fallout from these was what led to the questions in the House of Commons. Hilda Pickard-Cambridge was clearly an exemplary hospital searcher. Many of those recruited to the task failed miserably. Most did not appear to make visits or conduct interviews; others filled in the forms without including the necessary detail. Only 80 of the 750 searchers appointed by April 1941 filed any reports at all, and of those only 20 percent were correctly completed. A meeting was held at Red Cross headquarters, after which a circular to county committees was issued under the name of Lady Ampthill, chairman of the department, recording the failings of the hospital searching service as it then stood.[79] In July 1941 the chief searcher, a Mr. Lewis, produced a comprehensive account of the factors that he considered had given rise to the failings of the service (under his leadership). One of the chief factors, in his account, was the lack of a director of searching; the last incumbent had left in the autumn of 1940.[80] Following a meeting of the principal officers on July 15, Lady Trenchard was appointed director of the section, and Mr. Lewis resigned as chief searcher. In April 1942 matters took "a surprising turn": Mr. Lewis resurfaced, together with his former assistant at the Red Cross, Mrs. Beadle, in the employment of the War Office Casualty Branch, apparently threatening to set up a rival searching service and to force the one at the Red Cross to close. Lewis seems to have had friends in the House of Commons who were prepared to take up the matter for him in Parliament and cast aspersions on the Red Cross's efficiency. This was not the only internal dispute recorded in the *Confidential Supplement*. A disagreement later arose between Lady Ampthill and Lady Trenchard over the reorganization of the records of the Missing and Wounded Department. Lady Trenchard saw fit to involve the War Office in an attempt to convince the Red Cross of her views, without success. She resigned in August 1943. By then, personal disagreements aside, it had been agreed by the War Office that the Red Cross hospital searching should continue, and in October 1943 searchers were provided with official authorization to visit casualties.[81]

Despite such personality clashes, the women involved in Red Cross work undoubtedly gave great service under challenging conditions. There is an undeniable impression that they enjoyed their work too. Hilda Pickard-Cambridge notes that the hospital searching work was "sad, very sad," but she ends her account by noting: "I have loved my work, and I think the other searchers have loved their work too."[82] This comes across from her writing, for example, in her account of visits to the Royal Victoria Hospital, Netley, Hampshire:

> We were all very sorry when the Americans took over the whole of Netley Hospital and we could no longer go there. I loved the long drives through the country lanes passing many picturesque Hampshire villages. At first I was bewildered by all the twists and turns of the road, but I soon learnt to find my way. The hospital grounds sloped down to the sea where they had their own landing stage. It was such an immense building. The wards were easy to find.[83]

Although perhaps not aristocrats like the first women volunteers with the Red Cross back in the nineteenth century, these women were often led by titled ladies at the head of the departments and sections of the British Red Cross War Organisation—the Dowager Lady Ampthill as chairman of the Wounded, Missing and Relatives Department in June 1940, for example[84]—and they could aspire to honors and decorations after the war; OBEs and CBEs were common. Hilda Pickard-Cambridge carefully pastes into her album letters of congratulation on her OBE from the Dowager Lady Ampthill; Field Marshal Lord Chetwode, chairman of the Red Cross Executive Committee; the Countess of Limerick, deputy chairman; and the Duchess of Northumberland, county president of the Red Cross for Surrey alongside letters from family and friends. She records with pride the visit of the queen to the Surrey Branch, and an invitation to lunch with Lord O'Hagan at the House of Lords. Philanthropy and the obligations and aspirations of rank continued to run alongside one another.

Historical Recoveries

In the aftermath of the Second World War, search parties from the various armies combed the areas over which they had fought in an attempt to locate and identify the remains of those missing in action. The techniques and methods used—and the attitude to the repatriation of remains in particular—varied from army to army. The United States had search and recovery operations that covered battlefields around the world—Europe, Russia, the Middle East, China, Japan, Africa, the Pacific—and involved specially trained units of Grave Registration Service personnel. They carried out "sweeps" combing terrain that had been fought over and examining the landscape closely for signs of graves or unburied remains, and they enlisted the help of local inhabitants to provide information that could be followed up. These operations met with mixed success.[85] In four years of work in Europe, the United States recovered 16,649 remains; a recovery search in the Pacific, lasting more than six months, from June 1948 to March 1949, recovered 109 remains.[86] These sweeps ended in 1950.

As we have seen, it is the development of forensic techniques—DNA analysis in particular—that extends the possibilities of searching for the missing beyond the written records contained in the card indexes and the archives of the Red Cross and the concentration camps to the bones of the disappeared. Some exhumations had been carried out in the immediate aftermath of the war. For example, the routes of the death marches were tracked, witness statements taken, and bodies of those who died along the way exhumed from mass graves and reburied.[87] In April 1945 prisoners were on the move in their thousands, force-marched under guard from concentration camps that were about to be overrun by Allied armies. They took erratic routes, trains they were traveling on were bombed, barns in which they sheltered burned, and many died of exhaustion or were simply shot for failing to keep up. In some cases the corpses that were exhumed could be identified by the concentration camp numbers the prisoners bore, and lists were made. What happened to these records is not clear.

Techniques developed for the exhumation of bodies in the mass graves of more recent conflicts in Europe—in the Balkans in particular—were used in the investigations at Fromelles, as we have seen. These techniques have also begun to be used to identify remains of those killed in massacres in Slovenia after the end of the Second World War. Many of those killed were displaced persons returned to Yugoslavia against their will by the British authorities. The complexities of the history behind their flight have meant that there is still a reluctance to acknowledge what happened on the part of the relatives of those killed, as well as a silence with regard to the involvement of the British, who were supposedly in charge of helping displaced persons, not sending them to their deaths. John Corsellis was one of the British helpers in the displaced persons camps at the time, and he has written many years later of what happened.[88]

At the beginning of May 1945, as the German army was retreating, Slovenian members of the *domobranci,* the Slovenian Home Guard—a military organization of Catholic Slovenes who had been fighting the Communist Partisans in collaboration with the Germans in what was effectively a civil war in Yugoslavia—fled Slovenia over mountain passes into British-occupied Austria. Accompanying them were their families and Catholic civilians. They surrendered to the British forces, giving up their weapons and entering the displaced persons camp at Viktring—a camp with separate military and civilian sections. The British supported the Partisans—led by Tito—contrary to what many Slovenes had expected, and the Yalta agreement, which mandated the return of Soviet citizens to the Soviet zone in Germany also mandated the return of Yugoslavs to Yugoslavia. Despite the fact that the *domobranci* had surrendered in good faith to the British—and thus in theory should have been treated as prisoners of war—the British decided to return them to Yugoslavia, and to Tito's Partisans, and what is more, they decided to do this by deception. The *domobranci* were to be told that they were being moved to a camp in Italy, then locked into trains and taken back to Slovenia, whence they had so recently escaped:

> Our guardsmen slid together the doors of the cattle trucks when they were full and padlocked them. . . . The wagons were old and through the cracks in the boarding the [*domobranci*] could see exactly what was happening. They began hammering on the inside of the wagon walls, shouting imprecations . . . at us, who had betrayed them, lied to them and sent at least the men among them to a certain death. This scene was repeated day after day, twice a day.[89]

During the first of these transports, several people escaped and returned to the camp to tell the others what was happening. Still, out of fidelity, according to Corsellis and Ferrar's account, most of the remaining surrendered soldiers accepted their fate and submitted to the transports. Some escaped, most commonly by donning civilian clothing and joining the other section of the camp. They almost met the same fate. Orders had apparently been given that civilians were to be returned too: "They must be ready at 5am. They'll be transported by trucks to the stations, where trains will await them."[90] At this point the officer in charge of the camp, who had until then apparently been kept in the dark about the true destination of the transports, was told by the Slovenes what had been happening, and protested. In the meantime the British Red Cross assistant commissioner for civilian relief in Austria, John Selby-Bigge, had voiced his disapproval to senior military officers. Selby-Bigge and his colleagues shared the view that "as Red Cross workers, the position was untenable," and in his report to his superiors, which he showed to army commanders too, he was unequivocal: "The British Zone in Austria is not a suitable field of operations for the BRC."[91] As a result of his persuasion, the army changed its mind—too late for the *domobranci,* but in time to save the civilians.

Many of the civilians eventually emigrated to Argentina. The *domobranci* were force-marched, beaten, killed, and buried in mass graves. In 1991 Slovenia became independent, and the emigrants were able to return if they wished. But "during the 45 years of communism...the *domobranci,* the emigrants and the post-war massacres could not be discussed." Things were not much different after 1991, and even after more than seventeen years of independence the events of the war and the postwar period are far from resolved. There are mass graves throughout Slovenia: "The British Army sent back some 11,850 Slovenes, of whom just over 11,000 were *domobranci....*Some 4,000 to 5,000 *domobranci* lie in Kocevski Rog, with another 5,000 in disused mineshafts at Hrastnik in the east, close to the Teharje concentration camp. The rest were killed at various sites elsewhere in the country." The hills of Kocevski Rog were the site of Partisan encampments during the war: "Nature created rocky pits and chasms among these rolling hills. Mankind has filled many of them up, with dead bodies.[92]

Gradually, after independence, people began visiting the mass graves, whose locations were known though not spoken about. Memorials began to be erected by municipalities to the *domobranci,* though not without difficulties. Some families objected to having the name of a relative displayed in public on such a memorial—even to the extent of painting over the name in an attempt to erase it.[93] A government Commission on Concealed Mass Graves has now been set up in Slovenia, headed by Joze Dezman. Work is in progress mapping and marking the location of each of the hundreds of mass graves, and forensic archaeologists have been working on recovering and in some cases identifying remains, using DNA techniques.[94] Relatives remain reluctant in many cases to provide DNA for possible matching, but can if they wish, and an ossuary has been set up where remains can be stored.[95] Dezman estimates some eighty thousand people may have been killed in Slovenia after the war, including Croatians, Germans, Serbians, and Montenegrins.[96] In this case of the missing in action not only were the *domobranci* missing—their bodies lying unidentified in mass graves—but their story was unacknowledged: by the British who sent them to their deaths, by those who killed them, and by their families, who in some cases remain unwilling to accept them. The younger generation, I am told, does not see the point of the identification and exhumation exercise. For them it is time to move on.[97]

Forensic techniques are routinely in use now in the continuing search for the missing in action or in cases where remains are found by chance. Fromelles is a good example in which it seems to be accepted without question that DNA identifications are appropriate. Though these developments have opened up the possibility of identification where it could not have been attempted before, attempts to find and identify missing servicemen and servicewomen in any case did not stop with the end of official "sweeps" in the late 1940s and early 1950s.

In more recent conflicts, methods of dealing with military casualties or disappearances have changed. Bodies are now routinely returned or repatriated during conflicts, not afterward. The nature of wars in Korea, Vietnam, and other places made this necessary: action moves to and fro, and ground once held by one side is recaptured by the enemy, so that temporary burials are no longer feasible. And repatriation is now the norm. Even countries such as the United Kingdom now repatriate war dead. Service personnel still go missing in action, but there seems to be less willingness to accept the uncertainty that this involves. Both families and perhaps especially the military expect extensive, and expensive, efforts to be made to determine the fate of the missing and ideally to identify and repatriate their remains. There seems in some cases at least to be no limit on the time frame or cost of this work.

Vietnam offers a particularly compelling example of a search without limits. On July 23, 2010, four days after the ceremony in Fromelles, Hillary Clinton, United States secretary of state, stood on the tarmac at Hanoi airport in Vietnam to witness the remains of three American servicemen being loaded onto a plane to be flown to Hickham Air Force base in Hawaii for identification.[98] Fifteen years after the normalization of relations between the United States and Vietnam, and many more since the Paris Peace Accords of 1973, which signaled the end of the conflict, over 1,700 U.S. personnel are listed as missing in action in Vietnam, and the search for remains continues.[99]

The search for the missing in action in Vietnam has been interpreted in one of two ways, according to Thomas Hawley. On the one hand, the search is seen as necessary because soldiers reported as missing may be alive, either abandoned by the Americans at the end of the war or held on to as prisoners by the Vietnamese. On the other hand, the search is interpreted as a symptom of a cultural malaise that will not let the United States accept defeat and draw a line under the conflict. Hawley points out that resources devoted to the search in Vietnam are disproportionate to the numbers of missing. The search "actively contributes to the continuation" of "the hostilities and ambiguities handed down by the Vietnam War." Not only that, but in its reliance on ever-smaller fragmented remains the quest for certainty in identification fails: a tooth may have been found and identified, or a hand, but what is to say that the owner of that hand or tooth is not still alive? What counts as a body in this context? Hawley argues that the search for certainty becomes "a war unto itself" and one that not only cannot relieve "broader political and cultural issues related to the defeat in Vietnam" but also produces its own casualties, among those engaged in the search.[100]

The attitude of members of the U.S. armed forces to recovery of remains from conflicts long ended differs sharply from that of members of the public. While "servicepersons feel that the search should continue indefinitely and that cost should be of little consideration,"[101] members of the public are likely to feel differently. Michael Sledge calculates that recoveries in Southeast Asia cost "slightly over $1.2 million per identified remains."[102] Capdevila and Voldman note what they call "the paradox of those killed in wars in the West during the twentieth century":[103] "At the same time as DNA tests now enable us to identify scientifically those killed in war, though they may have been buried for many years, military technology has the capacity to completely pulverize the bodies of those it hurls into its deadly vortex."[104] Not only military technology, of course, as the collapse of the World Trade Center in 2001 bears witness.

The demand, first voiced in the American Civil War and again in the First World War, that the missing in action be treated equally, and as civilians, and that their remains be returned to family and home in a process of "demobilization" of the dead, led to enduring changes in the way the military dealt with its missing soldiers. The bodies of the missing and information about their fates were a site of struggle over ownership: did they belong to the military or to the families? The answer that appears to have been arrived at, at least in the United States and France, that the next of kin have the right to decide, remains subject to dispute. The contemporary exhumation of remains is still a source of contention. Some regard it as unnecessary, others as an absolute duty. The claim for equality of treatment of the person-as-such has perhaps been incorporated into a social order that now regards even the unique person as something that needs to be subject to control and assimilation into an order of hierarchy and discrimination. Equality has perhaps been replaced by uniformity, but, as we have seen, disagreement remains.

One of the striking things about the search for the missing in action is the involvement—or in some cases, the lack of involvement—of women. The British Red Cross in the Second World War, like the American Red Cross in the late nineteenth century, was an organization largely led and staffed by women. In his speech in the House of Commons debate in 1920, Viscount Wolmer said of the constitution of the Imperial War Graves Commission:

> It is exceedingly unfortunate that there is not a single woman upon that Commission. I listened with admiration to the eloquent passage in the speech of the hon. Member for Westminster when he spoke about the women of England. Why are they not represented upon the Commission? Of the hundreds of letters that I have received the greater part of them come from women. Women feel more acutely upon this question than men. That is only natural. Why are the women not represented on the War Graves Commission?[105]

He received no answer to his question. Whether it is correct that "women feel more acutely" on the question of the missing, it does seem to be the case that women's involvement in searching brings a different approach into play. For many of the women involved in hospital searching, this was an opportunity for service that was open to them, and they took it. We have seen in a similar way how women saw volunteering for service in the displaced persons camps or tracing services after the Second World War as an opportunity for adventure and escape as well as service. We also saw how they were critical of the depersonalized way camps were run, and of what they saw as the heartless disregard of those searching for missing family members. In the next chapter, where we turn to the disappeared in Argentina, we again find women in hugely important—and political—roles.

CHAPTER 7

Disappeared, Argentina

> When they tried to turn us into a marginalized group
> of imbeciles, we didn't retreat into seclusion; instead
> we went out to scream our pain and to protest in
> every corner of the world.
>
> —Matilde Mellibovsky, *Circle of Love over Death*

In Argentina's so-called dirty war from 1976 to
1983 over thirty thousand people were "disappeared" by the military regime.[1]
This was, as Lawrence Weschler writes, "a diabolically effective tactic." If the
aim was "to take people who had started behaving like subjects...and turn them
back into good little mute and neutered objects once again," then as a tactic it
could not have been bettered. Not only were opponents of the regime elimi-
nated; their friends and relatives who might otherwise have been working in
opposition to the regime too were instead reduced "to ever more desperate and
futile and isolating efforts at search and rescue."[2] The disappearances produced a
spreading fragmentation and mistrust and were impossible to pin on the regime
or its officers. Laurel Reuter observes: "Fear stalks the population, invades like a
cancer, spreads like a plague.... Fear possesses the world."[3] The culture of fear in
Argentina was particularly strong because "the repression was clandestine and
illegal. There were no soldiers in the street, nor were there any public spectacles.... The authorities constantly proclaimed their respect for human rights."[4]

It is only now, many years later, that many of the most difficult stories
of that time are beginning to emerge: stories, for example, of the children
of the missing who were seized by those who had abducted their parents
and adopted by families connected to or involved in the military regimes.
It is only now that some of them have discovered their "origins" and been
reunited with their surviving blood relatives.

A vast literature documents the disappearances, efforts to protest them, and the question of justice for the disappeared.[5] As is well known, disappearances have taken place in other countries in Latin America and, more recently, in places such as Pakistan.[6] The United Nations Working Group on Enforced or Involuntary Disappearances has documented historic instances, including Sri Lanka, Iraq, Bosnia and Herzogovina, and more recent cases, including, as well as Pakistan, Chechnya, Colombia, Nepal, and Algeria.[7] In all these places, arbitrary detention, torture, and killing were deliberately used by military dictatorships or authoritarian regimes as a tactic to generate fear. The calculated action of military and government authorities involved "disappearing" thousands of people, who were abducted, tortured, and killed, and whose relatives met with denials and rebuttals when they attempted to find out what had happened.

In the case of the disappeared in Argentina, the hope is kept alive—and the story open—by demands that the missing be returned alive. Photographs play a central role in these demands, making the absent present not only in the homes of relatives, but in demonstrations on the streets. In her poem "Buenos Aires," Marjorie Agosin recounts how a mother talks almost as if her daughter were living:[8]

When she showed me her photograph,
she said,
this is my daughter,
she still hasn't come home
She hasn't come home in ten years.
But this is her photograph.
Isn't it true that she's very pretty?

The demand that the disappeared be returned alive, and a refusal to allow them to be reconstituted as merely the dead, were central to the protests and political activism that ensued. They can be seen as an *encircling of trauma*: a refusal of anything that might "heal" the pain of loss, and a demand that what happened be remembered instead in all its traumatic impact.[9] This is very different from the idea of trauma as a purely individual psychological problem that should be overcome.[10] An encircling of trauma is a challenge to forms of political order based on wholeness or completion and the fantasy of security, an order that relies on tidy categories, stories of continuity, and the exclusion of anything or anyone that does not fit—forms of order like those that are described by Giorgio Agamben as sovereign power or Jacques Rancière as police order.[11]

Despite the apparent effectiveness of the tactic of disappearances, it can be seen as a method that backfired.[12] It led to the rise of organizations protesting the disappearances, most notably the Madres of the Plaza de Mayo, which carried on the work of opposition and the demand for reform that had animated those who were disappeared in the first place. Not only did the protests demand the return of the disappeared, and their children, they insisted on justice and prosecutions of those responsible, and continuing political reform. The form of the protests, and the people who organized them, can be seen as having had a considerable impact on the face of politics in Argentina—and as being of broader importance in the world at large too. If torture is, as Elaine Scarry argues,[13] an unmaking of the world, then "out of this massive 'unmaking' came an imaginative remaking," and, moreover, as we shall see, one "in which women were major actors."[14]

Madres of the Plaza de Mayo

Graciela Mellibovsky, a political economist, teacher, and translator, was disappeared on September 25, 1976, at the age of twenty-nine.[15] That Saturday she and her mother had met for a chat; later, she was planning to see a movie with friends. The friends gathered at three in the afternoon; shortly afterward, the group was kidnapped. Her mother had a phone call at around four, from someone who didn't identify himself. She heard nothing else that day, but early the following morning soldiers in civilian dress forced their way into the parents' apartment, ransacked the place, and took away belongings of Graciela's. There had been a mix-up, and this was a second group looking for Graciela. Not finding her at her parents' place, they forced the mother to let them into two other apartments owned by the family, which they also turned upside down, before letting her return home. The parents then "began a desperate round of visits to the police, the military, embassies, human rights and Jewish organisations. There was no official trace of Graciela. Yet there was a sign that she was alive. Five days after being kidnapped, Graciela called." At the end of that conversation her mother asked, "'When will I see you, will I see you again?' Graciela answered, 'No, mama, never.'"[16]

Graciela's story emerges from conversations Marguerite Feitlowitz had with Graciela's mother, Matilde, and her father, Santiago, in July 1990. Matilde Mellibovsky became one of the founding Madres of the Plaza de Mayo; Santiago Mellibovsky collects and prints photographs of the disappeared to be displayed on the walls of the Madres' offices and paraded in their processions.[17] Feitlowitz had come to be involved through her work as a writer, and, more specifically, the translator of plays by Griselda Gambaro.[18] Her interest was in "how disaster—and the memory and dread of disaster—affects our relationship to language: to narrative form, the making of images, the rhetorical framing of theatre." She spent extended periods of time in Argentina talking to survivors and relatives of the disappeared, recording and transcribing her interviews in an attempt to convey "the nuances of every voice."[19]

When she first met Matilde, Feitlowitz was introduced to Graciela—or rather to her portrait hanging in the living room: "Graciela is a beautiful girl... [but] also nervous, obsessive, agitated, doing everything at once. I don't want to 'improve' or 'recreate' her... I want her with all of her faults." They talk of the daughter, of what happened: "They came of age during '68.... They wanted to change the world, and why not?" And of Matilde, of how she dreams of her daughter, and thinks of how she died, and of what Matilde did next: "They took my daughter and the next day I was a Mother of the Plaza de Mayo. There was no other choice." Feitlowitz sums up her own thoughts: "Matilde has learned to inhabit a zone where past, present, life, death, lucidity, madness have changed, intermarried. At once present and absent, sustaining and sustained, Graciela is *there*."[20]

In 1976, when Graciela was kidnapped and killed, the Madres of the Plaza de Mayo were not yet engaged in public protest. The majority of the disappeared were young adults at the time, many of them active in movements for social change, some with husbands and young children of their own. Their parents were middle-aged men and women, generally not themselves involved in any political activity. It was during 1977, as the disappearances became more numerous and those searching for missing adult children realized they were not alone, that a group of mothers got together and began to organize.[21] As Madres, they still carry on their work, well over thirty years later. There were three groups in the beginning: the Madres (Mothers) of the Plaza de Mayo, the Abuelas (Grandmothers) of the Plaza de Mayo, and the Familiares (Relatives). The Abuelas focused on the search for the children of the disappeared, who were their grandchildren, and who had been abducted with their parents or born in detention; the Familiares eventually provided a meeting place for a new organization, the Children of the Disappeared, or H.I.J.O.S. The Madres split in the 1980s into two groups, the original Madres and the Linea Fundadora, as we shall see shortly.[22]

The human rights movement as a whole played a crucial role in ending the military dictatorship. In 1983 Raúl Alfonsín was elected president, and a period of transition began. During this time, however, although there were trials of top generals and admirals involved in the repression of the years of military dictatorship, a complex struggle began between those who wanted to see some form of closure of the past, and those who opposed reconciliation without accountability.[23] Official policies at the beginning of the 1990s included impunity and presidential pardons; by the mid-1990s, "the public confessions of a number of perpetrators brought the past right back onto the front pages of the newspapers."[24] Throughout this period, the work of the Madres and other relatives and human rights organizations continued, though with changing aims and strategies—and with internal disagreements, as we shall see.

March 24, 1996, the twentieth anniversary of the military coup, was the first time that the Madres demonstrations involved a wholesale "taking back of public space, making visible the history that long was hidden."[25] In one event the previous autumn not only were trees festooned with photographs of the disappeared; tables were set up where material mementos from their lives—diplomas, possessions, souvenirs—were displayed. As Rene Epelbaum, one of the Madres, remarked,

> How and when they died is something too many of us still don't know, but no one, no one, shall deny that our children *lived*. These very particular lives should not be subsumed in any abstract category, even one as legally and morally potent as *desaparecido*. Their disappearance was someone else's crime, not our children's identity.[26]

The Madres, with their slogan "They took them away alive; we want them back alive," refuse to allow the trauma of disappearance, the unmaking of the world, to be covered over or forgotten.[27] They refuse to be silenced, or to accept the incorporation of their children into the categorizations that form part of the authorized account of the dirty war. They insist on their children as people, with all their faults, and as people who lived their lives—their *political* lives.

In some sense they had no choice but to act. Their children had disappeared. They had been taken away, violently, yet, afterward, no one in authority would admit that anything of the sort had happened. Their inquiries—of the police, of hospitals, of the government—were fruitless. In some cases, those who kidnapped the children also removed evidence of their existence: photographs, certificates, and the like. There were to be no funerals, no public acknowledgment of their loss. They couldn't even talk about it to friends and neighbors: everyone was too frightened. So, if they did nothing, did not protest, did not act, then it would be as if their children had not only disappeared but had never existed, never *lived*. That is the dread that haunts the search for the missing in other contexts, as we have seen in earlier chapters.

In the face of public silence, the families had no choice but to carry "the burden of keeping the memories of the loved ones alive, documenting that they had names, jobs, homes, children and friends."[28] The alternative would be to surrender to the madness of believing their children had never existed—people don't just disappear, do they, so maybe they didn't exist in the first place. This "terrible task" of preserving the symbolic space and "presence for the disappeared in the life of the family and community" consumed their lives.[29]

It was a while before the Madres first marched with the now-iconic posters carrying huge images of their children's faces, and bearing their names, ages, and dates of disappearance. But this proved an enormously powerful form of protest, bringing the truth of the disappearances home to those who watched. These were not just photographs; "they demonstrated an unquestionable existence that had to be restored."[30] And marches with the children continue. On March 24, 2003, the twenty-sixth anniversary of the military coup in Argentina, a demonstration organized by a number of different groups marched through the streets carrying images of the disappeared on an enormous banner held between the rows of marchers.[31] The disappeared joined the protests: they were present. Later, in 2010, their images could be seen seated in the public gallery at the trial of those accused of being responsible for torture and killings at the Campo de Mayo detention center.[32]

The children are kept alive, present, in the homes of the Madres, in their offices as part of the struggle, and on the streets in public protests, through photographs. Their photographs move between these spaces, demanding their integration. The Madres' turn to open, public demonstrations and fearless demands for justice—the fact that *they* wouldn't go away, *they wouldn't disappear,* they would remain visible—challenged the strategies of terror of the authoritarian regime at its heart, and, later, the desire of the successor democracy to move on and to forget.

The initial protests not only took back public space; they also *encircled the trauma.* The Madres encircled the Plaza de Mayo and its central monument, formerly a monument to sovereign power and masculine authority:

> Since 1976, groups of women have met in the Plaza to circle one of the most public and political spots in the city: the place where men from Juan Perón to General Videla presented the "official"—that is to say, masculine—story. . . . At first, there were only fourteen mothers; now there are hundreds. The fourteen heads covered with kerchiefs and necks bearing photographs of the missing multiplied, and the Plaza was filled with kerchiefs, flowers, and women greeting each other. Every Thursday they march around the obelisk, a phallic symbol that they transformed into something feminine. The Mothers took over the Plaza.[33]

The Madres have appropriated the Plaza's name and rewritten it, not as a monument to the authority of the state and sovereign power but as a site where the disappeared, those reduced to bare life, are made present and visible as a part of the life of the city, part of its politics. The Madres inscribed themselves as ones who count; they demand the count of the disappeared.[34]

The Madres did this in part through their bold assumption that they had a right to be heard, that they were entitled to information about their children. Their initial inquiries operated on the basis that people indeed do not just disappear, that someone in authority must know their whereabouts, and that as mothers they had a right to know what had happened. They took the regime's declarations of support for human rights at face value and sought a response: "They did not question the government or the Catholic church but regarded themselves as good citizens and church members."[35]

The authorities used the demand of the mothers that their cases be investigated as an opportunity to extract more information about those they regarded as subversives, and about the networks of friends in which they were involved. The mothers came to seek information, but what happened was that information was extracted from them, and they were given nothing.[36] But that wasn't all that happened. Women searching for their children began to recognize each other in the endless queues day after day at bureaucratic offices of one sort or another. Having thought they were alone in their tragedy, they began to realize that this wasn't the case. Their search was shared by other mothers.

Discovering that they shared each other's anguish, and a common search for their missing children, mothers started meeting, first privately, and then more publicly, in the Plaza de Mayo. The Plaza, historically the center of political action and the location of government offices, banks, and other official buildings, was first chosen as a gathering place because they planned to present a petition to the ministry. Eventually the mothers started to meet in the Plaza de Mayo every Thursday at three thirty in the afternoon. They had become an organization determined "to work openly against a regime that enforced secrecy and total compliance, and...to claim space for truth and dissent in the very setting of governmental power."[37]

In her book, *Circle of Love over Death: Testimonies of the Mothers of the Plaza de Mayo*, Matilde Mellibovsky, mother of Graciela, does more than give us testimonies or tell us stories of the mothers and their circle.[38] Whereas other books, books in English, written by those who share a solidarity with the mothers or who want to give them voice—even those like Feitlowitz who want to preserve the nuance of voice—tell us about what happened and when, and sometimes why, Mellibovsky's book is different.[39] It takes us beyond the possibility of relating in any straightforward way what happened, and demands that we, we outsiders, listen with care.

The title of Mellibovsky's book sounds sentimental—motherly even; redemptive too perhaps—until you read the poem that it is taken from, one of several poems she includes in her book. It is a poem by Pedro Orgambide called "Circulate..." Here is an excerpt:

> Circulate the policeman said,
> and they started to march on that Thursday
>
> . . . .
>
> Circulate, he said
> and didn't know he was winding up an endless dance
> a circle of love over death
> a wedding ring with time
> a ring around his own neck.[40]

Mellibovsky tells us that when she determined to write the book she decided "I would no longer talk to myself. I would shout in what I was writing, and my scream would gather strength with every reader that stays with me.... With thirty thousand 'disappeared' there was no time for syntax. With a slash of a sabre they paralysed our lives and our culture." But she tried "to pause and think 'syntactically'. To recount and to demand." To provide an account that would let future generations "know how we felt and how we lived out this part of Argentina's history, which scarred our families for ever."[41]

The testimonies in the book tell us of the children: their separate but shared concern for social justice and the needs of others, those who didn't have enough; their activism and their work; and their parents' worries over what might happen. But parents' support, nevertheless, for their children's desire to change the world. As one mother puts it, at their age "who does not have a spirit of rebellion when faced with injustice?"[42] In some cases the kidnappings did not come as a complete surprise, but rather as the confirmation of a long-felt but silent dread that something might happen.

What was it like when the children disappeared? Nothing had prepared people for what happened: "When we deal with one of the 'disappeared,' an unknown, culturally uncharted relationship is established." When someone dies, their story is known, in all its details; "when someone disappears by force, everything remains surrounded with a tangle of conjectures, indeterminacies, doubts."[43] The years passed, and the protests continued, though the Madres were "growing exhausted by the authorities' silences and their brutal indifference"; they felt desperate, displaced, and marginalized.[44] However, they did not stop; they didn't do what they were supposed to do. As Mellibovsky points out,

> We were supposed to keep our mouths shut: we made accusations.
> We were supposed to be submissive: we unmasked them.

We were supposed to be quiet: we screamed with all our might.

They needed to bury things: we dug them up.

Above all, we were supposed to stay very quietly at home: but we went out, walked around, got into unimagined places.[45]

When they first went to the Plaza de Mayo, they were scared but felt compelled to go. Meeting and talking with other mothers, walking arm in arm around the obelisk, was a time when they could talk about the only thing that was on their minds—their children. But they were also continually under threat and close surveillance.[46]

Some have seen problems with the Madres' use of their image as mothers, in that it plays into a culture of violent patriarchy. Diana Taylor argues that "much as the military's performance was a display of virility, the Madres' spectacle was a public display of *lack*."[47] Taylor sees this as evidence that the Madres are trapped in "bad scripts," narratives that reproduce the male as powerful and the female as at best "just housewives" and at worst part of a "collective fantasy" of women's negativity.[48] However, if military authoritarianism, perhaps more than any other form of sovereign power or any social order based on exclusion and control, relies on the pretense or fantasy of wholeness, as Slavoj Žižek and Jacques Rancière among others argue, then the exposure of the inevitable *lack* that haunts such an order can be explosive.[49] And, as Taylor herself points out, the disappeared themselves are another sign of that lack:

> Ironically, the women made invisible by patriarchy and disappeared into the home became the spokespeople for the disappeared. By "outing" the disappearance of their children they came out as disappeared themselves. They appeared as the disappeared. The women, by exposing the missing, also exposed themselves.[50]

The Madres exposed the lack or absence upon which the repression was founded, and claimed the right, on behalf of the disappeared, of recognition, and of recognition not as one category among others but as persons with names, faces, and political views. By playing into right-wing notions of family, they were able to lay claim to the space to articulate and demand the right to a different politics, as equal speaking beings.[51]

Aparición con vida! Appearance alive!

In 1984, following the fall of the military dictatorship and the election of Alfonsín as president, the new government established a National Commission on the Disappeared (Comisión Nacional sobre la Desparición de Personas, or CONADEP). Its job was to "investigate the fate and the whereabouts of the disappeared."[52] Human rights organizations, and the Madres in particular, were profoundly disappointed that the commission had no substantive powers to subpoena witnesses, but only to gather such testimony as it could, and then perhaps pass cases on to the courts.[53] It became clear that Alfonsín wanted compromise, not the resolute pursuit of those responsible for the repression that he had promised. His aim was to punish some human rights abuses, but not alienate the military during the transition to democracy.[54]

Instead of what the Madres had hoped for, then—that the end of the dictatorship would bring them news of their missing and, in particular, details of who was responsible for their disappearance—the focus of investigations was on gathering information about the disappeared, not their persecutors.[55] As part of this, exhumations were beginning. Horrific images of the excavation of mass graves appeared on television and in the press. Matilde Mellibovsky writes: "It was Thursday. I don't know whether it was before I went to the Plaza. I saw it on TV. It was simply horrible. In an excavated plot among lumps of earth, a huge machine like some sort of crane was digging with its teeth—was enlarging a hole and then heaving out to one side...bones, human bones."[56] Not only were these images shocking, particularly for relatives, but the exhumations, apparently ordered by federal tribunals, were destroying evidence that could have identified the remains and provided material for prosecutions: "The exhumations were done by people without expertise, such as firefighters or cemetery keepers, and in a rapid manner, often under the direction of forensic doctors. In some cases they used bulldozers on entire sections of the cemeteries. As a result, many bones were lost, mixed up, left in the grave, or broken."[57]

There was little know-how within Argentina at that time for dealing with the exhumation of such graves: forensic archaeology or anthropology wasn't something people had wanted to risk being involved in, and the forensics people there were were likely to have been complicit in the original abuses through their links with the police. The need for expert help from outside became obvious, and CONADEP, under pressure from the Abuelas of the Plaza de Mayo among others, sought advice from the Human Rights and Science Program at the American Association for the Advancement of Science.[58] A delegation of forensic specialists under the leadership of Clive Snow was sent to Argentina; as soon as members of the delegation saw the results of what was happening, they called for an immediate stop to existing exhumations. In addition to carrying out some investigations themselves, they began training local forensic specialists who would eventually form the

Argentine Forensic Archaeology Team (Equipo Argentino de Antropologia Forense, or EAAF). A proper process of careful excavation, recording, and analysis of the remains was established.[59]

Despite the clandestine nature of abduction, detention, torture, and killing under the military dictatorship, bureaucratic organizations had maintained records of deaths and burials throughout the period. Some bodies were dumped at sea or in rivers in the infamous "death flights"; others were left on the streets or on wasteland to be picked up later by police. Somewhat surprisingly, when these bodies were found

> the police carried out almost all the routine procedures, as established by legal protocols. These procedures include writing a description of the find, taking photographs, fingerprinting the corpse, conducting an autopsy or external examination of the body, writing a death certificate, making an entry in the local civil register, and issuing a certificate of burial.[60]

The victims were then buried as "NN"—unknown persons with no name—in plots routinely set aside for that purpose in public cemeteries. People who lived nearby reported seeing military and police vehicles bringing the bodies in on a regular basis. Once access to files became possible, the bureaucratic records helped forensic teams in the location of graves; details from families and other witnesses established which detainees were held at which centers, and provided antemortem data. Identifications were made on the basis of evidence such as dental records, fingerprints, or the remains of surgical procedures.

It was not until 2007 that DNA analysis began to be widely used in the identification of remains. Under a project called The Latin American Initiative for the Identification of the "Disappeared"(LIID), funded by the U.S. Congress, techniques developed first in the Balkans and later in the aftermath of September 11 began to be used to apply genetic testing on a large scale in Argentina.[61] By that time, impunity laws enacted at various points since 1983 had been annulled, and prosecutions resumed.[62] Blood samples were being collected from the relatives of the disappeared, and advertising campaigns were promoting the plan, which would include a DNA analysis of six hundred skeletons that had been recovered but not identified.[63]

The start of exhumations in the early 1980s led to severe disagreements among the families of the disappeared, and the Madres in particular, disagreements that eventually led to a split in that organization. At first, despite concern at the methods being used, there was general support for the idea that the missing would finally be located and identified, but later, when it became clear that identifications would take place without prosecutions, that support was withdrawn.[64] The leader of the Madres, Hebe de Bonafini, expressed doubts that there was a political will to prosecute.[65] At one point the Madres organized a protest at the site of an ongoing excavation. According to an account by María Julia Bihurriet, one of the volunteers with the EAAF team,

> We could see a large group of people standing round the partially opened grave. There must have been about fifteen of them, mostly women.... A policeman came up and told us [they] were members of the Madres. They wouldn't let anyone near the graves that we had dug. He said that when he and his men approached, they hurled stones at them so they backed off.[66]

One of the graves being excavated that day was purported to be that of Ana Maria Torti, whose mother, a member of the Madres, had filed a petition saying that she did not wish the grave to be opened.[67] The judge who had ordered the exhumations suspended them after the protests. According to the Madres, this judge, Judge Pedro Hooft, had been working during the years of repression and had failed to investigate the case of at least one disappeared whose family came to him for help.[68]

The police attended the exhumations—supposedly just to keep order and ensure the safety of the archaeologists and their finds—but their attendance was disturbing. It "created a threatening presence... marking the excavations as a dangerous place."[69] These were men who had probably been involved in the burial of the bodies in the first place, and certainly men who knew about the bullets found in the graves. The police surveillance exacerbated the concerns of relatives and human rights groups, as well as emphasizing to the young volunteer archaeologists how precarious their own position was in a fledgling democracy.[70]

Many of the Madres came to the conclusion that the excavations and identifications were an attempt by the authorities to draw a line under the past, but without prosecuting those responsible for the disappearances. If the mothers and other relatives could be assured that their missing were indeed dead, and could hold funerals and bury the remains, then they could all move on—or this was the theory. Surviving relatives would become resigned to what had happened and no longer feel the need to take political action.[71]

Those who took this view decided that the way to continue their struggle, and to fight for the justice they demanded—both the social justice their children had fought for and the criminal conviction of those who had participated in the disappearances and killings—was to refuse to allow exhumations and identifications without prosecutions. They would not accept the compromises of the Alfonsín government, which they felt was yielding to pressure from the military to bury the past. Not all the Madres agreed with this position. Some wanted above all to reclaim the names of their sons and daughters and give them a proper burial, at last. In 1986, the strains caused in part at least by these differing views among the Madres led to a split and the formation of a breakaway group that called itself the Linea Fundadora (Founding Line) of the Madres of the Plaza de Mayo. The new group, which included some who had been part of the original Madres, supported exhumations by forensic experts and continued their work, but "within the political system as an interest group rather than as a radical opposition group that continued demonstrating and marching against the government."[72]

The slogan of the Madres was *Aparición con vida!* (Appearance alive!), which had been misunderstood as a sign that they really were as mad as the dictatorship had described them in the early days of their protests. They were labeled as Las Locas de Plaza de Mayo, the Madwomen of Plaza de Mayo, a term of abuse that the Madres turned back on the dictatorship by using it themselves.[73] Surely they must realize by now that their children were dead? What was the use of continuing to demand that they be returned alive?

Antonius C. G. M. Robben argues that there are two ways of coping when an adult child dies: "A mother can turn her grief inward through identification or externalise her anger on those responsible for the loss." With a disappeared child, the loss is made worse by the absence of details of what happened, and the way that "the parent is thrown between hope for life and resignation to death." Drawing from Freudian psychoanalytic work on mourning and loss, Robben argues that the split in the Madres reflected what are commonly seen as two responses to the "separation anxiety" felt by a mother at the loss of a child: projection and introjection. He sees the mothers who rejected exhumations as "introjecting" the suffering of the disappeared, identifying with their ideals and regarding themselves "as the embodiment of their children's ideals and struggles." Those who buried their children were, by contrast, able to become reconciled to their loss, projecting their feelings onto the bodies and ending their search. However, Robben notes that despite these two responses "the realisation that justice was not served, and that those responsible for the disappearances are scot-free, keeps troubling them." Importantly, he argues that the trauma of the past, where the relations of trust between people and between people and the authorities were broken, cannot be dealt with until both the missing are recovered *and* those responsible punished.[74]

The way the disappeared were abducted—this most usually involved an armed invasion and ransacking of the home—is seen by Robben as a deliberate erasure of the separation between public and private. The actions of the Madres—bringing their grief to the Plaza de Mayo—is a movement in the opposite direction, one that domesticates the public realm.[75] Their political platform, which embraces "the suffering of all victims of political violence" and tackles social problems such as poverty, Robben argues, is an extension of the "maternal protection they had been unable to provide their own children . . . to all victims of repression."[76]

But to what extent were the Madres doing what came "naturally" to them, and to what extent was what they did the result of a perceptive reading of the political situation they found themselves in, one that demanded they depart from the role expected of them as "mothers"? Women are not expected to be proficient political players. And it is precisely the separation of the public sphere from the private sphere to which women are confined that embodies this expectation. Women are not given a political voice; they have to demand it, which is what the Madres did. And they demanded a political voice on their own terms. Not as the "mothers" they were supposed to be, but as political beings who demanded to be heard as equal speaking beings. Those equal speaking beings did not have to, and indeed could not, accept their allotted place, or their allotted silence, as we have seen.

Their refusal to accept exhumations and identifications was part of their insistence on being heard own their own terms, as equal speaking beings, not as mothers of victims of the repression, and part of the ultimate refusal to be silenced before their demands for justice—social, individual, and intergenerational—were met.

The refusal was effective, as Zoë Crossland tells us.[77] The slogan *Aparición con vida!* was not a reflection of a mistaken belief that the disappeared were still alive, but a demand that kept open the space for political action and protest. Those abducted were alive when they were taken away. As Mercedes Mereno explains, "I'm asking for her alive, because if she isn't, I want to know who killed her and I want that assassin put in jail. If I ask for her as a corpse, then *I* am killing her, not the one who assassinated her."[78] In the period after the installation of a civilian government, some relatives received telephone calls from their children: some were still alive at that time and were killed later.[79] But most mothers accepted that their children were dead. They disagreed with the exhumations because, as Graciela de Jeger put it, "With the exhumations they want to eradicate the problem of the disappearances, because then there are no more *desaparecidos,* only dead people." Disappearance was a crime without limitations, whereas murder was not.[80] De Jeger continued: "We don't want the names of the victims. We know who they are. We want the names of the murderers. We want them to tell us what happened. They have to explain what they don't want to explain. This is the meaning of *Aparición con vida!*"[81]

By keeping their children disappeared, the Madres maintained their children's public visibility: "In order to claim the spaces left by the disappeared, the Mothers filled the spaces with embodied public representations of the disappeared as they remembered them in life."[82] Their demand was for no identification, no resumption of the police order; they insisted that the gap opened up by the disappearances, the gap in the social order, be maintained, the trauma visible.

If they had accepted their children's remains, admitted that they were dead and buried, the children would have been nothing but bare life, life that had been killed without the need for justice. Their children would have disappeared a second time. The children would have been returned to parents, returned to the home, the private sphere, but their political life, and the political voice of the Madres, would have ended. The only way to keep the disappeared alive politically—and after all, it was their politics that had killed them—was to refuse to allow exhumations and identifications. The Madres wanted to remember their children's lives, not their deaths, as political activists, not as victims.

The proper recovery of the disappeared would mean not just that they be counted, that their deaths be recorded, or that their killers and tormentors be brought to justice, but that they be recognized for who they were: people with particular views who were working for particular goals. The demand that the disappeared be returned alive was an insistence that their lives count, not just their deaths, that they be accepted not as victims, but as "subjects who had made a political choice," as Martin Caparros puts it.[83] The Madres achieved this by continuing their children's political work themselves. The protests of the Madres, and later those of the *Hijos por la Identidad, la Justicia, contra el Olvido y el Silencio* (Children for Identity and Justice, against Oblivion and Silence), known as H.I.J.O.S., were a demand for a place for opposition in the politics of Argentina, and a demand that the people—the poor and the vulnerable—count.

It was during the demonstrations to mark the twentieth anniversary of the coup—March 24, 1996—that the H.I.J.O.S. took to the streets for the first time.[84] As well as taking part in demonstrations with other groups, the H.I.J.O.S. organized a new form of protest, *escraches,* marches focused on exposing former torturers and assassins in the neighborhoods where they were living—making those responsible appear—and thus challenging the culture of impunity.[85] This organization marked a generational change, a taking up of the baton of the Madres by their grandchildren, the children of those persecuted and killed by the dictatorship.

The passing of the baton had skipped a generation, it seemed, but it was at this time that it finally became possible for the generation of the disappeared themselves to talk openly about the activism of the disappeared—the so-called subversion—and their own involvement as brothers and sisters, friends and colleagues, and survivors. The twentieth-anniversary march, following as it did the public confessions of Adolfo Scilingo, a navy captain who had served during the military dictatorship, marked this turning point, and the march was widely supported.[86] The participation of the younger generation, the children of the disappeared, "rejuvenated the human rights movement, importantly contributing to a renewed public presence."[87] And somehow it freed those of their parents' generation who were not disappeared but who returned or who were never abducted to begin to recover their own memories.

A number of books published in the late 1990s began to portray the disappeared as particular people, young people of the idealistic bent typical of the period who were engaged in work on behalf of the dispossessed, ranging from charitable work in the slums to more militant activism. As discussed earlier in the chapter, Matilde Mellibovsky's *Circle of Love over Death,* with its accounts in the form of testimonies by mothers of their children's lives, first published in 1997, was an attempt to give voice to those who were there, who lived through the period of the disappearances, so that they should not be forgotten.

Eric Carlson, author of *I Remember Julia,* published in 1996, sees his purpose as being similar, but in his case the testimonies he collects are in the main from Julia's own generation, people who knew her.[88] In Carlson's book, as in Mellibovsky's, the story is not a smooth linear narrative such as might appear in an academic account of what happened, but a tale of gaps, inconsistencies, and troubling, ambiguous loss. Memories don't add up to anything complete; we are left with only glimpses of Julia. In a disturbing undercurrent, the book testifies to the corrosive impact one person's disappearance can have on those around them.

Carlson includes the account of Ester Saavedra, a psychologist who describes herself as part of the same generation as the disappeared. She uses the term "living-dead" and sees disappearance as very particular: "It's a missing person whose absence one doesn't want to be made an accomplice to. This would be the equivalent to decreeing the disappearance, decreeing the death of the loved one." There was a need almost to deny that disappearances were happening, at least at first, and later just not to talk about what had happened: "The disappeared person brings something that disturbs the natural order of things.... The disappeared person takes, let's say, symbolically, many parts of other people.... [The disappeared person] sucks away vital aspects of the people that were left behind."[89]

When Julia's remains were identified in 1991, thirteen years after she disappeared, Laura, who had been a very good friend of Julia's and who worked at the same children's home, found herself unable to go to Julia's funeral. She was afraid to talk about Julia. "I don't want anything to happen to me," she said. "My daughter is married. I want, I want peace." She wouldn't go to the funeral, she said, because "I remember the last time I saw her, and, for me, she still remains alive. . . . The last time she was at home and said 'Well, I've got to go to work.'. . .I never saw her again. It's like I wait for her, and she's going to return." An ex-boyfriend of Julia's is so obsessed with her memory that his house is covered with pictures of her, although he broke up with her before she disappeared, and married someone else. Other friends lived in fear of being taken themselves once Julia had been abducted, "many denying for years that they ever knew Julia." Some searched for her later when they were in exile and met others they had worked with who had also escaped. Two women who had been held in detention centers with Julia but were later released told their memories of that time. But there were many people that Carlson spoke to who didn't want Julia's story to be told, "not only the soldiers and policemen responsible for Julia's death but also many of those who knew her as friends."[90] They thought it better to forget, to leave it be, to remain safe.

It was at this same time that Marcelo Brodsky produced his widely exhibited photographic essay, *Buena Memoria*, also published as a book. The essay tells the story of Brodsky's generation through photographs of his class at the Colegio Nacional de Buenos Aires, a class "marked by two 'missing' students," as well as the story of his brother Fernando, another of the disappeared.[91] In the first essay in the book, Martin Caparros points out that in the past when speaking of this generation, in order

> to avoid speaking of them as subjects who had made a political choice, it was better to turn them into victims, into the objects of other people's decisions. . . . We spoke of how they were the objects of kidnapping, torture, and murder, and we barely spoke of how they were when they were subjects, when they chose to live destinies that included the danger of death, because they felt they had to do so. Those versions of history were, among other things, a way to make the *desaparecidos* disappear yet again. . . . In the end we realised that all of us disappeared with that second disappearance. Our stories were lost with theirs, which no one told.[92]

In a volume filled with an immense sadness, Brodsky shows us pictures of his classmates as they were twenty years after the class photograph was taken. They are each photographed with an object they chose—a sign of their profession or of their interests—in front of the class photograph. The notes record ordinary lives lived, or, in some cases, lives disrupted by exile, emigration, or homecoming. And for two of them, lives cut short when they were abducted or killed. The class photograph, annotated with Brodsky's notes about his contemporaries, was displayed in the hall of the school itself, twenty years later, and Brodsky took photographs of the class of 1993, their sunlit faces reflected in the glass of the original class photograph as they gaze at the picture of the class of 1973. These images represent for him "the instants of the transmission of experience from one generation to another."[93] Members of the new generation write of how seeing the photograph made them sense how close they were to those other children, in that other time, and how it made them think very differently about what happened.

When Carlson wrote *I Remember Julia,* he still felt it necessary to conceal the name of the person he was talking about, and the names of some of her friends whom he interviewed for the book. The book is a tale that began when Julia's brother Manuel showed Carlson a box containing her personal things. They had been retrieved from her office after she disappeared, and then were packed away in his cupboard and not opened since. They were fragments of a life, like the fragments of so many other lives that lie untouched because families would rather not face the story, would rather forget. For Carlson "there is too much silence."[94] And yet, at the end of his story, his visits to those who remember Julia and give their accounts of her that break the silence, he reflects that he still cannot answer the question, Who was Julia?: "Does this collection of anecdotes and visions come close to describing her? Or are these stories merely echoes sounding against the dark wall of memory, a few scattered glimpses, and then nothingness?"[95] He concludes that, "as with any personality, full of contradictions and complexities, Julia cannot be seen in her entirety." And her brother will continue "finding Julia, bits and pieces of her.... His search for Julia will never end."[96] Like Oscar Munoz's image of the face continually being drawn, fading and being redrawn, we are continually trying to grasp the person, and failing.[97]

In his inaugural speech following his election as president in 2003, Néstor Kirchner laid claim to his own identity as "part of a decimated generation."[98] He made a commitment to the human rights movement and the demand for justice, appealing to "a shared identity and a shared history of militancy, loss and persecution."[99] In his first appearance at the United Nations, he proclaimed: "We are the sons and daughters of the Mothers and Grandmothers of the Plaza de Mayo."[100] Organizations such as the Madres responded by working with rather than against the government, and by finally accepting that their children were dead.

In a deposition given in 1984, one Antonio Francisco Valdez gave information about his claimed involvement in Graciela Mellibovsky's torture. According to Feitlowitz's report of her conversations with Graciela's mother, this was part of a deal-making strategy designed to get Valdez out of prison.[101] According to another source, her father had enlisted the help of the American Statistical Association, which had placed advertisements in the Argentine press offering a reward for information, and Valdez responded.[102] He gave graphic details of Graciela's ordeal and told how she was later taken out and shot. Until this time, her parents had held onto the hope that she was alive. Valdez offered to tell the parents where she was buried—for a price. They refused. They later discovered from other witnesses that she was buried in a mass grave in a city just outside Buenos Aires, alongside some five hundred other bodies. They did not request an exhumation: they would have needed permission from the relatives of the other five hundred.[103]

Graciela's story is more complex and more interesting than we might have thought from the accounts we have looked at so far. Her "crime" was that while working as an economist for the Argentine government she produced a statistical study of conditions in the slums of Buenos Aires that was profoundly embarrassing to her employers: "It was publically singled out by the Junta leader, General Jorge Vileda, as an example of the infiltration of subversives into government."[104] In 2008 Jana Asher, David Banks, and Fritz Scheuren dedicated their volume *Statistical Methods for Human Rights* to Graciela's memory. A chapter in this volume records how the International Statistical Institute held a session in Buenos Aires in 1981, shortly after Graciela's abduction and the disappearance of another Argentinian statistician, Carlos Noriega, director of the Argentine National Statistical Office, who had been forced out of his post when he refused to tamper with official statistics.[105] Members of the American Statistical Association (ASA) set up an Ad Hoc Committee on Scientific Freedom and Human Rights, which debated whether or not to boycott the meeting. In the end there was no boycott, but various activities were organized to coincide with it: a petition was prepared and presented to the authorities and the press, and meetings with human rights activists held.[106] The ad hoc committee is now fully established as the ASA Committee on Scientific Freedom and Human Rights; it monitors "violations of and threats to the scientific freedom and human rights of statisticians and other scientists throughout the world."[107]

The demand for the reappearance of the disappeared is not just a demand for the tracing of the missing or for a determination of their fate. Rather it is a protest against the injustice of the disappearances and a demand that the disappeared be restored to their existence as fully political beings—beings who lived lives, fought political battles, had children and families. Those searching for them were insisting: since they've been missing for all these years, you can't just return them to us now, dead, and claim that it is all fine. You treated them as lives of no value, lives not worth living. If we accept their bones, and nothing else, then we are tacitly accepting that too.

But there is no way that complete restitution is possible. There is no going back, no retrieval of the past. Memories are incomplete, new political systems flawed, relationships fragile and ambiguous. And people in any case cannot be fully fathomed. All that is possible, perhaps, is to recognize with the H.I.J.O.S. that "the men and women of that generation were not... martyrs, nor perfect heroes with perfect projects. They were persons who decided to commit themselves, organise and give it all"—in other words, equal speaking beings.[108] That recognition would bring the person-as-such back into politics. *Aparición con vida!* is more than a demand for justice in the form of trials and retribution; it is a demand for that new politics.

CHAPTER 8

Ambiguous Loss

> With ambiguous loss, there is no closure; the challenge is to learn to live with the ambiguity.
>
> —Pauline Boss, author of *Ambiguous Loss*

When people go missing in the aftermath of the violence of wars or disasters, it is likely that they did not go missing voluntarily. Authoritarian regimes may try to persuade relatives of the disappeared that those they are concerned about have absconded of their own will, as happened in Argentina, but it is highly unlikely to be the case. But when people go missing in other circumstances, it can be deliberate; only very few are likely to be victims of abduction or murder. This chapter considers instances in which people abscond or voluntarily break contacts with families and friends. They do so for a variety of reasons: to escape from what is seen as an intolerable or abusive situation; to avoid capture or prosecution, for example as perpetrators of war crimes or as enemy nationals; to give up children for adoption. The chapter looks first at people reported missing in the United Kingdom, and the evolution of systems to help relatives trace them. Different organizations are involved, and pressure from families left behind has led to changes in the procedures adopted. The chapter traces the way in which government authorities in the United Kingdom moved from a refusal to engage with those reported missing, except where a crime is suspected or in the case of minors, to a more active engagement of police in quotidian cases, largely as a result of pressure from voluntary organizations. The debates reflect differing assessments of the right to disappear versus the right of relatives to know what has happened.

When people go missing, details of their lives and motivations are picked over in the hunt for some clue as to what might have happened. Their last moves are traced, their friendships and connections mapped. Despite whatever is brought to light—the intimate scraps of a life—there remains something unfathomable. Someone has disappeared, unaccountably, but was there perhaps a sense in which that person was missing anyway? It turns out that no one knew them well. But then do we really know ourselves? Or those we are closest to? The later parts of the chapter look at accounts of those who have sought to trace their missing family long after the event. The questions and ambiguities remain after years have passed, seeming to compel people to attempt to resolve them. Often, extensive searching reveals only that many questions remain, and are, perhaps inevitably, unanswerable.

Reported Missing

It used to be the case that when people were reported missing in circumstances other than a disaster such as the World Trade Center collapse or the London bombings, the police paid little attention, on the basis that the vast majority of those reported missing return home unharmed within a short space of time.[1] Most of the missing in Britain are unlikely to be *victims* of a crime—or criminals—so *who* they are is unimportant, and the desire of relatives and friends to locate them can be disregarded. For some years now there have been campaigns to persuade the police to take more urgent action. Questions about missing persons were first asked in the House of Commons in the aftermath of the Second World War, when, as we have seen in the first half of this book, many millions of people had been separated from their families. Norman Dodds, MP, first raised the question in a more general context in 1953, suggesting the establishment of a central missing persons bureau, and remarking that other countries kept such a register.[2] In 1963 the case of Herman Woolf, who was apparently hit by a car, taken into police custody, arrested apparently on suspicion of drug offenses, and who later died in the hospital, prompted an inquiry. Woolf's ex-wife had reported him missing but received no information from the police until after his death—a story that sounds familiar—despite the fact that her former husband was carrying a diary listing her name and contact information, for use in case of emergency. There was also concern that he had been beaten up by police.[3] The failure to contact the ex-wife was put down to an administrative error on the part of the police, and the public was assured that steps had been taken to prevent this happening again. Greville Janner, MP, raised the question of the missing in 1973 and again, ten years later, in 1983, repeating the demand for centralized record-keeping and querying the accuracy of the statistics he had been given.[4] During the late 1980s the number of questions in the House of Commons on the topic of missing persons increased, and in December 1988 it was reported that the Association of Chief Police Officers had recommended that there be a national register of missing persons.[5] The slowness in the implementation of services in response to public demand recalls the position of authorities after the Second World War.

However, while laudable for some reasons—to protect the vulnerable, for example, and prevent the recurrence of instances like the Muswell Hill murders of fifteen young men in London in 1983 and the Cromwell Street murders in Gloucester, where the bodies of a series of young women, some of whom had been reported missing, were found[6]—systems to track and locate the missing can lead in uncomfortable directions. They can lead to the impossibility of escape for people who have good reason to flee abusive or unsatisfactory relationships in which they are ensnared, or for those seeking to avoid state control and deportation, such as asylum seekers. Such systems can also add fuel to the demand for identity cards and DNA databases applied to everyone in the population.

The pressure for change in the police approach has come from those often described as "left behind," and from the voluntary agencies dedicated to helping them. When someone goes missing, it is no comfort to those left behind to know that the chances are the person will return unharmed or will turn out to have left voluntarily. For the families of the missing under everyday circumstances, as for those after war or disaster, time and life are put on hold. "The unexpected absence of a family member produces a situation that is saturated with uncertainty," and there is an urgent and compelling need to know what happened.[7] The families of the missing suffer what Pauline Boss has called "ambiguous loss," a particularly distressing form of loss.[8] In such circumstances, statistics, probabilities, and calculations of risk are of no comfort. "Missing persons" in general may not be greatly at risk of harm, but it is the very particular instance, the unique human being, that is of concern to the family, not some general category of "missing persons."

For those who go missing—certainly for those who leave of their own free will—there may indeed be a desire to leave permanently, to disappear from their existing life, and to reinvent themselves in a different context. They may want to vanish without trace, without leaving any comforting message or reassurance behind; to cut the ties that bind and ensure that tracing them is hopeless.[9] According to journalist Doug Richmond, author of a "how-to" book on disappearance, there seem to be two chief reasons why middle-aged men choose to disappear: either an unhappy marriage combined with "boredom and frustration," or possible criminal prosecution or disgrace.[10] Closing the possibility of disappearance, through the linking of official data held in various places and by different agencies and through an increasingly proactive search process, may make escape, other than through suicide, out of the question. Yet it is still recognized that adults in the United Kingdom have the right to go where they wish, without telling anyone, if that is what they desire.

Voluntary agencies have played a significant role in searching for the missing in the United Kingdom, working alongside and sometimes in tension with the police and social services. The British Red Cross has long been involved in such searches, as we have seen in earlier chapters, though its focus is those separated by war or conflict—particularly, missing members of the armed forces. For some time the Salvation Army was the sole other agency offering tracing services, though it deals only with adults. Its work, motivated by a desire to redeem those it considered in danger of moral corruption, through prostitution for example, and to help bring families back together again, began at the end of the nineteenth century.[11] Its interventions designed to compel runaway fathers to support their wives and children were controversial, leading sociologist T. H. Huxley to object to the methods used and the way in which the Salvation Army constituted itself as judge and jury in such cases.[12] On the whole, though, the Salvation Army's tracing services were operated, and continue to be operated, in a way that is sensitive to the confidentiality of both its inquirers and those who are missing. It no longer tries to compel absconders to return, though it works to reunite families through persuasion.[13]

The impetus to tighten systems for tracing in the United Kingdom, and to make such procedures part of the governmental apparatus, often comes from highly publicized cases in which missing persons turn out to have been the victims of foul play. The disappearance of London estate agent Suzy Lamplugh in 1986 led to a series of significant changes in the resources available for both those missing and those searching for them.[14] At that time, services for tracing both young people and adults who had gone missing were almost nonexistent, apart from the continuing work of the Salvation Army.[15] Demands for increased services, such as the demands of Greville Janner, MP, went unanswered. Police searching was limited, and the number of people officially recorded as missing was relatively small. Suzy's parents, Paul and Diane Lamplugh, established a trust in her name, and Mary Asprey, who had known Suzy, and Mary's sister Janet Newman were instrumental in establishing a helpline for families. The service was initially set up by a former police officer who had worked on the case, Nick Carter, and it was made permanent in 1990 under the name National Missing Persons Helpline.[16]

Registered as a charity in 1992, the service expanded gradually until 1994, changing its name to Missing People a few years later. There was a huge increase in calls in 1994 after the discovery of bodies at 25 Cromwell Street in Gloucester, where Fred and Rosemary West lived. The couple had, between them, murdered at least twelve young women and buried their dismembered remains in the cellar and garden of the house.[17] It turned out that some of the women involved had been reported missing up to twenty years earlier, and calls from concerned families to the missing persons helpline resulted in the location of over a hundred missing persons whose disappearance was unrelated to the case, as well as the identification of several of the Wests' victims.[18]

As well as an increase in services, there was an increase in research and academic work attempting to analyze the question of the missing. In the early 1990s, Malcolm Payne introduced terminology that has remained in use to a certain extent since. The missing were categorized, "in a terminology designed to be memorable," as runaways (missing people), throwaways (rejected missing people), pushaways (people forced to go missing), fallaways (people who have lost contact), and takeaways (people forced out of contact).[19] Though useful in drawing attention to the variety of circumstances that can lead to someone being missing, this attempt at categorization fails to capture the complexity of the individual case. Runaway young people often see themselves as having been pushed out or rejected by their families and may be vulnerable in similar ways to those originally taken away or forcefully abducted. They may not intend to cut all ties with their families but over a period of time may turn out to have lost the possibility of regaining contact.[20]

Further research was sponsored in one way or another by the organization Missing People or its predecessor, and a number of reports were produced, most notably *Lost from View,* which remains a particularly interesting overview.[21] The report notes that, despite considerable work on runaway children,[22] research on missing adults has been sparse, and that reliable figures for the number of missing people, and indeed any useful definition of "missing," are elusive.[23] The study was based on the files of the National Missing Persons Helpline and included a survey of missing people who had been traced, asking them about their reasons for going missing and their experiences. The snippets of testimony of the "formerly missing" provide rare insight into their "complex and multilayered" views and motivations.[24] Nearly two-thirds of missing adults in the survey had decided to leave, and around a third of these had done so because of a breakdown in relationships—often a long process, with a particular argument sometimes being the final trigger. Others saw going missing as a way of escaping from multiple problems, including health or financial difficulties, violence or crime, and wanted to make a new start. A few of those who chose to go missing intended to commit suicide or had mental health problems. Many of the missing, around one in five, had simply drifted out of contact with relatives, seemingly without any particular decision to do so, and one in six were unintentionally absent—elderly people with dementia, for example. Being forced to leave was rare: only 1 in 100 was the victim of a crime or was forced away by others.

Other academic research has focused on the question from the perspective of the police and analyzed the degree of risk to which particular categories of missing persons are exposed.[25] In order to allocate scarce resources of police time sensibly, officers need to make judgments as to the likely vulnerability of the person reported missing. The police have produced reports on the question of the missing and issued detailed guidance to officers.[26] As well as highlighting the need for means of identifying "suspicious missing persons" or those to whom more resources needed to be devoted, a 1999 report noted the problem of contradictory requirements: "the well-being of the missing person; respect for the right of an individual to go missing; compassionate treatment of relatives...; the likelihood that the missing persons may have been the victim of a crime; and the preservation...of evidence."[27] The report recommended more standardization between police forces and a review of overlaps between police and other services, as well highlighting the fact that no organization held a comprehensive national list of missing persons.

Comprehensive guidance, recognizing the various responsibilities to the missing and to families, and the need to work with other organizations, was produced by the police in 2002 and updated in 2005.[28] A new Code of Practice was issued in April 2009, and in 2008 the work of the Missing Persons Bureau was transferred from the Metropolitan Police to the National Policing Improvement Agency (NPIA).[29] The NPIA will "maintain a database of all persons, including foreign nationals, missing in the UK and those UK citizens who are reported missing overseas."[30] The press release announcing the move noted that Missing People (formerly the National Missing Persons Helpline) was the only UK charity working with the missing, but a website (look4them.org.uk), a joint initiative of seven organizations working with missing people, including the police service, clarifies their various responsibilities. The Salvation Army traces adult relatives in the United Kingdom and overseas; Missing People deals with young runaways and missing people; Reunite handles abduction and international custody disputes; Norcap supports adults affected by abduction; the British Red Cross helps relatives separated by war and disasters; the police service in the United Kingdom deals with safety and welfare; and the Association of British Investigators offers commercial services.[31]

The International Committee of the Red Cross runs a campaign for the missing under the slogans End the Silence and The Right to Know.[32] The ICRC is concerned that governments recognize their obligations in situations of conflict to ensure that the missing are identified—by, for example, providing identity tags for all military personnel. These slogans work in the context of war and disaster, but in the case of those who go missing, perhaps of their own accord, the right to know has to be balanced with the right to disappear—the rights of those who vanish versus the rights of those left behind—and this complicates the work of agencies trying to help.

But even this rendering of the problem is too simple. It isn't just a conflict between the rights of the person who has decided to go missing and the rights of those left behind. The decision to leave may indeed be a decision that should be respected—unless, as the website for Missing People tells us, those missing might harm themselves or others—but such decisions may not always be clear-cut. In some sense, if we recognize that what we do is not transparent, even to ourselves—and indeed that we "ourselves," as selves, are not fixed and immutable beings that simply exist, are present, are not "missing"—then the decisions we make, the things that we do, are not something that we have fully conscious choice about or control over. It is clear from reading the stories of missing people who have been traced and who resume contact with their families that in some cases at least, perhaps even in many, although people had *decided* to disappear from view, they were nevertheless relieved to be offered the chance to return. Doug Richmond's "how-to" book for those who want to "disappear completely and never be found" makes the lives of those he calls "disappearees" sound pretty desperate, not just because of the potential loneliness but because of the inevitable and continual need to take care to do nothing that will risk discovery of the deception involved in their new identity.[33] Voluntarily renewing contact, should the disappeared choose to do so, can be difficult, and the various agencies seem to have an important role as mediators. In well over half of cases, though, people who have eventually been located have been adamant that there was no going back, and many didn't want to reestablish any contact at all with those they had left behind.[34]

If former member of Parliament John Stonehouse's account of his own faked suicide and disappearance—and how he was tracked down by police in Australia—is to be believed at all, it reveals a man undecided about what to do and in the end tortured by the multiple identities he assumes.[35] Stonehouse recounts how on several occasions he left his clothes on the beach and made elaborate preparations to move to a different hotel under an assumed name ready to emigrate to Australia only to find himself returning to retrieve his old identity—he had not been missed—and take up the threads of his old life. Even when he finally did go through with the fake suicide, at something like the fourth attempt, and flew to Australia, he returned to Copenhagen shortly afterward to observe the reaction to his disappearance in the United Kingdom—and presumably, though he tells us nothing of this in his autobiography, to meet up with his lover and later second wife, Sheila Buckley. Stonehouse records his relief when his deception is finally discovered by the police.

Stories of the missing can be strangely compelling and heartrending and provide fertile ground for crime writers and those interested in mysterious disappearances, as well as for accounts based on particular cases.[36] In these stories there is generally little sense of what the uncertainty of "ambiguous loss" entails, though Stewart O'Nan's novel *Songs for the Missing* is an exception, stepping outside the genre to present a grueling feel for what losing a child might be like.[37] There are also several "how-to" manuals designed to help people who want to undertake tracing on their own of friends or others they have lost touch with.[38] The interest in resuming contact with old school friends is paralleled by a huge interest in genealogy. Television programs based on stories of the missing, and containing appeals for information, have an avid following, and viewers phone in with sightings of the missing. The series *Missing Live,* produced by Leopard Films and broadcast on BBC One daytime TV in early 2009 attracted a 23.1 percent share of the audience: 1.05 million viewers.[39] A drama series recounting the story of a fictional police missing-persons unit was produced by the same organization and attracted 1.55 million viewers.

When the missing reappear, they reveal how the impact of their disappearance reverberates down the years. Ian McEwan relates how the reappearance of an elder brother, in late middle age, revealed so much that had been semivisible in his early life but not understood or grasped.[40] The brother, born before his parents had married and when his mother's first husband was still alive, had been given up for adoption. McEwan never missed his brother—he did not know a brother existed, so how could he? But his relationship with his parents was scarred by mysterious and problematic stories untold. He talks of the "great burden of shame and silence" his parents must have carried, but concludes, speaking of what led his mother to give away his brother on the platform at Reading Station: "To understand fully this singular, painful event would require the resources of an omniscient god. The full story is beyond our reach." The brother always knew that there was a mystery in his origins; McEwan did not. The discovery of a brother led, McEwan tells us, to "a forced and continuing reappraisal of the past.... Small instances keep offering themselves up for recalibration."[41] And the larger story of his childhood had to be rethought, and new conjectures put in place as to the possible motivations and feelings that led to this or that. The presence of what was unspoken was there, all the time, in evasions, if not in lies. His brother's unacknowledged absence meant that those in the family who were there were in a sense missing to each other—more missing than they might have been otherwise. Their story was incomplete, lacking in essential particulars, colored by what they could not talk about—without McEwan knowing it.

As Jason Cowley's narrator, in the midst of his search for his long-missing father, observes, "It occurred to me... that the solution to my quest was that there was no solution: other people in all their tortured interiority were essentially other, mysteries ultimately even to themselves."[42] It may be the endless fascination with this mystery that leads to the curious addiction to missing person stories, and the continuing attempt to bring the missing home, to conceal the impossibility of ever knowing the answer, perhaps, or, maybe, to reassure ourselves that our own sense of ourselves as ungraspable is not misplaced. Or, possibly, both. Those who seem to deal best with ambiguous loss, Pauline Boss tells us, are those who are able to hold on to two contradictory notions simultaneously: the idea that the missing person is dead yet also might nevertheless walk through the door one fine day.[43]

The Continuing Search

Generations pass, geopolitics shift, parameters change, but the searching goes on, for some people at least. Archives that were closed for a period of time are opened to searchers; restrictions in the former Soviet Union and in Eastern Europe are lifted, and access to new archives becomes possible.[44] More advanced identification techniques are developed—DNA makes identification possible when bodies are found, even after decades have passed. Controversies and ambiguities remain too, alongside human remains, and have implications for the politics of tracing in the present. Why indeed should we still want to know what happened, after all this time?

Some sixty years after the end of the Second World War and a couple of generations later, few of those whose relatives worked with or were members of the Nazi Party have written openly about their experience. Indeed, some of the Germans interviewed for Mark Wyman's 1989 book on the displaced,

DPs: Europe's Displaced Persons, chose to remain anonymous.[45] The beginnings of such writing, in the 1970s, took the form of biographies of the authors' fathers.[46] Other stories are told as fiction: Christa Wolf's *A Model Childhood,* for example, and Rachel Seiffert's *The Dark Room.*[47] Seiffert's book tells three stories of Germans during and in the aftermath of the war. The second story concerns five children who make their way from Bavaria to Hamburg, to the ruins of their grandmother's house, after their parents are arrested by the occupying forces. They are unaware of why they are regarded with suspicion by those they encounter, and are assisted on the journey by a young man who helps them cross the borders between military zones and teaches them how to beg for food and shelter and avoid the attention of the military. Only later, when he has disappeared, do they discover that their companion was traveling under identity documents stolen from a Jew who died in the camps. They are left with "a sick feeling" that the man who saved them and was like a brother to them was "both right and wrong, good and bad; both at the same time."[48] *A Model Childhood* is not fiction, although names and places are replaced. Eric Santner explores how the narrator of Wolf's story excavates from her childhood traces of moments when her Nazi father, a soldier home from the front, betrays rapidly concealed emotions of empathy and protest, as, for example, when he hears of the execution of five Polish hostages.[49] Santner describes how such parents are absent to their children, "psychologically speaking, always elsewhere," with the result that their children's development is disrupted.[50] The parents are unable to show emotion in relation to past events. They can relate the facts but not "reveal any sign of an emotional involvement in the events, any indication [of] contrition, shame or mourning, anything resembling an *affective* memory to accompany the memory of facts and events."[51] Wolf's excavations of the traces of affect, Santner argues, open the possibility of "a self that feels entitled to play with its boundaries" and can relate to "the oppressed of history";[52] a self that can live with an impure, uncanny identity, with missingness.

In Katrin FitzHerbert's autobiographical account—a history of her family across two world wars that recounts their movement to Germany after the First World War and back again after the Second World War—the author tells of how she had to attempt to reconcile a Nazi upbringing with her subsequent life in Britain. Born in 1936 in Berlin and raised as Katrin Thiele, she assumed the name Kay Norris after her arrival in the United Kingdom in 1946.[53] Her grandparents on her mother's side had been forced to return to Germany in 1918—her grandfather was German, and her grandmother British. They became committed Germans, her grandfather working as an official at the Nazi headquarters in Berlin, and their daughter, Katrin's mother, Elfreda, married a "dedicated Nazi," an officer in the Wehrmacht, Eberhard Thiele, who worked with the Nazi Party and the Hitler Youth.[54] Katrin herself was equally dedicated to the values she absorbed, and when defeat came, the nine-year-old decided she would hold fast to her Nazi ideals, although inwardly, while outwardly conforming with whatever was required. There was no help, no one she could talk to about what to do or what to think.

The family fled from the advancing Russians—mother and children by car and by train, grandparents leaving Berlin later, on foot, when the Nazi headquarters ceased functioning—and sought refuge at a solitary farm in Süppling, in the U.S. zone. Her father went into hiding, until her mother persuaded him to give himself up to the American authorities, although "if he had decided to avoid captivity [he] could have done so. His SS officer brother and many others like him managed it easily. . . . [He] shredded his identity papers and made his way to a relative in a village where nobody else knew him . . . and within a very short time he had become a pillar of the local community."[55] But for some reason Katrin's father was being hunted urgently by the Americans, and her mother, not knowing why he was being sought, feared for the safety of the rest of the family if he remained in hiding. On parting, they made an agreement that a best friend of her mother's, Kätchen Beume, would be a point of contact.

When, some time later, Eberhard Thiele wrote to Kätchen Beume from his prisoner of war camp, and later as a civilian internee, "she decided not to reveal to either of my parents the whereabouts of the other," Katrin discovered afterward.[56] Her mother, Elfreda, had in the meantime used her fluent English to find herself a job working as a translator with the British, hiding her activities as a wartime broadcaster for the Nazis and pretending that her soldier-husband had been reported missing on the Russian front years before. She had no desire to be reunited with her husband and was making a new life for herself as an independent woman, something she had never been able to be before. Elfreda decided to apply for "repatriation" with her two children to England and eventually married a British officer she had met through her work.

In the meantime, Katrin's father had "picked himself up, dusted himself down and become a perfectly successful citizen of the new West Germany", as had most of the millions of former Nazi Party members.[57] Eventually he and Kätchen Beume married and emigrated to Canada, partly in the hope that his children could join him there. What his daughter Katrin could never understand was what had happened to his Nazism. Had he renounced his beliefs, as everyone else in Germany seemed to have done, or locked them away in his heart or, like her, "tried to sort out for himself what had been daft and what had made sense about it all"?[58] She never felt able to talk to him about it. When they met, even many years afterward, they would always slip back into the old relationship of father and nine-year-old daughter, papa and his little girl.

But Katrin didn't want to entirely give up on her German identity, which caused problems in the thoroughly Anglicized family hers had become. While others were freezing out the wartime period, she didn't want to do that. At school and later at college she had to face the assumption that her family must either have been in the camps or have been involved in the July plot against Hitler—so that she was deserving of sympathy for the horrible time she must have had—and that all other Germans were uniformly bad: "British post-war culture hadn't equipped the population for dealing with the overwhelming majority of Germans, including us, who had supported their country's war effort, but had not been involved in, or allowed themselves to know about, Nazi mass murder."[59]

Her account ends with a discussion of how, eventually, in 1992, she began to research her family history. It was only at that point that she realized why her father had been so urgently sought by the Americans when the family was at Süppling. A few miles away, a thousand camp inmates on the march from Auschwitz had been herded into a barn and burned, and the man in charge was named Gerhard Thiele. She tells of her relief when she discovers that this was a case of mistaken identity; she is eventually sent a photograph of Gerhard Thiele, who looks not the least like her father, Eberhard Thiele.[60] Her father was not, as she had dreaded during her research, a mass murderer.

This is too easy though. What if he had been? Would it then have been obvious to his wife and children that he was a monster? Bernard Schlink tackles these difficult questions in his book *The Reader*.[61] The narrator of the novel tries to resolve his love for an older woman, Hanna—a woman who had been involved in just such an atrocity as Gerhard Thiele. As one of the guards in charge of a group of women prisoners on a march from Auschwitz, she had stood by as the women, locked into a church overnight, had burned to death when the church was bombed and caught fire:

> I wanted simultaneously to understand Hanna's crime and to condemn it. But it was too terrible for that. When I tried to understand it, I had the feeling I was failing to condemn it as it must be condemned. When I condemned it as it must be condemned, there was no room for understanding. But even as I wanted to understand Hanna, failing to understand her meant betraying her all over again. I could not resolve

this. I wanted to pose myself both tasks—understanding and condemnation. But it was impossible to do both.[62]

Disappeared Children

In Argentina too, the story continues, with its complexities and ambiguities.
In addition to the search for remains, the trials that ensue, and the debates over
memory and memorials, another thread remains to be unraveled: the fate of
the disappeared children of the disappeared. There were many young women
among those abducted, some of them pregnant. The common practice of
their abductors was to detain and torture the mother until she had given birth
and then to seize the baby for adoption by families involved in or sympathetic
to the repression. Sometimes, babies were adopted innocently by families
who had no idea of the children's origins. Sometimes, small children were
abducted with their parents and similarly seized for adoption. The aim was to
save the children from becoming the next generation of "subversives," and to
place them with families in which they would be brought up differently.[63]

The fight to find and restore children to their birth families was led by the
Abuelas (Grandmothers) of the Plaza de Mayo, an organization founded at
the same time as the Madres, and for the same reason—the coming together
of a group of women with the same aim: the search for the children of their
disappeared children. Their work has had considerable impact.[64] They were
instrumental in the use of forensic archaeology in the exhumation of the disappeared, and in the foundation of the Argentine Forensic Archaeology Team
(*Equipo Argentino de Antropologia Forense*, or EAAF). It became clear that
there were techniques that could not only determine whether a baby or a
fetus was buried with its mother but also confirm whether a woman had
given birth before her death. When it became clear that a method of confirming identity was necessary, that circumstantial evidence would not be
enough, it was the Abuelas who realized the possibility of blood tests and
DNA matching in establishing identities.[65] They were instrumental in setting
up a National Bank of Genetic Data (BNDG) to collect samples from parents
of the disappeared and from children in doubt as to their origins.[66] It was also
the work of the Abuelas that led to the inclusion of the right to identity in
the UN Declaration of the Rights of the Child. During the period of impunity, the fight for the restitution of children to their birth families went on,
in parallel with the prosecution of those who had abducted them as babies.
Impunity did not extend to those crimes.

By 2010 the Abuelas had "located and returned their true identity to
101 of the estimated 400 persons born in captivity and given away by the

military to childless couples."[67] Alicia Zubasnabar, one of the founders and first president of the Abuelas, died in 2008 without locating her grandchild.[68] One of those who was located and returned was the son of Abel Pedro Madariaga, who had worked since his return from exile in 1985 as secretary to the Abuelas. His wife, a surgeon who treated the poor in Buenos Aires and was twenty-eight when she was abducted and killed, gave birth to a boy before she died. One day in February 2010, that boy was one of those who "appeared." He contacted the Abuelas when eventually, aged thirty-three, he discovered from his adoptive mother, by then separated from her violent husband, that he had been illegally adopted. Tests showed that his father was Abel Pedro Madariaga. His son, Francisco Madariaga Quintela, commented: "For the first time, I know who I was. Who I am."[69]

However, things were not usually this straightforward.[70] Not all children were happy with their new identity as children of the disappeared, or the implications of separation from their adoptive parents, who were often imprisoned when the facts of their illegal appropriation of children emerged. Even though since 1987 judges had been able to order genetic testing in cases where there was strong circumstantial evidence, and then prosecute appropriators for abduction of minors among other offenses, cases still often took many years and in some instances were not resolved. Opponents of the process argued that restoration of a child to its biological family might constitute a second trauma, while others contended that allowing appropriation to continue meant a child living in "a virtual state of slavery."[71] The detective stories behind the searches and their emotional complexities captured the imagination in a way the search for the disappeared themselves did not. Two films, The Official Story and Cautiva, draw on such stories.[72]

Although children who refuse DNA tests can be compelled to surrender material or clothing that contains DNA, tests on belongings don't necessarily work. This is what happened in the case of Marcela and Felipe Noble Herrera, in which the samples were contaminated.[73] The case of the Noble children is particularly contentious. Marcela and Felipe Noble Herrera are the adopted children of Ernestina Herrera de Noble, media tycoon and owner of the publishing group Clarín and an opponent of the current president of Argentina, Cristina Fernández de Kirchner.[74] The children claim that their identity is a private matter, not for anyone else to determine.[75] Marcela has been quoted as saying that if they discovered they were the children of disappeared Argentines, they would try "to assimilate it, it's up to us to prepare ourselves and it's up to us to see what we want to do. Only we will know how we'll feel."[76] The case had been ongoing for twenty years, since the Abuelas first suspected that the two might be children of the disappeared.[77] Estela de Carlotto, president of the Abeluas, regretted that the case had turned into a "war," but stressed that they wanted to know the truth. If it turned out that they were the children of abducted parents, they would still be able "to live with whoever they want, follow their usual lives," and enjoy their inheritance. The case, she said, was not "a war between the government and the opposition Clarín news media," but a human question.[78] However, this seems disingenuous. The appropriations were political—part of the fight against "subversion." Thus the recovery of those children can only be political too—part of the recovery of their parents and families as speaking beings with the right to their own political views.

Even when finding or exposing their story as children of ambiguous origins may be complex and dangerous—both to them and to those around them—many people do seem compelled to make the attempt. Alex Kurzem, who as a boy escaped the extermination of Jewish women and children in his home village of Koidanov near Minsk in the Second World War, survived by avoiding exposure and making sure no one discovered his identity. Alex—aged five at the time—fled into the forest during the night before the massacre, only to be found and "adopted" by a Latvian brigade, later part of the SS and almost certainly responsible for many massacres themselves. Alex was adopted as the brigade's lucky mascot and later became part of a Latvian Nazi family who fled to Australia after the war. Thinking his father dead, and having witnessed the slaughter of his mother and siblings, Alex made a new life in Australia under the name given him by the Latvian brigade and never spoke of this part of his past even to his own wife and family. He had always been a great storyteller, telling his wife and his children gripping accounts of his early life, with props drawn from a small suitcase he kept locked at all times, but no one realized that he concealed much about his own childhood, as well as hiding the extent of what he didn't know but suspected. Eventually this posture became impossible for him to maintain, and he confided to his son Mark that he wanted his help to find out who he was. The search that ensued led back to the village where Alex had been brought up, to an unexpected half brother and to villagers who remembered him as a child. Only at this point did he discover that his father had survived capture and imprisonment at Auschwitz and Dachau and returned home to Koidanov. By the time Alex discovered his true identity, his father was dead, leaving only the half brother by a second marriage. Alex's father had believed that all three of his children by his first marriage had been killed, along with his wife. The search overturned what had been a quiet family life in Australia, prompted interventions from those who didn't want old skeletons uncovered, and left many questions unresolved. Alex had his story now, but it was as if there had been two persons in his body, "the Alex everybody knows and... another Alex who was a secret."[79] In the end, after all the searching, and all the disruption of family that revealing his hidden background caused, there was "no resolution, no absolution, no closure, no moving on, no getting over it.... Only an accommodation of the past."[80]

One of the most poignant areas of tracing work during the immediate aftermath of the Second World War was the search for children stolen by the SS as part of its attempt to increase the stock of what it saw as good blood in the face of losses at the front and a declining German birthrate. First indications were that some fifty thousand Swedish, Czech, Norwegian, French, Dutch, and Polish children had been taken from their parents to be raised as Germans.[81] But it turned out that as many as two hundred thousand children may have been abducted from Poland alone. Searching was difficult. Many children had settled with their adoptive parents and did not want to return—or if they did return, did so unhappily. And the new parents quite naturally did not want to give up their children and obstructed the searchers where they could. Even when children were traced to their new addresses, their names had been changed, and they no longer spoke anything but German—they had been thoroughly Germanized. Some thirty thousand of the Polish children were traced, but in 1948 the program ended. For UNRRA it was no longer policy to add to the "biological military strength of the enemy"—that of the new enemy, that is.[82]

Perhaps equally poignant is the search still taking place much later, and only begun much more recently, by those born and reared in Nazi orphanages as part of the SS-run *Lebensborn* program. Their search is for the truth about their origins and their birth parents. Contrary to what was believed for many years afterward, the *Lebensborn* homes were not "stud farms" where women were made pregnant by unknown SS men, but part of an attempt by the Nazis to provide places where women could give birth to "racially valuable" children to increase the German population.[83] As part of this plan, some tens of thousands of married and unmarried women of what were judged to be sound Aryan characteristics were encouraged to bear their children, who in the case of the unmarried had often been fathered by married German officers, rather than have abortions.[84] These women were enabled to give birth discreetly and give the child for adoption if they wished (or even, in some cases, if they didn't).[85] As adults by then in their sixties, these children and those stolen from their natural parents in occupied countries, began to meet and talk about what had happened to them.[86] Their stories are of lies and evasions, of half truths and suspicions that not all was as it should be, and finally of having to come to terms with their ambiguous origins—as children of the SS, but as simultaneously its victims.[87]

Most of the birth records of the *Lebensborn* program have been destroyed or lost, though some survive. Dorothee Schmitz-Köster interviewed many *Lebensborn* children and reports that they "remember a vague feeling of something wrong in their early childhood," but although "they asked again and again...after a while they stopped asking because they received only evasive answers": "They started their search without even knowing exactly what they were looking for. They rummaged through drawers and closets, looked desperately into documents and photographs, eavesdropped on adults' discussions—without any result. The longer the situation lasted, the more insecure the children felt."[88]

Instead of blaming their parents, they regarded themselves as inferior and responsible for their own treatment. It was only when much older, and with their own families grown too, that they had begun to investigate their origins thoroughly. But this process was full of ambiguity and ambivalence. As one of Schmitz-Köster's interviewees, Anne M., remarked: "You never know whom you will find....You cannot be sure whether or not you will take a liking to the person you find, whether or not you want to give him or her the place of a father or mother."[89] Anne M. searched through military and other archives and in cemeteries and phoned everyone with her mother's maiden name. Finally, through a chance meeting with a historian who shared her mother's name and had an archive containing the name and address of her mother's sister, she discovered that her mother had died six months earlier. She met her half brothers and sisters, who had known of an elder half sister, and who told her that her mother had always regretted having parted with her.[90] Other cases were less comforting, with difficulties, like the epithet "Nazi bastard," reverberating down the generations. Hedda W., born in a *Lebensborn* home, refused to disavow the National Socialist official her mother had later married, and her own son broke off all contact with her, unable to live with the contradiction and accept that as far as his mother was concerned his step-grandfather, who was convicted and executed after the war, could have been a loving father.[91]

Adrianna Cavarero argues that it is through telling the stories of our lives to each other that we find our uniqueness and express our desire for some form of unity as a singular being.[92] Who we are is exposed through this shared telling of stories, accounts of what has happened, where and when, in all its particular detail, rather than through a recitation of our various identities, or the roles that we play in what we call social reality.[93] We all have a role to play—indeed many different roles to play—as mothers, breadwinners, teachers, lovers. But we cannot sum up the uniqueness of a person by summarizing the range of roles that they play. Roles may tell us *what* someone is or what they "do," but not *who* they are, in all their irreplaceability. There is always something more, something not encompassed by the social role, or something less, something required by the role that the particular person does not quite fit. Nor can we say *who* someone is by summarizing their characteristics or attributes: blue eyes, long hair, a degree in sociology, wears sandals. When we love someone it is not because of their eye color or qualifications, but because of some indescribable something. We love the *who* and not the *what*.[94] Philosophers may seek to address the question of *what* a human being is (or political philosophers what a citizen is or economists what a consumer is, for example), and respond by evoking universals and abstractions. In contrast, the story, or the exchange of stories—for the telling of a story is not a solitary occupation—concerns *who* we are, as particular, unique, embodied beings who are born and live a life. As the reflection of ourselves in the eyes of others gives us a sense of wholeness, so the telling of our story by other people affirms for us that unity of self that we so desire.[95] We cannot get that affirmation from a solitary recounting of our own narrative—it has to come to us as a gift from someone else. Nor can we wait until our story is finished—we need the tale while we are still alive.[96] Neither autobiography nor biography is what is at stake.

When we are unable to take part in this exchange of stories, we do not know who we are. When someone dies, their story is recounted to others by those who miss them, or told and retold among those who already know it, as a form of commemoration: "As if the link with the absent consisted in the thread of the tale, the story gets repeated until it is broken by forgetfulness."[97] When someone goes *missing,* to tell their story in this way—in the absence of the main proponent—would be a denial of the hope that they might one day return to be the participant once more in their own story, or a refusal to admit that their story may be continuing in another place, among a different group of people.

In telling our stories, we never master or decide who we are: "The story... does not have at its centre a compact and coherent identity [but rather] an unstable and insubstantial unity, longed for by a desire that evokes...the unmasterable design—of a life whose story only others can recount."[98] The *who* in that sense is always *missing.* We are not, then, present to ourselves but rather always in search of ourselves, or of some accommodation with what we might be. At the end of his story of the search for who he really was, for his origins as a child and a determination of his responsibility or otherwise for the things he was made to do in order to survive, Alex Kurzem found "only an accommodation with the past." All that was possible, for him and for his son Mark too, was "to find a way of living, comfortably or not," with who they might be.[99] Telling his story, through Mark's book, was for Alex Kurzem perhaps just one way of trying to find that accommodation. In this sense maybe we are all *missing persons*—persons who, through stories told to each other and through a recognition of the impossibility of a final end to those stories, a final answer to the question of who we are, come to an accommodation with ourselves and each other as in some sense ultimately *missing*. A politics based on that accommodation, and the relations in which it is inevitably entwined, would be a different politics from the one we have at the moment. A politics based on regard for the *who* and not the *what*, a politics based not on categorization, determination and the search for certainty, but one based perhaps on "the infinity of encounters of millions of singular worlds."[100] Or, in Paul Kottman's words, a politics "that is attentive to *who* one is, rather than *what* one is."[101] In the politics of those who are displaced, go missing, or are disappeared, which is what the chapters of this book explore, we can perhaps find traces of such a politics already in existence—and signs of the struggle for such a politics in the face of those who would try to return to the safety of a politics founded on the control of identifiable persons.

Conclusion

> Political being-together is a being-between: between
> identities, between worlds.
>
> —Jacques Rancière, *Disagreement: Politics and*
> *Philosophy*

Although much recent political theory and philosophy has focused on critical analyses of contemporary politics and forms of governance, there have been a number of attempts to think about a different politics, a politics that does not objectify the person but works with uniqueness and singularity.[1] Such a politics would entail forms of community very different from those that are built on the assumption of community as the coming together of separate individuals who share something in common. Is such a thing possible? How would it work? What does it mean to think in such terms?

This book has been an exploration of these questions not through philosophical debate and discussion but through a detailed study of missing persons and their treatment, a study based as much on story and anecdote as on analysis and explanation. To operate otherwise would be to already objectify the person, to work with categories or roles and not with the person-as-such. The person-as-such can be approached only through paying attention to particular actions in particular places at particular times; the person-as-such is not generalizable. Politics, as Jacques Rancière reminds us, "is always local and occasional."[2] If we are to identify practices "driven by the assumption of equality between any and every speaking being and by a concern to test this equality," we need to examine particular practices.[3] Such practices, which "give rise to a meeting of police logic and egalitarian logic," are what make a thing "political."[4]

When people disappear or go missing, practices of action and activism take place that contest the instrumentalization or objectification of the person and the production of a police logic. In chapter 1, we looked at the missing posters produced in New York in the aftermath of September 11 and saw that the continued display of the posters long after it became clear that the missing were not going to return could be seen as a form of political dissent. The posters protested the appropriation of the missing as heroes by the federal authorities and demanded they be seen as people with their own particularities and political views, views that might differ markedly from the views of the government. The appearance of the posters, on every wall and window in Manhattan, proclaimed the sudden visibility of lives until then rendered invisible by the corporate architecture of the towers, and the emergence of what Giorgio Agamben calls "bare life"—life produced by sovereign power as without voice—on to the streets.[5] People, ordinary people, gathered in parks to discuss and debate what had happened, and to mourn the missing. The authorities responded by urging people to go home and hug their children—and leave politics to those in command. But the posters, and the protests, remained.

The person in present-day politics in the West tends to be seen as the object of administration and governance rather than someone of value as such. Politics has been replaced by biopolitics—the governance and administration of populations.[6] Or, as Agamben would argue, politics in the West has always relied on separations and exclusions—in particular on the separation between political life and the life of the home, producing the life of the home as bare life, a form of life that in contemporary times inhabits the camp.[7] We saw in chapter 2 how those in displaced persons camps in the aftermath of the Second World War were treated as bare life—life with no political voice—lives to be saved, nothing more. Jacques Rancière argues that what we have is a police order, where persons are defined by what they are and what roles they have in the accepted mode of "human being-together," which is defined as the only one possible.[8] This order can be challenged, he argues, by "the production through a series of actions of a body and a capacity for enunciation not previously identifiable within a given field of experience, whose identification is thus part of the reconfiguration of the field of experience."[9] This challenge happened in the DP camps, where those within the camps refused to be treated as bare life. They made their voices heard, demanding that their relatives be traced, or just setting about it themselves. This, they insisted, was more important than food or shelter. It happened in the actions of the Red Cross workers who insisted that families and relatives count, and that their distress demanded a response, as we saw in chapter 3. The search was a search for particular people, never mind the category in which they were placed by the camp or administering authorities. This assumption of the importance of the person-as-such challenged the tidy arrangements of the occupying authorities and demanded that persons and their relationships count.

For those searching, missing persons are missed for *who* they are—in all their specificity—not for *what* they are or what role they play. However, we saw in chapter 4 that in the aftermath of the London bombings in 2005 the concern of the authorities was not who the missing were but what they were. Their first priority was to identify those responsible for the bombings, and they would not release any information whatsoever to worried relatives in the meantime. The call for attention to be paid to persons not process, made in the London Assembly report, did not have much impact, but questions have been raised again about treatment of relatives. It has been disclosed that even the details of those who survived the blast for long enough to give their names to their rescuers or in the hospital were not passed to those searching for them. The procedures in place for responding to disasters do not focus on people but on procedures. They miss the person-as-such, and the web of relations in which the person is embedded.

In the case of the London bombings, it was not forensic difficulties that prevented the identification of the missing for so long. In New York, the situation was very different. Existing techniques had to be extended, and new systems developed, and the scale of the tragedy was a challenge in itself. As chapter 5 explored, the process was profoundly ambiguous. On the one hand, vast resources were spent in the attempt to identify the remains of those missing in the collapse of the towers, in what could be seen as a reimposition of a police order of categorization without remnant; on the other, the attempt was bound to fail. Even if remains were identified, they were fragmented and incomplete, insufficient on their own to reclaim the person-as-such. The process was complicated, as in the case of the missing in action, which we explored in chapter 6, by the way in which those lost, labeled as "heroes," seem almost, like military personnel, to belong not to their families, but to the authorities. Produced as something like Agamben's *homo sacer,* service personnel exist in a no-man's-land between life and death, a place where killing does not count as homicide. They are no longer persons-as-such. When they are missing in action, it is the military authorities who assume the right to determine whether they are to be presumed dead. And it is these same authorities in many cases who claim the ownership of the bodies of the missing and the right to decide how they should be buried and their "sacrifice" commemorated. However, we saw that, particularly since the First World

War, families have contested this claim and asserted their own ownership of their kin. Sometimes families have prevailed, and the dead have been "demobilised"; sometimes they have not.

An examination of *the politics of missing persons* has revealed a struggle between two different politics: contemporary politics, which can be seen as a politics that instrumentalizes the individual, *a politics that misses the person,* and a politics of the person-as-such. Protesting the missing can be seen as a demand for this different form of politics. In the protests in Argentina after disappearances during the "dirty war," which we looked at in chapter 7, the insistence that the missing be returned alive was central. The refusal of identification and reburial was of course linked to the pursuit of prosecutions of those responsible, but it was also, and perhaps more fundamentally, a call for the disappeared to be returned as fully political lives, persons who were activists in one way or another, committed to their political beliefs. It wasn't enough for the authorities to return a bag of bones and claim that this was the end of it. Yet at the same time, we saw how, in Eric Carlson's *I Remember Julia,* the memories of those who knew Julia did not add up; it was impossible to produce a complete picture of who she was.

It turns out in the end that a politics of the person-as-such is a politics that is open to the way in which in some sense we are all "missing persons." The person-as-such can never be fully known, completely specified, or tied down. As we saw in the stories we followed in chapter 8, stories of those who went missing deliberately for one reason or another or who were abducted as children, and those who tried to trace them years afterward, there is always something imponderable, some lack or gap in our grasp, whether of each other or of ourselves. A politics that acknowledges this is what I am calling *a politics of the person as missing.* It is a politics that not only traces the absent but recognizes that the person-as-such is in some sense never fully present.

What I have traced in this book are instances of such a politics taking place, making space for itself within another politics based on administration and control. I have shown how this other politics, whether we describe it as a police order, sovereign power, or biopolitics, is disturbed by a politics of the person-as-such, though of course it fights back. Missing persons, the displaced, and the disappeared, who are neither present nor fully absent but inhabit a world between the living and the dead, are an exemplary site of such disturbance.

.

Notes

Preface

1. Report, Rheda, 30 May 1945, UN Archives, S-0413–0002-07.

2. Wisława Szymborska, "Starvation Camp near Jaslo," in *Poems New and Collected* (Orlando, FL: Harcourt, 1998), 42.

3. When I use the terms "object" and "person" I do not intend to deny the possibility of personhood to what we generally think of as inanimate things. As far as I am concerned, things can enjoy "personhood" too. The distinction between the animate and the inanimate is deeply problematic.

Introduction

1. This argument is developed in detail in my *Trauma and the Memory of Politics* (Cambridge: Cambridge University Press, 2003).

2. I borrow this phrase of course from Jean-Luc Nancy, *The Inoperative Community*, trans. Peter Connor, Lisa Garbus, Michael Holland, and Simona Sawhney (Minneapolis: University of Minnesota Press, 1991).

3. W. G. Sebald, *Vertigo*, trans. Michael Hulse (London: Harvill, 1999), 262–63.

4. Primo Levi's poem "If This Is a Man" begins with the lines "You who live safe / In your warm houses." Primo Levi, *"If This Is a Man" and "The Truce,"* trans. Stuart Woolf (London: Abacus, 1979), 17.

5. Paul Burstow, "Dying Alone: Assessing Isolation, Loneliness, and Poverty," http://www.paulburstow.org.uk/resources/index/; John Waite, "A Death Unnoticed," Face the Facts, BBC Radio 4, 23 July 2009, http://www.bbc.co.uk/programmes/b00lr2g8#synopsis.

6. Himadeep Muppidi, *The Politics of the Global* (Minneapolis: University of Minnesota Press, 2004); Muppidi, "Shame and Rage: International Relations and the World School of Colonialism," in *Interrogating Imperialism: Conversations on Gender, Race, and War*, ed. Robin L. Riley and Naeem Inayatullah (New York: Palgrave, 2006), 51–62.

7. I am indebted to Himadeep Muppidi for this point.

8. Jenny Edkins, "Humanitarianism, Humanity, Human," *Journal of Human Rights* 2, no. 2 (2003): 253–58.

9. Judith Butler, *Frames of War: When Is Life Grievable?* (London: Verso, 2009), 1; see also Butler, *Precarious Life: The Powers of Mourning and Violence* (London: Verso, 2004).

10. Nancy Scheper-Hughes, *Death without Weeping: The Violence of Everyday Life in Brazil* (Berkeley: University of California Press, 1992).

11. Ralph Ellison, *Invisible Man* (London: Penguin, 2001).

12. Frantz Fanon, *Black Skin, White Masks,* trans. Charles Lam Markmann (London: Pluto, 1986), 109, 112.

13. Muppidi, "Shame and Rage," 3.

14. Alinah Kelo Segobye, "Missing Persons, Stolen Bodies, and Issues of Patrimony: The El Negro Story," *Pula: Botswana Journal of African Studies* 16, no. 1 (2002): 16.

15. Butler, *Frames of War,* 1.

16. Ellison, *Invisible Man,* 3–4.

17. Adil Jussawalla, *Missing Person* (Mumbai: Clearing House, 1976); Fanon, *Black Skin, White Masks.*

18. Vinay Dharwadker, "Poetry of the Indian Subcontinent," in *A Companion to Twentieth-Century Poetry,* ed. Neil Roberts (Oxford: Blackwell, 2003), 273.

19. Nor is the person necessarily a living being—inanimate objects can be persons in the sense I mean here too—though clearly if it is rare to treat a person as a person not an object, an object is even more likely to be objectified.

20. Mary Douglas and Stephen Nay, *Missing Persons: A Critique of the Social Sciences* (Berkeley: University of California Press, 1998).

21. Mary Evans, *Missing Persons: The Impossibility of Auto/Biography* (London and New York: Routledge, 1999), 1.

22. Carolyn Steedman, *Dust* (Manchester: Manchester University Press, 2001).

23. Ibid., 68.

24. Butler, *Precarious Life,* 22–23.

25. Douglas and Nay, *Missing Persons.*

26. Butler, *Precarious Life,* 22.

27. Marie Fatayi-Williams, foreword to *Terrorism and the Politics of Response,* ed. Angharad Closs Stephens and Nick Vaughan-Williams (London and New York: Routledge, 2009), x–xii.

28. Jacques Rancière, *Disagreement: Politics and Philosophy,* trans. Julie Rose (Minneapolis: University of Minnesota Press, 1999).

29. See, for example, Slavoj Žižek, *The Sublime Object of Ideology* (London: Verso, 1989); Jacques Lacan, *Écrits: A Selection,* trans. Alan Sheridan (London: Routledge, 1977).

30. Jacques Rancière, *Dissensus: On Politics and Aesthetics,* trans. Steven Corcoran (London: Continuum, 2010), 36.

31. Rancière, *Disagreement,* 41.

32. Ibid., 40.

33. Giorgio Agamben, *Homo Sacer: Sovereign Power and Bare Life,* trans. Daniel Heller-Roazen (Stanford, CA: Stanford University Press, 1998), 7.

34. Agamben, *Homo Sacer,* 153.

35. Rancière, *Disagreement,* 39.

36. International Committee of the Red Cross (ICRC), *The Missing: ICRC Progress Report* (Geneva: ICRC, 2006), 2.

37. Search Bureau, Control Commission for Germany (BE) Bunde, British Army of the Rhine, "General Instructions for All Officers Engaged in Tracing and Search," 10 September 1945, the National Archives, Kew, FO 945/557.

38. The encyclopaedia divides animals into the following categories: "(a) belonging to the Emperor, (b) embalmed, (c) tame, (d) sucking pigs, (e) sirens, (f) fabulous, (g) stray dogs, (h) included in the present classification, (i) frenzied, (j) innumerable, (k) drawn with a very fine camelhair brush, (l) *et cetera*, (m) having just broken the water pitcher, (n) that from a long way off look like flies." Michel Foucault, *The Order of Things: An Archaeology of the Human Sciences* (London: Tavistock/Routledge, 1970), xv.

39. Foucault, *Order of Things*, xviii.

40. Rancière, *Disagreement*, 41.

41. Žižek, *Sublime Object of Ideology*, 131.

42. Agamben, *Homo Sacer*.

43. Ibid., 115.

44. Agamben, *The Coming Community*, trans. Michael Hardt (Minneapolis: University of Minnesota Press, 1993), 87.

1. Missing Persons, Manhattan

1. "In the matter of courage (a morally neutral virtue): whatever may be said of the perpetrators of Tuesday's slaughter, they were not cowards." Susan Sontag, The Talk of the Town, *New Yorker*, 24 September 2001; see also Sontag, "Of Courage and Resistance," *Nation*, 5 May 2003. For a fascinating discussion of courage, see Anna Funder's lecture on courage: Sydney PEN Voices: The 3 Writers Project, November 2008, on SlowTV, *The Monthly: Australian Politics, Society, and Culture*, http://www.themonthly.com.au/node/1330.

2. See Laura Kurgan, *New York, September 11, 2001: Four Days Later...*, an installation using high-resolution Ikonos satellite imagery of New York on September 15, 2001, Control_Space, ZKM, Karlsruhe, Germany, October 2001, http://www.l00k.org/september_11th_project.

3. At the same time this impossibility is made apparent; see Jean-Luc Nancy, *Le regard du portrait* (Paris: Galilee, 2000). The subject is exposed as nonpresent to itself. I discuss this more fully in "Exposed Singularity," *Journal for Cultural Research* 9, no. 4 (October 2005): 359–86.

4. Roland Barthes, *Camera lucida*, trans. Richard Howard (London: Vintage, 1993), 5.

5. Jane Gross and Jenny Scott, "The Missing: Hospital Treks, Fliers, and the Cry: Have You Seen...?" *New York Times*, 13 September 2001.

6. These gatherings, and some of the discussions, were recorded on video. The New-York Historical Society exhibited a selection of this material in September 2002.

7. Museum of the City of New York, Virtual Union Square, 2001; see also Josie Appleton, "A Very Strange Time Capsule," 14 March 2002, http://www.spiked-online.com/Printable/00000002D466.htm; for a discussion, see Joel McKim, "New York's Spontaneous 9/11 Memorials and the Politics of Ambivalence," *Borderlands e-journal* 9, no. 2 (2010).

8. There is video material of the Union Square gatherings, for example, in Steven Rosenbaum, *7 Days in September* (2002); and Ken Jacobs, *Circling Zero, Part*

One: "We See Absence" (2002). See also the video of Union Square exhibited at the New-York Historical Society in March 2002.

9. David Usborne, "It Has Taken Me My Whole Life to Find Him," *Independent,* 14 September 2001; and Usborne, "Normal Life Resumes," *Independent,* 15 September 2001.

10. David Friend, *Watching the World Change: The Stories behind the Images of 9/11* (New York: Picador, 2006), 40.

11. Ibid.

12. Patty Lampert, quoted in Friend, *Watching the World Change,* 45.

13. Jonathan Wallace, "The Missing," *Year Zero,* 29 September 2001, The Ethical Spectacle, http://www.spectacle.org/yearzero/missing.html.

14. As Diana Taylor remarks, the photographer Lorie Novak noted that the images in the missing posters do not show people in standard gender roles. Diana Taylor, *The Archive and the Repertoire: Performing Cultural Memory in the Americas* (Durham, NC: Duke University Press, 2003), 249.

15. Fred Abrahams and Eric Stover, *A Village Destroyed, May 14, 1999: War Crimes in Kosovo* (Berkeley: University of California Press, with Human Rights Watch and the Human Rights Center at the University of California, Berkeley, 2001), 108–9.

16. Jeshajahu Weinberg and Rina Elieli, *The Holocaust Museum in Washington* (New York: Rizzoli, in collaboration with the United States Holocaust Memorial Museum, 1995).

17. The Tower of Faces, the Yaffa Eliach Shtetl Collection, United States Holocaust Memorial Museum, Photograph #N03043, http://www.ushmm.org/uia-cgi/uia_doc/query/10?uf=uia_RdpfZw.

18. Billie Jones, "Employing Identification in Online Museums." Paper presented at Museums and the Web 2000, Minneapolis, 17–19 April 2000. http://www.archimuse.com/mw2000/papers/jones/jones.html.

19. Richard Crownshaw, "Performing Memory in Holocaust Museums," *Performance Research* 5, no. 3 (2000): 18–27.

20. Mark Wigley, "Insecurity by Design," in *After the World Trade Center: Rethinking New York City,* ed. Michael Sorkin and Sharon Zukin (New York: Routledge, 2002), 69–85.

21. Ibid., 71.

22. Elaine Scarry, *The Body in Pain: The Making and Unmaking of the World* (New York: Oxford University Press, 1985), 281.

23. Ibid., 307.

24. Wigley, "Insecurity by Design," 72.

25. Ibid., 75.

26. Eric Darton, "The Janus Face of Architectural Terrorism: Minoru Yamasaki, Mohammed Atta, and Our World Trade Centre," in Sorkin and Zukin, *After the World Trade Centre,* 89, 88–89.

27. Wigley, "Insecurity by Design," 72.

28. Judith Butler, *Precarious Life: The Powers of Mourning and Violence* (London: Verso, 2004).

29. Wigley, "Insecurity by Design," 84.

30. For a paper that includes many of these images, see David Eng, "The Value of Silence," *Theatre Journal* 54, no. 1 (2002): 85–94.

31. Wigley, "Insecurity by Design," 82–83.

32. "Bare life" is Giorgio Agamben's term: Giorgio Agamben, *Homo Sacer: Sovereign Power and Bare Life,* trans. Daniel Heller-Roazen (Stanford, CA: Stanford University Press, 1998).

33. Taylor, *The Archive and the Repertoire,* 247–48.

34. Angelika Bammer, "Memory Sites: Destruction, Loss, and Transformation— A Reflection in Words and Images," image panels, The Schatten Gallery, Robert W. Woodruff Library, Emory University, 9 September to 9 November 2003, http:// web.library.emory.edu/libraries/schatten/previous/memorysites/.

35. See, for example, Kieran Murray, "Poor Migrant Workers among Victims of US Attacks," Reuters, 12 September 2001, http://www.tepeyac.org/sep12reuters. htm; and Steven Greenhouse and Mireya Navarro, "Those at Towers' Margin Elude List of Missing: The Hidden Victims," *New York Times,* 17 September 2001.

36. Mirian Ching Louje, "The 9/11 Disappeareds," *Nation,* 3 December 2001.

37. See Asociación Tepeyac de New York, http://www.tepeyac.org.ns50.alentus. com/intro.asp; and for a collection of newspaper clippings from the time, http:// www.tepeyac.org/notasprensa.htm.

38. James Ziglar, Immigration and Naturalization Service Commissioner, quoted in Suzanne Gamboa, "Victims May Include Illegal Aliens," *Newsday,* 20 September 2001.

39. Center for History and New Media and American Social History Project/ Center for Media and Learning, The September 11 Digital Archive, Asociación Tepeyac de New York Collection, List of WTC Missing Victims, http://911digitalarchive. org/repository.php?collection_id=18.

40. Edwin Andrés Martínez Tutek, "Undocumented Workers Uncounted Victims of 9/11," *Chicago Tribune,* 7 September 2006, http://redeye.chicagotribune.com/ am-gone0907,0,2135361.story.

41. Center for History and New Media and American Social History Project/ Center for Media and Learning, The September 11 Digital Archive, Asociación Tepeyac de New York Collection, Missing but Not Counted, http://911digitalarchive. org/repository.php?collection_id=18.

42. Jean Baudrillard, *The Spirit of Terrorism* (London: Verso, 2002), 16.

43. The absence of bodies was exaggerated by the self-censorship of the U.S. media, which stopped showing images of people falling from the World Trade Center towers very early on, and refused to cover the retrieval of body parts (Malcolm Hamer, personal communication, 23 October 2001).

44. Address by the President to a Joint Session of Congress and the American People, 20 September 2001, quoted in Maja Zehfuss, "Forget September 11!" *Third World Quarterly* 24, no. 3 (2003): 525.

45. Marshall Sella, "Missing: How a Grief Ritual Is Born," *New York Times Magazine,* 7 October 2001.

46. Vivian Gorlick, "First Person: Why the Posters Haunt Us Still," *New York Times,* 23 September 2001.

47. Amy Waldman, "A Nation Challenged: The Fliers; Posters of the Missing Now Speak of Losses," *New York Times,* 29 September 2001.

48. Friend, *Watching the World Change,* 36–37.

49. *New York Times,* "Joanne Ahladiotis: Going All Out, All the Time," 29 November 2001.

50. Janice Hume, "'Portraits of Grief,' Reflectors of Values: The *New York Times* Remembers Victims of September 11," *Journalism and Mass Communication Quarterly* 80, no. 1 (2003): 166–82.

51. David Simpson, *9/11: The Culture of Commemoration* (Chicago: University of Chicago Press, 2006), 23.

52. Ibid., 51.

53. Judith Greenberg, "Wounded New York," in *Trauma at Home: After 9/11,* ed. Judith Greenberg (Lincoln: University of Nebraska Press, 2003), 23.

54. Hume, "'Portraits of Grief,'" 170.

55. David Usborne, "The Most Important Story of My Life," *The Independent Saturday Review,* 15 September 2001.

56. September 11 Photo Project, "The September 11 Photo Project Launches National Tour at Washington, D.C.'s Military Women's Memorial," Press release, 12 February 2002, http://www.sep11photo.org/. The September 11 Photo Project is now part of the collection of the New York Public Library.

57. Michael Feldschuh, ed., *The September 11 Photo Project* (New York: Regan Books, HarperCollins, 2002).

58. Michael Feldschuh, interview with author, New York, 13 November 2002.

59. Alice Rose George, Gilles Peress, Michael Schulan, and Charles Traub, *Here Is New York: A Democracy of Photographs* (Zurich: Scalo, 2002).

60. Michael Schulan, interview with author, New York, 21 November 2002.

61. George et al., *Here Is New York.*

62. Artists Network of Refuse and Resist, "Our Grief Is Not a Cry for War," artists performance 2001, http://www.refuseandresist.org/newresistance/092301grief.html.

63. Lower Manhattan.info, "Memorial Draws Comments from Fire-Fighters, Others," 29 May 2003, http://www.lowermanhattan.info/news/memorial_draws_comments_from_87335.asp#top.

64. Amber Amundson, "A Widow's Plea for Non-Violence," *Chicago Tribune,* 25 September 2001.

65. Ibid.

66. See, for example, Bill Moyers, "Bill Moyers Interview with Mrs. Admundsen," *Now with Bill Moyers,* PBS, 25 January 2002, http://www.pbs.org/now/transcript/transcript102_full.html.

67. Not in Our Name, "The Pledge of Resistance," 2003, http://www.notinourname.net/index.php?option=com_content&view=article&id=20&Itemid=5. The project closed in 2008.

68. Jeanne Henry, "What Madness Prompts, Reason Writes: New York City September 11–October 2, 2001," *Anthropology and Education Quarterly* 33, no. 3 (2002): 285.

69. Sella, "Missing."

70. City Lore, "Missing: Streetscape of a City in Mourning," http://www.citylore.org/911_exhibit/911_home.html. See Karen J. Kroslowitz, "Spontaneous Memorials: Forums for Dialogue and Discourse," *Museums and Social Issues* 2, no. 2 (2007): 243–56.

71. Laura Flanders, Live reports from Manhattan, filed 10.35pm EST Tues September 11 2001, Working Assets, WorkingforChange, http://www.workingforchange.com/printitem.cfm?itemid=11899.

72. Ibid., filed 1.05pm EST Weds September 12 2001.

73. Jenny Edkins, "The Rush to Memory and the Rhetoric of War," *Journal of Political and Military Sociology* 31, no. 2 (2003): 231–51.

74. Greenberg, "Wounded New York," 23.

75. CBS News, "Many WTC Remains Are Unidentified," August 14, 2003, http://www.cbsnews.com/stories/2003/08/14/attack/main568168.shtml.

76. Marguerite Guzman Bouvard, *Revolutionizing Motherhood: The Mothers of the Plaza de Mayo* (Lanham, MD: SR Books, 1994). The Madres and their protests are discussed in chapter 7.

77. Associated Press, "Final WTC Death Toll Said Down to 2,749," 23 January 2004, http://www.voicesofsept11.org/medical_examiner/012304.html. See also Eric Lipton, "New York Settles on a Number That Defines Tragedy: 2,749 Dead in Trade Center Attack," *New York Times,* 23 January 2004.

78. Marianne Hirsch, "I Took Pictures: September 2001 and Beyond," in Greenberg, *Trauma at Home,* 69.

79. U.S. Department of State, International Information Programs, *New York City: Three Months After: Pictorial Essays Developed during Three Days in December 2001 Capture the City's—and the Nation's—Indomitable Spirit,* http://usinfo.state.gov/topical/pol/terror/album/newyork/.

80. Louis Nevaer, *Missing: Last Seen at the World Trade Center on September 11, 2001,* a touring exhibition of missing person fliers, funded by the Mesoamerica Foundation, http://www.bronston.com/missing/.

81. Patricia Yaeger, "Rubble as Archive, or 9.11 as Dust, Debris, and Bodily Vanishing," in Greenberg, *Trauma at Home,* 189.

2. Displaced Persons, Postwar Europe

1. Mark Wyman, *DPs: Europe's Displaced Persons, 1945–1951* (Ithaca, NY: Cornell University Press, 1989; Associated University Presses, 1998 [with a new introduction]), 17, 19. These figures are disputed. I am grateful to R. Gerald Hughes for his comments on this chapter and the next. For other accounts of displaced persons in the postwar period, see in particular Malcolm J. Proudfoot, *European Refugees, 1939–1952: A Study in Forced Population Movement* (London: Faber and Faber, 1957); and Michael R. Marrus, *The Unwanted: European Refugees in the Twentieth Century* (New York: Oxford University Press, 1985); see also Anna C. Bramwell, ed., *Refugees in the Age of Total War* (London: Unwin Hyman, 1988); Johannes-Dieter Steinert and Inge Weber-Newth, eds., *European Immigrants in Britain, 1933–1950* (Munich: K. G. Saur, 2003); Ian Connor, *Refugees and Expellees in Post-War Germany* (Manchester: Manchester University Press, 2007); and on forced population transfers in the East, Joseph B. Schechtman, *European Population Transfers, 1939–1945* (New York: Oxford University Press, 1946); and Alfred J. Reiber, ed., *Forced Migration in Central and Eastern Europe, 1939–1950* (London: Frank Cass, 2000).

2. The existence of the concentration camps, and the deportations and massacres, had been known since 1942. See, for example, Caroline Moorehead's account of the discussions within the International Committee of the Red Cross in the autumn of 1942: *Dunant's Dream: War, Switzerland, and the History of the Red Cross* (London: HarperCollins, 1998), xxv-xxxi. The British Foreign Office received a telegram containing a message from Gerhart Reigner, secretary of the World Jewish Congress, on

10 August 1942, detailing plans for the extermination of the Jews and the resolution of the Jewish question in Europe. A Foreign Office lawyer called this a "rather wild story." Tom Bower, *Blind Eye to Murder: Britain, America, and the Purging of Nazi Germany—A Pledge Betrayed* (London: Andre Deutsch, 1981), 43. By December, a declaration and condemnation had been issued by the foreign secretary (United Nations Declaration, House of Commons Debate, 17 December 1942, *Hansard,* vol. 385, cols. 2082–87).

3. Contemporary report quoted in F. S. V. Donnison, *Civil Affairs and Military Government: North West Europe, 1944–1946* (London: HMSO, 1961), 220.

4. Donnison, *Civil Affairs and Military Government,* 220.

5. Evelyn Bark, *No Time to Kill* (London: Robert Hale, 1960), 50.

6. Primo Levi, *"If This Is a Man" and "The Truce,"* trans. Stuart Woolf (London: Abacus, 1979), 188.

7. Ibid., 189–90.

8. Donnison, *Civil Affairs and Military Government,* 353.

9. Extracts from report for period April 10 to April 14 [1945] by Mr. E. C. Nottingham, Public Safety Branch, on his tour of AEF Operational Zone, *Post-War Europe: Refugees, Exile, and Resettlement, 1945–1950.* Online archive, FO 1052/336.

10. Donnison, *Civil Affairs and Military Government,* 355.

11. Levi, *"If This Is a Man" and "The Truce,"* 194.

12. Ibid., 374–78.

13. Ibid., 262.

14. Ibid., 275.

15. Ibid., 378.

16. Donnison, *Civil Affairs and Military Government,* 342–43.

17. Moorehead, *Dunant's Dream,* 502; Jessica Reinisch, "Preparing for a New World Order: UNRRA and the International Management of Refugees," in *Post-War Europe: Refugees, Exile, and Resettlement, 1945-1950* (Reading: Thomson Learning EMEA Ltd., 2007), 3, http://www.tlemea.com/postwareurope/essay4.asp.

18. Reinisch, "Preparing for a New World Order." For an official history of UNRRA, see George Woodbridge, *The History of the United Nations Relief and Rehabilitation Administration* (New York: Columbia University Press, 1950).

19. Reinisch, "Preparing for a New World Order," 5.

20. Herbert Lehman address before the Washington Chapter, February 1945, UN Archives, S-1021-0143-35,14, cited in Reinisch, "Preparing for a New World Order," 4. Lehman was UNRRA's first director-general.

21. Jessica Reinisch, "'We Shall Build Anew a Powerful Nation': UNRRA, Internationalism, and National Reconstruction in Poland," *Journal of Contemporary History* 43, no. 3 (2008): 466.

22. UNRRA European Regional Office, "Fifty Facts about the UNRRA," (London: HMSO, 1946), European Navigator, Centre Virtuel de la Connaissance sur l'Europe (CVCE), http://www.ena.lu.

23. The "Fifty Facts" brochure, copiously illustrated with images of well-designed "assembly centres" and appealing children, in the manner of much humanitarian literature to this day, appears designed to counter these criticisms.

24. United Nations (Relief Administration), *Hansard,* 25 January 1944, Commons Sitting.

25. Reinisch, "Preparing for a New World Order," 7.

26. P. G. Cambray and G. G. B. Briggs, *The Official Record of the Humanitarian Services of the War Organisation of the British Red Cross Society and Order of St. John of Jerusalem, 1939–1947* (London: Red Cross and St John, 1949), 479.

27. Francesca M. Wilson, *Aftermath: France, Germany, Austria, Yugoslavia, 1945 and 1946* (West Drayton, Middlesex: Penguin Books, 1947), 31.

28. Ibid., 10.

29. Ibid., 25.

30. Ibid., 32.

31. Ibid.

32. Ibid., 34.

33. Ibid., 37.

34. Prior to that, the house at Feldafing had been the home of Fay von Hassell, a woman from a privileged German background imprisoned in the Nazi camps herself after her father, a former diplomat, was executed for his involvement in the plot to assassinate Hitler in July 1944. She tells of her own experiences in her autobiography *A Mother's War* (London: John Murray, 2003) and I return to her account later in the chapter. Her story, together with that of Francesca Wilson, is included in David Stafford, *Endgame 1945: Victory, Retribution, Liberation* (London: Little, Brown, 2007), an account that draws on the diaries and memoirs of a small number of those caught up in the immediate period after the end of the war.

35. Wilson, *Aftermath,* 40–41 (spelling standardized).

36. Moorehead, *Dunant's Dream,* 500.

37. Wilson, *Aftermath,* 43.

38. Ibid., 133 n. 1.

39. Kathryn Hulme, *The Wild Place* (New York: Cardinal, 1960), 211.

40. Ibid., 8–9.

41. Wilson, *Aftermath,* 139–41.

42. Notes on Visit of Lt. Col. R. B. Longe to Hohne Assembly Centre on 14 Feb 46, 16 February 1946, *Post-War Europe: Refugees, Exile, and Resettlement, 1945–1950.* Online archive, FO 1052/336.

43. For a fuller discussion of the problems of this sort, and the renaming of Belsen as Hohne by the British, see Rainer Schulze, "'A Continual Source of Trouble': The Displaced Persons Camp Bergen-Belsen (Hohne), 1945–1950," in *Post-War Europe: Refugees, Exile, and Resettlement, 1945–1950* (Reading: Thomson Learning EMEA Ltd., 2007), http://www.tlemea.com/postwareurope/essay1.asp. For a discussion of the campaigns among displaced persons at the camp, see Michael Brenner, "Displaced Persons and the Desire for a Jewish National Homeland," in *Post-war Europe: Refugees, Exile and Resettlement, 1945–1950,* http://www.tlemea.com/postwareurope/essay2.asp.

44. "Flow chart: Inside an Assembly Centre for United Nations DPs," Displaced Persons Branch G-5 SHAEF, April 1945, the National Archives, Kew, FO 945/591.

45. See Wyman, *DPs,* 62–63, for a discussion of the Yalta pact and subsequent agreements relating to the separation and repatriation of Soviet DPs; for the controversy about British repatriations, see Nikolai Tolstoy, *Victims of Yalta* (London: Hodder and Stoughton, 1977); see also Proudfoot, *European Refugees,* 152–57; Marrus, *The Unwanted,* 313–16.

46. Jenny Edkins, "Sovereign Power, Zones of Indistinction, and the Camp," *Alternatives* 25, no. 1 (2000): 3–25.

47. Schulze, "'A Continual Source of Trouble.'"

48. Wilson, *Aftermath,* 132.

49. Moorehead, *Dunant's Dream,* 507.

50. Wilson, *Aftermath,* 132–33. Estimates were that thirteen million children in Europe had lost or been separated from their guardians (Moorehead, *Dunant's Dream,* 503).

51. Extracts from report, Mr. E. C. Nottingham, *Post-War Europe: Refugees, Exile, and Resettlement, 1945–1950.* Online archive, FO 1052/336.

52. Wyman, *DPs,* 55.

53. Levi, *"If This Is a Man" and "The Truce,"* 378.

54. Moorehead, *Dunant's Dream,* 528.

55. Bark, *No Time to Kill,* 53.

56. Wilson, *Aftermath,* 52 (spelling standardized). Teresienstadt, Auschwitz, and Dachau were all concentration camps.

57. Wyman, *DPs,* 55.

58. "Central Tracing Bureau Finds Many Missing DPs," *[UNRRA] Team News,* 22 March 1947, p. 5 (abridged from Oscar Schisgall, "'T' Stands for Dead: UNRRA Traces Hitler's Victims," *Coronet* 20, no. 6 (1946)); British Red Cross Archives, London, Ref. 735/1.

59. Wilson, *Aftermath,* 54.

60. Report on visit by reps AP and UP to Hohne camp, 18 December 1945, *Post-War Europe: Refugees, Exile, and Resettlement, 1945–1950.* Online archive, FO 1052/336.

61. Moorehead, *Dunant's Dream,* 513.

62. Ibid., 512.

63. Ibid., 513.

64. Von Hassell, *Mother's War,* 113.

65. Ibid., 196.

66. I. F. Stone, *Underground to Palestine* (New York: Boni and Gaer, 1946), 87–88, cited in Wyman, *DPs,* 55.

67. Quoted in Wyman, *DPs,* 55.

68. Hester Hardwick, interview with author, September 2008.

69. Hulme, *Wild Place,* 10.

70. Moorehead, *Dunant's Dream,* 513.

71. Ibid., 528–29.

72. See the discussion in chapter 8 of how Alex Kurzem remained missing (Mark Kurzem, *The Mascot: The Extraordinary Story of a Jewish Boy and an SS Extermination Squad* [London: Rider, 2007]).

73. Maja Zehfuss, *Wounds of Memory: The Politics of War in Germany* (Cambridge: Cambridge University Press, 2007), 203–8.

74. Richard von Weizsäcker, politician and later president of Germany (1984–1994), writing in 1970, quoted in Zehfuss, *Wounds of Memory,* 204. For his role in the 1980s, see Bill Niven, *Facing the Nazi Past: United Germany and the Legacy of the Third Reich* (London: Routledge, 2001), 105–6.

75. Hulme, *Wild Place,* 6; Moorehead, *Dunant's Dream,* 540–41.

76. Moorehead, *Dunant's Dream,* 538; see James Bacque's contentious book *Crimes and Mercies: The Fate of German Civilians under Allied Occupation, 1944–1950* (Vancouver: Talonbooks, 2007). Bacque also gives figures (which are contested) for the number of German civilians in the occupied zones who died as a result of punitive starvation rations and neglect. See also Alfred M. De Zayas, *Nemesis at Potsdam: Anglo-Americans and the Expulsion of the Germans* (London: Routledge and Kegan Paul, 1977).

77. Bower, *Blind Eye to Murder,* 56.

78. Ibid., 113.

79. Ibid., 116.

80. See, for example, the accounts of Benjamin (Beryl) Ferencz, collected in the United States Holocaust Memorial Museum, Holocaust Encyclopedia, Personal Stories, War Crimes Trials, http://www.ushmm.org/wlc/media_oi.php?lang=en&ModuleId=10005140&MediaId=4959

81. See also David Cesarani, *Justice Delayed: How Britain Became a Refuge for Nazi War Criminals* (London: Phoenix Press, 2001).

82. Bower, *Blind Eye to Murder,* 129.

83. Ibid., 198.

84. Ibid.

85. Ibid., 202.

86. Norbert Frei, *Adenauer's Germany and the Nazi Past: The Politics of Amnesty and Integration,* trans. Joel Golb (New York: Columbia University Press, 2002), 346 n. 27; see also 97–119.

87. Bower, *Blind Eye to Murder,* 117. IBM Hollerith machines had been used by the Nazis too (Götz Aly and Karl Heinz Roth, *The Nazi Census: Identification and Control in the Third Reich* [Philadelphia: Temple University Press, 2004]).

88. Supreme Headquarters, Allied Expeditionary Force (SHAEF), *CROWCASS (Central Registry of War Criminals and Security Suspects): Wanted Lists* (Uckfield: Naval & Military Press, 2005), reprint of 1947 original document held at the National Archives, Kew, London.

89. David McKittrick, "Nazi Background of Prominent Irish Publisher Exposed," *Independent,* 4 January 2007; House of Commons, *Hansard,* Written Answers for 29 January 2007, "War Criminals"; "War Crimes of the Second World War," Research Guides, The National Archives, http://www.nationalarchives.gov.uk/catalogue/RdLeaflet.asp?sLeafletID=33.

90. Simon Wiesenthal Center and the Targum Shlishi Foundation's joint "Operation: Last Chance" campaign, offering financial rewards for information leading to the arrest and conviction of Nazi war criminals, was launched in 2002. http://www.operationlastchance.org/index.htm.

91. Wilson, *Aftermath.*

92. Susan T. Pettiss, *After the Shooting Stopped: The Memoir of an UNRRA Welfare Worker, Germany 1945–1947* (Bloomington, IN: Trafford Publishing, 2004), 8.

93. Letter from Evelyn Bark to Dr. W. Stuart Stanbury, Canadian Red Cross Society, 21 February 1952, British Red Cross Archives, London Ref. 1344 11/9A.

94. Letter from Chairman, British Red Cross, to Sir Paul Gore-Booth, Under-Secretary of State, Foreign Office, 11 July 1966, British Red Cross Archives, London, Ref. 1344 11/9A.

3. Tracing Services

1. Davide Panagia and Jacques Rancière, "Dissenting Words: A Conversation with Jacques Rancière," *Diacritics* 30, no. 2 (2000): 116.

2. Primo Levi, *"If This Is a Man" and "The Truce,"* trans. Stuart Woolf (London: Abacus, 1979), 208.

3. Caroline Moorehead, *Dunant's Dream: War, Switzerland, and the History of the Red Cross* (London: HarperCollins, 1998), 518.

4. UNRRA, European Regional Office, *Communication Between Displaced Persons and Their Families—Enquiries, Tracing, and Registration of Missing Persons,* UN 1244; TDP/E(44)18; (Revised) 22.8.44, p. 1, the National Archives, Kew, HO 213/1071.

5. Ibid., p. 3.

6. Ibid., p. 1.

7. John Corsellis and Marcus Ferrar, *Slovenia 1945: Memories of Death and Survival after World War II* (London: I. B. Tauris, 2006). I return to this case later.

8. Supreme Headquarters, Allied Expeditionary Force (SHAEF), *Outline Plan for Refugees and Displaced Persons* (All Operations), AG 383.7-1 GE-AGM, 3 June 1944, p. 1, the National Archives, Kew, FO 945/591.

9. Organisation Todt was set up to use conscripted or slave labor, initially German and later from occupied countries and concentration camps, in civil and military engineering projects. See Michael Thad Allen, *The Business of Genocide: The SS, Slave Labor, and the Concentration Camps* (Chapel Hill: University of North Carolina Press, 2005).

10. SHAEF, *Outline Plan,* p. 1.

11. Ibid., p. 9.

12. Ibid.

13. Lt. Col. L. R. Hulls, Director, Refugee Branch, ACC Italy, *Memorandum to Displaced Persons Branch,* G-5, SHAEF, 9 June 1944, the National Archives, Kew, FO 945/591.

14. Ibid.

15. Supreme Headquarters, Allied Expeditionary Force (SHAEF), *Displaced Persons and Refugees in Germany,* Administrative Memorandum no. 39, 18 November 1944, the National Archives, Kew, FO 945/591.

16. See, for example, UNRRA Committee of Council for Europe, *Statement of Categories of Displaced Persons,* CCE (44) 67/U.N. a. 441, 11 November 1944, copy in FO 945/591; Paul Mason, Foreign Office Refugee Department, to C. B. P. Peake, SHAEF, 22 January 1945, the National Archives, Kew, FO 945/591.

17. *The Central Tracing Bureau,* May 1947, typescript, British Red Cross Archives, London, Ref. 656/1. This document, described in the catalogue as a historical account citing original documents, Jan. 1944–April 1946, has no indication of an author. It belonged to Miss Susan Mustard, formerly of the International Tracing Service, 1947–1969, and was transferred to the British Red Cross Archives via one of their Branches (Emily Oldfield, Information Assistant, British Red Cross Museum and Archives, London, personal communication, 27 November 2008).

18. Foreign Office to Berne, Outward Telegram No. 3187, 26 September 1944, the National Archives, Kew, HO 213/1071.

19. The International Committee of the Red Cross is commonly known today by its acronym, ICRC; in the period I am writing of here, it was also, and more usually, known as the International Red Cross (IRC) or the International Committee. A separate body, the League of Red Cross Societies (LORCS), was founded under American Red Cross leadership after the first World War, as a rival organization to the ICRC (see Moorhead, *Dunant's Dream,* 258–91). By the time of the second World War, LORCS's influence had declined and its work had been limited to times of peace. To add to the terminological confusion, LORCS is now the International Federation of Red Cross and Red Crescent Societies (IFRC).

20. Moorehead, *Dunant's Dream,* 377. For a detailed history of the ICRC Central Tracing Agency and its work with prisoners of war from 1870, see Gradimir Djurović, *The Central Tracing Agency of the International Committee of the Red Cross: Activities of the ICRC for the Alleviation of the Mental Suffering of War Victims,* trans. Muriel Monkhouse and Dominique Cornwell (Geneva: Henry Dunant Institute, 1986).

21. International Committee of the Red Cross, Draft International Convention on the Condition and Protection of Civilians of Enemy Nationality Who Are on Territory Belonging to or Occupied by a Belligerent, Tokyo, 1934, http://www.icrc. org/ihl.nsf/INTRO/320?OpenDocument. The draft adopted at the XVth International Conference of the Red Cross in Tokyo in 1934 was to have been discussed at a conference in 1940, which did not take place because of the outbreak of war. ICRC proposals that the belligerents nevertheless recognize the draft were not accepted.

22. Moorehead, *Dunant's Dream,* 413.

23. Ibid., 417–18. Sir Anthony Eden made his famous speech as foreign secretary in the House of Commons at this time.

24. Moorehead, *Dunant's Dream,* 420–25. A declaration was issued by the United Nations governments on 17 December 1942, noting and condemning what was happening (House of Commons Debates, United Nations Declaration, *Hansard,* vol. 385, 17 December 1942, cols. 2082–87).

25. André Durand, *From Sarajevo to Hiroshima: History of the International Committee of the Red Cross* (Geneva: Henry Dunant Institute, 1984), 579–601; for a discussion of Moorehead's conclusions about ICRC inaction in 1942, see Kenneth Anderson, "First in the Field: The Unique Mission and Legitimacy of the Red Cross in a Culture of Legality," *Times Literary Supplement Book Review,* 31 July 1998.

26. Durand, *From Sarajevo to Hiroshima,* 626.

27. International Committee of the Red Cross, "Dispersed Families," in: ICRC, *Report of the International Committee of the Red Cross on Its Activities during the Second World War (September 1, 1939–June 30, 1947),* report presented at the XVIIth International Red Cross Conference, Stockholm, August 1948. Volume II: The Central Agency for Prisoners of War, No. 2A (Geneva: ICRC, 1948), 308–15. See also Djurović, *Central Tracing Agency,* 175–78.

28. International Committee of the Red Cross, "Dispersed Families," 313.

29. Minutes of Meeting of Mlle Ferriere, Member of the ICRC, and Messrs Carter and Youngdahl of the Displaced Persons Division of the UNRRA on the 6th February 1945 in Geneva, UN Archives, New York, S-0402-0004-03.

30. "Enquiries by Displaced Persons in Germany about Their Missing Relatives," Memorandum to SHAEF, G-5, D.P. and Welfare Branch, Versailles, from UNRRA

and the International Red Cross Committee, 2 June 1945, signed by Eyre Carter, UNRRA, and M. Thudichum, International Red Cross Committee, UN Archives, New York, S-0402-0004-03.

31. *Central Tracing Bureau,* 7.

32. *Tracing of Missing Persons in Germany on an International Scale,* Central Tracing Bureau Study, 6 July 1946, UN Archives, New York, S-0402-0004-03; and revised version of this report.

33. *Central Tracing Bureau,* 20.

34. An example of the tension to which contradicting priorities gave rise is the refusal of UNRRA officials to provide lists of their nationals to governments concerned to secure repatriation. A request from the Yugoslav liaison officer for lists of Yugoslav nationals in UNRRA camps was refused by Colonel Bowring in March 1946 (Letter from Col. Bowring, 21 March 1946, UN Archives, New York, S-0413-0001-13).

35. Paul Mason, Foreign Office, to Under-Secretary of State, Home Office, Ref. WR/1027/9/48, 26 September 1944, the National Archives, Kew, HO 213/1071.

36. Aliens Department, Home Office, Proposals by UNRRA for Setting Up of Machinery for Tracing Whereabouts of Displaced Persons in Europe, minute sheet, 5 October 1944, the National Archives, Kew, HO 213/1071.

37. Its full title was The United Kingdom Search Bureau for German, Austrian and Stateless Persons from Central Europe.

38. Aliens Department, Home Office, minute sheet, 5 October 1944, the National Archives, Kew, HO 213/1071.

39. P. G. Cambray and G. G. B. Briggs, *The Official Record of the Humanitarian Services of the War Organisation of the British Red Cross Society and Order of St. John of Jerusalem, 1939–1947* (London: Red Cross and St. John 1949), 464.

40. Minutes of Meeting to Discuss Establishment of Centralised Search Bureau, 25 November 1943, the National Archives, Kew, HO 294/169. At the initial meeting, called by the Central Office for Refugees, there was a discussion of the importance of everyone using a standard-sized of card—which raises not only a parallel with issues of computer compatibility these days, but also the specter of the ideal displaced person as uniform too.

41. Evelyn Bark, *No Time to Kill* (London: Robert Hale, 1960), 38.

42. Moorehead, *Dunant's Dream,* 517.

43. Cambray and Briggs, *Official Record,* 470–71.

44. Information from SHAEF REAR D.P. Branch, 19 December 1944, the National Archives, Kew, FO 945/591.

45. *Central Tracing Bureau,* 2b.

46. Ibid.

47. L. M. Livingstone, CRW, British Red Cross Commission, to Paul Mason, Foreign Office, 2 July 1945, the National Archives, Kew, FO 945/557.

48. Lt. Col. F. C. Davies, Displaced Persons Branch PW & DP Division Control Commission for Germany (BE), Records of and Enquiries concerning United Nations Nationals in Germany, memorandum to Lt. Col. V. M. Hammer, CA/DP War Office, 11 July 1945, the National Archives, Kew, FO 945/557.

49. From SHAEF (Main) to Foreign Office, Telegram no. 67 Saving, 26 June 1945, from Mr Kirkpatrick, the National Archives, Kew, FO 945/557.

50. Minutes, Conference on 11 July 1945 on Central Records Office for Displaced Persons in Germany, the National Archives, Kew, FO 945/557.

51. Allied Force Headquarters APO512, To Commanding Generals/Officers in Italy, Austria, Rumania, Bulgaria, Albania, Greece, and Yugoslavia, *Inquiries concerning the Whereabouts and Welfare of Individuals,* by Command of Field Marshal Alexander, Signed Col. C. W. Christenberry, AG 091.4/211 GEC-O, 5 July 1945, the National Archives, Kew, FO 945/557.

52. S. J. Warner, Director, Foreign Relations Department, Red Cross, to N. S. Gosling, British Red Cross Foreign Relations Section Austria, 20 July 1945, the National Archives, Kew, FO 945/557.

53. Ibid.

54. S. J. Warner, Director, Foreign Relations Department, Red Cross, to Lt. Col. E. M. Hammer, War Office, Civil Affairs, 20 July 1945, the National Archives, Kew, FO 945/557.

55. Ibid.

56. J. W. O. Davidson, Prisoners of War Department, Foreign Office, to Hammer, 18 August 1945, the National Archives, Kew, FO 945/557.

57. Warner to Hammer, 20 July 1945.

58. Ibid.

59. Col. A. H. Moffitt, Combined Displaced Persons Executive at G-5 Division, USFET, "Central Tracing Bureau and Central Records Office," Circular GE-CDPX 383.7, 24 July 1945, to HQ 21 Army Group for Military Government, Third US Army for G-5, Seventh US Army for G-5, First French Army for Military Government, the National Archives, Kew, FO 945/557.

60. Thomas Parrington, Circular to All Departments of British Red Cross Commission North West Europe, Re: Tracing Missing Persons, 23 August 1945, the National Archives, Kew, FO 945/557.

61. J. R. Bowring, Col., Director, Search Bureau, Bunde, "The Tracing of Missing Persons of Allied Nationality throughout Germany," Ref. PWDP/55700, 13 August 1945, the National Archives, Kew, FO 945/557.

62. Ibid.

63. Col. A. H. Moffitt. Combined Displaced Persons Executive at G-5 Division, USFET. "Tracing Service in Germany," Circular GE-CDPX 383.7 (4.33), 26 August 1945, to Foreign Relations Department, British Red Cross, the National Archives, Kew, FO 945/557.

64. Minutes of Meeting of Working Group on Central Tracing Service, 30 August 1945, the National Archives, Kew, FO 945/557.

65. S. J. Warner, Director, Foreign Relations Department, Red Cross, to Col. A. H. Moffitt, Combined Displaced Persons Executive at G-5 Division, USFET, 12 September 1945, the National Archives, Kew, FO 945/557.

66. Allied Control Authority, Coordinating Committee, Establishment of a Missing Persons Tracing Service, CORC/P(45)54, 13 September 1945, the National Archives, Kew, FO 945/557.

67. Lt. Col. F. C. Davies, PW & DP Division, Control Commission for Germany, to Hammer, 16 September 1945, the National Archives, Kew, FO 945/557.

68. Col. J. R. Bowring to Executive Director, British Red Cross, 28 November 1945, UN Archives, New York, S-0413-0004-08.

69. UNRRA 1076, UN Archives, New York, S-1058-0001-01-83 to S-1058-0001-01-89.

70. Caption: "Hoechst, Germany, 1945. Colonel John R Bowring stands before a chart showing how National Tracing Bureaus in the different European countries tie in with UNRRA's Central Tracing Bureau"; UNRRA 1069, UN Archives, New York, S-1058-0001-01-82.

71. Caption: "Hoechst, Germany, 1945. Records room"; UNRRA 1072, UN Archives, New York, S-1058-0001-01-85.

72. Caption: "Hoechst, Germany, 1945. UNRRA Central Tracing Bureau Correspondence room"; UNRRA 1071, UN Archives, New York, S-1058-0001-01-84.

73. S. J. Warner to Col. Bowring, 30 August 1946, the National Archives, Kew, FO 945/558.

74. S. J. Warner to Sir George Rendal, Foreign Office, 4 September 1946, the National Archives, Kew, FO 945/558.

75. Warner to Hammer, 20 July 1945.

76. Cambray and Briggs, *Official Record,* 466, 469.

77. J. W. O. Davidson, Foreign Office Prisoners of War Department, to Lt. Col. H. J. Phillimore, War Office Directorate of Prisoners of War, 26 June 1945; minutes, Conference on 11 July 1945 on Central Records Office for Displaced Persons in Germany, the National Archives, Kew, FO 945/557.

78. Outward Telegram from Foreign Office to Washington, no. 8874, 27 August 1945, WR.2289/1/48, the National Archives, Kew, FO 945/557.

79. Notes of conversation, Barrell-Hammer, 12 September 1946, the National Archives, Kew, FO 945/558.

80. *Central Tracing Bureau,* 9.

81. Ibid., 13.

82. *The Tracing of Missing Persons in Germany on an International Scale,* 6 July 1946.

83. *The Tracing of Missing Persons in Germany on an International Scale with Particular Reference to the Problem of UNRRA,* prepared for the personal information of the Chief of Operations for Germany, [Revised version of 6 July 1946 Central Tracing Bureau Study], Section IIA, UN Archives, New York, S-0413-0006-04.

84. Ibid., Section IB(2).

85. Ibid., Section IIB.

86. Ibid., Section IIA.

87. *Tracing of Missing Persons in Germany on an International Scale,* Central Tracing Bureau Study, 6 July 1946, p. 8. Not all of the unofficial organizations were concerned with tracing "enemy nationals," who could not be helped by UNRRA. A paper notes that a number of organizations representing former concentration camp inmates had also sprung up, and some of them had in their possession concentration camp records; see *A Review of the Tracing Situation from the Point of View of the Central Tracing Bureau—* UNRRA, CTB, Arolsen, 3 March 1946, p. 8, UN Archives, New York, S-0413-0005-05 (this appears to be a preliminary draft of the report of 6 July 1946).

88. Foundation Haus der Geschichte der Bundesrepublik Deutschland, Permanent Exhibition / Exhibit Highlights / Missing Persons Tracing Service, http://www.hdg.de/index.php?id=1687&L=1&Fsize=2.

89. Ibid., The Idea of a Tracing Service.

90. Ibid., Private Tracing Services—Cashing in on Human Feelings.

91. *Tracing of Missing Persons in Germany,* Section VE.1.

92. Ibid., Section VE.1b.

93. Ibid., Section VE.2.

94. Frank Biess, *Homecomings: Returning POWs and the Legacies of Defeat in Post-war Germany* (Princeton, NJ: Princeton University Press, 2006), 183–84.

95. Moorehead, *Dunant's Dream,* 345–57; German Red Cross, Tracing Service Munich, http://www.drk-suchdienst.eu/content/content2.php?CatID=61&NewsID=45&lang=en.

96. German Red Cross, Tracing Service Munich, History, http://www.drk-suchdienst.eu/content/content2.php?CatID=61&NewsID=45&lang=en.

97. Ibid., The Missing of World War II: Expert Opinions, http://www.drk-suchdienst.eu/content/content2.php?CatID=53&NewsID=120&lang=en.

98. Ibid., Missing in the Second World War, http://www.drk-suchdienst.eu/content/categoryshow.php?CatID=53.

99. Ibid. For the continuing work and history of the German Red Cross Tracing Service, see, for example, Klaus Mittermaier: *Vermißt wird—: Die Arbeit des deutschen Suchdienstes* (Berlin: Links Publisher, 2002).

100. International Tracing Service, *Annual Report 2007* (Bad Arolsen: ITS, 2008).

101. An early description of the operations of the ITS, with illustrations, is available in Hugh G. Elbot, "Manhunt for 6,000,000," in *Information Bulletin* (Office of the U.S. High Commissioner for Germany Office of Public Affairs, Public Relations Division, APO 757, US Army) May 1951, 7–10, http://digital.library.wisc.edu/1711.dl/History.omg1951May; and "New Home for the International Tracing Service at Arolsen," *Information Bulletin,* September 1952, http://digital.library.wisc.edu/1711.dl/History.omg1952Sept.

102. For historical accounts of the ITS, see chapter 7 of Gradimir Djurović, *The Central Tracing Agency of the International Committee of the Red Cross: Activities of the ICRC for the Alleviation of the Mental Suffering of War Victims,* trans. Muriel Monkhouse and Dominique Cornwell (Geneva: Henry Dunant Institute, 1986), 179–88; and two accounts published for its fiftieth anniversary: Paul Reynard, "The International Committee of the Red Cross and the International Tracing Service in Arolsen," *International Review of the Red Cross,* no. 296 (1993): 457–63; and Charles-Claude Biedermann, "International Tracing Service: 50 Years of Service to Humanity," *in the same issue,* 447–56.

103. Paul A. Shapiro, "The History of the International Tracing Service and Its Archival Collection," paper presented at opening session of Beyond Camps and Forced Labour: Current International Research on Survivors of Nazi Persecution, Third International Multidisciplinary Conference at the Imperial War Museum, London, 7–9 January 2009. The account in this section draws heavily on this paper and the discussion that followed, though obviously the interpretations and conclusions are my own. For an account of Shapiro's work, see Helen Stephenson, "Opening the Archives—Closure for Holocaust Victims," *Prescott News,* 23 February 2008.

104. In 1945, Yugoslavia had requested a list of its nationals in DP camps. The then Central Tracing Bureau, precursor to the ITS and at that point run by Colonel Bowring, had refused to provide such information, again fearing its misuse.

105. Paul A. Shapiro, interview with author, 7 January 2009.

106. The guidelines for researchers on the ITS website in 2009 are not the most welcoming.

107. "International Task Force Supports Decision to Open Bad Arolsen Archives for Scholarly Research by the End of the Year," 9 June 2004; "International Task Force Calls for Concrete Steps to Open Holocaust-Era Archives of the International Tracing Service in Germany," 16 December 2004; "International Holocaust Task Force Urges Opening of Bad Arolsen Archive," 30 June 2005; http://www.holo causttaskforce.org/about/index.php?content=press/.

108. Greg Gordon, "Pressure Mounts to Open Holocaust Records," *Minneapolis-St. Paul Star Tribune,* 9 May 2005.

109. Frank-Uwe Betz, "Das andere Mahnmal," *Die Zeit,* 19 May 2005 (translation with help from Maja Zehfuss).

110. Roger Cohen, "U.S.-German Flare-Up Over Vast Nazi Camp Archives," *New York Times,* 20 February 2006; Sam Loewenberg and Julian Borger, "Closed Archive Leads to Holocaust Denial Claim," *Guardian,* 21 February 2006; *Washington Post,* "A Holocaust Denial," 25 March 2006. For links to other published material, see United States Holocaust Memorial Museum, International Tracing Service Archive.

111. Luke Harding, "Germany to Release Archive Files on Millions of Nazi Victims," *Guardian,* 20 April 2006.

112. Anna Funder, "Secret History," *Guardian,* 16 June 2007.

113. Ibid.

114. Some survivors have questioned the choice of the USHMM as an appropriate home for the ITS records and demanded Internet accessibility. See the links at Edwin Black, "Secret Bad Arolsen Holocaust Archive—A Trove of Revelations about Holocaust Insurance, Corporate Complicity, and IBM Involvement," http://www. ibmandtheholocaust.com/BadArolsenArticles.php.

115. United States Holocaust Memorial Museum, International Tracing Service Inventory Search—About the ITS Inventory, general description, http://resources. ushmm.org/itsinventory/help_description.php.

116. Shapiro, interview, 7 January 2009.

117. ITS, *Annual Report 2007,* 38.

118. ITS, *Annual Report 2008* (Bad Arolsen: ITS, 2009).

119. ITS, *Annual Report 2007,* 4.

120. ICRC, official statement (opening ceremony of the International Tracing Service in Bad Arolsen, 30 April 2008), http://www.icrc.org/web/eng/siteeng0.nsf/ htmlall/int-tracing-service-statement-300408.

121. ITS, "Debate on the Future of ITS Is Well Underway" (press release, 20 May 2009), http://www.its-arolsen.org/en/press/press_releases/index.html?expand=251 4&cHash=d89ea8fe93.

122. U.K. Foreign and Commonwealth Office, International Commission for the International Tracing Service, 18 May 2009, http://www.fco.gov.uk/en/news room/latest-news/?view=News&id=17969182.

123. S. J. Warner, Foreign Relations Department, War Organisation of the British Red Cross Society, to E. B. Boothby, Refugees Department, Foreign Office, 19 February 1947, the National Archives, Kew, FO 371/66721.

124. Arthur Rucker, Deputy Executive Secretary, Preparatory Commission of the IRO, to Secretary of State for Foreign Affairs, 6 August 1947, the National Archives, Kew, FO 371/66721.

125. Preparatory Commission for the IRO, Fourth Part of First Session: Resolution on the Establishment of an International Tracing Service, PREP/146/Rev.1, 31 October 1947, the National Archives, Kew, FO 371/66721.

126. S. J. Warner, "The Tracing of Missing Persons," memorandum, 17 May 1946, the National Archives, Kew, FO 945/557.

127. Bark, *No Time to Kill,* 32.

128. S. J. Warner to Colonel Bowring, 21 January 1947, British Red Cross Archives, London, Ref. 735/1.

129. Bark, *No Time to Kill,* 32.

4. Missing Persons, London

1. Rachel North—a passenger in the carriage that was bombed at Russell Square/King's Cross—wrote a book about her experiences when the emergency services failed to arrive, and when, much longer after the event, there proved to be very ineffectual support for those who had been caught up in the bombings: Rachel North, *Out of the Tunnel* (London: Friday Books, 2007). Another account is Peter Zimonjic, *Into the Darkness: An Account of 7/7* (London: Vintage Books, 2008). John Tulloch, an academic caught up in the events of that day, also wrote of his experiences; he sat opposite one of the bombers on the tube: John Tulloch, *One Day in July: Experiencing 7/7* (London: Little, Brown, 2006). The full extent of the aid offered by passengers to each other is revealed in the accounts presented at the inquests into the victims, ongoing as revisions to this book were being completed. For transcripts of the hearings, see Coroner's Inquests into the London Bombings of 7 July 2005, http://7julyinquests.independent.gov.uk, which includes witness statements by Zimonjic and Tulloch; and for an overview, Alexandra Topping, "7/7 Inquest: Coroner Is Inspired by Tales of Heroism," *Observer,* 5 December 2010. The inquests also confirmed suspicions of delays to the emergency service response for fear of contamination (Topping, "7/7 Inquest Hears of Fire and Ambulance Crew Delays," *Guardian,* 25 November 2010).

2. See, for example, Adrian Kear and Deborah Lynn Steinberg, *Mourning Diana: Nation, Culture, and the Performance of Grief* (London: Routledge, 1999), 51.

3. The family received compensation of £11,000 (Alan Travis, "Victims of 7/7 Bombs Were Not Given Enough Help, Ministers Admit," *Guardian,* 23 September 2006).

4. Sandra Laville, "Mother's Fury at 'Slaughter of the Innocents,'" *Guardian,* 12 July 2005; Marie Fatayi-Williams, *For the Love of Anthony: A Mother's Search for Peace after the London Bombings* (London: Hodder & Stoughton, 2006).

5. *Guardian,* "Straight from the Heart," 13 July 2005.

6. London Assembly, Richard Barnes AM (Chair) "Report of the 7 July Review Committee," June 2006, vol. 1, "Report," paragraph 9.3, p. 98.

7. BBC News, "Missing People Sought after Bombs," 10 July 2005, http://news.bbc.co.uk/1/hi/england/london/4666679.stm. See also Thomas Ikimi, *The Homefront,* film (London, 2007), 81 mins.

8. London Assembly, "Report," vol. 1, paragraph 7.3, p. 84.

9. London Assembly, Richard Barnes AM (Chair), "Report of the 7 July Review Committee," June 2006, vol. 3, "Views and Information from Individuals," p. 43.

10. London Assembly, "Report," vol. 1, paragraph 7.2, p. 84.

11. Metropolitan Police, "'One Week Anniversary' bombings appeal," http://cms.met.police.uk/news/major_operational_announcements/terrorist_attacks/one_week_anniversary_bombings_appeal.

12. London Assembly, "Report," vol. 1, paragraph 9.9, p. 99.

13. Ibid.

14. Ibid.

15. Ibid., p. 98.

16. Melanie Henwood makes similar points in "The Emergency Response to 7/7: Flaws with the Family Assistance Centre," 23 November 2006, http://www.communitycare.co.uk/Articles/2006/11/23/102302/the-emergency-response-to-77.-flaws-with-the-family-assistance.html; see also Rachel North, "The July 7 Questions That Still Haunt Victims," *Times,* 18 December 2005. A DVD produced by the Metropolitan Police, *Messages from 7/7* (London: HMSO, 2006), looks at the establishment of the Resilience Mortuary and Family Assistance Centre after 7/7.

17. Duncan Gardham and Nicole Martin, "How Much Blood Must Be Spilled? A Mother Asks," *Daily Telegraph,* 13 July 2005.

18. Ibid.

19. Nana Sifa Twum, "Wundowa's Body Released to Family," Modern Ghana.com, 19 July 2005, http://www.modernghana.com/news/82274/1/wundowas-body-released-to-family.html.

20. Emily Nash, "Our Lost Loved Ones," *Mirror News,* 9 July 2005.

21. Audrey Gillan and Owen Bowcott, "Families Feel Pain of Name Delay: First Victim Is Identified but Frustration Grows among Those Waiting to Hear Fate of the Missing," *Guardian,* 12 July 2005.

22. Ibid.

23. Tom Geoghegan, "Trying Not to Harbour Hatred," BBC News, 3 July 2006, http://news.bbc.co.uk/1/hi/uk/5130044.stm.

24. Yusuph Olaniyonu and Frank Kintum, "Anthony Fatayi-Williams Body Recovered," Online Nigeria, 15 July 2005, http://nm.onlinenigeria.com/templates/?a=3831&z=12.

25. "Inquest into Oil Executive Opens," *Daily Telegraph,* 14 July 2005.

26. Fatayi-Williams, *For the Love of Anthony,* 38.

27. Ibid., 48.

28. London Assembly, "Report," vol. 3, p. 223.

29. Paula Dear, "Don't Wait for Me Tonight, Mum," BBC News, http://news.bbc.co.uk/1/hi/uk/5098448.stm,.

30. Gillan and Bowcott, "Families Feel Pain of Name Delay."

31. London Assembly, "Report," vol. 1; vol. 2, "Views and Information from Organisations"; vol. 3.

32. London Assembly, "Report," vol. 1, paragraph 9.3, p. 98. *The Guardian* had noted on 12 July that following the Madrid bombings in 2004, in which more than 190 people died, most of the bodies were identified within twenty-four hours, and most were buried within three days of the attacks (Giles Tremlett, "Spanish Reaction: Admiration Mingled with Astonishment over Calm Response," *Guardian,* 12 July 2005).

33. UK Cabinet Office, John Reid (Home Secretary) and Tessa Jowell (Culture Secretary), "Addressing the Lessons from the Emergency Response to the 7th July 2005 London Bombings: What We Learned and What We Are Doing about It," 22 September 2006.

34. Ibid., paragraph 49, p. 12.

35. The International Criminal Police Organization—INTERPOL, "Disaster Victim Identification," http://www.interpol.int/Public/DisasterVictim/Default.asp. The manual is available at http://www.interpol.int/Public/DisasterVictim/guide/default.asp.

36. The forms are available at http://www.interpol.int/Public/DisasterVictim/Forms/Default.asp.

37. The fact that there is no space for a name on the form that the authorities recovering bodies use could explain why even when the victim gave a name before dying it was not linked with the body.

38. The categories are the same as those used in 1945.

39. Marie Fatayi-Williams confirms that this was the case; she was asked repeatedly whether Anthony was wearing a watch. Since she had not been staying with him on the morning of the bombings, she did not know. Marie Fatayi-Williams, interview with author, 7 December 2006.

40. Travis, "Victims of 7/7 Bombs."

41. Jason Bennetto, "Terror in London: Police Identifying Victims of Asian Tsunami Switch," *Independent,* 12 July 2005.

42. Ibid.

43. David Hare, *The Permanent Way or La Voie Anglaise* (London: Faber & Faber, 2003).

44. Disaster Action, www.disasteraction.org.uk.

45. Disaster Action, "When Disaster Strikes—Disaster Victim Identification: Issues for Families and Implications for Police Family Liaison Officers (FLOs) and Coroner's Officers (COs)," http://www.disasteraction.org.uk/guidance.htm.

46. Shiya Ribowsky and Tom Shachtman, *Dead Center: Behind the Scenes at the World's Largest Medical Examiner's Office* (New York: Harper, 2007), 165–67.

47. Federal Bureau of Investigation, "The FBI Releases 19 Photographs of Individuals Believed to Be the Hijackers of the Four Airliners That Crashed on September 11, 01," press release, 27 September 2001, http://www.fbi.gov/pressrel/pressrel01/092701hjpic.htm.

48. Robert C. Shaler, *Who They Were: Inside the World Trade Center DNA Story; The Unprecedented Effort to Identify the Missing* (New York: Free Press, 2005), 300.

49. BBC News, "In Full: Blair on Bomb Blasts; Statement from Downing Street, 1730 BST 7 July 2005," http://news.bbc.co.uk/1/hi/uk/4659953.stm.

50. London Assembly, "Report," vol. 1, paragraph 11.6.

51. Ribowsky and Shachtman, *Dead Center,* 103–4.

52. Metropolitan Police, "'One Week Anniversary' Bombings Appeal."

53. The need for general reform of the coroners' system in England and Wales is recognized, and there have been a number of reports. See, for example, House of Commons Constitutional Affairs Committee, "Reform of the Coroners' System and Death Certification: Eighth Report of Session 2005–06; Report, together with Formal Minutes," HC 902–I (London: The Stationery Office Limited, 2006); Tom Luce, *Death Certification and Investigation in England, Wales, and Northern Ireland: The Report of a Fundamental Review, 2003,* Cm. 5831 (London: HMSO, 2003); Philip Hasleton, "Reforming the Coroner and Death Certification Service," *Current Diagnostic Pathology* 10, no. 6 (December 2004): 453–62; Gordon H. H. Glasgow, "The Campaign for Medical Coroners in Nineteenth-Century England and Its Aftermath: A Lancashire Focus on Failure, Part II," *Mortality* 9, no. 3 (August 2004): 223–34.

54. Sean O'Neill, "Book by Former Anti-terror Chief Andy Hayman Banned from Shops," *Times,* 3 July 2009; Sandra Laville, "Government Bans Former Anti-terror Chief's Tell-all Book: Court Injunction on Andy Hayman's *The Terrorist Hunters,* Which Includes Details of De Menezes and Litvinenko Cases," guardian.co.uk, 2 July 2009.

55. Andy Hayman, "No Warning, No Links, No Leads: 7/7 Bombings Were a Bolt out of Nowhere," *Times,* June 20, 2009.

56. Intelligence and Security Committee, "Could 7/7 Have Been Prevented? Review of the Intelligence on the London Terrorist Attacks on 7 July 2005," Chairman Kim Howells, Cm. 7617, May 2009, pp. 15–16, http://www.cabinetoffice.gov.uk/intelligence/special_reports.aspx.

57. London Assembly, "Report," vol. 1, paragraph 9.1.

58. Ibid., Paragraph 9.3.

59. Sam Greenhill, "I've Just Seen Hell on Earth: Four Years after 7/7, a Never-before-Seen Picture of the Horror That Confronted Police on the Tube Ripped Apart by Terrorists," *Daily Mail,* 8 July 2009.

60. European Hospital, EHOnline, "The London Tube and Bus Bombings: UK Government Now Supports Forensic Radiography Response Team Training," 27 March 2009, http://www.european-hospital.com/topics/article/5568.html.

61. Greenhill, "I've Just Seen Hell."

62. *Guardian,* "Bomb Victim IDs May Take Weeks—Coroner," 15 July 2005.

63. Joshua Rozenberg, "Relatives of Tube Bomber Want Another Post Mortem," *Daily Telegraph,* 29 October 2005.

64. Shiv Malik, "My Brother the Bomber," *Prospect,* 30 June 2007.

65. BBC News, "Funeral Service for London Bomber," 3 November 2005.

66. Richard Norton-Taylor, "Victim of 7/7 'Might Have Been Saved,'" *Guardian,* 27 April 2010.

67. Coroner's Inquests into the London Bombings of 7 July 2005, Hearing transcripts, 26 April 2010, Morning, pp. 76–79, http://7julyinquests.independent.gov.uk/hearing_transcripts/26042010am.htm

68. Duncan Gardham, "Families of July 7 Bombing Victims Fear They May Never Learn the Truth," *Telegraph,* 20 May 2009.

69. Coroner's Inquests into the London Bombings of 7 July 2005, http://7julyinquests.independent.gov.uk/index.htm.

70. Mary Dejevsky, "Heroes Born the Day 999 Let Us Down," *Independent,* 3 December 2010.

71. Dejevsky, "Heroes Born the Day 999 Let Us Down."

72. The Rt. Hon. Lady Justice Hallett DBE, Decision following Pre-Inquest Hearing from 26 to 30 April 2010, p. 12, http://7julyinquests.independent.gov.uk/directions_decs/decision-april-2010.htm.

73. Hearing Transcripts, 11 October 2010, Morning Session, http://7julyinquests.independent.gov.uk/hearing_transcripts/11102010am.htm. The report was said to include a witness statement from a Commander Bracken, "who was either involved in or in charge of matters at Ladbroke Grove, the Selby disaster, Potters Bar, Hatfield and the south-east Asian Tsunami." The report will be provided to the coroner in due course (Eddie Townsend, Press Bureau, Scotland Yard, personal communication, 6 December 2010).

74. Intelligence and Security Committee, "Could 7/7 Have Been Prevented?"

75. Ibid., 15.

76. Ibid., 26.

77. Ibid., 41.

78. Eric Stover and Rachel Shigekane, "The Missing in the Aftermath of War: When Do the Needs of Victims' Families and International War Crimes Tribunals Clash?" *International Review of the Red Cross* 84, no. 848 (2002): 845–66. See also Fred Abrahams, Gilles Perez, and Eric Stover, *A Village Destroyed: May 14, 1999; War Crimes in Kosovo* (Berkeley: University of California Press, 2001), 85, 95. A detailed account of the work of identifying the missing in Bosnia is given by Sarah E. Wagner, *To Know Where He Lies: DNA Technology and the Search for Srebrenica's Missing* (Berkeley: University of California Press, 2008).

79. Prime Minister Tony Blair, Statement 17.30 7 July 2005, http://news.bbc.co.uk/1/hi/uk/4659953.stm.

80. For the development of a similar idea about how "responding to threat requires the time of government to be politically corrected," see Brian Massumi, "The Future Birth of the Affective Fact," browse.reticular.info/text/collected/massumi.pdf. Thanks to Nick Vaughan-Williams for drawing my attention to the similarities here.

81. London Assembly, "Report," vol. 1, paragraph 1.15, p. 9.

82. Ibid., paragraph 1.17, p. 9.

83. Giorgio Agamben, *Homo Sacer: Sovereign Power and Bare Life,* trans. Daniel Heller-Roazen (Stanford, CA: Stanford University Press, 1998).

84. Tulloch, *One Day in July,* 222.

85. Ibid., 219.

86. Ibid., 222.

87. John Berger, review of a Francis Bacon retrospective, quoted in Tulloch, *One Day in July,* 213.

88. Joseba Zulaika and William A. Douglass, *Terror and Taboo: The Follies, Fables, and Faces of Terrorism* (New York: Routledge, 1996), 195.

89. Ibid., 226.

5. Forensic Identification

1. William Langewiesche, *American Ground: Unbuilding the World Trade Center* (London: Scribner, 2003). The name Ground Zero, which appears to have been given to the site by the media within twenty-four hours of the collapse of the towers, has stuck, despite the fact that for those working there the site was called by other names. Initially known simply as "the pile," as work progressed it became (for obvious reasons) "the hole" or "the pit." Technically the term "ground zero" relates to a nuclear explosion. It designates the position on the earth's surface immediately above or below the point of detonation of a nuclear bomb. Peter Schwenger, "Circling Ground Zero," *PMLA-Publications of the Modern Language Association of America* 106, no. 2 (1991): 253.

2. Eric W. Rothenbuhler, "The Symbolics of Touch on 9/11 and After" (paper presented at Making Sense of September 11: News Media and Old Metaphors, Ohio University, Athens, Ohio, September 21, 2002; Rothenbuhler, "Ground Zero, the Firemen, and the Symbolics of Touch on 9/11 and After," in *Media Anthropology*, ed. Eric W. Rothenbuhler and Mihai Coman (New York and London: Sage, 2005), 176–87.

3. John E. Czarnecki, "Unlikely Collaboration of Architects Design Viewing Platform (David Rockwell, Diller+Scofidio, and Kevin Kennon Collaborate on the Platform for the Public Overlooking Ground-Zero)," *Architectural Record* 190, no. 2 (2002): 26.

4. Laura Kurgan, *Around Ground Zero* (New York: New York New Visions; Coalition for the Rebuilding of Lower Manhattan, 2001); Kevin Lerner, "Architect Creates Map to Orient Ground-Zero Visitors (Laura Kurgan's Map Includes Pedestrian Routes, Open Views, and Area Buildings Condition Information)," *Architectural Record* 190, no. 2 (2002): 28.

5. Kevin Bubriski, *Pilgrimage: Looking at Ground Zero* (New York: powerHouse Books, 2002), 11.

6. "Mariette," World Trade Center Viewing Platform, 26 January 2002.

7. Ken Jacobs, "Circling Zero, Part One: 'We See Absence': Program Note" (Paper presented at the Attack and Aftermath: Documenting 9/11, American Museum of the Moving Image, New York, September 7–11, 2002).

8. Ibid.

9. Sarah E. Wagner, *To Know Where He Lies: DNA Technology and the Search for Srebrenica's Missing* (Berkeley: University of California Press, 2008).

10. Rene Marcus, American Red Cross Museum Stories, rc_story11.xml, 27 October 2003, September 11 Digital Archive. http://911digitalarchive.org/repository_object.php?object_id=422.

11. Shiya Ribowsky and Tom Shachtman, *Dead Center: Behind the Scenes at the World's Largest Medical Examiner's Office* (New York: Harper, 2007), 191.

12. Robert N Munson, American Red Cross Museum Stories, rc_story14.xml, 2 October 2003, September 11 Digital Archive. http://911digitalarchive.org/repository_object.php?object_id=427.

13. Ibid.

14. Ibid.

15. Ibid.

16. Marcus, American Red Cross Museum Stories, story 11.

17. Ibid.

18. Caroline Moorhead, *Dunant's Dream: War, Switzerland and the History of the Red Cross* (London: HarperCollins, 1998), 87–118.

19. These words remain in the 2007 revision of the Charter, which is available at www2.redcross.org/images/pdfs/charter.pdf. The revision followed a congressional review of ARC's performance in response to hurricane Katrina (Kevin R. Kosar, *The Congressional Charter of the American National Red Cross: Overview, History, and Analysis, CRS Report for Congress RL33314,* 15 March 2006 [Washington: Congressional Research Service, Library of Congress, 2006], www.fas.org/sgp/crs/misc/RL33314.pdf).

20. American Red Cross, History, The Federal Charter of the American Red Cross, http://www.redcross.org/portal/site/en/menuitem.d229a5f06620c6052b1ec fbf43181aa0/?vgnextoid=39c2a8f21931f110VgnVCM10000089f0870aRCRD.

21. Grant Williams, "Red Cross Faces Sharp Criticism over Spending and Management," *The Chronicle of Philanthropy,* 17 October 2001, http://philanthropy.com/free/update/2001/10/2001101702.htm.

22. Ibid.

23. CNN, "Red Cross Defends Handling of Sept. 11 Donations," 6 November 2001, http://archives.cnn.com/2001/US/11/06/rec.charity.hearing.

24. Grant Williams, "Red Cross President Resigns under Pressure from Board," *The Chronicle of Philanthropy,* 26 October 2001, http://philanthropy.com/free/update/2001/10/2001102601.htm.

25. Deborah Sontag, "Who Brought Bernadine Healy Down?" *New York Times,* 23 December 2001.

26. Williams, "Red Cross President Resigns."

27. Sontag, "Who Brought Bernadine Healy Down?"

28. Ibid.

29. Ibid.

30. CNN, Red Cross Briefing on Liberty Fund, live event/special, 14 November 2001, http://transcripts.cnn.com/TRANSCRIPTS/0111/14/se.03.html.

31. Ibid.

32. American Red Cross, September 11th Response and Recovery, Liberty Fund, The Liberty Fund Controversy, Clip 1: George Mitchell, recorded April 28, 2006, http://www.redcross.org/911recovery/.

33. American Red Cross, Liberty Disaster Relief Fund, Financial Statements, 30 June 2004, http://www.redcross.org/portal/site/en/menuitem.d8aaecf214c576bf9 71e4cfe43181aa0/?vgnextoid=0bf26a5e61dce110VgnVCM10000089f0870aRCRD &vgnextfmt=default#report.

34. Ibid.

35. CNN, Red Cross Briefing on Liberty Fund, 14 November 2001.

36. House Committee on Homeland Security, Subcommittee on Management, Integration, and Oversight, Testimony of Leigh A. Bradley, American Red Cross, 12 July 2006, p. 16, http://www.redcross.org/portal/site/en/menuitem.53fabf6cc033 f17a2b1ecfbf43181aa0/?vgnextoid=d2366b9128c2b110VgnVCM10000089f0870a RCRD&currPage=bbe75d795323b110VgnVCM10000089f0870aRCRD.

37. American Red Cross, September 11th Response and Recovery, Liberty Fund, Fraud, http://www.redcross.org/911recovery/.

38. Rothenbuhler, "Symbolics of Touch."

39. Ibid., 2.

40. Ibid., 3.

41. Ibid., 4.

42. Ibid., 5.

43. Mark Wigley, "Insecurity by Design," in *After the World Trade Center: Rethinking New York City,* ed. Michael Sorkin and Sharon Zukin (New York: Routledge, 2002), 73.

44. One of the strongest family groups in the aftermath of September 11 was an organization for the safety of skyscrapers (The Skyscraper Safety Campaign: A Project of Parents and Families of Firefighters and WTC Victims, http://www.sky scrapersafety.org/).

45. Elaine Scarry, *The Body in Pain: The Making and Unmaking of the World* (New York: Oxford University Press, 1985).

46. Langewiesche, *American Ground,* 146.

47. Dennis Smith, *Report from Ground Zero: The Heroic Story of the Rescuers at the World Trade Center* (London: Doubleday, 2002), 340.

48. Ibid., 349.

49. Ibid., 352.

50. Rothenbuhler, "Symbolics of Touch," 12.

51. Giorgio Agamben, *Homo Sacer: Sovereign Power and Bare Life,* trans. Daniel Heller-Roazen (Stanford, CA: Stanford University Press, 1998).

52. Rothenbuhler, "Symbolics of Touch," 16.

53. Ibid., 17.

54. There were three missing persons by the name of Michael Lynch, two of whom were firefighters (Ribowsky and Shachtman, *Dead Center,* 186).

55. The Michael Lynch Memorial Foundation, About Us, http://www.mlynch. org/ml/about.htm.

56. Mike Wallace, *A New Deal for New York* (New York: Bell & Weiland in association with Gotham Center for New York City History, 2002).

57. Laura Kurgan, interview with author, New York, 20 November 2002.

58. Robert Lee Hotz, "Probing the DNA of Death," *Los Angeles Times,* October 9, 2002.

59. Ibid.

60. Timothy Thompson and Susan Black, eds., *Forensic Human Identification: An Introduction* (Boca Raton, FL: CRC Press, 2007), xiv.

61. Ibid., xv.

62. William Goodwin and Sibte Hadi, "DNA," in Thompson and Black, *Forensic Human Identification,* 6, 8.

63. Robin Williams and Paul Johnson, *Genetic Policing: The Use of DNA in Criminal Investigations* (Cullompton: Willan, 2008), 33.

64. Nancy Ritter, "Identifying Remains: Lessons Learned from 9/11," *National Institute of Justice Journal* 256 (2007): 20–26; National Institute of Justice, "Lessons Learned from 9/11: DNA Identification in Mass Fatality Incidents," (Washington, DC: US Department of Justice, Office of Justice Programs, 2006); L. G. Biesecker et al., "DNA Identification after the World Trade Center Attack," *Science* 310,

no. 5751 (2006): 1122–23; Elaine Marchi and T. Z. Chastain, "The Sequence of Structural Events That Challenged the Forensic Effort of the World Trade Center Disaster," *American Laboratory,* December 2002, 13–17; Elaine Marchi, "Methods Developed to Identify Victims of the World Trade Center Disaster," *American Laboratory,* March 2004, 30–36; Zoran M. Budimlija et al., "World Trade Center Human Identification Project: Experiences with Individual Body Identification Cases," *Croatian Medical Journal* 44, no. 3 (2003): 259–63; Gaille Mackinnon and Amy Z. Mundorff, "The World Trade Center—September 11, 2001," in Thompson and Black, *Forensic Human Identification,* 485–99.

65. Mackinnon and Mundorff, "World Trade Center," 491.

66. Quoted in David Friend, *Watching the World Change: The Stories behind the Images of 9/11* (New York: Picador, 2006), 67.

67. Robert C. Shaler, *Who They Were: Inside the World Trade Center DNA Story; The Unprecedented Effort to Identify the Missing* (New York: Free Press, 2005), 52.

68. Ibid., 55.

69. Ibid., 148.

70. Ribowsky and Shachtman, *Dead Center,* 224.

71. Shaler, *Who They Were,* 145.

72. Ibid., 152–53. Misidentifications also happened in other ways. For example, instances of people carrying IDs that were not their own led to mistakes that were not discovered until DNA testing was completed (Ribowsky and Shachtman, *Dead Center,* 214).

73. Shaler, *Who They Were;* Ribowsky and Shachtman, *Dead Center.*

74. National Institute of Justice, "Lessons Learned from 9/11"; Shaler, *Who They Were,* 110–13.

75. Shaler, *Who They Were,* 115.

76. Mackinnon and Mundorff, "World Trade Center," 491–92.

77. Budimlija et al., "World Trade Center Human Identification Project."

78. National Institute of Justice, "Lessons Learned from 9/11," 83.

79. Ibid., 84.

80. Ayaz Nanji, "Ground Zero Forensic Work Ends," CBS News, 23 February 2005, http://www.cbsnews.com/stories/2005/02/23/national/main675839.shtml.

81. Eric Lipton, "At the Limits of Science, 9/11 ID Effort Comes to End," *New York Times,* 3 April 2005.

82. Eric Lenkowitz, "9/11 Victim ID'd 6 Yrs Later," *New York Post,* 14 September 2007.

83. 9-11 Research, Missing Bodies, http://911research.wtc7.net.wtc/evidence/bodies.html.

84. CBS News, "Latest NYC 9/11 Search Finds 72 Human Remains," 23 June 2010, http://www.cbsnews.com/stories/2010/06/22/ap/national/main6608278.shtml

85. This is Judith Butler's term: Judith Butler, *Precarious Life: The Powers of Mourning and Violence* (London: Verso, 2004).

86. Ribowsky and Shachtman, *Dead Center.*

87. Ibid., 194.

88. Ibid.

89. The missing of 9/11 are not the only, or even the most numerous, missing persons in the United States; there is a "silent mass disaster": those who go missing every day. Nancy Ritter, "Missing Persons and Unidentified Remains: The Nation's Silent Mass Disaster," *National Institute of Justice Journal* 256 (2007): 2–7.

90. Friend, *Watching the World Change,* 73–77.

91. Ibid., 76.

92. Ibid., 77.

93. Ibid., 37.

94. Ribowsky and Shachtman, *Dead Center,* 195.

95. Ibid., 196.

96. Mackinnon and Mundorff, "World Trade Center," 488.

97. Ribowsky and Shachtman, *Dead Center,* 166.

98. Charles Lawrence, "Remains of 9/11 Victims 'to Spend Eternity' in City Rubbish Dump," *Daily Telegraph,* 10 October 2004.

99. David W. Dunlap, "Renovating a Sacred Place, Where the 9/11 Remains Wait," *New York Times,* 29 August 2006.

100. Office of the Chief Medical Examiner, "Update on the Results of DNA testing of Remains Recovered at the World Trade Center Site and Surrounding Area," Press release, 1 February 2009, http://www.ci.nyc.ny.us/html/ocme/html/pa/pa.shtml. See also OCME press releases dated 1 May 2009.

101. Ribowsky and Shachtman, *Dead Center,* 199.

102. Ibid., 237. The figure relates to Phase I.

103. Jasmina Husanović, "'Therapeutic' Regimes of Governing Trauma and the Dea(r)th of the Political: Politics of Missing Persons and ICMP's 'Bosnian Technology'" (seminar paper, Goldsmiths College, London, March 2009).

104. Ribowsky and Shachtman, *Dead Center,* 195.

6. Missing in Action

1. Michael Sledge also poses this question. Michael Sledge, *Soldier Dead: How We Recover, Identify, Bury, and Honor Our Military Fallen* (New York: Columbia University Press, 2005), 29.

2. Sledge, *Soldier Dead,* 143.

3. Giorgio Agamben, *Homo Sacer: Sovereign Power and Bare Life,* trans. Daniel Heller-Roazen (Stanford, CA: Stanford University Press, 1998).

4. Jacques Rancière, *Dissensus: On Politics and Aesthetics,* trans. Steven Corcoran (London: Continuum, 2010), 36.

5. Giorgio Agamben, *Profanations,* trans. Jeff Fort (New York: Zone Books, 2007).

6. Luc Capdevila and Daniele Voldman, *War Dead: Western Societies and the Casualties of War,* trans. Richard Veasey (Edinburgh: Edinburgh University Press, 2006), 55.

7. Capdevila and Voldman, *War Dead,* 47.

8. Ibid., 46.

9. Ibid., 47.

10. Ibid., 52.

11. Drew Gilpin Faust, *The Republic of Suffering: Death and the American Civil War* (New York: Vintage Books, 2008).

12. Sledge, *Soldier Dead,* 135–49.

13. Capdevila and Voldman, *War Dead.*

14. See, for example, Dilip Sarkar, *Missing in Action: Resting in Peace?* (Worcester: Victory Books International, 2006), for an account of amateur recovery of RAF missing; and for official searches for missing air crew, Stuart Hadaway, *Missing Believed Killed: The Royal Air Force and the Search for Missing Aircrew, 1939–1952* (Barnsley: Pen and Sword Aviation, 2008).

15. Sledge, *Soldier Dead,* 29.

16. Commonwealth War Graves Commission, "Order of Service: Dedication and Burial; Fromelles (Pheasant Wood) Military Cemetery," 19 July 2010, http://www.cwgc.org/fromelles/?page=english/diary-events/view/news190710; The Hon. Alan Griffin MP, Australian Minister for Veterans' Affairs and Defence Personnel, "Final Fromelles Soldier Laid to Rest," press release, 41/2010, 19 July 2010, http://www.minister.defence.gov.au/Griffintpl.cfm?CurrentId=10634. See also Julie Summers, Louise Loe, and Nigel Steel, *Remembering Fromelles: A New Cemetery for a New Century* (Maidenhead: CWGC Publishing, 2010).

17. Commonwealth War Graves Commission, "New Cemetery Becomes Final Resting Place for 250 Soldiers in Dedication Led by HRH Prince of Wales," press release, 19 July 2010, http://www.cwgc.org/fromelles/?page=english/diary-events/view/news190710.

18. Tim Whitford and Tony Pollard, "For Duty Done: A WWI Military Medallion Recovered from the Mass Grave Site at Fromelles, Northern France," *Journal of Conflict Archaeology* 5, no. 1 (2009): 201–29; Commonwealth War Graves Commission, "Getting Us Here—Building the Case, http://www.cwgc.org/fromelles/?page=english/background/getting_us_here&pageno=2.

19. Whitford and Pollard, "For Duty Done"; Peter Barton, "The Historian's Role," http://www.cwgc.org/fromelles/?page=english/background/getting_us_here; see also at http://www.cwgc.org/fromelles/: "Reaction and Response—The Next Step"; "Recovery and Reburial in 1919"; "The GUARD Investigations—Proving the Case."

20. Barton, "Historian's Role."

21. Strangely, reports of these two GUARD investigations do not seem to be available. There are links to the GUARD Report on two other sites, but they are no longer active; see Commonwealth War Graves Commission, "The GUARD Investigations—Proving the Case," http://www.cwgc.org/fromelles/?page=english/background/getting_us_here; Missing Soldiers of Fromelles Discussion Group, "Military, Media, and Exploratory Dig," 23 February 2009, http://www.docstoc.com/docs/35340103/The-Military-Media-and-Exploratory-Dig.

22. Kate Brady, "Fromelles: A Report from Oxford Archaeology's Finds Manager"; Steve Martin and Tracey Vennai, "Fromelles: The Story So Far," 14 September 2009; "The Fromelles Recovery: Oxford Archaeology's Role"—all available at http://www.cwgc.org/fromelles/?page=english/the-project/getting_going.

23. Martin and Vennai, "Fromelles."

24. Florian Westphal, Head of Public and Media Relations, International Committee of the Red Cross, personal communication, 26 July 2010; Robert Hall, "Piecing Together the Past," BBC News, 13 March 2009, http://news.bbc.co.uk/2/hi/uk_news/7940540.stm. This archive forms part of the Archives of the International Agency for Prisoners of War of the ICRC. The ICRC aims to publish the whole of

the agency's archives in early 2014: "So far, the documents—some 500 000 pages with lists of prisoners and 6 millions of index cards—have undergone important preservation treatments because many of the items were severely damaged. The digitization of the documents is about to start and will last for 30 months. A partial release of documents is expected for 2012 and will include most documents about British prisoners." Martin Morger, International Committee of the Red Cross, Archives Division, personal communication, 27 August 2010. See http://www.icrc.org/web/eng/siteeng0.nsf/html/archives-feature-160310.

25. Martin and Vennai, "Fromelles," 4.

26. Commonwealth War Graves Commission, "Remembering Fromelles: The Project," http://www.cwgc.org/fromelles/?page=english/the-project/project/1; "Remembering Fromelles: Questions and Answers," http://www.cwgc.org/fromelles/?page=english/the-project/questions.

27. Julian Ware, "WWI: Finding the Lost Battalions," broadcast on Channel 4, 19 July 2010, Darlow Smithson Productions, produced and directed by Janice Sutherland.

28. Missing Soldiers of Fromelles Discussion Group, "Military, Media, and Exploratory Dig."

29. "Remembering Fromelles: Questions and Answers," http://www.cwgc.org/fromelles/?page=english/the-project/questions.

30. Ware, "WWI: Finding the Lost Battalions."

31. Ibid.

32. BBC News, "DNA Tests Fail to Identify Unknown WWI Soldiers," 17 March 2010, http://news.bbc.co.uk/1/hi/uk/8572381.stm.

33. Commonwealth War Graves Commission, "Who We Are," http://www.cwgc.org/content.asp?menuid=1&id=1&menuname=Who%20We%20Are&menu=main.

34. Commonwealth War Graves Commission, Facts & Statistics, http://www.cwgc.org/content.asp?menuid=2&submenuid=50&id=50&menuname=Facts%20and%20figures&menu=sub.

35. Julie Summers, *Remembered: The History of the Commonwealth War Graves Commission* (London: Merrell, 2007), 12.

36. Ibid., 16–17.

37. Imperial War Graves Commission, House of Commons Debate, 4 May 1920, *Hansard,* vol. 128, cols. 1929–72.

38. Ibid., col. 1940.

39. Ibid., col. 1942.

40. Ibid., col. 1971.

41. Ibid, col. 1972.

42. Stephen Robb, "Fromelles Dead Offer Reminder of 'Preciousness of Life,'" BBC News UK, 19 July 2010, http://www.bbc.co.uk/news/uk-10661923.

43. P. G. Cambray and G. G. B. Briggs, *The Official Record of the Humanitarian Services of the War Organisation of the British Red Cross Society and Order of St. John of Jerusalem, 1939–1947* (London: Red Cross and St. John 1949), 341.

44. Ibid., 339.

45. Ibid., 340–41.

46. R. A. Lewis (War Organisation Wounded Missing and Relatives Department) to Mrs. Pickard-Cambridge, 24 October 1940, album compiled by Hilda

Pickard-Cambridge, containing letters, forms, handwritten accounts of the work of the Searchers for the Wounded and Missing, 1939–1945, Archives of the British Red Cross, Ref. 2305/4.

47. *Red Cross and St. John War Organisation, 1939–1947, Official Record, Confidential Supplement* [supplement to P. G. Cambray and G. G. B. Briggs, *The Official Record of the Humanitarian Services of the War Organisation of the British Red Cross Society and Order of St. John of Jerusalem, 1939–1947* (London: Red Cross and St. John 1949)], British Red Cross Archives Library, 514.

48. Missing Soldiers (Tracing), *Hansard*, 19 December 1941, Commons Sitting; Cambray and Briggs, *Official Record*, 347.

49. Cambray and Briggs, *Official Record*, 348.

50. *Red Cross and St. John War Organisation…Confidential Supplement*, 512–19.

51. Cambray and Briggs, *Official Record*, 3–4.

52. Ibid.

53. Caroline Moorehead, *Dunant's Dream: War, Switzerland, and the History of the Red Cross* (London: HarperCollins, 1998), 52.

54. Ibid., 87.

55. Ibid., 89.

56. Ibid.

57. Missing Soldiers (Tracing), *Hansard*, 10 February 1942, Commons Sitting.

58. History Cas. (L) [War Office Casualty Branch (Liverpool)], p. 28, the National Archives, Kew, WO 162/205.

59. Ibid.

60. History Cas. (L) [War Office Casualty Branch (Liverpool)], p. 62, the National Archives, Kew, WO 162/205.

61. Losses on PS "Gracie Fields," the National Archives, Kew, WO 361/12.

62. Losses on PS "Gracie Fields," note signed JH, 9 February 1941, the National Archives, Kew, WO 361/12

63. Statement by 3528991 Pte. Clegg. H. with regard to 3513516 Pte. MAILE.H., the National Archives, Kew, WO 361/12.

64. Cambray and Briggs, *Official Record*, 351–53.

65. Mrs. Hilda M. Pickard-Cambridge, St. Catherines, Marley, near Haslemere in Surrey, has left not only this account, but also an amazing scrapbook of information: "British Red Cross Search for the Missing, 1940–1945," British Red Cross Archives, London, Ref. 2305/4. Mrs. Pickard-Cambridge was chief searcher for the Surrey Joint War Organisation. During World War II she traced missing persons by visiting hospitals and gathering information from the wounded. After the war she put together this two-hundred-page account of her work. She was kept going by the compliments of the soldiers who expressed their gratitude for the work the Red Cross was doing (Hilda Pickard-Cambridge, "Account of the Searching," in "British Red Cross Search for the Missing, 1940–1945," 8).

66. Cambray and Briggs, *Official Record*, 349.

67. Ibid., 350.

68. *Red Cross and St. John War Organisation, 1939–1947, Official Record: Appendices to Official History* [P. G. Cambray and G. G. B. Briggs, *The Official Record of the Humanitarian Services of the War Organisation of the British Red Cross Society and Order of St. John of Jerusalem, 1939–1947* (London: Red Cross and St. John 1949)] *and Confidential*

Supplement, British Red Cross Archives Library. See also *Hospital Searching for "Missing" Men: The Work of the Searching Service, Wounded and Missing Department, Red Cross and St. John War Organisation,* reprinted from the "Summary of Work," no. 96, 12 June 1943, British Red Cross Archives, London, Ref. 2156/13.

69. Pickard-Cambridge, "Account of the Searching," 2.

70. Ibid., 2–3.

71. Letter from the Director, Searchers Department, Red Cross and St. John War Organisation, for Distribution to Searchers by Chief Searchers, 3 June 1943, Pickard-Cambridge, "British Red Cross Search for the Missing," 30, British Red Cross Archives, London, Ref. 2305/4.

72. Pickard-Cambridge, "Account of the searching," 7.

73. Ibid., 3–4.

74. Cambray and Briggs, *Official Record,* 350, my emphasis.

75. History Cas. (L) [History of the War Office Casualty Branch (Liverpool)], p. 16, the National Archives, Kew, WO 162/205.

76. See, for example, the account in Cambray and Briggs, *Official Record,* 360, of how Red Cross workers visited the injured in hospital and conveyed messages and information about how they were doing to relatives.

77. Canadian Letters and Images Project, Vancouver Island University in partnership with The University of Western Ontario, http://www.canadianletters.ca/letters.php?letterid=2325&docid=1&collectionid=153&warid=3.

78. Cambray and Briggs, *Official Record,* 353.

79. *Red Cross and St. John War Organisation…Confidential Supplement,* 520.

80. Ibid., 521–22.

81. Ibid., 523–29.

82. Pickard-Cambridge, "Account of the Searching," 9.

83. Pickard-Cambridge, "British Red Cross Search for the Missing," 104.

84. Cambray and Briggs, *Official Record,* 339.

85. Sledge, *Soldier Dead,* 66–82.

86. Ibid., 77, 73.

87. The plan seems to have been for a detailed investigation of each march, as the papers preserved in the archives relating to the investigation of the Fossenberg to Cham death march show (UNRRA Bureau of Documents and Tracing, US Zone, 23 March 1946, Fossenberg—Cham Death March, Report of the Commissariat Belge au Repatriement, UN Archives S-0436-20-3). Other maps of the routes of death marches also survive in the files, but with much less detail, as if the investigations were never fully completed (UNRRA Central Tracing Bureau, Documents Intelligence, 15 July 1946, Death Marches: Routes and Distances, vols. I–III, UN Archives S-0413-0002-04 to S-0413-0002-07). Photographs of some of the exhumations and reburials survive (United States Holocaust Memorial Museum, Holocaust Encyclopedia, Photography, Death Marches, http://www.ushmm.org/wlc/media_ph.php?lang=en&ModuleId=10005162&MediaId=6126).

88. John Corsellis and Marcus Ferrar, *Slovenia 1945: Memories of Death and Survival after World War II* (London: I. B. Tauris, 2005). I am indebted to Andreja Zevnik for alerting me to this case, and for helping in the research.

89. Nigel Nicholson, *Long Life* (London: Weidenfeld and Nicholson, 1997), 121, quoted in Corsellis and Ferrar, *Slovenia 1945,* 52.

90. Corsellis and Ferrar, *Slovenia 1945,* 60.

91. Ibid., 63.

92. Ibid., 201, 205.

93. Andreja Zevnik, personal communication, 1 December 2008.

94. Damir Marjanovic et al., "DNA Identification of Skeletal Remains from the World War II Mass Graves Uncovered in Slovenia," *Croat Medical Journal* 48 (2007). Of the remains of twenty-seven individuals, four persons were identified. The work demonstrated that techniques developed in identifying missing persons in Bosnia and Herzegovina and Croatia could be used for much older remains.

95. RTS, Odprtje Kostnice žrtev povojnih pobojev, 28 October 2008, video (Slovenian), http://www.tele-59.si/novice/2064/?results=40.

96. Government Communication Office, Republic of Slovenia, "Commission: Important Steps Made in Revealing Post-WWII Killings," Ljubljana, 14 October 2008, http://www.ukom.gov.si/eng/slovenia/publications/slovenia-news/7252/7262/.

97. Andreja Zevnik, personal communication, 1 December 2008.

98. Karen DeYoung, "On the Tarmac, Clinton Attends Ceremony for Americans MIA in Vietnam," *Washington Post,* blog, 23 July 2010.

99. For a description of the process in several cases, see Lisa Hoshower-Leppo, "Missing in Action: Searching for America's War Dead," in *Matériel Culture: The Archaeology of Twentieth-Century Conflict,* ed. John Schofield, William Gray Johnson, and Colleen M. Beck (London: Routledge, 2002), 80–90.

100. Thomas M. Hawley, *The Remains of War: Bodies, Politics, and the Search for American Soldiers Unaccounted for in Southeast Asia* (Durham, NC: Duke University Press, 2005), 10–11, 4, 12, 114.

101. Sledge, *Soldier Dead,* 93.

102. Ibid.

103. Capdevila and Voldman, *War Dead,* 180.

104. Ibid., 182–83.

105. Imperial War Graves Commission, House of Commons Debate, 4 May 1920, 7.

7. Disappeared, Argentina

1. Thirty thousand is the number produced by human rights organizations; on the difficulty of counting in the case of Argentina, see Alison Brysk, "The Politics of Measurement: The Contested Count of the Disappeared in Argentina," *Human Rights Quarterly* 16, no. 4 (1994): 676–92. A figure of "at least 9,000" is commonly cited by forensic archaeologists.

2. Lawrence Weschler, Preface to *Los Desaparecidos / The Disappeared,* by Laurel Reuter (Milan: Charta, 2006), 9.

3. Laurel Reuter, *Los Desaparecidos / The Disappeared* (Milan: Charta, 2006), 25.

4. Emilio F Mignone, "Beyond Fear: Forms of Justice and Compensation," in *Fear at the Edge: State Terror and Resistance in Latin America,* ed. Juan E Corradi, Patricia Weiss Fagen, and Manuel Antonio Garretón (Berkeley: University of California Press, 1992), 253.

5. For material in English, see, for example, on the disappearances in Argentina, Argentine National Commission on the Disappeared, *Nunca Mas: Report of*

the Argentine National Commission on the Disappeared (New York: Farrar, Straus and Giroux, 1986) (similar reports are available for other South American countries); Patricia Marchak, *God's Assassins: State Terrorism in Argentina in the 1970s* (Montreal: McGill-Queen's University Press, 1999); on Brazil and Uruguay, Lawrence Weschler, *A Miracle, a Universe: Settling Accounts with Torturers* (Chicago: University of Chicago Press, 1990); on Guatemala, Archdiocese of Guatemala, Human Rights Office, *Guatemala: Never Again! Recovery of Historical Memory Project (Remhi): The Official Report* (Maryknoll, NY: Orbis Books, 1999); on Argentina and Chile, Thomas C. Wright, *State Terrorism in Latin America: Chile, Argentina, and International Human Rights* (Lanham, MD: Rowman and Littlefield, 2007); and Tina Rosenberg, *Children of Cain: Violence and the Violent in Latin America* (New York: William Morrow, 1991). There are also many films and novels, as well as art exhibitions.

6. Ziad Zafar, *Missing in Pakistan,* documentary, 2007, http://video.google.com/videoplay?docid=-854791386997728455; Declan Walsh, "Without a Trace," *Guardian,* 16 March 2007.

7. María Fernanda Pérez Solla, *Enforced Disappearances in International Human Rights* (Jefferson, NC: McFarland and Company, 2006), 7.

8. Marjorie Agosin, "Buenos Aires," extracted in Weschler, Preface, 8.

9. Jenny Edkins, *Trauma and the Memory of Politics* (Cambridge: Cambridge University Press, 2003), 15–17; Slavoj Žižek, *For They Know Not What They Do: Enjoyment as a Political Factor* (London: Verso, 1991), 272.

10. Inger Agger and Soren Buus Jensen, for example, focus on "healing," despite recognizing the role political context and political demands play in the healing process: survivors need to "reframe or de-privatise their traumatic experiences" and society at large needs to go through a process of "healing and democratisation" that they call "rituals of social reparation." Inger Agger and Soren Buus Jensen, *Trauma and Healing under State Terrorism* (London: Zed Books, 1996), 201–2.

11. Giorgio Agamben, *Homo Sacer: Sovereign Power and Bare Life,* trans. Daniel Heller-Roazen (Stanford, CA: Stanford University Press, 1998); Jacques Rancière, *Dissensus: On Politics and Aesthetics,* trans. Steven Corcoran (London: Continuum, 2010).

12. Antonius C. G. M. Robben, "The Assault on Basic Trust: Disappearance, Protest, and Reburial in Argentina," in *Cultures under Siege: Collective Violence and Trauma,* ed. Antonius C. G. M. Robben and Marcelo M. Suárez-Orozco (Cambridge: Cambridge University Press, 2000), 71; see also Robben, *Political Violence and Trauma in Argentina* (Philadelphia: University of Pennsylvania Press, 2005), 297–98.

13. Elaine Scarry, *The Body in Pain: The Making and Unmaking of the World* (New York: Oxford University Press, 1985).

14. Jean Franco, "Gender, Death, and Resistance: Facing the Ethical Vacuum," in Corradi, Fagen, and Garretón, *Fear at the Edge,* 112.

15. Marguerite Feitlowitz, *A Lexicon of Terror: Argentina and the Legacies of Torture* (Oxford: Oxford University Press, 1988), 90–109; see also Jorge Gaggero, *Graciela está en nosotros: Memoria de todos* (Buenos Aires: Colihue, 2007).

16. Feitlowitz, *Lexicon of Terror,* 97.

17. Ibid., 94; Silvia Malagrino, *Burnt Oranges,* film (United States: www.librememdia.com, 2006).

18. Griselda Gambaro, *Information for Foreigners,* trans. Marguerite Feitlowitz (Evanston, IL: Northwestern University Press, 1992); see also Annette H. Levine, *Cry for Me, Argentina: The Performance of Trauma in the Short Narratives of Aida Bortnik, Griselda Gambaro, and Tununa Mercado* (Madison, NJ: Fairleigh Dickinson University Press, 2009).

19. Feitlowitz, *Lexicon of Terror,* x, xi.

20. Feitlowitz, *Lexicon of Terror,* 90, 93.

21. Marguerite Guzmán Bouvard, *Revolutionising Motherhood: The Mothers of the Plaza de Mayo* (Lanham, MD: SR Books, 1994).

22. Marchak, *God's Assassins,* 163–65.

23. Saskia P. C. van Drunen, *Struggling with the Past: The Human Rights Movement and the Politics of Memory in Post-Dictatorship Argentina (1983–2006)* (Amsterdam: Rozenberg Publishers, 2010), gives a detailed account of this struggle.

24. Van Drunen, *Struggling with the Past,* 81.

25. Feitlowitz, *Lexicon of Terror,* 186.

26. Ibid.

27. Nora Amalia Femenía, "Argentina's Mothers of Plaza De Mayo: The Mourning Process from Junta to Democracy," *Feminist Studies* 13, no. 1 (1987): 15.

28. Ibid., 13.

29. Ibid.

30. Matilde Mellibovsky, *Circle of Love over Death: Testimonies of the Mothers of the Plaza de Mayo,* trans. Maria Prosser and Matthew Prosser (Willimantic, CT: Curbstone Press, 1997), 134.

31. Malagrino, *Burnt Oranges.*

32. Memory in Latin America, blog, http://memoryinlatinamerica.blogspot.com/2010/02/argentina-campo-de-mayo-trial-update.html.

33. Marjorie Agosin, "Cities of Life, Cities of Change," *Human Rights Quarterly* 12, no. 4 (1990): 554–58.

34. Franco, "Gender, Death, and Resistance."

35. Bouvard, *Revolutionising Motherhood,* 62; see also Marysa Navarro, "The Personal Is Political: Las Madres de Plaza Mayo," in *Power and Popular Protest: Latin American Social Movements,* ed. Susan Eckstein (Berkeley: University of California Press, 2001), 241–58.

36. Bouvard, *Revolutionising Motherhood,* 68.

37. Ibid., 69.

38. Mellibovsky, *Circle of Love over Death.*

39. As well as Feitlowitz, *Lexicon of Terror,* I am thinking here of Jo Fisher, *Mothers of the Disappeared* (London: Zed Books, 1989) and Bouvard, *Revolutionising Motherhood.*

40. Cited in Mellibovsky, *Circle of Love over Death,* 81.

41. Mellibovsky, *Circle of Love over Death,* ix, x.

42. Ibid., 9. Van Drunen points out that it was only in the 1990s that it became possible to speak of the activism of the disappeared, rather than present them as innocent victims (van Drunen, *Struggling with the Past*).

43. Mellibovsky, *Circle of Love over Death,* 27.

44. Ibid., 52.

45. Ibid.

46. Ibid., 85.

47. Diana Taylor, *Disappearing Acts: Spectacles of Gender and Nationalism in Argentina's "Dirty War"* (Durham, NC: Duke University Press, 1997), 204.

48. Ibid., 203–5.

49. Slavoj Žižek, *The Sublime Object of Ideology* (London: Verso, 1989); Jacques Rancière, *Disagreement: Politics and Philosophy,* trans. Julie Rose (Minneapolis: University of Minnesota Press, 1999).

50. Taylor, *Disappearing Acts,* 198.

51. Rancière, *Disagreement,* 33. See also Debra B. Bergoffen's argument that the Madres "played the patriarchal card" in her "Engaging Nietzsche's Women: Ofelia Schutte and the Madres de la Plaza de Mayo," *Hypatia* 19, no. 3 (2004): 165–66); Bouvard's extensive discussion in the final chapters of *Revolutionising Motherhood;* and Zoë Crossland, "Violent Spaces: Conflict over the Reappearance of Argentina's Disappeared," in *Matériel Culture: The Archaeology of Twentieth-Century Conflict,* ed. John Schofield, William Gray Johnson, and Coleen M. Beck (London: Routledge, 2002), 118.

52. Van Drunen, *Struggling with the Past,* 60. The commission's report was published in 1984 (Argentine National Commission on the Disappeared, *Nunca Mas*).

53. Bouvard, *Revolutionising Motherhood,* 134–35.

54. Van Drunen, *Struggling with the Past,* 59.

55. Crossland, "Violent Spaces," 121.

56. Mellibovsky, *Circle of Love over Death,* 161.

57. Argentine Forensic Archaeology Team / Equipo Argentino de Antropologia Forense (EAAF), *Annual Report, 2007,* 20.

58. Mercedes Doretti and Jennifer Burrell, "Gray Spaces and Endless Negotiations: Forensic Anthropology and Human Rights," in *Anthropology Put to Work,* ed. Les W. Field and Richard G. Fox (Oxford: Berg, 2007), 45–64.

59. See, for example, reports of the Argentine Forensic Archaeology Team / Equipo Argentino de Antropologia Forense (EAAF), http://eaaf.typepad.com/eaaf_reports/; and Mauricio Cohen Salama, *Tumbas anónimas: Informe sobre la identificación de restos de víctimas de la represión ilegal* [Anonymous Graves: Report on Identification of Remains of Victims of Illegal Repression] (Buenos Aires: Catalogos Editora, 1992). See also Christopher Joyce and Eric Stover, *Witnesses from the Grave: The Stories Bones Tell* (London: Grafton, 1993).

60. Argentine Forensic Anthropology Team, *Biannual Report, 1996–97,* 15, http://eaaf.typepad.com/eaaf_reports/.

61. EAAF, *Annual Report, 2007,* 131–32.

62. For a history of impunity laws and their annulment, see EAAF, "The Right to Truth," in *Annual Report, 2007,* 102–19; and van Drunen, *Struggling with the Past.*

63. EAAF, "The Latin American Initiative for the Indentification of the 'Disappeared' (LIID)," in *Annual Report, 2007,* 130–35.

64. Van Drunen, *Struggling with the Past,* 62–63; Antonius C. G. M. Robben, "Mourning and Mistrust in Civil-Military Relations in Post-Dirty War Argentina," in *Multidisciplinary Perspectives on Peace and Conflict Research: A View from Europe,* ed. Francisco Ferrandiz and Antonius C. G. M. Robben (Bilbao: University of Deusto, 2007), 253–70; 263; Crossland, "Violent Spaces," 119.

65. Robben, "Assault on Basic Trust," 91.

66. Joyce and Stover, *Witnesses from the Grave*, 258.

67. Ibid., 257; Bouvard, *Revolutionising Motherhood*, 149.

68. Bouvard, *Revolutionising Motherhood*, 172 n. 37.

69. Crossland, "Violent Spaces," 127.

70. Ibid., 128; Joyce and Stover, *Witnesses from the Grave*, 259; see also Karen Kissane, "Bringing back the dead," *The Age*, 11 October 2008, http://www.theage.com.au/world/bringing-back-the-dead-20081010-4yb9.html?page=-1.

71. Robben, "Assault on Basic Trust," 92.

72. Bouvard, *Revolutionising Motherhood*, 163.

73. Ibid., 79.

74. Robben, "Assault on Basic Trust," 87, 88, 91, 93, 94, 96.

75. Ibid., 81–82.

76. Ibid., 93–94.

77. Crossland, "Violent Spaces," 119–23.

78. Mercedes Mereno, quoted in Bouvard, *Revolutionising Motherhood*, 139, my emphasis.

79. Fisher, *Mothers of the Disappeared*, 127–28.

80. Fernando J. Bosco, "Human Rights Politics and Scaled Performances of Memory: Conflicts among the *Madres De Plaza De Mayo* in Argentina," *Social and Cultural Geography* 5, no. 3 (2004): 390.

81. Graciela de Jeger, cited in Fisher, *Mothers of the Disappeared*, 129.

82. Crossland, "Violent Spaces," 122.

83. Martin Caparros, "Apariciones/ Reappearances," in *Buena Memoria/Good Memory*, ed. Marcelo Brodsky (Buenos Aires: La Marca Editora, 2006), 13–14.

84. Van Drunen, *Struggling with the Past*, 91–92.

85. See, for example, Susana Kaiser, "*Escraches:* Demonstrations, Communication, and Political Memory in Post-Dictatorial Argentina," *Media, Culture, and Society* 24, no. 4 (2002): 499–516.

86. Van Drunen, *Struggling with the Past*, 89-91.

87. Ibid., 93.

88. Eric Stener Carlson, *I Remember Julia: Voices of the Disappeared* (Philadelphia: Temple University Press, 1996).

89. Ibid., 46, 49.

90. Ibid., 82, 83, xvi, xv.

91. Marcelo Brodsky, *Buena Memoria/Good Memory*, 4th ed. (Buenos Aires: La Marca Editora, 2006), 10.

92. Caparros, "Apariciones/ Reappearances," 13–14.

93. Brodsky, *Buena Memoria*, 58.

94. Carlson, *I Remember Julia*, 183.

95. Ibid., 181.

96. Ibid., 183.

97. Reuter, *Los Desaparecidos / The Disappeared*, 104–5.

98. Van Drunen, *Struggling with the Past*, 212.

99. Ibid., 217.

100. Ibid., 218.

101. Feitlowitz, *Lexicon of Terror*, 96–97. In Feitlowitz the name is given as Andres Francisco Valdez.

102. Jana Asher, David Banks, and Fritz Scheuren, eds., *Statistical Methods for Human Rights* (New York: Springer, 2008), v. See also Pete Larson, Freewheel Burning, blog, 2 May 2010, http://peterslarson.com/2010/05/02/graciela-mellibovsky-saidler/.

103. Feitlowitz, *Lexicon of Terror,* 95–96.

104. Asher, Banks, and Scheuren, *Statistical Methods for Human Rights,* v.

105. Ibid., 182.

106. Ibid., 184.

107. ASA Committee on Scientific Freedom and Human Rights, http://www.amstat.org/committees/commdetails.cfm?txtComm=CCNPRO05.

108. Van Drunen, *Struggling with the Past,* 121.

8. Ambiguous Loss

1. Association of Chief Police Officers and National Centre for Policing Excellence, "Guidance on the Management, Recording, and Investigation of Missing Persons" (London: National Centre for Policing Excellence, 2005).

2. Commons Sitting: Police, House of Commons Debates, 16 July 1953, *Hansard,* vol. 517, cols. 2219–20.

3. Woolf Enquiry Evidence, House of Commons Debate, 15 May 1964, *Hansard,* vol. 695, col. 837.

4. Missing Persons, House of Commons Debate, 25 May 1973, *Hansard,* vol. 857, cols. 950–62; Missing Persons (Statistics), House of Commons Debate, 31 March 1983, *Hansard,* vol. 40, cols. 524–30.

5. Missing Persons, House of Commons Debate, 19 December 1988, *Hansard,* vol. 144, cols. 139–42W.

6. Brian Masters, *Killing for Company: Case of Dennis Nilsen* (London: Arrow Books, 1995).

7. Susan Hogben, "Life's on Hold: Missing People, Private Calendars, and Waiting," *Time & Society* 15, no. 2/3 (2006): 327–42.

8. Pauline Boss, *Ambiguous Loss: Learning to Live with Unresolved Grief* (Cambridge, MA: Harvard University Press, 1999).

9. Jason Cowley's novel, *Unknown Pleasures* (London: Faber and Faber, 2000), explores why one person may have gone missing; see also Cowley, "Where Are They Now?" *Observer,* 18 June 2000.

10. Doug Richmond, *How to Disappear Completely and Never Be Found* (New York: Carol Publishing Group, 1995). Richmond's conclusions from anecdotal evidence coincide with those of the report *Lost from View,* which is discussed below.

11. Richard Williams, *Missing! A Study of the World-Wide Missing Persons Enigma and Salvation Army Response* (London: Hodder and Stoughton, 1969).

12. Williams, *Missing!* 54–56.

13. For a secular account from the early 1960s that demonstrates many of the same concerns as Williams's account, see Mary Ellison, *Missing from Home* (London: Pan Books, 1964).

14. Andrew Stephens, *The Suzy Lamplugh Story* (London: Faber and Faber, 1988). Suzy Lamplugh's family has disowned this book, though it originally commissioned Stephens to write it.

15. Malcolm Payne, "Understanding 'Going Missing': Issues for Social Work and Social Services," *British Journal of Social Work* 25 (1995): 333–48.

16. Missing People, "Our History," http://wwww.missingpeople.org.uk/about/ history.

17. John Bennett and Graham Gardner, *The Cromwell Street Murders: The Detective's Story* (Stroud, Gloucestershire: Sutton Publishing, 2006).

18. Missing People, "Our History."

19. Payne, "Understanding 'Going Missing,'" 336–37.

20. Andrew O'Hagan, *The Missing* (London: Faber and Faber, 1995).

21. In addition to *Lost from View,* see Lucy Holmes, "Living in Limbo: The Experiences of, and Impacts on, the Families of Missing People" (London: Missing People, 2008), http://www.missingpeople.org.uk/supportus/livinginlimbo/detail. asp?dsid=1847; Missing People, "Research to Date" (London: Missing People, 2007), http://www.missingpeople.org.uk/media-centre/downloads/.

22. For recent work, see, in the United Kingdom, PACT, "Every Five Minutes: A Review of the Available Data on Missing Children in the UK" (London: PACT [Parents & Abducted Children Together], 2005); and in the United States, Heather Hammer, David Finkelhor, Andrea J. Sedlak, and Lorraine E. Porcellini, "National Estimates of Missing Children: Selected Trends, 1988–1999," in *NISMART Bulletin Series* (Washington, DC: Office of Juvenile Justice and Delinquency Prevention, 2004).

23. Nina Biehal, Fiona Mitchell, and Jim Wade, *Lost from View: Missing Persons in the UK* (Bristol: The Policy Press, 2003).

24. Ibid., 14.

25. Geoff Newiss, "Understanding the Risk of Going Missing: Estimating the Risk of Fatal Outcomes in Cancelled Cases," *Policing: An International Journal of Police Strategies and Management* 29, no. 2 (2006): 246–60; Newiss, "A Study of the Characteristics of Outstanding Missing Persons: Implications for the Development of Police Risk Assessment," *Policing and Society* 15, no. 2 (2005): 212–25.

26. Geoff Newiss, "Missing Presumed…? The Police Response to Missing Persons," ed. Barry Webb, Police Research Series Paper 114 (London: Policing and Reducing Crime Unit, 1999).

27. Ibid., 9.

28. Association of Chief Police Officers and National Centre for Policing Excellence, "Guidance."

29. National Policing Improvement Agency, "Collection of Missing Persons Data: A Code of Practice for the Police Service on Collecting and Sharing Data on Missing Persons with Public Authorities" (London: HMSO, 2009), http://www. official-documents.gov.uk/document/other/9787777146872/9787777146872.asp; NPIA, "Missing Persons Bureau Moves to NPIA," press release, 1 April 2008, http:// www.npia.police.uk/en/10266.htm.

30. NPIA, "Missing Persons Bureau."

31. Look4them—tracing missing persons, locating relatives, searching parents, http://www.look4them.org.uk.

32. International Committee of the Red Cross (ICRC), *The Missing: ICRC Progress Report* (Geneva: ICRC, 2006).

33. Richmond, *How to Disappear Completely;* see also Evan Ratliff, "Gone/Vanish: How to Disappear," *Wired,* December 2009, 144–53, 184–88.

34. Biehal, Mitchell, and Wade, *Lost from View,* 36, 39–45.

35. John Stonehouse, *Death of an Idealist* (London: W. H. Allen, 1975).

36. See, for example, Paul Begg, *Into Thin Air: People Who Disappear* (London: David and Charles, 1979), and David Clark, *Vanished! Mysterious Disappearances* (London: Michael O'Mara Books, 1990), which focus on famous cases, and Barry Cummins, *Missing: Missing without Trace in Ireland* (Dublin: Gill & Macmillan, 2003), which looks at cases of girls abducted and murdered. Jon Krakauer, *Into the Wild* (London: Pan Books, 2007), now made into a film, is an account of the case of Chris McCandless.

37. Stewart O'Nan, *Songs for the Missing: A Novel* (New York: Viking Adult, 2008).

38. For example, Colin Rogers, *Tracing Missing Persons: An Introduction to Agencies, Methods, and Sources in England and Wales* (Manchester: Manchester University Press, 1986), which, in addition to providing resources for searching, gives an overview of the missing-person question in the mid-1980s; R. Scott Grasser, *Findsomeone.Com* (Woburn, MA: Butterworth-Heinemann, 1998); Karen Bali, *The People Finder: Reuniting Relatives, Finding Friends—A Practical Guide to Finding People You've Lost Touch With* (London: Nicholas Brealey Publishing, 2007).

39. Leopard Films, "Missing Drama Dominates Its Slot on BBC 1," http://www.leopardfilms.com/news/leopard-uk/missing-drama-dominates-its-slot-on-bbc. Thanks to Simona Rentea for drawing my attention to this program, and for sharing with me her fascinating analysis of what it reveals about the missing.

40. Ian McEwan, Foreword to *Complete Surrender,* by Dave Sharp and John Parker (London: John Blake, 2008).

41. Ibid., xx, xiv, xvii.

42. Cowley, *Unknown Pleasures,* 90.

43. Boss, *Ambiguous Loss.*

44. The period immediately after the war has recently become a focus for historians too, for example, the group at Birkbeck (Balzan Project at Birkbeck College, directed by David Feldman (Birkbeck) and Mark Mazower (Columbia), "Reconstruction in the Immediate Aftermath of War: A Comparative Study of Europe, 1945–1950," First Balzan Workshop, Comparing Europe's Post-War Reconstructions, 28 October 2005, report by Jessica Reinisch, http://www.balzan.bbk.ac.uk/page14.html); the report of their first workshop draws attention to the need to look at this period from various perspectives. There is also an online archive dealing with the period: *Post-War Europe: Refugees, Exile, and Resettlement, 1945-1950,* ed. Dan Stone (Reading: Thomson Learning EMEA Ltd., 2007), http://www.tlemea.com/postwareurope/.

45. Mark Wyman, *DPs: Europe's Displaced Persons, 1945–1951* (Ithaca, NY: Cornell University Press, 1989; Associated University Presses, 1998 [with a new introduction]). See, for example, the interview on p. 168 with a German woman who recalls her feeling at the time that "DPs had everything they wanted" while the Germans got "hungrier and hungrier."

46. Eric Santner, *Stranded Objects: Mourning, Memory, and Film in Postwar Germany* (Ithaca, NY: Cornell University Press, 1990), 36. For other discussions of postwar German identity and memory, see, for example, Maja Zehfuss, *Wounds of Memory: The Politics of War in Germany* (Cambridge: Cambridge University Press, 2007); Frank Biess, *Homecomings: Returning POWs and the Legacies of Defeat in Postwar Germany* (Princeton, NJ: Princeton University Press, 2006); Dagmar Barnouw, *The War in the Empty Air: Victims, Perpetrators, and Postwar Germans* (Bloomington: Indiana University

Press, 2005); and Mary Fulbrook, *German National Identity after the Holocaust* (Cambridge: Polity, 1999).

47. Christa Wolf, *A Model Childhood,* trans. Ursule Molinaro and Hedwig Rappolt (London: Virago, 1995); Rachel Seiffert, *The Dark Room* (London: Vintage, 2005).

48. Seiffert, *Dark Room,* 210.

49. Santner, *Stranded Objects,* 159–60.

50. Ibid., 37.

51. Ibid., 44.

52. Ibid., 162.

53. Katrin FitzHerbert, *True to Both My Selves: A Family Memoir of Germany and England in Two World Wars* (London: Virago, 1997).

54. Ibid., 50, 163.

55. Ibid., 127.

56. Ibid., 259.

57. Ibid., 260. See Norbert Frei, *Adenauer's Germany and the Nazi Past: The Politics of Amnesty and Integration,* trans. Joel Golb (New York: Columbia University Press, 2002) for an account of how the denazification processes of the Allied occupation were reversed, and amnesties put in place. Thanks to R. Gerald Hughes for drawing my attention to this point.

58. FitzHerbert, *True to Both My Selves,* 260.

59. Ibid., 284.

60. Ibid., 293.

61. Bernard Schlink, *The Reader,* trans. Carol Brown Janeway (London: Phoenix, 1997).

62. Schlink, *Reader,* 156. Compare the attempt made by Gitta Sereny with Albert Speer: Gitta Sereny, *Albert Speer: His Battle with Truth* (London: Picador, 1996).

63. Rita Arditti, *Searching for Life: The Grandmothers of the Plaza de Mayo and the Disappeared Children of Argentina* (Berkeley: University of California Press, 1999), 1.

64. As well as the account in Arditti, *Searching for Life,* see the Abuelas' website at http://www.abuelas.org.ar/english/history.htm.

65. See, for example, Victor B. Penchaszadeh, "Abduction of Children of Political Dissidents in Argentina and the Role of Human Genetics in Their Restitution," *Journal of Public Health Policy* 13, no. 3 (1992): 291–305.

66. Arditti, *Searching for Life,* 144–58.

67. Télam: National News Agency of Argentina, "Grandmothers of Plaza de Mayo Head Regrets That 'Noble Case' Turned into a War," April 1, 2010, http://english.telam.com.ar/index.php?option=com_content&view=article&id=8897:grandmothers-of-plaza-de-mayo-head-regrets-that-qnoble-caseq-turned-into-a-war&catid=34:society.

68. *Times,* "Alicia Zubasnabar: Founder of Grandmothers of the Plaza de Mayo," 30 June 2008, http://www.timesonline.co.uk/tol/comment/obituaries/article 4236351.ece.

69. Michael Warren, "Argentine Father and Son Reunited 33 Years after Military Kidnapped, Killed Imprisoned Mother," *Washington Examiner,* 23 February 2010.

70. Penchaszadeh, "Abduction of Children," 299–301; Arditti, *Searching for Life,* 125–43.

71. Penchaszadeh, "Abduction of Children," 301–2.

72. Luis Puenzo, *The Official Story / La Historia Oficial,* film (Argentina, 1985), 104 mins.; Gastón Biraben, *Cautiva / Captive,* film, (Argentina, 2005), 109 mins.

73. David Usborne, "Argentine Media Heirs Face 'Adoption' DNA Tests," 8 June 2010, http://www.independent.co.uk/news/world/americas/argentine-media-heirs-face-adoption-dna-tests-1994125.html; Memory in Latin America, blog, "This Week in Argentina," 3 July 2010, http://memoryinlatinamerica.blogspot.com/2010/07/this-week-in-argentina.html.

74. The relationship between Cristina Kirchner and Clarín is complex and controversial. See, for example, "Kirchner and Clarín: Argentina Media Fight Gets Personal," *Huffington Post,* 13 September 2009, http://www.huffingtonpost.com/2009/09/13/kirchner-and-clarin-argen_n_285105.html; Alvaro Vargas Llosa, "Newsprint Matters," Real Clear Politics, 1 September 2010, http://www.realclearpolitics.com/articles/2010/09/01/newsprint_matters_106964.html.

75. Usborne, "Argentine Media Heirs Face 'Adoption' DNA Tests."

76. Ibid.

77. Télam, "Grandmothers of Plaza de Mayo Head."

78. Ibid.

79. Mark Kurzem, *The Mascot: The Extraordinary Story of a Jewish Boy and an SS Extermination Squad* (London: Rider, 2007), 334. Thanks are due to Susan Lillienthal for alerting me to this account.

80. Kurzem, *Mascot,* 335.

81. Caroline Moorehead, *Dunant's Dream: War, Switzerland, and the History of the Red Cross* (London: HarperCollins, 1998), 432–36, 522–29; Wyman, *DPs,* 91–95.

82. UNRRA memorandum quoted in Moorehead, *Dunant's Dream,* 525–26.

83. Kåre Olsen, "Under the Care of the Lebensborn: Norwegian War Children and Their Mothers," in *Children of World War II: The Hidden Enemy Legacy,* ed. Kjersti Ericsson and Eva Simonsen (Oxford: Berg, 2005), 15–16.

84. Ericsson and Simonsen, *Children of World War II.* See also Michelle Mouton, *From Nurturing the Nation to Purifying the Volk: Weimar and Nazi Family Policy, 1918–1945* (Cambridge: Cambridge University Press, 2007); and Lisa Pine, *Nazi Family Policy, 1933–1945* (Oxford: Berg, 1997).

85. David Crossland, "Nazi Program to Breed Master Race: Lebensborn Children Break Silence," *Spiegel Online,* 11 July 2006, http://www.spiegel.de/international/0,1518,druck-446978,00.html; Jess Smee, "Victims of Hitler's Plan for a Master Race: Climate of Shame Suppressed Discussion of Third Reich's Social Impact," *Guardian,* 6 November 2006.

86. Dorothee Schmitz-Köster, "A Topic for Life: Children of German Lebensborn Homes," in Ericsson and Simonsen, *Children of World War II,* 213.

87. See the autobiographical account of Gisela Heidenreich, *Das endlose Jahr* (Frankfurt: Scherz, 2002), and the following novels: Nancy Huston, *Fault Lines* (London: Atlantic Books, 2008) and Sara Young, *My Enemy's Cradle* (London: HarperCollins, 2008).

88. Schmitz-Köster, "Topic for Life," 219.

89. Ibid., 223.

90. Ibid., 224.

91. Ibid., 225.

92. Adriana Cavarero, *Relating Narratives: Storytelling and Selfhood,* trans. Paul A. Kottman (London: Routledge, 2000).

93. "What we call social reality" is Slavoj Žižek's useful phrase; it draws attention to the way in which the social order is a fantasy, a response to our desire for completeness (Slavoj Žižek, *The Sublime Object of Ideology* [London: Verso, 1989]). The Lacanian account that Žižek develops sees the entry into the social order—into language and subjectivity—as inevitably producing a problem of "fit": a lack or an excess.

94. As Jacques Derrida tells us in an interview with Amy Kofman. Kirby Dick and Amy Ziering Kofman, *Derrida,* film (Jane Doe Films Inc., 2002), 85 mins.

95. In Jacques Lacan's account of the mirror stage, the infant perceives itself as whole when it sees its own reflection in the mirror or in the gaze of its mother. This is a misperception, but it drives a desire for completion and unity that persists throughout life. Jacques Lacan, "The Mirror Stage as Formative of the Function of the I," in *Écrits,* trans. Alan Sheridan (London: Routledge, 1977), 1–7.

96. Cavarero, *Relating Narratives,* 32–33.

97. Ibid., 100–101.

98. Ibid., 23, 63. Cavarero goes on to emphasize that "the *who*—as exposed, relational, altruistic—is totally external" (89). This is reminiscent of Jean-Luc Nancy's analysis of the way the subject is produced—exposed—in the portrait (Jean-Luc Nancy, *Le regard du portrait* [Paris: Galilee, 2000]) and Roland Barthes' figuration of the photograph (like Cavarero's story told by another) as *"the impossible science of the unique being"* (Roland Barthes, *Camera lucida,* trans. Richard Howard [London: Vintage, 1993], 71).

99. Kurzem, *Mascot,* 335.

100. Costas Douzinas, "2 July, 7 July, and Metaphysics," in *Terrorism and the Politics of Response,* ed. Angharad Closs Stephens and Nick Vaughan-Williams (London: Routledge, 2009), 208.

101. Paul A. Kottman, "Translator's Introduction," in Cavarero, *Relating Narratives,* xxiii.

Conclusion

1. Though they all use different terminology, for writers who grapple with such questions, see, for example, Giorgio Agamben, *The Coming Community,* trans. Michael Hardt (Minneapolis: University of Minnesota Press, 1993); Maurice Blanchot, *The Unavowable Community* (Barrytown: Station Hill, 2006); Jean-Luc Nancy, *The Inoperative Community,* trans. Peter Connor, Lisa Garbus, Michael Holland, and Simona Sawhney (Minneapolis: University of Minnesota Press, 1991); Eric L. Santner, *On Creaturely Life: Rilke, Benjamin, Sebald* (Chicago: University of Chicago Press, 2006); Slavoj Žižek, Eric L. Santner, and Kenneth Reinhard, *The Neighbor: Three Enquiries in Political Theology* (Chicago: University of Chicago Press, 2005).

2. Jacques Rancière, *Disagreement: Politics and Philosophy,* trans. Julie Rose (Minneapolis: University of Minnesota Press, 1999), 139.

3. Ibid., 30.

4. Ibid., 32.

5. Giorgio Agamben, *Homo Sacer: Sovereign Power and Bare Life,* trans. Daniel Heller-Roazen (Stanford, CA: Stanford University Press, 1998).

6. Michel Foucault, *The History of Sexuality,* vol. 1, *An Introduction,* trans. Robert Hurley (Harmondsworth: Penguin Books, 1990), 139.

7. Agamben, *Homo Sacer.*

8. Rancière, *Disagreement,* 27.

9. Ibid., 35.

Bibliography

Archival Material

British Red Cross Archives, London

Ref. 656/1. *The Central Tracing Bureau.* May 1947. Typescript. Historical account citing original documents, Jan. 1944–April 1946.

Ref. 656/2. Paper re the re-organisation of the Central Tracing Bureau [c 1947].

Ref. 656/4. Photograph: Chart depicting organisation of tracing services c1947 (1) National Tracing Bureaux, (2) Central Tracing Bureau, (3) Zonal Tracing Bureaux.

Ref. 735/1. Central Tracing Bureau, Germany 1946–1947.

Ref. 1064/1 (29) Personal file: Warner, Miss Sydney Jeanetta.

Ref. 1344 11/9A. Personal file: Bark, Evelyn.

Ref. 2305/4. Hilda M. Pickard-Cambridge, "British Red Cross Search for the Missing," 1940–1945. Album compiled by Hilda Pickard-Cambridge, containing letters, forms, handwritten accounts of the work of the Searchers for the Wounded and Missing, 1939–1945.

Ref. 2156/13. *Hospital Searching for "Missing" Men: The Work of the Searching Service, Wounded and Missing Department, Red Cross and St. John War Organisation.* Reprinted from the "Summary of Work," no. 96, 12 June 1943.

Canadian Letters and Images Project, Vancouver Island University in partnership with The University of Western Ontario. http://www.canadianletters.ca.

Center for History and New Media and American Social History Project/ Center for Media and Learning. The September 11 Digital Archive. http://911 digitalarchive.org/.

American Red Cross Museum Stories.
Asociación Tepeyac de New York Collection.

Center for Holocaust and Genocide Studies. http://www.chgs.umn.edu.

Hansard. House of Commons

Debates. Commons Sitting, 1920–88. http://hansard.millbanksystems.com/ commons/.
Written Answers. http://www.publications.parliament.uk/.

Post-War Europe: Refugees, Exile, and Resettlement, 1945–1950. Online archive of primary source materials from the National Archives of the UK and the Wiener Library, London. http://www.tlemea.com/postwareurope/.

FO 1052/336. Reports on DP Camps. Control Office for Germany and Austria and Foreign Office: Control Commission for Germany (British Element), Prisoners of War/Displaced Persons Division. Registered files (PWDP and other series).

WO 202/609. War Office: British Military Missions in Liaison with Allied Forces. Military Headquarters Papers, Second World War.

The National Archives, Kew

FO 371/66721. Foreign Office: Political Departments; General Correspondence from 1906–1966. POLITICAL: REFUGEES (WR); Refugees (48). Establishment of an International Tracing Service. 1947.

FO 945/557. Control Office for Germany and Austria and Foreign Office, German Section: General Department. Displaced Persons Section. Germany: Proposals for handling enquiries on whereabouts of missing persons. 1945–1946.

FO 945/558. Control Office for Germany and Austria and Foreign Office, German Section: General Department. Displaced Persons Section. Germany: Proposals for handling enquiries on whereabouts of missing persons. 1946–1947.

FO 945/591. Control Office for Germany and Austria and Foreign Office, German Section: General Department. Displaced Persons Section. SHAEF (Supreme Headquarters, Allied Expeditionary Force): Outline plan for displaced persons and refugees. 1944–1945.

HO 213/1071. Home Office: Aliens Department; General (GEN) Files and Aliens' Naturalization and Nationality (ALN and NTY Symbol Series) Files. National Tracing Bureau undertaken by Foreign Relations Dept. and British Red Cross. 1944.

HO 294/169. Czechoslovak Refugee Trust: Records. United Kingdom Search Bureau for German, Austrian, and Stateless Persons from Central Europe: Minutes and correspondence. 1943–1948.

WO 162/205. Commander-in-Chief and War Office: Adjutant General's Department; Papers. History of Casualty Branch (Liverpool) (Cas L). 1945.

WO 361/12. War Office: Department of the Permanent Under-Secretary of State; Casualties (L) Branch: Enquiries into Missing Personnel, 1939–45 War. Evacuation of Dunkirk: Losses on hospital carrier *Gracie Fields*, 30 May 1940. 1940 Jan 01–1941 Dec 31.

United Nations Archives, New York

S-0402. United Nations Relief and Rehabilitation Administration (UNRRA)/Germany: Central Headquarters, Department of Field Operations, Repatriation Section. Subject files of the Repatriation Section at Central Headquarters. 1945–.

S-0413. United Nations Relief and Rehabilitation Administration (UNRRA)/Germany Mission: Central Headquarters (Arolsen), Department of Field Operations, Central Tracing Bureau. Subject files of the Central Tracing Bureau at Central Headquarters. 1945–.

S-0436. United Nations Relief and Rehabilitation Administration (UNRRA)/Germany Mission: United States Zone (Pasing), Area Teams. District, team, and camp files of the United States Zone. 1945–.

S-1021. Series consists of reports, documents, and reference papers relating to studies on the organization and functions of UNRRA. UNRRA—Records of the Office of the Historian—Monograph Collection. 1942–.

S-1058. UNRRA Germany Mission photographs. Taken by a variety of UNRRA photographers, for the UNRRA Visual Information Office, Washington, D.C.

United States Holocaust Memorial Museum. http://www.ushmm.org/

Holocaust Encyclopedia. Personal Stories, War Crimes Trials.
Holocaust Encyclopedia. Photography, Death Marches.
International Tracing Service Archive.

Books and Articles

Abrahams, Fred, Gilles Perez, and Eric Stover. *A Village Destroyed, May 14, 1999: War Crimes in Kosovo.* Berkeley: University of California Press, 2001.

Agamben, Giorgio. *The Coming Community.* Translated by Michael Hardt. Minneapolis: University of Minnesota Press, 1993.

———. *Homo Sacer: Sovereign Power and Bare Life.* Translated by Daniel Heller-Roazen. Stanford, CA: Stanford University Press, 1998.

———. *Profanations.* Translated by Jeff Fort. New York: Zone Books, 2007.

Agger, Inger, and Soren Buus Jensen. *Trauma and Healing under State Terrorism.* London: Zed Books, 1996.

Agosin, Marjorie. "Beyond the Dawn." *Human Rights Quarterly* 10 (1988): 133.

———. "Buenos Aires." Extracted in Lawrence Weschler, preface to *Los Desaparecidos / The Disappeared,* by Laurel Reuter, 8. Milan: Charta, 2006.

———. "Cities of Life, Cities of Change." *Human Rights Quarterly* 12 (1990): 554–58.

———. "The Generation of Disenchantment." *Human Rights Quarterly* 14 (1992): 135–41.

Allen, Michael Thad. *The Business of Genocide: The SS, Slave Labor, and the Concentration Camps.* Chapel Hill: University of North Carolina Press, 2005.

Aly, Götz, and Karl Heinz Roth. *The Nazi Census: Identification and Control in the Third Reich.* Philadephia: Temple University Press, 2004.

Anderson, Kenneth. "First in the Field: The Unique Mission and Legitimacy of the Red Cross in a Culture of Legality." *Times Literary Supplement,* 31 July 1998.

Arditti, Rita. *Searching for Life: The Grandmothers of the Plaza De Mayo and the Disappeared Children of Argentina.* Berkeley: University of California Press, 1999.

Asher, Jana, David Banks, and Fritz Scheuren, eds. *Statistical Methods for Human Rights.* New York: Springer, 2008.

Bacque, James. *Crimes and Mercies: The Fate of German Civilians under Allied Occupation, 1944–1950.* Vancouver: Talonbooks, 2007.

Bali, Karen. *The People Finder: Reuniting Relatives, Finding Friends.* London: Nicholas Brealey Publishing, 2007.

Bark, Evelyn. *No Time to Kill.* London: Robert Hale, 1960.

Barnouw, Dagmar. *The War in the Empty Air: Victims, Perpetrators, and Postwar Germans.* Bloomington: Indiana University Press, 2005.

Barthes, Roland. *Camera lucida.* Translated by Richard Howard. London: Vintage, 1993.

Barton, Peter. "The Historian's Role." http://www.cwgc.org/fromelles/?page=english/background/getting_us_here.

Baudrillard, Jean. *The Spirit of Terrorism.* London: Verso, 2002.

Begg, Paul. *Into Thin Air: People Who Disappear.* London: David and Charles, 1979.

Bennett, John, and Graham Gardner. *The Cromwell Street Murders: The Detective's Story.* Stroud, Gloucestershire: Sutton Publishing, 2006.

Bergoffen, Debra B. "Engaging Nietzsche's Women: Ofelia Schutte and the Madres de la Plaza de Mayo." *Hypatia* 19, no. 3 (2004): 157–68.

Biedermann, Charles-Claude. "International Tracing Service: 50 Years of Service to Humanity." *International Review of the Red Cross* 296 (1993): 447–56.

Biehal, Nina, Fiona Mitchell, and Jim Wade. *Lost from View: Missing Persons in the UK.* Bristol: The Policy Press, 2003.

Biesecker, L. G., et al. "DNA Identification after the World Trade Center Attack." *Science* 310, no. 5751 (2006): 1122–23.

Biess, Frank. *Homecomings: Returning POWs and the Legacies of Defeat in Postwar Germany.* Princeton, NJ: Princeton University Press, 2006.

Black, Edwin. "Secret Bad Arolsen Holocaust Archive—A Trove of Revelations about Holocaust Insurance, Corporate Complicity, and IBM Involvement." http://www.ibmandtheholocaust.com/BadArolsenArticles.php.

Blanchot, Maurice. *The Unavowable Community.* Barrytown: Station Hill, 2006.

Bosco, Fernando J. "Human Rights Politics and Scaled Performances of Memory: Conflicts among the *Madres De Plaza De Mayo* in Argentina." *Social and Cultural Geography* 5, no. 3 (2004): 381–402.

Boss, Pauline. *Ambiguous Loss: Learning to Live with Unresolved Grief.* Cambridge, MA: Harvard University Press, 1999.

Bouvard, Marguerite Guzman. *Revolutionizing Motherhood: The Mothers of the Plaza de Mayo.* Lanham, MD: SR Books, 1994.

Bower, Tom. *Blind Eye to Murder: Britain, America, and the Purging of Nazi Germany—A Pledge Betrayed.* London: Andre Deutsch, 1981.

Brady, Kate. "Fromelles: A Report from Oxford Archaeology's Finds Manager." http://www.cwgc.org/fromelles/?page=english/the-project/getting_going.

Bramwell, Anna C., ed. *Refugees in the Age of Total War.* London: Unwin Hyman, 1988.

Brenner, Michael. "Displaced Persons and the Desire for a Jewish National Homeland." In *Post-War Europe: Refugees, Exile, and Resettlement, 1945–1950.* Reading: Thomson Learning EMEA Ltd., 2007. http://www.tlemea.com/postwareurope/essay2.asp.

Brodsky, Marcelo. *Buena Memoria/Good Memory.* 4th ed. Buenos Aires: La Marca Editora, 2006.

Brysk, Alison. "The Politics of Measurement: The Contested Count of the Disappeared in Argentina." *Human Rights Quarterly* 16, no. 4 (1994): 676–92.

Bubriski, Kevin. *Pilgrimage: Looking at Ground Zero.* New York: powerHouse Books, 2002.

Budimlija, Zoran M., et al. "World Trade Center Human Identification Project: Experiences with Individual Body Identification Cases." *Croatian Medical Journal* 44, no. 3 (2003): 259–63.

Burstow, Paul. "Dying Alone: Assessing Isolation, Loneliness, and Poverty." http://www.paulburstow.org.uk/resources/index/.

Butler, Judith. *Frames of War: When Is Life Grievable?* London: Verso, 2009.

———. *Precarious Life: The Powers of Mourning and Violence.* London: Verso, 2004.

Cambray, P. G., and G. G. B. Briggs. *The Official Record of the Humanitarian Services of the War Organisation of the British Red Cross Society and Order of St. John of Jerusalem, 1939–1947.* London: Red Cross and St. John 1949.

Caparros, Martin. "Apariciones/ Reappearances." In *Buena Memoria/Good Memory,* edited by Marcelo Brodsky, 12–17. Buenos Aires: La Marca Editora, 2006.

Capdevila, Luc, and Daniele Voldman. *War Dead: Western Societies and the Casualties of War.* Translated by Richard Veasey. Edinburgh: Edinburgh University Press, 2006.

Carlson, Eric Stener. *I Remember Julia: Voices of the Disappeared.* Philadelphia: Temple University Press, 1996.

Cavarero, Adriana. *Relating Narratives: Storytelling and Selfhood.* Translated by Paul A. Kottman. London and New York: Routledge, 2000.

Cesarani, David. *Justice Delayed: How Britain Became a Refuge for Nazi War Criminals.* London: Phoenix Press, 2001.

Clark, David. *Vanished! Mysterious Disappearances.* London: Michael O'Mara Books, 1990.

Connor, Ian. *Refugees and Expellees in Post-War Germany.* Manchester: Manchester University Press, 2007.

Corsellis, John, and Marcus Ferrar. *Slovenia 1945: Memories of Death and Survival after World War II.* London: I. B. Tauris, 2006.

Cowley, Jason. *Unknown Pleasures.* London: Faber and Faber, 2000.

Crossland, Zoë. "Violent Spaces: Conflict over the Reappearance of Argentina's Disappeared." In *Matériel Culture: The Archaeology of Twentieth-Century Conflict,* edited by John Schofield, William Gray Johnson, and Colleen M. Beck, 115–31. London: Routledge, 2002.

Crownshaw, Richard. "Performing Memory in Holocaust Museums." *Performance Research* 5, no. 3 (2000): 18–27.

Cummins, Barry. *Missing: Missing without Trace in Ireland.* Dublin: Gill & Macmillan, 2003.

Czarnecki, John E. "Unlikely Collaboration of Architects Design Viewing Platform (David Rockwell, Diller+Scofidio, and Kevin Kennon Collaborate on the Platform for the Public Overlooking Ground-Zero)." *Architectural Record* 190, no. 2 (2002): 26.

Darton, Eric. "The Janus Face of Architectural Terrorism: Minoru Yamasaki, Mohammed Atta, and Our World Trade Center." In *After the World Trade Center: Rethinking New York City,* edited by Michael Sorkin and Sharon Zukin, 88–95. New York: Routledge, 2002.

Dede, Martha. "Blood and Money: The American Red Cross and the Terrorist Attacks of September 11, 2001." California State University Long Beach, Spring 2008. www.csulb.edu/colleges/cba/ucel/ . . . /martha-dede-2007-2.doc.

Dejevsky, Mary. "Heroes Born the Day 999 Let Us Down." *Independent,* 3 December 2010.

De Zayas, Alfred M. *Nemesis at Potsdam: Anglo-Americans and the Expulsion of the Germans.* London: Routledge and Kegan Paul, 1977.

Dharwadker, Vinay. "Poetry of the Indian Subcontinent." In *A Companion to Twentieth-Century Poetry,* edited by Neil Roberts, 264–80. Oxford: Blackwell, 2003.

Djurović, Gradimir. *The Central Tracing Agency of the International Committee of the Red Cross: Activities of the ICRC for the Alleviation of the Mental Suffering of War Victims.* Translated by Muriel Monkhouse and Dominique Cornwell. Geneva: Henry Dunant Institute, 1986.

Donnison, F. S. V. *Civil Affairs and Military Government: North West Europe, 1944–1946.* London: HMSO, 1961.

Doretti, Mercedes, and Jennifer Burrell. "Gray Spaces and Endless Negotiations: Forensic Anthropology and Human Rights." In *Anthropology Put to Work,* edited by Les W. Field and Richard G. Fox, 45–64. Oxford: Berg, 2007.

Douglas, Mary, and Stephen Nay. *Missing Persons: A Critique of the Social Sciences.* Berkeley: University of California Press, 1998.

Douzinas, Costas. "2 July, 7 July and Metaphysics." In *Terrorism and the Politics of Response,* edited by Angharad Closs Stephens and Nick Vaughan-Williams, 190–210. London: Routledge, 2009.

Durand, André. *From Sarajevo to Hiroshima: History of the International Committee of the Red Cross.* Geneva: Henry Dunant Institute, 1984.

Edkins, Jenny. "Exposed singularity." *Journal for Cultural Research* 9, no. 4 (2005): 359–86.

———. "Humanitarianism, Humanity, Human." *Journal of Human Rights* 2, no. 2 (2003): 253–58.

———. "The Rush to Memory and the Rhetoric of War." *Journal of Political and Military Sociology* 31, no. 2 (2003): 231–51.

———. "Sovereign Power, Zones of Indistinction, and the Camp." *Alternatives* 25, no. 1 (2000): 3–25.

———. *Trauma and the Memory of Politics.* Cambridge: Cambridge University Press, 2003.

Elbot, Hugh G. "Manhunt for 6,000,000." In *Information Bulletin* (Office of the U.S. High Commissioner for Germany, Office of Public Affairs, Public Relations Division, APO 757, US Army), May 1951, 7–10. http://digital.library.wisc.edu/1711.dl/History.omg1951May.

Ellison, Mary. *Missing from Home.* London: Pan Books, 1964.

Ellison, Ralph. *Invisible Man.* London: Penguin, 2001.

Eng, David. "The Value of Silence." *Theatre Journal* 54, no. 1 (2002): 85–94.

Ericsson, Kjersti, and Eva Simonsen, eds. *Children of World War II: The Hidden Enemy Legacy,* Oxford: Berg, 2005.

Evans, Mary. *Missing Persons: The Impossibility of Auto/Biography.* London: Routledge, 1999.

Fanon, Frantz. *Black Skin, White Masks.* Translated by Charles Lam Markmann. London: Pluto, 1986.

Fatayi-Williams, Marie. Foreword to *Terrorism and the Politics of Response,* edited by Angharad Closs Stephens and Nick Vaughan-Williams, x–xii. London: Routledge, 2009.

———. *For the Love of Anthony: A Mother's Search for Peace after the London Bombings.* London: Hodder & Stoughton, 2006.

Faust, Drew Gilpin. *The Republic of Suffering: Death and the American Civil War.* New York: Vintage Books, 2008.

Feitlowitz, Marguerite. *A Lexicon of Terror: Argentina and the Legacies of Torture.* Oxford: Oxford University Press, 1988.

Feldschuh, Michael, ed. *The September 11 Photo Project.* New York: Regan Books, HarperCollins, 2002.

Femenía, Nora Amalia. "Argentina's Mothers of Plaza De Mayo: The Mourning Process from Junta to Democracy." *Feminist Studies* 13, no. 1 (1987): 9–18.

Fisher, Jo. *Mothers of the Disappeared.* London: Zed Books, 1989.

FitzHerbert, Katrin. *True to Both My Selves: A Family Memoir of Germany and England in Two World Wars.* London: Virago, 1997.

Foucault, Michel. *The History of Sexuality.* Vol. 1, *An Introduction.* Translated by Robert Hurley. Harmondsworth: Penguin Books, 1990.

———. *The Order of Things: An Archaeology of the Human Sciences.* London: Tavistock/Routledge, 1970.

Franco, Jean. "Gender, Death, and Resistance: Facing the Ethical Vacuum." In *Fear at the Edge: State Terror and Resistance in Latin America,* edited by Juan E. Corradi, Patricia Weiss Fagen, and Manuel Antonio Garretón, 104–18. Berkeley: University of California Press, 1992.

Frei, Norbert. *Adenauer's Germany and the Nazi Past: The Politics of Amnesty and Integration.* Translated by Joel Golb. New York: Columbia University Press, 2002.

Friend, David. *Watching the World Change: The Stories behind the Images of 9/11.* New York: Picador, 2006.

Fulbrook, Mary. *German National Identity after the Holocaust.* Cambridge: Polity, 1999.

Gaggero, Jorge. *Graciela está en nosotros: Memoria de todos.* Buenos Aires: Colihue, 2007.

Gambaro, Griselda. *Information for Foreigners.* Translated by Marguerite Feitlowitz. Evanston, IL: Northwestern University Press, 1992.

George, Alice Rose, Gilles Peress, Michael Schulan, and Charles Traub. *Here Is New York: A Democracy of Photographs.* Zurich: Scalo, 2002.

Glasgow, Gordon H. H. "The Campaign for Medical Coroners in Nineteenth-Century England and Its Aftermath: A Lancashire Focus on Failure, Part II." *Mortality* 9, no. 3 (August 2004): 223–34.

Goodwin, William, and Sibte Hadi. "DNA." In *Forensic Human Identification: An Introduction,* edited by Timothy Thompson and Susan Black, 5–27. Boca Raton: CRC Press, 2007.

Grasser, R. Scott. *Findsomeone.Com.* Woburn, MA: Butterworth-Heinemann, 1998.

Greenberg, Judith. "Wounded New York." In *Trauma at Home: After 9/11,* edited by Judith Greenberg, 21–35. Lincoln: University of Nebraska Press, 2003.

Hadaway, Stuart. *Missing Believed Killed: The Royal Air Force and the Search for Missing Aircrew, 1939–1952.* Barnsley: Pen and Sword Aviation, 2008.

Hammer, Heather, David Finkelhor, Andrea J. Sedlak, and Lorraine E. Porcellini. "National Estimates of Missing Children: Selected Trends, 1988–1999."

NISMART Bulletin Series, NCJ 206179. Washington, DC: U.S. Department of Justice, Office of Juvenile Justice and Delinquency Prevention, 2004.

Hare, David. *The Permanent Way or La Voie Anglaise.* London: Faber & Faber, 2003.

Hasleton, Philip. "Reforming the Coroner and Death Certification Service." *Current Diagnostic Pathology* 10, no. 6 (2004): 453–62.

Hawley, Thomas M. *The Remains of War: Bodies, Politics, and the Search for American Soldiers Unaccounted for in Southeast Asia.* Durham, NC: Duke University Press, 2005.

Heidenreich, Gisela. *Das endlose Jahr.* Frankfurt: Scherz, 2002.

Henry, Jeanne. "What Madness Prompts, Reason Writes: New York City, September 11–October 2, 2001." *Anthropology and Education Quarterly* 33, no. 3 (2002): 283–96.

Henwood, Melanie. "The Emergency Response to 7/7: Flaws with the Family Assistance Centre," 23 November 2006. http://www.communitycare.co.uk/Articles/2006/11/23/102302/the-emergency-response-to-77.-flaws-with-the-family-assistance.html.

Hirsch, Marianne. "I Took Pictures: September 2001 and Beyond." In *Trauma at Home: After 9/11,* edited by Judith Greenberg, 69–86. Lincoln: University of Nebraska Press, 2003.

Hogben, Susan. "Life's on Hold: Missing People, Private Calendars, and Waiting." *Time & Society* 15, no. 2/3 (2006): 327–42.

Holmes, Lucy. "Living in Limbo: The Experiences of, and Impacts on, the Families of Missing People." London: Missing People, 2008. http://www.missingpeople.org.uk/supportus/livinginlimbo/detail.asp?dsid=1847.

Hoshower-Leppo, Lisa. "Missing in Action: Searching for America's War Dead." In *Matériel Culture: The Archaeology of Twentieth-Century Conflict,* edited by John Schofield, William Gray Johnson, and Colleen M. Beck, 80–90. London: Routledge, 2002.

Hulme, Kathryn. *The Wild Place.* New York: Cardinal, 1960.

Hume, Janice. "'Portraits of Grief,' Reflectors of Values: The *New York Times* Remembers Victims of September 11." *Journalism and Mass Communication Quarterly* 80, no. 1 (2003): 166–82.

Husanović, Jasmina. "'Therapeutic' Regimes of Governing Trauma and the Dea(r)th of the Political: Politics of Missing Persons and ICMP's 'Bosnian Technology.'" Seminar paper, Goldsmiths College, London, March 2009.

Huston, Nancy. *Fault Lines.* London: Atlantic Books, 2008.

Jacobs, Ken. "Circling Zero, Part One: 'We See Absence': Program Note." Paper presented at "The Attack and Aftermath: Documenting 9/11," American Museum of the Moving Image, New York, September 7–11, 2002.

Jones, Billie. "Employing Identification in Online Museums." Paper presented at "Museums and the Web 2000," Minneapolis, 17–19 April 2000. http://www.archimuse.com/mw2000/papers/jones/jones.html.

Joyce, Christopher, and Eric Stover. *Witnesses from the Grave: The Stories Bones Tell.* London: Grafton, 1993.

Jussawalla, Adil. *Missing Person.* Mumbai: Clearing House, 1976.

Kaiser, Susana. "*Escraches:* Demonstrations, Communication, and Political Memory in Post-Dictatorial Argentina." *Media, Culture, and Society* 24, no. 4 (2002): 499–516.

Kear, Adrian, and Deborah Lynn Steinberg. *Mourning Diana: Nation, Culture, and the Performance of Grief.* London: Routledge, 1999.

Kottman, Paul A. "Translator's Introduction." In *Relating Narratives: Storytelling and Selfhood,* edited by Adriana Cavarero, vii–xxxi. London: Routledge, 2000.

Krakauer, Jon. *Into the Wild.* London: Pan Books, 2007.

Kroslowitz, Karen J. "Spontaneous Memorials: Forums for Dialogue and Discourse." *Museums and Social Issues* 2, no. 2 (2007): 243–56.

Kurgan, Laura. *Around Ground Zero.* New York: New York New Visions; Coalition for the Rebuilding of Lower Manhattan, 2001.

Kurzem, Mark. *The Mascot: The Extraordinary Story of a Jewish Boy and an SS Extermination Squad.* London: Rider, 2007.

Lacan, Jacques. *Écrits: A Selection.* Translated by Alan Sheridan. London: Routledge, 1977.

———. "The Mirror Stage as Formative of the Function of the I." In *Écrits,* 1–7.

Langewiesche, William. *American Ground: Unbuilding the World Trade Center.* New York: Farrar, Straus and Giroux, 2002.

Lerner, Kevin. "Architect Creates Map to Orient Ground-Zero Visitors (Laura Kurgan's Map Includes Pedestrian Routes, Open Views, and Area Buildings Condition Information)." *Architectural Record* 190, no. 2 (2002): 28.

Levi, Primo. *"If This Is a Man" and "The Truce."* Translated by Stuart Woolf. London: Abacus, 1979.

Levine, Annette H. *Cry for Me, Argentina: The Performance of Trauma in the Short Narratives of Aida Bortnik, Griselda Gambaro, and Tununa Mercado.* Madison NJ: Fairleigh Dickinson University Press, 2009.

Mackinnon, Gaille, and Amy Z. Mundorff. "The World Trade Center—September 11, 2001." In *Forensic Human Identification: An Introduction,* edited by Timothy Thompson and Susan Black, 485–99. Boca Raton: CRC Press, 2007.

Marchak, Patricia. *God's Assassins: State Terrorism in Argentina in the 1970s.* Montreal: McGill-Queen's University Press, 1999.

Marchi, Elaine. "Methods Developed to Identify Victims of the World Trade Center Disaster." *American Laboratory,* March 2004, 30–36.

Marchi, Elaine, and T. Z. Chastain. "The Sequence of Structural Events That Challenged the Forensic Effort of the World Trade Center Disaster." *American Laboratory,* December 2002, 13–17.

Marjanović, Damir, et al. "DNA Identification of Skeletal Remains from the World War II Mass Graves Uncovered in Slovenia." *Croat Medical Journal* 48 (2007) 513–19.

Marrus, Michael R. *The Unwanted: European Refugees in the Twentieth Century.* Oxford: Oxford University Press, 1985.

Martin, Steve, and Tracey Vennai. "Fromelles: The Story So Far." Commonwealth War Graves Commission, The Project, 14 September 2009. http://www.cwgc.org/fromelles/?page=english/the-project/getting_going.

Massumi, Brian. "The Future Birth of the Affective Fact." Conference Proceedings, "Genealogies of Biopolitics," October 2005. http://browse.reticular.info/text/collected/massumi.pdf.

Masters, Brian. *Killing for Company: Case of Dennis Nilsen.* London: Arrow Books, 1995.

McEwan, Ian. Foreword to *Complete Surrender,* by Dave Sharp and John Parker. London: John Blake, 2008.

Mellibovsky, Matilde. *Circle of Love over Death: Testimonies of the Mothers of the Plaza de Mayo.* Translated by Maria and Matthew Prosser. Willimantic, CT: Curbstone Press, 1997.

Mignone, Emilio F. "Beyond Fear: Forms of Justice and Compensation." In *Fear at the Edge: State Terror and Resistance in Latin America,* edited by Juan E. Corradi, Patricia Weiss Fagen, and Manuel Antonio Garretón, 250–63. Berkeley: University of California Press, 1992.

Mittermaier, Klaus. *Vermißt wird—: Die Arbeit des deutschen Suchdienstes.* Berlin: Links Publisher, 2002.

Moorehead, Caroline. *Dunant's Dream: War, Switzerland, and the History of the Red Cross.* London: HarperCollins, 1998.

Mouton, Michelle. *From Nurturing the Nation to Purifying the Volk: Weimar and Nazi Family Policy, 1918–1945.* Cambridge: Cambridge University Press, 2007.

Muppidi, Himadeep. *The Politics of the Global.* Minneapolis: University of Minnesota Press, 2004.

——. "Shame and Rage: International Relations and the World School of Colonialism." In *Interrogating Imperialism: Conversations on Gender, Race, and War,* edited by Robin L. Riley and Naeem Inayatullah, 51–62. New York: Palgrave, 2006.

Nancy, Jean-Luc. *The Inoperative Community.* Translated by Peter Connor, Lisa Garbus, Michael Holland, and Simona Sawhney. Minneapolis: University of Minnesota Press, 1991.

——. *Le regard du portrait.* Paris: Galilee, 2000.

Navarro, Marysa. "The Personal Is Political: Las Madres de Plaza Mayo." In *Power and Popular Protest: Latin American Social Movements,* edited by Susan Eckstein, 241–58. Berkeley: University of California Press, 2001.

Newiss, Geoff. "Missing Presumed...? The Police Response to Missing Persons." Edited by Barry Webb. Police Research Series Paper 114. London: Policing and Reducing Crime Unit 1999.

——. "A Study of the Characteristics of Outstanding Missing Persons: Implications for the Development of Police Risk Assessment." *Policing and Society* 15, no. 2 (2005): 212–25.

——. "Understanding the Risk of Going Missing: Estimating the Risk of Fatal Outcomes in Cancelled Cases." *Policing: An International Journal of Police Strategies and Management* 29, no. 2 (2006): 246–60.

Nicolson, Nigel. *Long Life.* London: Weidenfeld and Nicolson, 1997.

Niven, Bill. *Facing the Nazi Past: United Germany and the Legacy of the Third Reich.* London: Routledge, 2001.

North, Rachel. *Out of the Tunnel.* London: Friday Books, 2007.

O'Hagan, Andrew. *The Missing.* London: Faber and Faber, 1995.

Olsen, Kåre. "Under the Care of the Lebensborn: Norwegian War Children and Their Mothers." In *Children of World War II: The Hidden Enemy Legacy,* edited by Kjersti Ericsson and Eva Simonsen, 15–34. Oxford: Berg, 2005.

O'Nan, Stewart. *Songs for the Missing: A Novel.* New York: Viking Adult, 2008.

Panagia, Davide, and Jacques Rancière. "Dissenting Words: A Conversation with Jacques Rancière." *Diacritics* 30, no. 2 (2000): 113–26.

Payne, Malcolm. "Understanding 'Going Missing': Issues for Social Work and Social Services." *British Journal of Social Work* 25 (1995): 333–48.

Penchaszadeh, Victor B. "Abduction of Children of Political Dissidents in Argentina and the Role of Human Genetics in Their Restitution." *Journal of Public Health Policy* 13, no. 3 (1992): 291–305.

Pérez Solla, María Fernanda. *Enforced Disappearances in International Human Rights.* Jefferson, NC: McFarland and Company, 2006.

Pettiss, Susan T. *After the Shooting Stopped: The Memoir of an UNRRA Welfare Worker, Germany 1945–1947.* Bloomington, IN: Trafford Publishing, 2004.

Pine, Lisa. *Nazi Family Policy, 1933–1945.* Oxford: Berg, 1997.

Proudfoot, Malcolm J. *European Refugees, 1939–1952: A Study in Forced Population Movement.* London: Faber and Faber, 1957.

Rancière, Jacques. *Disagreement: Politics and Philosophy.* Translated by Julie Rose. Minneapolis: University of Minnesota Press, 1999.

———. *Dissensus: On Politics and Aesthetics.* Translated by Steven Corcoran. London: Continuum, 2010.

Ratliff, Evan. "Gone/Vanish: How to Disappear." *Wired,* December 2009, 144–53, 184–88.

Reiber, Alfred J., ed. *Forced Migration in Central and Eastern Europe, 1939–1950.* London: Frank Cass, 2000.

Reinisch, Jessica. "Preparing for a New World Order: UNRRA and the International Management of Refugees." In *Post-War Europe: Refugees, Exile, and Resettlement, 1945–1950.* Reading: Thomson Learning EMEA Ltd., 2007. http://www.tlemea.com/postwareurope/essay4.asp.

———. "'We Shall Build Anew a Powerful Nation': UNRRA, Internationalism, and National Reconstruction in Poland." *Journal of Contemporary History* 43, no. 3 (2008): 451–76.

Reuter, Laurel. *Los Desaparecidos / The Disappeared.* Milan: Charta, 2006.

Reynard, Paul. "The International Committee of the Red Cross and the International Tracing Service in Arolsen." *International Review of the Red Cross* 33, no. 296 (1993): 457–63.

Ribowsky, Shiya, and Tom Shachtman. *Dead Center: Behind the Scenes at the World's Largest Medical Examiner's Office.* New York: Harper, 2007.

Richmond, Doug. *How to Disappear Completely and Never Be Found.* New York: Carol Publishing Group, 1995.

Ritter, Nancy. "Identifying Remains: Lessons Learned from 9/11." *National Institute of Justice Journal* 256 (2007): 20–26.

———. "Missing Persons and Unidentified Remains: The Nation's Silent Mass Disaster." *National Institute of Justice Journal* 256 (2007): 2–7.

Robben, Antonius C. G. M. "The Assault on Basic Trust: Disappearance, Protest, and Reburial in Argentina." In *Cultures under Siege: Collective Violence and Trauma,* edited by Antonius C. G. M. Robben and Marcelo M. Suárez-Orozco, 70–101. Cambridge: Cambridge University Press, 2000.

———. "Mourning and Mistrust in Civil-Military Relations in Post-Dirty War Argentina." In *Multidisciplinary Perspectives on Peace and Conflict Research: A View from Europe,* edited by Francisco Ferrandiz and Antonius C. G. M. Robben, 253–70. Bilbao: University of Deusto, 2007.

———. *Political Violence and Trauma in Argentina.* Philadelphia: University of Pennsylvania Press, 2005.

Rogers, Colin. *Tracing Missing Persons: An Introduction to Agencies, Methods, and Sources in England and Wales.* Manchester: Manchester University Press, 1986.

Rosenberg, Tina. *Children of Cain: Violence and the Violent in Latin America.* New York: William Morrow, 1991.

Rothenbuhler, Eric W. "Ground Zero, the Firemen, and the Symbolics of Touch on 9/11 and After." In *Media Anthropology,* edited by Eric W. Rothenbuhler and Mihai Coman, 176–87. New York: Sage, 2005.

———. "The Symbolics of Touch on 9/11 and After." Paper presented at Making Sense of September 11: News Media and Old Metaphors, Ohio University, Athens, Ohio, September 21, 2002.

Salama, Mauricio Cohen. *Tumbas anónimas: Informe sobre la identificación de restos de víctimas de la represión ilegal* [Anonymous Graves: Report on Identification of Remains of Victims of Illegal Repression]. Buenos Aires: Catalogos Editora, 1992.

Santner, Eric L. *On Creaturely Life: Rilke, Benjamin, Sebald.* Chicago: University of Chicago Press, 2006.

———. *Stranded Objects: Mourning, Memory, and Film in Postwar Germany.* Ithaca, NY: Cornell University Press, 1990.

Sarkar, Dilip. *Missing in Action: Resting in Peace?* Worcester: Victory Books International, 2006.

Scarry, Elaine. *The Body in Pain: The Making and Unmaking of the World.* New York: Oxford University Press, 1985.

Schechtman, Joseph B. *European Population Transfers, 1939–1945.* New York: Oxford University Press, 1946.

Scheper-Hughes, Nancy. *Death without Weeping: The Violence of Everyday Life in Brazil.* Berkeley: University of California Press, 1992.

Schisgall, Oscar. "'T' Stands for Dead: UNRRA Traces Hitler's Victims." *Coronet* 20, no. 6 (1946). (Abridged in "Central Tracing Bureau Finds Many Missing DPs," *[UNRRA] Team News,* 22 March 1947, p. 5; British Red Cross Archives, London, Ref. 735/1, Central Tracing Bureau, Germany 1946–1947.)

Schlink, Bernard. *The Reader.* Translated by Carol Brown Janeway. London: Phoenix, 1997.

Schmitz-Köster, Dorothee. "A Topic for Life: Children of German Lebensborn Homes." In *Children of World War II: The Hidden Enemy Legacy,* edited by Kjersti Ericsson and Eva Simonsen, 213–28. Oxford: Berg, 2005.

Schulze, Rainer. "'A Continual Source of Trouble': The Displaced Persons Camp Bergen-Belsen (Hohne), 1945–1950." In *Post-War Europe: Refugees, Exile, and Resettlement, 1945–1950.* Reading: Thomson Learning EMEA Ltd., 2007. http://www.tlemea.com/postwareurope/essay1.asp.

Schwenger, Peter. "Circling Ground Zero." *PMLA-Publications of the Modern Language Association of America* 106, no. 2 (1991): 251–61.

Sebald, W. G. *Vertigo.* Translated by Michael Hulse. London: Harvill, 1999.

Segobye, Alinah Kelo. "Missing Persons, Stolen Bodies, and Issues of Patrimony: The El Negro Story." *Pula: Botswana Journal of African Studies* 16, no. 1 (2002): 14–18.

Seiffert, Rachel. *The Dark Room*. London: Vintage, 2005.

Sereny, Gitta. *Albert Speer: His Battle with Truth*. London: Picador, 1996.

Shaler, Robert C. *Who They Were: Inside the World Trade Center DNA Story: The Unprecedented Effort to Identify the Missing*. New York: Free Press, 2005.

Shapiro, Paul A. "The History of the International Tracing Service and Its Archival Collection." Paper presented at opening session of Beyond Camps and Forced Labour: Current International Research on Survivors of Nazi Persecution, Third International Multidisciplinary Conference at the Imperial War Museum, London, 7–9 January 2009.

Simpson, David. *9/11: The Culture of Commemoration*. Chicago: University of Chicago Press, 2006.

Sledge, Michael. *Soldier Dead: How We Recover, Identify, Bury, and Honor Our Military Fallen*. New York: Columbia University Press, 2005.

Smith, Dennis. *Report from Ground Zero: The Heroic Story of the Rescuers at the World Trade Center*. London: Doubleday, 2002.

Stafford, David. *Endgame 1945: Victory, Retribution, Liberation*. London: Little, Brown, 2007.

Steedman, Carolyn. *Dust*. Manchester: Manchester University Press, 2001.

Steinert, Johannes-Dieter, and Inge Weber-Newth, eds. *European Immigrants in Britain, 1933–1950*. Munich: K. G. Saur, 2003.

Stephens, Andrew. *The Suzy Lamplugh Story*. London: Faber and Faber, 1988.

Stone, Dan, ed. *Post-War Europe: Refugees, Exile, and Resettlement, 1945–1950*. Reading: Thomson Learning EMEA Ltd., 2007. http://www.tlemea.com/postwareurope/.

Stone, I. F. *Underground to Palestine*. New York: Boni and Gaer, 1946.

Stonehouse, John. *Death of an Idealist*. London: W. H. Allen, 1975.

Stover, Eric, and Rachel Shigekane. "The Missing in the Aftermath of War: When Do the Needs of Victims' Families and International War Crimes Tribunals Clash?" *International Review of the Red Cross* 84, no. 848 (2002): 845–66.

Summers, Julie. *Remembered: The History of the Commonwealth War Graves Commission*. London: Merrell, 2007.

Summers, Julie, Louise Loe, and Nigel Steel. *Remembering Fromelles: A New Cemetery for a New Century*. Maidenhead: CWGC Publishing, 2010.

Szymborska, Wisława. "Starvation Camp near Jasło." In *Poems New and Collected*, 42. Orlando, FL: Harcourt, 1998.

Taylor, Diana. *The Archive and the Repertoire: Performing Cultural Memory in the Americas*. Durham, NC: Duke University Press, 2003.

———. *Disappearing Acts: Spectacles of Gender and Nationalism in Argentina's "Dirty War."* Durham, NC: Duke University Press, 1997.

Thompson, Timothy, and Susan Black, eds. *Forensic Human Identification: An Introduction*. Boca Raton, FL: CRC Press, 2007.

Tolstoy, Nikolai. *Victims of Yalta*. London: Hodder and Stoughton, 1977.

Tulloch, John. *One Day in July: Experiencing 7/7*. London: Little, Brown, 2006.

Van Drunen, Saskia P. C. *Struggling with the Past: The Human Rights Movement and the Politics of Memory in Post-Dictatorship Argentina (1983–2006)*. Amsterdam: Rozenberg Publishers, 2010.

von Hassell, Fay. *A Mother's War*. London: John Murray, 2003.

Wagner, Sarah E. *To Know Where He Lies: DNA Technology and the Search for Srebrenica's Missing.* Berkeley: University of California Press, 2008.

Wallace, Jonathan. "The Missing." *Year Zero,* 29 September 2001. The Ethical Spectacle. http://www.spectacle.org/yearzero/missing.html.

Wallace, Mike. *A New Deal for New York.* New York: Bell & Weiland in association with Gotham Center for New York City History, 2002.

Weinberg, Jeshajahu, and Rina Elieli. *The Holocaust Museum in Washington.* New York: Rizzoli in collaboration with the United States Holocaust Memorial Museum, 1995.

Weschler, Lawrence. *A Miracle, a Universe: Settling Accounts with Torturers.* Chicago: University of Chicago Press, 1990.

———. Preface to *Los Desaparecidos / The Disappeared,* by Laurel Reuter. Milan: Charta, 2006.

Whitford, Tim, and Tony Pollard. "For Duty Done: A WWI Military Medallion Recovered from the Mass Grave Site at Fromelles, Northern France." *Journal of Conflict Archaeology* 5, no. 1 (2009): 201–29.

Wigley, Mark. "Insecurity by Design." In *After the World Trade Center: Rethinking New York City,* edited by Michael Sorkin and Sharon Zukin, 69–85. New York: Routledge, 2002.

Williams, Grant. "Red Cross Faces Sharp Criticism over Spending and Management." *The Chronicle of Philanthropy,* 17 October 2001. http://philanthropy.com/free/update/2001/10/2001101702.htm.

———. "Red Cross President Resigns under Pressure from Board." *The Chronicle of Philanthropy,* 26 October 2001. http://philanthropy.com/free/update/ 2001/ 10/2001102601.htm.

Williams, Richard. *Missing! A Study of the World-Wide Missing Persons Enigma and Salvation Army Response.* London: Hodder and Stoughton, 1969.

Williams, Robin, and Paul Johnson. *Genetic Policing: The Use of DNA in Criminal Investigations.* Cullompton: Willan, 2008.

Wilson, Francesca M. *Aftermath: France, Germany, Austria, Yugoslavia, 1945 and 1946.* West Drayton, Middlesex: Penguin Books, 1947.

Wolf, Christa. *A Model Childhood.* Translated by Ursule Molinaro and Hedwig Rappolt. London: Virago, 1995.

Woodbridge, George. *The History of the United Nations Relief and Rehabilitation Administration.* New York: Columbia University Press, 1950.

Wright, Thomas C. *State Terrorism in Latin America: Chile, Argentina and International Human Rights.* Lanham, MD: Rowman and Littlefield, 2007.

Wyman, Mark. *DPs: Europe's Displaced Persons, 1945–1951.* Ithaca, NY: Cornell University Press, 1989; Associated University Presses, 1998 (with a new introduction).

Young, Sara. *My Enemy's Cradle.* London: HarperCollins, 2008.

Zehfuss, Maja. "Forget September 11!" *Third World Quarterly* 24, no. 3 (2003) 513–28.

———. *Wounds of Memory: The Politics of War in Germany.* Cambridge: Cambridge University Press, 2007.

Zimonjic, Peter. *Into the Darkness: An Account of 7/7.* London: Vintage Books, 2008.

Žižek, Slavoj. *For They Know Not What They Do: Enjoyment as a Political Factor.* London: Verso, 1991.

——. *The Sublime Object of Ideology*. London: Verso, 1989.

Žižek, Slavoj, Eric L. Santner, and Kenneth Reinhard. *The Neighbor: Three Enquiries in Political Theology*. Chicago: University of Chicago Press, 2005.

Zulaika, Joseba, and William A Douglass. *Terror and Taboo: The Follies, Fables, and Faces of Terrorism*. New York: Routledge, 1996.

Newspaper Articles, Online News Services, and News Broadcasts

Amundson, Amber. "A Widow's Plea for Non-Violence." *Chicago Tribune,* 25 September 2001.

Associated Press. "Final WTC Death Toll Said Down to 2,749." 23 January 2004. http://www.voicesofsept11.org/medical_examiner/012304.html.

BBC News. "DNA Tests Fail to Identify Unknown WWI Soldiers." 17 March 2010. http://news.bbc.co.uk/1/hi/uk/8572381.stm.

——. "In Full: Blair on Bomb Blasts; Statement from Downing Street, 1730 BST 7 July 2005." 7 July 2005. http://news.bbc.co.uk/1/hi/uk/4659953.stm.

——. "Missing People Sought after Bombs." 10 July 2005. http://news.bbc.co.uk/1/hi/england/london/4666679.stm.

Bennetto, Jason. "Terror in London: Police Identifying Victims of Asian Tsunami Switch." *Independent,* 12 July 2005.

Betz, Frank-Uwe. "Das andere Mahnmal." *Die Zeit,* 19 May 2005.

CBS News. "Latest NYC 9/11 Search Finds 72 Human Remains." 23 June 2010. http://www.cbsnews.com/stories/2010/06/22/ap/national/main6608278.shtml.

——. "Many WTC Remains Are Unidentified." 14 August 2003. http://www.cbsnews.com/stories/2003/08/14/attack/main568168.shtml.

CNN. "Red Cross Briefing on Liberty Fund." Live event/special, November 14, 2001. http://transcripts.cnn.com/TRANSCRIPTS/0111/14/se.03.html.

——. "Red Cross Defends Handling of Sept. 11 Donations." November 6, 2001. http://archives.cnn.com/2001/US/11/06/rec.charity.hearing.

Cohen, Roger. "U.S.-German Flare-Up Over Vast Nazi Camp Archives." *New York Times,* 20 February 2006.

Cowley, Jason. "Where Are They Now?" *Observer,* 18 June 2000.

Crossland, David. "Nazi Program to Breed Master Race: Lebensborn Children Break Silence." *Spiegel Online,* 11 July 2006. http://www.spiegel.de/international/0,1518,druck-446978,00.html.

Dear, Paula. "Don't Wait for Me Tonight, Mum." BBC News. 4 July 2006. http://news.bbc.co.uk/1/hi/uk/5098448.stm.

DeYoung, Karen. "On the Tarmac, Clinton Attends Ceremony for Americans MIA in Vietnam." *Washington Post,* blog, 23 July 2010. http://voices.washingtonpost.com/checkpoint-washington/2010/07/on_the_tarmac_clinton_attends.html.

Dunlap, David W. "Renovating a Sacred Place, Where the 9/11 Remains Wait." *New York Times,* 29 August 2006.

European Hospital, EHOnline. "The London Tube and Bus Bombings: UK Government Now Supports Forensic Radiography Response Team Training." 27 March 2009. http://www.european-hospital.com/topics/article/5568.html.

Flanders, Laura. Live reports from Manhattan. Filed 10.35pm EST Tues September 11 2001. Working Assets. WorkingforChange. http://www.workingfor change.com/printitem.cfm?itemid=11899.

———. Live reports from Manhattan. Filed 1.05pm EST Weds September 12 2001. Working Assets. WorkingforChange. http://www.workingforchange.com/ printitem.cfm?itemid=11899.

Funder, Anna. "Secret History." *Guardian,* 16 June 2007.

Gamboa, Suzanne. "Victims May Include Illegal Aliens," *Newsday,* 20 September 2001.

Gardham, Duncan. "Families of July 7 Bombing Victims Fear They May Never Learn the Truth." *Telegraph,* 20 May 2009.

Gardham, Duncan, and Nicole Martin. "How Much Blood Must Be Spilled? A Mother Asks." *Telegraph,* 13 July 2005.

Geoghegan, Tom. "Trying Not to Harbour Hatred." BBC News, 3 July 2006. http:// news.bbc.co.uk/1/hi/uk/5130044.stm.

Gillan, Audrey, and Owen Bowcott. "Families Feel Pain of Name Delay: First Victim Is Identified but Frustration Grows among Those Waiting to Hear Fate of the Missing." *Guardian,* 12 July 2005.

Gordon, Greg. "Pressure Mounts to Open Holocaust Records." *Minneapolis-St. Paul Star Tribune,* 9 May 2005.

Gorlick, Vivian. "First Person: Why the Posters Haunt Us Still." *New York Times,* September 23, 2001.

Greenhill, Sam. "'I've Just Seen Hell on Earth: Four Years after 7/7, a Never-before-Seen Picture of the Horror That Confronted Police on the Tube Ripped Apart by Terrorists." *Daily Mail,* 8 July 2009.

Greenhouse, Steven, and Mireya Navarro. "Those at Towers' Margin Elude List of Missing: The Hidden Victims." *New York Times,* 17 September 2001.

Gross, Jane, and Jenny Scott. "The Missing: Hospital Treks, Fliers, and the Cry: Have You Seen...?" *New York Times,* September 13 2001.

Guardian. "Bomb Victim IDs May Take Weeks—Coroner." 15 July 2005.

———. "Straight from the Heart." 13 July 2005.

Hall, Robert. "Piecing Together the Past." BBC News, 13 March 2009. http://news. bbc.co.uk/2/hi/uk_news/7940540.stm.

Harding, Luke. "Germany to Release Archive Files on Millions of Nazi Victims." *Guardian,* 20 April 2006.

Hayman, Andy. "No Warning, No Links, No Leads: 7/7 Bombings Were a Bolt out of Nowhere." *Times,* 20 June 2009.

Hotz, Robert Lee. "Probing the DNA of Death." *Los Angeles Times,* 9 October 2002.

International Committee of the Red Cross (ICRC). Official statement, opening ceremony of the International Tracing Service in Bad Arolsen, 30 April 2008. http://www.icrc.org/web/eng/siteeng0.nsf/htmlall/int-tracing-service-statement-300408.

Kissane, Karen. "Bringing Back the Dead." *The Age,* 11 October 2008.

Larson, Pete. Freewheel Burning, blog, 2 May 2010. http://peterslarson.com/2010/ 05/02/graciela-mellibovsky-saidler/.

Laville, Sandra. "Government Bans Former Anti-terror Chief's Tell-all Book: Court Injunction on Andy Hayman's *The Terrorist Hunters,* Which Includes Details of De Menezes and Litvinenko Cases." guardian.co.uk, 2 July 2009.

——. "Mother's Fury at 'Slaughter of the Innocents.'" *Guardian,* 12 July 2005.

Lawrence, Charles. "Remains of 9/11 Victims 'to Spend Eternity' in City Rubbish Dump." *Telegraph,* 10 October 2004.

Lenkowitz, Eric. "9/11 Victim ID'd 6 Yrs Later." *New York Post,* 14 September 2007.

Lipton, Eric. "At the Limits of Science: 9/11 ID Effort Comes to End." *New York Times,* 3 April 2005.

——. "New York Settles on a Number That Defines Tragedy: 2,749 Dead in Trade Center Attack." *New York Times,* 23 January 2004.

Loewenberg, Sam, and Julian Borger. "Closed Archive Leads to Holocaust Denial Claim." *Guardian,* 21 February 2006.

Louje, Mirian Ching. "The 9/11 Disappeareds." *Nation,* 3 December 2001.

Lower Manhattan.info. "Memorial Draws Comments from Fire-Fighters, Others," 29 May 2003. http://www.lowermanhattan.info/news/memorial_draws_comments_from_87335.asp#top.

Malik, Shiv. "My Brother the Bomber." *Prospect,* 30 June 2007.

McKittrick, David. "Nazi Background of Prominent Irish Publisher Exposed." *Independent,* 4 January 2007.

Memory in Latin America, blog. "Argentina Campo de Mayo Trial Update." 4 February 2010. http://memoryinlatinamerica.blogspot.com/2010/02/argentina-campo-de-mayo-trial-update.html.

——. "This Week in Argentina." 3 July 2010. http://memoryinlatinamerica.blogspot.com/2010/07/this-week-in-argentina.html.

Moyers, Bill. "Bill Moyers Interview with Mrs. Admundsen." *Now with Bill Moyers,* PBS, 25 January 2002. http://www.pbs.org/now/transcript/transcript102_full.html.

Murray, Kieran. "Poor Migrant Workers among Victims of US Attacks." Reuters, 12 September 2001. http://www.tepeyac.org/sep12reuters.htm.

Nanji, Ayaz. "Ground Zero Forensic Work Ends." CBS News, 23 February 2005. http://www.cbsnews.com/stories/2005/02/23/national/main675839.shtml.

New York Times. "Joanne Ahladiotis: Going All Out, All the Time." 29 November 2001.

North, Rachel. "The July 7 Questions That Still Haunt Victims." *Times,* 18 December 2005.

Norton-Taylor, Richard. "Victim of 7/7 'Might Have Been Saved.'" *Guardian,* 27 April 2010.

Olaniyonu, Yusuph, and Frank Kintum. "Anthony Fatayi-Williams Body Recovered." Online Nigeria, 15 July 2005. http://nm.onlinenigeria.com/templates/?a=3831&z=12.

O'Neill, Sean. "Book by Former Anti-terror Chief Andy Hayman Banned from Shops." *Times,* 3 July 2009.

Robb, Stephen. "Fromelles Dead Offer Reminder of 'Preciousness of Life.'" BBC News UK, 19 July 2010. http://www.bbc.co.uk/news/uk-10661923.

Rozenberg, Joshua. "Relatives of Tube Bomber Want Another Post Mortem." *Daily Telegraph,* 29 October 2005.

Sella, Marshall. "Missing: How a Grief Ritual Is Born." *New York Times Magazine,* 7 October 2001.

Smee, Jess. "Victims of Hitler's Plan for a Master Race: Climate of Shame Suppressed Discussion of Third Reich's Social Impact." *Guardian,* 6 November 2006.

Sontag, Deborah. "Who Brought Bernadine Healy Down?" *New York Times,* 23 December 2001.

Sontag, Susan. "Of Courage and Resistance." *Nation,* 5 May 2003.

——. The Talk of the Town, *New Yorker,* 24 September 2001.

Stephenson, Helen. "Opening the Archives—Closure for Holocaust Victims." *Prescott News,* 23 February 2008.

Télam: National News Agency of Argentina. "Grandmothers of Plaza de Mayo Head Regrets that 'Noble Case' Turned into a War." 1 April 2010. http://english.telam.com.ar/index.php?option=com_content&view=article&id=8897:grandmothers-of-plaza-de-mayo-head-regrets-that-qnoble-caseq-turned-into-a-war&catid=34:society.

Telegraph. "Inquest into Oil Executive Opens." 14 July 2005.

Times. "Alicia Zubasnabar: Founder of Grandmothers of the Plaza de Mayo." 30 June 2008.

Travis, Alan. "Victims of 7/7 Bombs Were Not Given Enough Help, Ministers Admit." *Guardian,* 23 September 2006.

Tremlett, Giles. "Spanish Reaction: Admiration Mingled with Astonishment over Calm Response." *Guardian,* 12 July 2005.

Tutek, Edwin Andrés Martínez. "Undocumented Workers Uncounted Victims of 9/11." *Chicago Tribune,* 7 September 2006.

Twum, Nana Sifa. "Wundowa's Body Released To Family." Modern Ghana.com, 19 July 2005. http://www.modernghana.com/news/82274/1/wundowas-body-released-to-family.html.

Usborne, David. "Argentine Media Heirs Face 'Adoption' DNA Tests." *Independent,* 8 June 2010. http://www.independent.co.uk/news/world/americas/argentine-media-heirs-face-adoption-dna-tests-1994125.html.

——. "It Has Taken Me My Whole Life to Find Him." *Independent,* 14 September 2001.

——. "The Most Important Story of My Life." *The Independent Saturday Review,* 15 September 2001.

——. "Normal Life Resumes." *Independent,* 15 September 2001.

Waldman, Amy. "A Nation Challenged: The Fliers; Posters of the Missing Now Speak of Losses." *New York Times,* 29 September 2001.

Walsh, Declan. "Without a Trace." *Guardian,* 16 March 2007.

Warren, Michael. "Argentine Father and Son Reunited 33 Years after Military Kidnapped, Killed Imprisoned Mother." *Washington Examiner,* 23 February 2010.

Washington Post. "A Holocaust Denial." 25 March 2006.

Reports, Press Releases, and Websites of Institutions

9-11 Research. Missing Bodies. http://911research.wtc7.net.wtc/evidence/bodies.html.

Abuelas of the Plaza de Mayo. http://www.abuelas.org.ar/english/history.htm.

American Red Cross. Charter. www2.redcross.org/images/pdfs/charter.pdf.

——. History, The Federal Charter of the American Red Cross. http://www.redcross.org/portal/site/en/menuitem.d229a5f06620c6052b1ecfbf43181aa0/?vgnextoid=39c2a8f21931f110VgnVCM10000089f0870aRCRD.

——. Liberty Disaster Relief Fund, Financial Statements, 30 June 2004. http://www.redcross.org/portal/site/en/menuitem.d8aaecf214c576bf971e4cfe43181aa0/?vgnextoid=0bf26a5e61dce110VgnVCM10000089f0870aRCRD&vgnextfmt=default#report.

——. September 11th Response and Recovery: Fraud. House Committee on Homeland Security, Subcommittee on Management, Integration, and Oversight. Testimony of Leigh A. Bradley, American Red Cross. 12 July 2006. http://www.redcross.org/911recovery/.

——. September 11th Response and Recovery: Liberty Fund: The Liberty Fund Controversy, Clip 1: George Mitchell, recorded 28 April 2006. http://www.redcross.org/911recovery/.

American Statistical Association Committee on Scientific Freedom and Human Rights. http://www.amstat.org/committees/commdetails.cfm?txtComm=CCNPRO05.

Archdiocese of Guatemala, Human Rights Office. *Guatemala: Never Again! Recovery of Historical Memory Project (Remhi); The Official Report.* Maryknoll, NY: Orbis Books, 1999.

Argentine Forensic Archaeology Team / Equipo Argentino de Antropologia Forense (EAAF). *Annual Report, 2007.* eaaf.typepad.com/eaaf/An07_Report.pdf

——. *Biannual Report, 1996–97.* http://eaaf.typepad.com/eaaf_reports/.

——. "The Latin American Initiative for the Identification of the 'Disappeared' (LIID)." In *Annual Report, 2007,* 130–35.

——. "The Right to Truth." In *Annual Report, 2007,* 102–19.

Argentine National Commission on the Disappeared. *Nunca Mas: Report of the Argentine National Commission on the Disappeared.* New York: Farrar, Straus and Giroux, 1986.

Asociación Tepeyac de New York. http://www.tepeyac.org.ns50.alentus.com/intro.asp; http://www.tepeyac.org/notasprensa.htm.

Association of Chief Police Officers and National Centre for Policing Excellence. "Guidance on the Management, Recording, and Investigation of Missing Persons." London: National Centre for Policing Excellence, 2005.

Balzan Project at Birkbeck College, directed by David Feldman (Birkbeck) and Mark Mazower (Columbia). "Reconstruction in the Immediate Aftermath of War: A Comparative Study of Europe, 1945–1950." First Balzan Workshop, Comparing Europe's Post-War Reconstructions, 28 October 2005. Report by Jessica Reinisch. http://www.balzan.bbk.ac.uk/page14.html.

Commonwealth War Graves Commission. Facts & Statistics. http://www.cwgc.org/content.asp?menuid=2&submenuid=50&id=50&menuname=Facts%20and%20figures&menu=sub.

——. "Getting Us Here—Building the Case." http://www.cwgc.org/fromelles/?page=english/background/getting_us_here&pageno=2.

——. "The GUARD Investigations—Proving the Case." http://www.cwgc.org/fromelles/?page=english/background/getting_us_here.

——. "New Cemetery Becomes Final Resting Place for 250 Soldiers in Dedication Led by HRH Prince of Wales." Press release, 19 July 2010. http://www.cwgc.org/fromelles/?page=english/diary-events/view/news190710.

——. "Order of Service: Dedication and Burial; Fromelles (Pheasant Wood) Military Cemetery, 19 July 2010." http://www.cwgc.org/fromelles/?page=english/diary-events/view/news190710.

——. "Remembering Fromelles: The Project." http://www.cwgc.org/fromelles/ ?page=english/the-project/project/1.

——. "Remembering Fromelles: Questions and Answers." http://www.cwgc.org/ fromelles/?page=english/the-project/questions.

——. "Who We Are." http://www.cwgc.org/content.asp?menuid=1&id=1&menu name=Who%20We%20Are&menu=main.

Congressional Research Service. *The Congressional Charter of the American National Red Cross: Overview, History, and Analysis.* 15 March 2006. Kevin R. Kosar. www. fas.org/sgp/crs/misc/RL33314.pdf.

Coroner's Inquests into the London Bombings of 7 July 2005. http://7julyinquests. independent.gov.uk/index.htm.

——. Hearing Transcripts, 26 April 2010, Morning. http://7julyinquests.independent. gov.uk/hearing_transcripts/26042010am.htm.

Disaster Action. "When Disaster Strikes—Disaster Victim Identification: Issues for Families and Implications for Police Family Liaison Officers (FLOs) and Coroner's Officers (COs)." http://www.disasteraction.org.uk/guidance.htm.

Federal Bureau of Investigation. "The FBI Releases 19 Photographs of Individuals Believed to Be the Hijackers of the Four Airliners That Crashed on September 11, 01." Press release, 27 September 2001. http://www.fbi.gov/pressrel/ pressrel01/092701hjpic.htm.

German Red Cross, Tracing Service Munich. History. http://www.drk-suchdienst. eu/content/content2.php?CatID=61&NewsID=45&lang=en.

——. Missing in the Second World War. http://www.drk-suchdienst.eu/content/ categoryshow.php?CatID=53.

——. The Missing of World War II: Expert Opinions. http://www.drk-suchdienst. eu/content/content2.php?CatID=53&NewsID=120&lang=en.

Government Communication Office, Republic of Slovenia. "Commission: Important Steps Made in Revealing Post-WWII Killings." Ljubljana, 14 October 2008. http:// www.ukom.gov.si/eng/slovenia/publications/slovenia-news/7252/ 7262/.

Griffin, Hon. Alan, MP, Australian Minister for Veterans' Affairs and Defence Personnel. "Final Fromelles Soldier Laid to Rest." Press release, 41/2010, 19 July 2010. http://www.minister.defence.gov.au/Griffintpl.cfm?CurrentId=10634.

Hallett, Rt. Hon. Lady Justice DBE. Decision following Pre-Inquest Hearing from 26 to 30 April 2010. http://7julyinquests.independent.gov.uk/directions_ decs/decision-april-2010.htm.

House of Commons Constitutional Affairs Committee. "Reform of the Coroners' System and Death Certification: Eighth Report of Session 2005–06; Report, together with Formal Minutes." HC 902–I. London: The Stationery Office Limited, 2006.

Intelligence and Security Committee. "Could 7/7 Have Been Prevented? Review of the Intelligence on the London Terrorist Attacks on 7 July 2005." Chairman Kim Howells. Cm. 7617. May 2009. http://www.cabinetoffice.gov.uk/ intelligence/special_reports.aspx.

International Committee of the Red Cross (ICRC). Draft International Convention on the Condition and Protection of Civilians of Enemy Nationality Who Are on Territory Belonging to or Occupied by a Belligerent. Tokyo, 1934. http:// www.icrc.org/ihl.nsf/INTRO/320?OpenDocument.

———. *The Missing: ICRC Progress Report*. Geneva: ICRC, 2006.

International Criminal Police Organization (INTERPOL). "Disaster Victim Identification." http://www.interpol.int/Public/DisasterVictim/Default.asp.

———. "Manual"; http://www.interpol.int/Public/DisasterVictim/guide/default.asp.

International Red Cross. *Report of the International Committee of the Red Cross on Its Activities during the Second World War (September 1, 1939–June 30, 1947)*. XXVIIth Conference, Stockholm, August 1948. Geneva: IRC, 1948.

International Tracing Service. *Annual Report 2007*. Bad Arolsen: ITS, 2008.

———. *Annual Report 2008*. Bad Arolsen: ITS, 2009.

———. "Debate on the Future of ITS Is Well Underway." Press release, May 20, 2009. http://www.its-arolsen.org/en/press/press_releases/index.html?expand=251 4&cHash=d89ea8fe93.

———. "New Home for the International Tracing Service at Arolsen." *Information Bulletin,* September 1952. http://digital.library.wisc.edu/1711.dl/History.omg 1952Sept.

London Assembly, Richard Barnes AM (Chair). "Report of the 7 July Review Committee." June 2006. Vol. 1, "Report." London: Greater London Authority.

———. "Report of the 7 July Review Committee." June 2006. Vol. 2, "Views and Information from Organisations." London: Greater London Authority.

———. "Report of the 7 July Review Committee." June 2006. Vol. 3, "Views and Information from Individuals." London: Greater London Authority.

Look4them—tracing missing persons, locating relatives, searching parents. http://www.look4them.org.uk.

Luce, Tom. *Death Certification and Investigation in England, Wales, and Northern Ireland: The Report of a Fundamental Review, 2003*. Cm. 5831. London: HMSO, 2003.

Metropolitan Police. *Messages from 7/7*. London: HMSO, 2006.

———. "'One Week Anniversary' Bombings Appeal." http://cms.met.police.uk/news/major_operational_announcements/terrorist_attacks/one_week_anniversary_bombings_appeal.

Michael Lynch Memorial Foundation. About Us. http://www.mlynch.org/ml/about.htm.

Missing People. "Our History." http://wwww.missingpeople.org.uk/about/history.

———. "Research to Date." London: Missing People, 2007. http://www.missing people.org.uk/media-centre/downloads.

Missing Soldiers of Fromelles Discussion Group. "Military, Media, and Exploratory Dig." 23 February 2009. http://www.docstoc.com/docs/35340103/The-Military_-Media-and-Exploratory-Dig.

National Institute of Justice. "Lessons Learned from 9/11: DNA Identification in Mass Fatality Incidents." Washington, DC: U.S. Department of Justice, Office of Justice Programs, 2006.

National Policing Improvement Agency (NPIA). "Collection of Missing Persons Data: A Code of Practice for the Police Service on Collecting and Sharing Data on Missing Persons with Public Authorities." London: HMSO, 2009.

———. "Missing Persons Bureau Moves to NPIA." Press release, 1 April 2008. http://www.npia.police.uk/en/10266.htm.

Not in Our Name. "The Pledge of Resistance," 2003. http://www.notinourname.net/index.html.

Office of the Chief Medical Examiner (OCME). "Update on the Results of DNA Testing of Remains Recovered at the World Trade Center Site and Surrounding Area." Press release, 1 February 2009. http://www.ci.nyc.ny.us/html/ocme/html/pa/pa.shtml.

Parents & Abducted Children Together (PACT). "Every Five Minutes: A Review of the Available Data on Missing Children in the UK." London: PACT, 2005.

Red Cross and St. John War Organisation, 1939–1947, Official Record: Appendices to Official History [P. G. Cambray and G. G. B. Briggs, The Official Record of the Humanitarian Services of the War Organisation of the British Red Cross Society and Order of St. John of Jerusalem, 1939–1947 (London: Red Cross and St. John 1949)] and Confidential Supplement. British Red Cross Archives Library.

Red Cross and St. John War Organisation, 1939–1947, Official Record: Confidential Supplement [to P. G. Cambray and G. G. B. Briggs, The Official Record of the Humanitarian Services of the War Organisation of the British Red Cross Society and Order of St. John of Jerusalem, 1939–1947 (London: Red Cross and St. John 1949)]. British Red Cross Archives Library.

September 11 Photo Project, "The September 11 Photo Project Launches National Tour at Washington, D.C.'s Military Women's Memorial." Press release, 12 February 2002. http://www.sep11photo.org/sep11version_2007.htm.

Simon Wiesenthal Center and the Targum Shlishi Foundation. "Operation: Last Chance" Campaign. http://www.operationlastchance.org/index.htm.

Skyscraper Safety Campaign: A Project of Parents and Families of Firefighters and WTC Victims. http://www.skyscrapersafety.org/.

Supreme Headquarters, Allied Expeditionary Force (SHAEF). CROWCASS (Central Registry of War Criminals and Security Suspects): Wanted Lists. Uckfield: Naval & Military Press, 2005. Reprint of 1947 original document held at the National Archives, Kew, London.

Task Force for International Cooperation on Holocaust Education, Remembrance, and Research (ITF). "International Task Force Supports Decision to Open Bad Arolsen Archives for Scholarly Research by the End of the Year," 9 June 2004; "International Task Force Calls for Concrete Steps to Open Holocaust-Era Archives of the International Tracing Service in Germany," 16 December 2004; "International Holocaust Task Force Urges Opening of Bad Arolsen Archive," 30 June 2005. http://www.holocausttaskforce.org/about/index.php?content=press/.

UK Cabinet Office, John Reid (Home Secretary) and Tessa Jowell (Culture Secretary). "Addressing Lessons from the Emergency Response to the 7 July 2005 London Bombings: What We Learned and What We Are Doing about It." 22 September 2006. Norwich: HMSO. www.londonprepared.gov.uk/.../homeoffice_lessonslearned.pdf.

UK Foreign and Commonwealth Office. International Commission for the International Tracing Service (18/05/2009). http://www.fco.gov.uk/en/newsroom/latest-news/?view=News&id=17969182.

UNRRA European Regional Office. "Fifty Facts about the UNRRA." London: HMSO, 1946. European Navigator, Centre Virtuel de la Connaissance sur l'Europe (CVCE). http://www.ena.lu.

U.S. Department of State, International Information Programs. *New York City: Three Months After; Pictorial Essays Developed during Three Days in December 2001 Capture the City's—and the Nation's—Indomitable Spirit.* http://usinfo.state.gov/topical/pol/terror/album/newyork/.

Films, Broadcasts, Exhibitions, Images

Artists Network of Refuse and Resist. "Our Grief Is Not a Cry for War." Artists performance 2001. http://www.refuseandresist.org/newresistance/092301grief.html.

Bammer, Angelika. "Memory Sites: Destruction, Loss, and Transformation." Image panels. The Schatten Gallery, Robert W. Woodruff Library, Emory University, 9 September to 9 November 2003. http://web.library.emory.edu/libraries/schatten/previous/memorysites/.

Biraben, Gastón. *Cautiva / Captive.* Film. Argentina, 2005. 109 mins.

City Lore. "Missing: Streetscape of a City in Mourning." Originally exhibited at the New York Historical Society, March–July 2002, now an online exhibit. http://www.citylore.org/911_exhibit/911_home.html.

Dick, Kirby, and Amy Ziering Kofman. *Derrida.* Film. Jane Doe Films Inc., 2002. 85 mins.

Foundation Haus der Geschichte der Bundesrepublik Deutschland. Permanent Exhibition / Exhibit Highlights / Missing Persons Tracing Service. http://www.hdg.de/index.php?id=1687&L=1&Fsize=2.

Funder, Anna. Sydney PEN Voices: The 3 Writers Project, November 2008, on SlowTV. *The Monthly: Australian Politics, Society, and Culture.* http://www.themonthly.com.au/node/1330.

Ikimi, Thomas. *The Homefront.* Film. London, 2007. 81 mins.

Kurgan, Laura. *New York, September 11, 2001: Four Days Later…*Installation using high-resolution Ikonos satellite imagery of New York on September 15, 2001. Control_Space, ZKM, Karlsruhe, Germany, opening October 2001. Catalogue. http://www.princeton.edu/~kurgan/sep15/text.html.

Leopard Films. "Missing Drama Dominates Its Slot on BBC 1." http://www.leopardfilms.com/news/leopard-uk/missing-drama-dominates-its-slot-on-bbc.

Malagrino, Silvia. *Burnt Oranges.* Film. United States: www.libremedia.com, 2006.

Nevaer, Louis. *Missing: Last Seen at the World Trade Center, September 11, 2001.* A touring exhibition of missing person fliers. Funded by the Mesoamerica Foundation. http://www.bronston.com/missing/.

Puenzo, Luis. *The Official Story / La Historia Oficial.* Film. Argentina, 1985. 104 mins.

Slovenia. RTS, Odprtje Kostnice žrtev povojnih pobojev, 28 October 2008. Video (Slovenian). http://www.tele-59.si/novice/2064/?results=40.

Waite, John. "A Death Unnoticed." Face the Facts, BBC Radio 4, 23 July 2009. http://www.bbc.co.uk/programmes/b00lr2g8#synopsis.

Ware, Julian. "WWI: Finding the Lost Battalions." Channel 4, 19 July 2010. Darlow Smithson Productions. Produced and directed by Janice Sutherland.

Zafar, Ziad. *Missing in Pakistan.* Documentary. 2007. http://video.google.com/videoplay?docid=-854791386997728455.

INDEX